Technical Java

Technical Java

Developing Scientific and Engineering Applications

Grant Palmer

Prentice Hall PTR
Upper Saddle River, NJ
www.phptr.com

Library of Congress Cataloging-in-Publication Data

A CIP catalog record of this book can be obtained from the Library of Congress

Production Supervisor: Wil Mara
Acquisitions Editor: John Neidhart
Cover Design: Nina Scuderi
Cover Design Director: Jerry Votta
Editorial Assistant: Brandt Kenna
Marketing Manager: Kate Hargett
Manufacturing Manager: Alexis Heydt-Long
Composition: Pine Tree Composition

© 2003 Pearson Education, Inc.
Publishing as Prentice Hall Professional Technical Rerefence
Upper Saddle River, New Jersey 07458

Prentice Hall books are widely used by corporations and government agencies for training, marketing, and resale.

Prentice Hall PTR offers excellent discounts on this book when ordered in quantity for bulk purchases or special sales. For more information, please contact: U.S. Corporate and Government Sales, 1-800-382-3419, corpsales@pearsontechgroup.com. For sales outside of the U.S., please contact: International Sales, 1-317-581-3793, international@pearsontechgroup.com.

Company and product names mentioned herein are the trademarks or registered trademarks of their respective owners.

All rights reserved. No part of this book may be reproduced, in any form or by any means, without permission in writing from the publisher.

Printed in the United States of America

First Printing

ISBN 0-13-101815-9

Pearson Education LTD.
Pearson Education Australia PTY, Limited
Pearson Education Singapore, Pte. Ltd.
Pearson Education North Asia Ltd.
Pearson Education Canada, Ltd.
Pearson Educación de Mexico, S.A. de C.V.
Pearson Education—Japan
Pearson Education Malaysia, Pte. Ltd.

Dedication

*This book is dedicated to Cheryl Richter,
my oldest and dearest friend.*

ABOUT THE FTP SITE

A companion FTP site has been provided for this book. You can access it through *http://authors.phptr.com/palmer/*. On the site you will find the source code and support files for every example in the book. The site is organized by chapter, making it easy to locate each example. Some of the source code files will be found in the TechJava/MathLib or TechJava/Gas directories. When this is the case, README files are provided to direct you to the files in question.

Contents

Preface xxi

Acknowledgments xxv

Chapter 1 Introduction to Java 1

A Brief History of Java 2
- Humble Beginnings 2
- Java 1.0 2
- Java 1.1 3
- Java 1.2 3
- Java 1.3 and Java 1.4 4
- The Future 4

What Java Is 5
- Simple and Familiar 5
- Object Oriented 5
- Interpreted and Platform Neutral 5
- Robust 6
- Secure 6

    Multithreaded   7

    Versatile and Expandable   7

Installing Java on Your Machine   7

Compiling and Running Java Programs   8

CHAPTER 2 Moving from Fortran to Java   11

Program Structure   12

Basic Syntax   13

Variables   14

Subroutines, Functions, and Methods   15

Arrays   16

Dynamic Memory Allocation   17

Pointers   17

Exception Handling   18

Libraries   18

Built-in Math Functions   19

Input/Output Capability   19

GUIs and Web-Based Applications   20

CHAPTER 3 Moving from C to Java   21

Program Structure   22

Basic Syntax   23

Java Classes vs. C Structs   23

Variables   24

Pointers   25

Functions and Methods   25

Arrays   26

Dynamic Memory Allocation   27

Exception Handling   28

C Libraries and the Java APIs   28

Strings   29

Built-in Math Functions   29

Basic Printing   30

Input/Output Capability   30

GUIs and Web-Based Applications   30

Chapter 4 Moving from C++ to Java   31

Basic Syntax   32

Preprocessor Directives   32

Data Types   33

Pointers   33

Structures, Unions, Enumerations   34

Inheritance and Interfaces   34

Built-In Math Functions   34

Standard I/O   35

Strings   35

Memory Management   35

Chapter 5 An Overview of Object-Oriented Programming Concepts   37

Objects   37

Classes   38

Encapsulation   38

Inheritance   39

Polymorphism   40

Chapter 6 Basic Syntax 41

General Syntax and a Simple Java Program 41
    Example: A Simple Java Program 42

Comments 43
    Example: Using Comments 43

Operators 44
    Arithmetic Operators 44
    Assignment Operators 45
    Increment/Decrement Operators 46
    Relational Operators 47
    Boolean Operators 48
    Bitwise Operators 50
    Miscellaneous Operators 51
    Operator Precedence 53

Loops and Other Flow of Control Structures 54
    `if-else` Statements 54
    `while` Loops 55
    `do-while` Loops 56
    `for` Loops 57
    `switch` Statements 59

Transfer of Control Statements 60
    `break` Statements 60
    `continue` Statements 61
    `return` Statements 62

Basic Printing and Keyboard I/O 62

Chapter 7 Classes 65

Class Declaration Syntax 66

Access Privileges 67

Objects 68

Declaring Fields 69

Declaring Methods 70

Constructors   72

Static Initialization Blocks   74

Making Copies of Objects   75

Nested Classes   77

    Static Nested Classes   78

    Instance Nested Classes   78

    Anonymous Inner Classes   80

Encapsulation   81

Inheritance   82

    Inheritance and Access Modifiers   84

    Inheritance and Method Arguments   85

    Member Hiding and Member Overriding   86

The `super` Keyword   86

The `this` Keyword   86

Abstract Classes   87

Final Classes   89

The Garbage Collector   89

Chapter 8 Variables   91

Primitive and Reference Type Variables   92

Instance and Class Variables   95

Creating Variables   98

Naming Conventions and Restrictions   101

Access Modifiers   102

Accessing Variable Values   103

Final Variables   105

Transient and Volatile Variables   106

Casting   106

Variable Scope   108

Chapter 9 Methods 111

Declaring Methods   112

Naming Conventions   114

Access Modifiers   114

Instance Methods   116

Static Methods   118

The `main()` Method   119

Input Parameters   121

    Passing Arguments to Methods   121

Abstract Methods   123

Final Methods   124

The `native` and `synchronized` Keywords   124

Method Chaining   124

Method Overloading   126

Method Overriding   127

The `return` Statement   129

Chapter 10 Interfaces 131

Differences Between Interfaces and Abstract Classes   132

Declaring an Interface   132

Interface Members   133

Implementing an Interface   134

Interfaces and Inheritance   136

Interface Instances as Input Parameters and Return Types   136

Chapter 11 Packages and JAR Files 139

Defining a Package   140

`import` Declarations   142

CLASSPATH Environment Variable   143

Packages and Access Control   144

JAR Files   145

Chapter 12 Exception Handling   149

The Exception Class Hierarchy   150

`try` Statements   151

    The `try` Statement   152

    The `catch` Clause   152

    The `finally` Clause   153

The `throw` and `throws` Keywords   155

Chapter 13 Arrays   159

One-Dimensional Arrays   160

Two-Dimensional Arrays   161

Arrays of More than Two Dimensions   164

Initializing Array Elements   164

Accessing Array Elements   166

Arrays as Method Arguments and Return Types   167

Array Length   169

Collection Classes in the Java API   170

Chapter 14 The Java Class Libraries   173

Package Naming Conventions   174

The Core J2SE Libraries   174

    java.io   174

    java.lang   175

    java.math   175

    java.util   175

The GUI Libraries 176
  java.awt 176
  java.awt.event 176
  javax.swing 177
  javax.swing.border 177
  javax.swing.event 177
  javax.swing.table 177
  javax.swing.text 178
  javax.swing.tree 178

CHAPTER 15 PRIMITIVE VARIABLE WRAPPER AND STRING CLASSES 179

Primitive Variable Wrapper Classes 180

Creating Primitive Variable Wrapper Class Objects 181

Converting a Wrapper Class Object to a Primitive Value 184

The `parse()` Methods 185

The `String` Class 186

Obtaining `String` Objects 187

Concatenating `Strings` 189

Other Important `String` Class Methods 190

Converting Primitive and Reference Types to `Strings` 193

Converting `Strings` to Primitive Values 193

CHAPTER 16 BUILT-IN MATH FUNCTIONS 197

`Math` and `StrictMath` Classes 198

Mathematical Constants 199

Absolute Value Methods 199

Power and Square Root Methods 201

Transcendental Math Functions 203

Trigonometric Methods 204

Conversion Methods   206

Minimum and Maximum Methods   208

Rounding and Remainder Methods   209

Random Number Generator Methods   211

The `java.math` Package   212

Comparing the Built-in Math Capability of C, C++, Fortran, and Java   212

References   214

Chapter 17 User-Defined Math Functions   215

Basic Plan of Attack   216

The `Math2` Class   216

Logarithm Methods   217

Hyperbolic Trigonometric Methods   218

The Gamma Function   219

The Final Version of the `Math2` Class   220

Compiling the `Math2` Class   222

Using `Math2` Class Methods   222

Comparing Java, C, and Fortran Values   223

References   224

Chapter 18 Building Class Hierarchies   225

Defining the State and Behavior of a Gas Mixture   226

The General Class Hierarchy Structure   227

`AbstractGas` Class   229

`PerfectGas` Class   230

`Air` Class   233

`RealGas` Class   234

`Species` Class   238

`N2` Class   240

`N` Class   241

`NitrogenGas` Class   242

Summary   245

References   246

Chapter 19 Solving Systems of Equations   247

General Considerations   248

The `EqnSolver` Class   249

Test Case   249

Pivoting   250

Gauss-Jordan Elimination   253

Gaussian Elimination   255

Lower-Upper Decomposition   257

Matrix Inversion   261

Testing the `EqnSolver` Class Methods   263

Real Gas Viscosity Method   265

Chapter 20 Solving Differential Equations   271

Ordinary Differential Equations   272

The `ODE` Class   273

Initial Value Problems   275

Runge-Kutta Schemes   276

Example Problem: Damped Spring Motion   280

　　`SpringODE` class   282

　　Solving the Spring Motion ODE   283

Embedded Runge-Kutta Solvers 285

Other ODE Solution Techniques 291

Two-Point Boundary Problems 292

Shooting Methods 292

Example Problem: Compressible Boundary Layer 296

    The `CompressODE` Class 300

    Solving the Compressible Boundary Layer Equations 303

Other Two-Point Boundary Solution Techniques 305

Partial Differential Equations 306

References 306

Chapter 21 Integration of Functions 307

General Comments 308

Trapezoidal Algorithms 309

Simpson's Rule 314

Solving Improper Integrals 317

Gaussian Quadrature Methods 322

General Integral Types 326

Example: Thin Airfoil Theory 326

References 331

Chapter 22 Fourier Transforms 333

The Fourier Transform 334

Discrete Fourier Transform 336

Analyzing Composite Signals 343

Sampling Theory 345

Spectral Leakage 347

Fast Fourier Transform 349

Chapter 23 Generic Class Libraries 355

Analyzing the Problem 356

Example: Least Squares Fit 356

Implementing the Generic Part 357

Implementing the Problem-Specific Part 358

Testing the Generic Class Library 361

Chapter 24 Data Modeling and Curve Fits 365

Least Squares Fit to a Polynomial Equation 366

The `DataModeling` Class 368

The `Polynomial` Class 369

Example Problem: Curve Fitting Specific Heat Data 370

Fitting to Nonpolynomial Equations 373

The `Power` Class 374

Other Data Modeling Techniques 378

References 379

Chapter 25 Java I/O 381

General Concepts 382

Byte Input Streams 384

    `InputStream` Class 385

    `BufferedInputStream` Class 385

    `ByteArrayInputStream` Class 386

    `DataInputStream` Class 386

    `FileInputStream` Class 387

    `FilterInputStream` Class 388

    `ObjectInputStream` Class 388

    Other `InputStream` Subclasses 389

Byte Output Streams 390
    `OutputStream` Class 391
    `BufferedOutputStream` Class 391
    `ByteArrayOutputStream` Class 392
    `DataOutputStream` Class 392
    `FileOutputStream` Class 393
    `FilterOutputStream` Class 394
    `ObjectOutputStream` Class 394
    `PrintStream` Class 395

Character Input Streams 396
    `Reader` Class 397
    `BufferedReader` Class 398
    `FileReader` Class 398
    `InputStreamReader` Class 399
    Other `Reader` Subclasses 399

Character Output Streams 400
    `Writer` Class 400
    `BufferedWriter` Class 401
    `FileWriter` Class 401
    `OutputStreamWriter` Class 402
    `PrintWriter` Class 402
    Other `Writer` Subclasses 404

Test Case: An Atmosphere Modeling Tool 404

Getting Input from Command Line Arguments 408

Using the Standard I/O Streams 410

Reading and Writing to a File 412

Saving and Restoring Objects 415

The `java.nio` Packages 418

References 418

Chapter 26 An Introduction to Java GUIs 419

The Java GUI Libraries 420

The `AtmGUI` Class 421

Choosing a Container 422

Selecting the GUI Components 423

Adding the Components to the Container 425

Event Handlers 427

Other GUI elements 430

The Final Form of the `AtmGUI` class 430

Chapter 27 Creating Web-Based Applications Using Java Servlets 435

Web-Based Application Basics 436

Java Servlets 437

Required Libraries and Tools 438

Example: A Web-Based Atmosphere Modeling Tool 438

`HttpServlet` Class 439

General Form of an `HttpServlet` Subclass 440

Extracting Input Parameters 441

Running Server-Based Applications 442

Sending Output Back to the Client Machine 443

The `AtmServlet` Class 443

Deploying the Web-Based Application 447

Appendix: Java Keywords 449

Index 453

Preface

This book was inspired by the following premise—Java is a great language for developing scientific and engineering applications. It's more powerful and versatile than Fortan or C. It's easier to learn, less redundant, and less prone to error than C++. I have been a scientific programmer at a NASA research center for 18 years. You would think such a place would be on the cutting edge of programming technology, but that is not the case. Most of the technical programmers there still program in Fortran or C. The reason is largely one of inertia. Those languages are what they have always used and they are comfortable with them. Some people have moved over to C++, and slowly but surely people are moving to Java as their technical programming language of choice.

The book is designed to break through the inertia and misconceptions that may have kept you from using Java for your scientific and engineering programming work. It will give you a good foundation in the basics of Java and demonstrate how Java can be applied to solve a number of mathematical analysis problems. The book will discuss migration issues from other languages to Java and provide an introduction to developing GUI- or web-based technical applications.

WHY IS JAVA A GOOD TECHNICAL PROGRAMMING LANGUAGE?

There are many features of Java that make it a good choice for your technical programming work. For one thing, Java is an object-oriented language. Because of this, it provides a structured framework for developing your programs. When a code is written in an object-oriented manner, it becomes easier to read and more modular. You can write programs that extend the capabilities of existing programs. When an analysis procedure is written as an object it can be easily incorporated into any number of different applications.

One of the design goals of the developers of Java was that the language be easy to learn and use. It borrows much of its basic syntax from C and C++, but the developers of Java simplified the language by removing redundancies that exist in C and C++, as well as removing potentially dangerous elements—such as multiple inheritance—that were of marginal value. It is much easier to learn and apply Java, for example, than it is to learn and apply C or C++.

Another powerful feature is Java's portability. Java programs are designed so that you can "compile once, run anywhere." You can develop a scientific application on a UNIX workstation, transfer it to an Apple or Windows-based laptop, and the application will run without having to recompile it. Java's portability opens up the power of the Internet to your technical programming work. You can easily develop your scientific or engineering applications as web-based programs.

There is a global support network for Java. You can get online support and documentation from the Sun Microsystems website and many other sources as well. There are Java User Groups (JUGs) pretty much anywhere you live in just about every country. These groups are very useful for solving problems and discussing programming techniques and issues.

It also is easy to develop code in Java. You can leverage existing classes and methods to develop new ones. In this book, we will demonstrate how simple it is to create user-defined mathematical functions. The object-oriented structure of a Java makes the code easy to read. A program that is easy to read is easier to maintain or modify.

The Structure of This Book

Think of this book in four parts. The first includes a general introduction to Java and its development history. Following this are chapters that discuss migration issues from Fortan, C, or C++ to Java. You will find that much of the basic syntax is the same between C, C++, and Java. There are some important differences, though, that these chapters will bring to light.

The second part goes over the basic elements of the Java language with an emphasis on topics pertinent to technical programming. Following a discussion of basic object-oriented programming concepts, there are chapters that discuss classes, methods, and variables. Interfaces, packages, and JAR files are also covered. There are chapters that discuss how Java treats arrays and strings. Finally, there are chapters on the math capability of Java—both the intrinsic functionality that comes with the Java API and a discussion of how to create user-defined math libraries.

Once we have a good understanding of the key elements of the Java language, we are ready to do some serious technical programming. The third part of this book discusses how Java can be applied to such tasks as solving systems of equations, differential equations, integral functions, and Fourier transforms. These chapters not only provide Java source code and real-life model problems, but also delve into the theory behind the solution techniques. This section of the book also includes chapters on developing data curve fits and generic class libraries.

The final part consists of three chapters covering important features you will probably make use of in your technical programming. Chapter 25 discusses the input/output capability of Java. The Java API provides a powerful and versatile I/O functionality for reading and writing both byte and character data. Java also gives you the ability to write GUI front ends to your technical programs. An introduction to how this is done is provided in Chapter 26. Another great feature of Java is that it gives you access to the power of the Internet. The final chapter of this book provides an introduction to how you can turn a program into a web-based application using Java servlets.

What This Book Is Not

This book will teach you the basic tools you will need to start writing technical programs in Java, but it will not cover every possible aspect of scientific or engineering programming. The book is not an exhaustive treatise on solving differential equations, integral functions, or Fourier transforms. Each of those topics is a book unto itself. This book will present the most commonly used techniques to solve those mathematical problems, but won't go into many specialized or super-advanced techniques.

The book also does not give a comprehensive description of all of the classes, methods, interfaces, and fields from the Java API. The Java libraries are enormous and a detailed look at even the Standard Edition libraries would take many hundreds of pages. This book does cover some Java API elements that are particularly relevant to technical programming. For a detailed look at the rest of the Java API, the reader is referred to the Sun Java doc pages.

Acknowledgments

A lot of time and effort from a lot of people goes in to creating a book such as this. I would like to acknowledge the efforts of some of those who worked very hard to make this book a reality. I would like to thank my editors at Prentice Hall, Karen McLean, John Neidhart, and Wil Mara, for helping me refine my idea for a book on technical programming with Java and for making sure everything went as smoothly as possible. I would also like to thank my technical reviewers Jim Huddleston, Anne Horton, Basil Hassan, Joe Olejniczak, James Brown, and Periklis Papadopoulos. Their insights, corrections, and suggestions helped to tighten up and strengthen the book. I learned a lot from them in the process. Finally, as always, I would like to thank my beautiful wife, Lisa, for the patience she shows when I'm writing my books.

INTRODUCTION TO JAVA

Before 1995 the average person thought Java was a large Indonesian island or perhaps a hot beverage you took with cream and sugar. Today anyone with any background in computer programming knows that Java is one of the most popular and influential programming languages. Java has become the standard for developing Web-based enterprise applications, particularly business and multimedia type programs. It is a very telling point that other languages, Fortran for example, are evolving to become more Java-like in form and function.

A lot of the same things that make Java a great programming language for business and multimedia applications—simplicity, flexibility, versatility, robustness—make Java a great language for developing scientific and engineering applications as well. In science and engineering, as in any other discipline, inertia is a powerful force. Technical programming is still dominated by two older languages, Fortran and C. But the world is changing, and more and more technical programmers are moving to Java as their language of choice. This book will teach you the basics of the Java language and show you how to apply Java to create sophisticated scientific and engineering applications.

This chapter will provide a big picture look at Java. We will talk about the history of Java, from its humble beginnings to how the rise of the Internet propelled Java into prominence in the programming world. We will cover the basic characteristics of the language, what Java is, and what it can do. Finally, this chapter will teach you some very basic things like how to load Java onto your computer and how to compile and run a Java program.

This chapter will cover—

- A brief history of Java
- What Java is
- Installing Java on your machine
- Compiling and running Java programs

A Brief History of Java

As Claude Rains said in the movie *Lawrence of Arabia*, "Big things have small beginnings." This was certainly true about Java. The history of Java is a story of how a brilliant and forward-seeing group of developers saw an opportunity to turn a small-scale development project into a language that would change the face of computer programming. This section will give a brief history of Java from its humble beginnings to the current state of the language.

Humble Beginnings

In 1991, developers at Sun Microsystems, Inc., started work on Oak, intended to be a platform-independent programming language for use in consumer electronic devices. The idea was to have one language that could run on a variety of CPUs under different operating systems. Thirteen people were involved in what was dubbed the "Green Project."

While this was going on, a revolutionary development called the Internet was emerging and gaining popularity. The Internet, as we all know, is an environment where media content (text, images, sound, and video) moves from one machine to another. People working on different machines under potentially different operating systems needed the ability to download content, perhaps even full-scale applications from the Internet, and run them on their local machines. The Sun developers realized that Oak had the potential to meet this need, and their focus switched from consumer electronics to Internet programming. In 1995, Sun developers changed the name of the language from Oak to Java.

Java 1.0

Initially released in 1995, Java built upon the capabilities and syntax of C and C++, removing some of the less worthwhile elements of those languages and adding important functionality that they lacked. Java was designed to be simple, familiar, versatile, secure, expandable, robust, and easy to learn.

The Java source code was initially released (appropriately enough) over the Internet. The Java developers were, in essence, sending their young child out into the world to see what people thought of her. Word spread within the developer community, and within a few months over 10,000 downloads of Java had occurred. The people who downloaded the code provided feedback to the Java developers about what they liked about the language, what they didn't like, and what they wanted added. Java was on its way.

Java 1.1

Java version 1.0 was a revolution in programming, but some deficiencies and idiosyncrasies soon became apparent. Some of the functionality didn't work in an optimum fashion and the language wasn't as standardized or expandable as it could be. Java 1.1, released in 1997, addressed the shortcomings of Java 1.0 and added a lot of functionality. Java 1.1 represented a second revolution in Java programming.

In Java 1.1, basic elements of the language—the method naming convention, for example—became standardized. Some parts of the language, such as the Graphical User Interface (GUI) classes and the Java event model, were reworked. Important new features, such as Remote Method Invocation (RMI), the Java Native Interface (JNI), and Java Database Connectivity (JDBC), were added. The concept of a JavaBean was introduced as a structured way to write software components. Reflection and serialization were added to the language, as were hundreds of new classes and interfaces.

Java 1.2

Version 1.2—more specifically Java 2 Platform version 1.2—was released in 1999. All subsequent Java releases also use the prefix Java 2 Platform. Java was now split into different branches—

- The standard Java packages make up the Java 2 Platform Standard Edition (J2SE).
- The classes and interfaces for creating enterprise software can be found in the Java 2 Platform Enterprise Edition (J2EE).
- The packages for developing applications for consumer electronic devices can be found in Java 2 Platform Micro Edition (J2ME). In this way, Java returned to its roots with version 1.2.

One of the major additions to the Java language under version 1.2 was the Swing packages which contain GUI components, containers, component models, and event handlers that are far more powerful, versatile, and customizable than their Java 1.1 GUI counterparts. The Swing components have access to a drag-and-drop capability added in Java 1.2. Security features were added to the language including support for X.509 certificates. The Accessibility API was added to the platform. Enhancements and additions were made to the collections, extensions, JavaBean, and input method frameworks. A number of performance enhancements to make Java programs run faster were also incorporated into the 1.2 release.

Java 1.3 and Java 1.4

The evolution of Java continued with the release of versions 1.3 and 1.4 with the development focusing on improving the performance and security of the language. Java 1.3 made enhancements to the security, networking, reflection, drag-and-drop, sound, and applet deployment capabilities. Additions were made to both the Abstract Window Toolkit (AWT) and Swing GUI libraries. The Java Naming and Directory Interface (JNDI) was added to the Java 2 platform, as was the CORBA Object Request Broker (ORB). Improvements were made to the `javac`, `jar`, `rmic`, `jarsigner`, and `javaw` compiler and utility tools.

Java 1.4 made additions and enhancements to the regular expressions, math, reflection, accessibility, I/O, logging, assertions, chained exceptions, preferences, and collections classes. The Java API for Extensible Markup Language (XML) processing was added to the Java 2 platform. Additional security capability was added to the Java 2 Software Development Kit (SDK) including the Java Cryptography Extension (JCE), Java Secure Socket Extension (JSSE), and Java Authentication and Authorization Service (JAAS). The Java Print Service API was introduced to the platform in version 1.4. More refinements and additions were made to the AWT and Swing GUI components including changes made to the drag-and-drop capability of Swing components. A new application-deployment technology named Java Web Start is bundled with the J2SE 1.4.0 release.

The Future

The future of Java is bright. Java is already the standard for developing Web-based, enterprise applications. It has replaced C++ as the language of choice for developing business and e-commerce programs. Java is expanding into other programming disciplines including a significant move into the scientific and engineering programming fields. It is a telling point that many high school computer classes in the U.S. are now taught in Java.

What Java Is

Now that we know Java's roots, let's talk about what Java is and what it can do. When the developers at Sun were creating Java, they had certain design guidelines in mind about the type of language they wanted to create. This section describes those concepts, giving you a feeling for the overall design philosophy of the language, what the developers did, and why. This section also lists some of the many advantages of Java.

Simple and Familiar

The creators of Java wanted the language to be simple and familiar. Java is based on C and C++ and borrows much in the way of basic syntax from those languages. The developers wanted to make Java a simple language by removing some of the complex elements of C and C++ that were potentially more trouble than they were worth. Programming entities not supported by Java include multiple inheritance, operator overloading, and publicly accessible pointers.

One criterion for removing elements was to minimize redundancy. C and, later, C++ evolved in a somewhat unstructured manner leading to overlapping features. Java tried to eliminate as much redundancy as possible while adding important features missing from C and C++.

Object Oriented

Java was designed from the ground up as a fully object-oriented programming language. The object-oriented paradigm has become the model of choice for modern programming languages in that it supports the needs of client/server and distributed software. Objects have portability and persistence. They can be created in one location and sent over a network connection to another location to be used or stored for future use. Java supports the object-oriented characteristics of encapsulation, inheritance, and polymorphism. These concepts are explained in more detail in Chapter 5.

Interpreted and Platform Neutral

The Internet was a major impetus in the development of Java. There was a need to be able to transmit applications from one machine to another over the Internet and there was no guarantee that the machines would be using the same operating system. When a Fortran, C, or C++ code is compiled and linked on a given system, the result is an executable file that can usually be run only on that system. You can't compile a program on a Microsoft Windows machine and run the executable under the Macintosh operating system, for instance. The implementation of many fundamental data types is machine and operating system dependent.

The designers of Java set out to develop a platform-independent language. When Java source code is compiled, the result is not a standard executable. Instead, what is produced is called *bytecode*. Bytecode, as the name would suggest, is a series of bytes that correspond to machine opcode instructions. A Java program is executed by sending its bytecode to the Java runtime system, which is called the Java Virtual Machine or JVM. The JVM interprets the bytecode and converts the bytes back into machine instructions. Because a Java program is run through a JVM interpreter, Java is known as an interpreted language.

There are many varieties of JVMs but all of them must adhere to a strictly defined specification. This ensures that bytecode generated on any machine running any operating system can be interpreted by a JVM on any other machine. A Java program can be compiled on a Windows machine and its bytecode can be sent over the Internet to a Linux box that will happily run the application.

Robust

Robustness, the ability of a program to run with low probability of a crash, is an increasingly important concern in the age of distributed and network applications. The Java compiler performs an extensive check for syntax-related errors and warnings, so problems can be identified before the program is deployed. Java is a strongly typed language. The type of each variable and parameter must be explicitly declared. This avoids type mismatch or casting errors.

Another big difference between C, C++, and Java is that the Java memory model precludes the possibility of overwriting locations in memory. This is due in part because Java does not support publicly accessible pointers. The compiler will also check array indices and will not permit a value that is out-of-bounds. Java has a sophisticated exception handling capability built into the language, so exceptions that would otherwise cause program termination can be dealt with.

Secure

With the rise of distributed and Web-based applications, security has become more and more important in modern software design. The Java compiler and runtime have built-in features to prevent application programmers from writing subversive code. One security enhancement is that Java does not support publicly accessible pointers. Because memory allocation is handled exclusively by the JVM, programmers cannot forge or manufacture pointers to memory locations. Because Java uses late binding of structures to memory, the physical memory layout of a class cannot be inferred by looking at the class declaration.

The Java class loader implements additional security procedures. When a class is loaded from across the network, it is put into a separate class partition based on its origin. This prevents a remote class from spoofing (pretending to be) a local class. Additional Java security mechanisms are provided by the bytecode verifier and by the interfaces contained in the Java networking package.

Multithreaded

Java is a multithreaded language. A Java program can start multiple threads of execution, each performing its own sequence of operations at the same time. The Java language provides all the tools for threads to acquire and release locks in a manner that minimizes deadlock conditions. Java also provides programming mechanisms to synchronize access to methods and develop functionality in a thread-safe manner.

Versatile and Expandable

One of the great advantages of Java is its versatility. The Java language covers a wide range of programming disciplines. You can perform network programming, develop GUIs, and create scientific and engineering applications using a single programming language. There is no more mixing and matching languages, no more Common Gateway Interface (CGI) scripts or language integration issues.

Another strength of Java is that it is expandable. New class libraries are constantly being made available for you to download and incorporate into your program development. Java provides all the framework and tools for you to develop your own class libraries too. New classes can easily be incorporated into the existing language framework.

INSTALLING JAVA ON YOUR MACHINE

The easiest way to install Java on your machine is to download the Java 2 SDK, available free from the Sun website at http://java.sun.com/j2se/downloads.html.

The SDK download includes the Java compiler, JVM, and the J2SE libraries. Also included are utility functions that can be useful when developing your programs. The Sun website has versions of the SDK for Windows, Solaris, and Linux operating systems. You can download the J2EE and J2ME libraries from the Sun Java website as well.

Other versions of the Java SDK are available from third-party sources. For example, you can download the SDK for Silicon Graphics' IRIX operating system from the SGI website. A collection of XML parser libraries can be obtained from the Apache Software Foundation website. Many other sources for Java class libraries exist and can be found by searching the Internet.

Compiling and Running Java Programs

The standard Java compiler is named `javac` and comes with the SDK. To compile a Java program, you type "javac," followed by any compiler options and the name of the source code to be compiled.

```
javac <options> <source_code>
```

You can specify more than one source file to be compiled. Table 1.1 lists the Java compiler options and what they do. You can also get this list by typing either "javac" or "javac –help." You will find that for many of your programs, you will simply use the `javac` keyword by itself without any options.

TABLE 1.1 Java Compiler Options

OPTION	DESCRIPTION
-g	Full debugging information
-g:none	No debugging information
-g:{lines,vars,source}	Only some debugging information
-O	Optimize. This option may hinder debugging and/or create larger .class files
-nowarn	Generates no warnings
-verbose	Verbose compiler output
-deprecation	Indicates where deprecated APIs are used
-classpath <path>	Indicates where compiler should look for .class files
-sourcepath <path>	Indicates where compiler should look for source files
-bootclasspath <path>	Overrides location of bootstrap class files
-extdirs <dirs>	Overrides location of installed extensions
-d <directory>	Specifies where .class files will be placed
-encoding <encoding>	Specifies character encoding scheme to be used
-source <release>	Checks source compatibility with specified release
-target <release>	Generates .class files for the specified Virtual Machine
-help	Prints the list of compiler options

The Java compiler is smart in that it will automatically compile any dependent source code. For example, let's say the `Blah.java` program makes use of source code contained in the `Foo.java` program. If you compile the `Blah.java` program by typing "javac Blah.java" the compiler will also, if necessary, compile the `Foo.java` code.

The output of the Java compiler is the bytecode of the compiled program. The bytecode file name will have the same name of the source code sent to the compiler with the ".class" extension. For example, to compile the `Blah.java` source code without any compiler options you would type

```
javac Blah.java
```

This will generate a bytecode file named `Blah.class`.

To run a Java program, you must send the appropriate bytecode to the JVM. You do this by typing "java," any JVM options, and the .class file name.

```
java <options> <class_file>
```

You do not type the .class extension. For example, to run the compiled `Blah.java` program without any JVM options, you would type—

```
java Blah
```

Some of the more commonly used standard JVM options are listed in Table 1.2.

TABLE 1.2 Virtual Machine Options	
OPTION	DESCRIPTION
-client	Specifies the client Virtual Machine
-server	Specifies the server Virtual Machine
-cp <directories>	
-classpath <directories>	Indicates where to look for classes and resources
-D <name>=<value>	Sets a system property
-verbose[:class|gc|in]	Enables verbose output
-version	Prints product version and exits
-showversion	Prints product version and continues with other commands
-?	
-help	Lists standard JVM options
-X	Lists nonstandard JVM options

MOVING FROM FORTRAN TO JAVA

If you are moving from Fortran to Java, there will be a learning curve. Java is a C and C++ based language, and the basic syntax used by Java is different than Fortran. What's more, Java is an object-oriented language. You will have to learn to think and program in an object-oriented manner. The good news is that simplicity was one of the design goals of the developers who created Java. It's much easier moving from Fortran to Java than it is to move from Fortran to a language like C++.

You will quickly realize that Java is more powerful and versatile than Fortran. There are more programming constructs and more ways of customizing programming elements. Java is a more comprehensive language as well. It offers a lot more features and can be used for a wider range of programming disciplines. The Fortran libraries are limited in scope, consisting mainly of mathematical functions. Java has enormous libraries covering almost every conceivable programming need. You will find when developing complicated multidisciplinary applications that a lot of the programming work has already been done for you.

This chapter will shed some light on the things you will have to learn and consider when moving to the Java world. It will focus not only on the basic syntactical differences but also touch briefly on object-oriented programming concepts that you will need to know. This chapter is not meant to be a comprehensive tutorial for either Fortran or Java. For a detailed description of the core elements of the Java language, look to Chapters 5–16.

The specific topics we will discuss in this chapter are—

- Program structure
- Basic syntax
- Variables
- Subroutines, functions, and methods
- Arrays
- Dynamic memory allocation
- Pointers
- Exception handling
- Libraries
- Built-in math functions
- Input/Output capabilities
- GUIs and web-based applications

Program Structure

Java is an object-oriented, C-based language. Fortran is neither. While some advocates of the more recent versions of Fortran (Fortran 90 and Fortran 95) have tried to pass the language off as being almost object oriented, in truth it models only some object-oriented features but does not directly support such important concepts as inheritance and dynamic dispatching. In addition, Fortran 90 and 95 are built upon legacy versions (Fortran 77 primarily) that aren't object oriented in the least. Java was designed from the ground up to be a true object-oriented language.

One of the big differences between Fortran and Java is the basic program structure of the two languages. A Fortran program consists of a main program section and zero or more subroutines or functions. Program execution starts at the top of the main program section. The main program section is terminated with `stop` and `end` statements. Subroutines and functions are terminated with `end` statements. A Fortran program usually consists of variable declarations and a series of subroutine and/or function calls.

Java is an object-oriented programming language. The fundamental building block of a Java program is a named block of code called a *class*. Classes are usually designed to be self-contained. They declare fields (i.e., variables) and methods (the Java equivalent of subroutines) that are used to access and manipulate these fields and perform other functions as well. All statements in a Java program must be placed inside a class or interface.

Classes define the structure of the objects that make Java object oriented. An object is an instance of a class. Java arrays are also objects although no explicit class defines them. An object will have its own copy of the nonstatic data members and methods defined by its class. Java programs will usually declare at least one variable that refers to an object. A Java application can contain more than one class, but one of the classes will declare a `main()` method. The `main()` method is the entry point for program execution. The system calls the `main()` method when the program is run.

BASIC SYNTAX

Java is a C-based language, which doesn't help you much coming from a Fortran background. There are significant differences in the basic syntax between Java and Fortran. Don't worry too much about this. The Java compiler is very good at pointing out if and where you slipped back into the Fortran way of doing things.

Both Fortran and Java allow free-form coding. You can indent the executable statements any way you like. Indentation is normally used to make a code more readable. Unlike Fortran, Java is case sensitive. All Java keywords (`new`, `public`, `final`, etc.) must be entered in lowercase. Identifiers are likewise case sensitive. For example, myVariable is not the same as MYVARIABLE or MyVariable to the Java compiler. All executable statements in Java are terminated with a semicolon. There are no `PARAMETER` or `DIMENSION` statements in Java. Java does not have common blocks.

In Java, blocks of code are designated using braces. Since Java classes and methods are named blocks of code, their contents are placed inside braces. You can designate blocks of code pretty much wherever you like. Code blocks define areas of scope. Variables exist only in the block of code in which they are declared. Once program execution leaves a block of code, any variables declared inside the block disappear.

Comment statements are different in Fortran and Java. Java defines both multiline or single line comments. A multiline comment starts with the characters `/*` and ends with the characters `*/`. As the name implies, a multiline comment can span multiple lines. Single line Java comments start with the characters `//`. Java also supports documentation comments. This type of comment can be incorporated into an HTML file describing the Java source code.

The basic mathematical and assignment operators, *, /, +, -, and =, are the same for both languages. Java supports additional types of operators including combination mathematical/assignment operators and operators used when working with objects. Java uses the symbolic Fortran relational operators (==, <, <=, >, and >=) rather than the original Fortran operators (.NE., .LT., .LE., .GT., and .GE.).

There are similarities and differences in the loop and flow control structures between the two languages. Fortran defines an `IF-END IF` conditional structure. Java defines a similar construct using the syntax `if-else`. The Fortran `DO-END DO` loop is similar in nature to the Java `for` loop. The Fortran `SELECT-CASE` structure is similar in nature to the Java `switch` statement. Java provides additional flow control structures that Fortran does not, including the `while` and `do-while` statements.

VARIABLES

Java and Fortran define a number of types to represent various boolean, character, numerical, and object data. The types supported by the languages are shown in Table 2.1.

Fortran has five intrinsic types. The three numerical types, INTEGER, REAL, and COMPLEX, represent integer, floating point, and complex number values. The LOGICAL type represents a boolean value. It can have values of .TRUE. and .FALSE. with periods on either side of the word. The CHARACTER type represents strings (sequences of characters).

TABLE 2.1	Types	
FORTRAN	JAVA	DESCRIPTION
LOGICAL	boolean	Boolean true or false value
N/A	byte	A single byte of data
N/A	char	A Unicode character
INTEGER	short, int, long	Integer numeric type
REAL	float, double	Floating point numeric type
COMPLEX	N/A	Complex integer or floating point number
CHARACTER	String	A sequence of characters
N/A	reference (object)	A class instance

Java defines more types than Fortran. Java has three integer types—`short`, `int`, and `long`, representing 16-, 32-, and 64-bit integer values. Java supports two floating point data types. The `float` type is single precision. The `double` type is double precision. Java supports the `byte` and `char` types that Fortran does not. On the other hand, Java does not have a complex number type. The Java `String` class represents a sequence of characters. The reference type represents an instance of a Java class or array.

Java is a *strongly typed* language, meaning that the type of every variable must be specified when the variable is declared. Java will not assume that a variable whose name starts with the letter *i* is an integer variable for example. Java variables must be declared before they are used. The basic syntax for declaring a variable in Java is the variable type, the variable name, and a semicolon—

```
variable_type variable_name;
```

A Java variable can be initialized when it is declared or it can be assigned a value later in the program. Java does not support global variables. A Java variable exists only in the block of code in which it is declared. Once the program execution leaves a block of code, any variables declared inside that block disappear.

Java variables can represent either primitive types such as integer and floating point types or reference types such as objects and arrays. Java variables can be assigned different characteristics and behavior by using one or more modifying keywords when the variable is declared. The keywords that can be used with variables include `public`, `private`, `protected`, `final`, `transient`, `volatile`, and `static`.

SUBROUTINES, FUNCTIONS, AND METHODS

A Fortran *subroutine* or *function* is a named section of code that can be called from somewhere else in a Fortran program. A subroutine or function declaration consists of the subroutine name and input argument list. The body of the subroutine or function follows the declaration and is terminated with an `END SUBROUTINE` statement. A Fortran subroutine or function is called using the `call` keyword followed by the subroutine or function name and input argument list.

A Java method is a named block of code that can be called from somewhere else in a Java program. A Java method declaration consists of the method return type, method name, input parameter list, and, optionally, one or more modifying keywords. The body of the method is enclosed in braces ({}). Java methods can be declared to be `public`, `private`, `protected` `static`, `abstract`, `final`, `native`, and `synchronized`.

Java methods can be instance or static. An instance method is associated with an instance of a class (an object). A static method is associated with a class rather than with an instance of a class. Static methods are sometimes referred to as class methods. Instance and static methods are called in different ways. Inside the class in which they are defined, both instance and static methods are called by simply typing the method name and providing the correct number and type of arguments. Outside of the class in which they are defined, instance methods are called by referencing a specific object. Static methods are called by typing the class name, a period, and then the method name.

All arguments to Java methods are passed by value. For arguments representing primitive data types, a copy of the argument value is sent to the method. Any changes made to the value inside the method will not be made to the original value. For arguments representing reference types (objects or arrays), a copy of the reference to the location in memory where the data for the object or array is stored is sent to the method. Any changes made using this reference inside the method will also be made to the original object.

Arrays

Java and Fortran represent and treat arrays in different ways. Fortran arrays are defined using the `dimension` keyword followed by the array name and array size in parentheses. Commas separate the dimension sizes of multidimensional arrays. For example, to create a 59x59 array named `data`, you could type

```
REAL DIMENSION(59,59):: data
```

Java arrays are reference types. They are created using the `new` keyword. You must specify the type of data stored in the array. The size of the array is specified using square brackets. One set of brackets is used for every dimension. For example, to create a 59x59 Java array named `data` that would contain elements of data type `double`, you could type

```
double data[][] = new double[59][59];
```

There are other array differences as well. Fortran array subscripts start from the number 1 by default but the range can be specified explicitly. Java array indices start from the number 0 and the range cannot be customized. Fortran array elements can be accessed by placing the desired subscript inside parentheses after the array name. For example, to assign the value 4.0 to the element in the first row and first column of the previously declared `data` array, you would type

```
data(1,1) = 4.0
```

You access an element of a Java array using a pair of square brackets ([]) around the index of the element to be accessed. You use a different pair of square brackets for every dimension. For example, to assign the value 4.0 to the element in the first row and first column of the Java `data` array, you would type

```
data[0][0] = 4.0;
```

Java always performs bounds checking for array access. Fortran does not bounds check by default although most compilers support this feature as an option.

DYNAMIC MEMORY ALLOCATION

Fortran allows you to dynamically allocate memory for arrays using the ALLOCATE statement. Any allocated memory can be deallocated using the DEALLOCATE statement. Dynamic memory allocation is useful if the size of an array won't be known until runtime in that you don't have to declare a really large array to take care of all possibilities. Dynamic memory allocation can also be dangerous in that you must be careful to deallocate all allocated memory when it is no longer needed. If you don't, your program will have a memory leak.

Java does not support explicit dynamic memory allocation and deallocation because it has a sophisticated memory management system as part of the Java runtime. Because memory for an array can be allocated anywhere in the program, you can wait to declare the array until you know what size it will be. A system thread called the *garbage collector* monitors the state of your program and automatically deallocates memory for objects that are no longer being used.

POINTERS

Fortran allows POINTER variables that are references to locations in memory. Java does not support publicly accessible pointers. The developers of Java felt that the dangers of pointers in terms of possible memory corruption and overwriting data outweighed any benefits that come from using them. The Java language is designed such that pointers are unnecessary.

Exception Handling

Exception handling allows you to respond to exceptions that might occur while your program is running. The Fortran language has no built-in exception handling. You can create your own exception handling in a Fortran program if you like. Normally this involves testing for exceptions using a series of `IF-ELSE IF` statements. The problem with this approach is you have to do all the work yourself. Unforeseen errors might slip through your exception handling code, and the exception handling must take place where the exception will occur. You can't pass the exception handling off to another part of the code.

Exception handling is an integral part of the Java language. Built-in classes and programming constructs make it easy to build exception handling into your programs. Exception handling is performed by defining specialized blocks of code. One type of block throws an exception to another type of block that catches and processes the exception. A third type of code block can be called after all the exception handling takes place. What's more, the exception handling can be passed on to another part of the program. The exception handling does not have to be performed where the exception occurs.

The Java compiler will check that you are handling certain types of exceptions. If the appropriate safeguards aren't built in to your program, the code won't compile. This sounds a bit annoying but is actually a nice feature. Sometimes errors occur but the program keeps running, generating garbage data. The Java compiler will alert you to potential exceptions, allowing you to make arrangements in your code to handle them.

Libraries

The code libraries available to Fortran programmers are limited in scope. The creators of the Numerical Algorithms Group (NAG) Fortran 90 Library boast of having more than 254 callable procedures. Almost all of these are mathematical or statistical analysis functions. If you want to do anything beyond mathematical analysis with Fortran, you are pretty much left to do all the work yourself.

One of the great strengths of the Java language is the enormous collection of code libraries that you can utilize when developing your programs. There are literally thousands of classes, interfaces, and constants at your disposal. The libraries cover almost every programming topic imaginable from math functions, to collections, to GUI components, to network programming. The libraries are generally free and easy to download and install on your system.

The libraries consist of classes and other programming structures grouped together in entities called *packages*. The packages are sorted by function. The `java.io` package, for example, contains classes used in Input/Output (I/O) operations. You can make part or all of a package available to your program by placing an `import` declaration at the top of the program

Built-In Math Functions

Fortran is superior to Java (or to C or C++ for that matter) in its mathematical functions that are either intrinsic to the language or available through the commercially available Fortran libraries. The NAG Fortran Libraries have functions to compute gamma functions, Bessel functions, error functions, Fresnel integrals, and elliptic integrals, to name a few.

The Java libraries provide built-in functions to compute absolute value, power, square root, transcendental, trigonometric, rounding, and other mathematical functions. The Java math methods are modeled after the algorithms found in the 1995 version of the Freely Distributable Math Library (`fdlibm`) package. There is nothing exotic in the Java math capability. There is nothing to compute a Bessel function or anything like that, for example.

That being said, there is nothing to prevent you or someone else from creating Java mathematical function libraries that match or exceed the Fortran capability. The Java Native Interface (JNI) can be used to call external native routines. Indeed, as more and more scientific and engineering programmers move over to Java, extensive math libraries will become available. We will see how to create user-defined Java math functions in Chapter 17.

Input/Output Capability

The I/O capability of Fortran is primitive. The basic I/O statements are READ, WRITE, and PRINT. The READ function can be used to read formatted or unformatted data either from a file or from standard input. The WRITE and

`PRINT` statements are used to write data. A `WRITE` statement can be used to write to a file.

Java provides an entire library devoted to I/O functionality. Java uses a stream-based I/O system. A stream is simply an abstraction that represents a connection between a data source and a destination. Java provides a wide array of specialized I/O stream classes in two general categories. Character streams are designed to read and write character data. The characters can be read in one at a time or an entire line of data can be read in as a `String`. Byte streams are intended to read and write binary data. The data can be read in one byte at a time or an entire buffer of byte data can be read. With Java, there is a convenient I/O class to read or write any type of data from any data source.

GUIs and Web-Based Applications

If you want to create a GUI with Fortran you are out of luck. Fortran does not have that capability. Java, on the other hand, can be used to create sophisticated GUI front-ends for your engineering or scientific applications. The Java standard libraries have entire packages devoted to GUI classes and interfaces. You can also develop your own custom GUI components. With Java you can write a GUI front-end for your scientific or engineering application without having to learn or use another programming language.

Java also has the capability to create web-based client/server applications. Using Java's network programming capability, you can place your scientific or engineering application on a central server and any number of client machines can access the application via their web browsers. A brief introduction to Java servlets is provided in Chapter 27.

3

MOVING FROM C TO JAVA

If you are a C programmer moving to Java, there is good news. Java is a C-based language, so much of the basic syntax is the same—you still put semicolons at the end of statements, array indices still start at 0, and so on. Every Java program will have a `main()` method that serves as the starting point of the program just as in C. Some of the built-in library functions share the same names in Java and C.

While Java and C share a number of similarities, there are new concepts to learn when moving to Java. The primary shift from C to Java is that you will have to learn how to think in an object-oriented sense. A C program is a collection of functions. A Java program is a collection of classes. A class is a block of code that provides the definition, or blueprint, for an object. Your Java programs will spend a lot of their time creating and manipulating objects.

You will also find that Java is more powerful and versatile than C. You can define how your methods and data can be accessed by outside users. You can create different types of methods and variables by applying modifying keywords to them. You can build sophisticated class hierarchies where classes share and build upon the capabilities of other classes. You can take advantage of the built-in exception handling capability of Java.

This chapter will help you on your way in moving from C to Java. It will provide a top-level look at some of the important similarities and differences between Java and C. This chapter is not meant to be a comprehensive tutorial for either C or Java. For a detailed review of the core elements of the Java language, see Chapters 6–16 of this book.

In this chapter we will discuss —

- Program structure
- Basic syntax
- Java classes versus C structs
- Variables
- Pointers
- Functions and methods
- Arrays
- Dynamic memory allocation
- Exception handling
- C libraries and Java APIs
- Strings
- Built-in math functions
- Basic printing
- Input/Output capability
- GUIs and web-based applications

Program Structure

One main difference between C and Java is the fundamental program structure of the two languages. C programs are function based. The function is the primary building block of a C program. All statements except for `#include` statements, function prototypes, and global variable declarations are placed inside functions. A C program execution will largely consist of a series of function calls.

Java is an object-oriented language. The class is the primary building block of a Java program. Classes aren't all that mysterious. In simplistic terms, classes are just named blocks of code that can define both methods (functions) and data. Classes provide the blueprints for the objects that make Java object oriented. All executable statements in Java must be placed inside a class. A Java program execution will normally consist of creating one or more objects and manipulating the objects.

One similarity between Java and C is that both languages use a `main()` function (or method) to define the entry point for program execution. The system calls the `main()` function when the program is run.

Basic Syntax

As mentioned before, Java is a C-based language and much of the basic syntax is the same. Both languages allow you to indent statements any way you like. Indentation is largely used to make code more readable. Both languages end statements with a semicolon. Braces are used to delimit blocks of code.

The mathematical, relational, assignment, and boolean operators are the same in Java and C. In addition to mathematical addition, Java uses the + operator to concatenate strings. Java does not use the address operator (&), dereference (*), or struct access (->) operators because it does not support publicly accessible pointers. Java and C use the same types of loop and flow control structures including `if-else`, `while`, `do-while`, `for`, and `switch` statements. Java also has the transfer of control statements `return`, `break`, and `continue`.

Java Classes vs. C Structs

Java is an object-oriented programming language. C is not. The C language does not support objects. The closest C comes to defining an object is the `struct` or `union` programming constructs. As you probably know, a `struct` is a collection of named data members. The data members can be of different types. You can declare a `struct` variable that is a reference to a `struct`. The values of the `struct` data members can be accessed by typing the `struct` variable name, a period, and the data member name.

If you are familiar with using `structs`, it shouldn't be too great a leap to become familiar with the concept of a class. A Java class is basically just a named block of code that defines a collection of both fields and methods. A class is more self-contained than a `struct` in that a class can (and should) define all the methods required to manipulate its data members. Java classes can make use of the powerful object-oriented concepts of inheritance, polymorphism, and encapsulation. There are many different types of classes according to whether one or more modifying keywords are applied to them. You can have `public` and `private` classes, `abstract` and `final` classes. You can nest a class definition inside another class definition

You can create instances of a class. A class instance is also known as an object. You can declare variables that are references to class instances. A class can define a class instance as one of its fields.

Variables

Both C and Java define a variety of data types. The types each language supports are shown in Table 3.1.

Some of the types supported by C are not supported by Java and vice versa. Java does not support `signed` or `unsigned` types. All Java integral types (including `char`) are signed. Java does not use the `long double` or `void` type. Java does not support pointers, so there are no pointer or function pointer types in Java. The same can be said of `struct` and `union` types.

Java does provide some useful data types that are not provided by C. The `boolean` type has a true or false value. Using a `boolean` variable is more convenient than using 0 for false and 1 for true as in C. Java provides the `byte` type that represents a single byte of data. Because Java is object oriented, you can declare variables that are references to class instances (objects).

When a C variable is declared outside of any function definition it is a global variable and is available anywhere inside a C program. Java does not support global variables. A Java class variable is one that is declared outside of any method definitions and is available anywhere inside the class in which it is declared. Both C and Java support local variables. A local variable is declared inside a method, a `for` statement, or other block of code and exists only inside the block in which it is defined.

TABLE 3.1 C and Java Types

TYPE	C	JAVA
boolean	No	Yes
byte	No	Yes
char	Yes	Yes
signed char, unsigned char	Yes	No
short, int, long	Yes	Yes
unsigned short, unsigned int, unsigned long	Yes	No
float, double	Yes	Yes
long double	Yes	No
void	Yes	No
pointer, function pointer	Yes	No
struct, union	Yes	No
reference	No	Yes

In both languages, variables must be declared before they are used. Variable declaration statements in C must be placed before any other executable statements in the block of code in which the variable is defined. A Java variable can be declared anywhere in the program as long as it is declared before it is used. The syntax for declaring C or Java variables is the same: the type, the variable name, and a semicolon.

```
type variable_name;
```

The variable can be initialized when it is declared or later in the program. Java and C are similar in that variables only have scope inside the block of code in which they are declared. A C variable can be declared to be `static` or `extern`. Java variables can be declared to be `static`, `final`, `public`, `private`, `protected`, `final`, `transient`, and `volatile`

POINTERS

A C program can make use of pointers to directly access locations in memory. Pointers can be used to change the value of a variable and are also routinely used to manipulate arrays. Pointers can be useful in certain situations but can also be dangerous in that pointers have the potential to do bad things such as corrupt memory.

Java does not support publicly accessible pointers. Java has been designed so that there is no reason to use pointers. A Java primitive type variable stores a single value. You can manipulate the value directly. A reference type variable holds the address where a class instance or array is stored. The reference type variable provides all the access you will need.

FUNCTIONS AND METHODS

In C they are called functions. Java calls them methods. Both are named blocks of code that can be called from somewhere else in a program. Functions are the basic building blocks of a C program. Java methods, on the other hand, are always declared inside of a class. Java methods do not have to be prototyped.

A C function declaration includes the return type, function name, and input parameter list. The only modifying keywords that can be applied to a C function are `extern`, which means the function is defined outside of the current file, or `static`, which means the function cannot be referenced from other files. The body of the function is enclosed in braces.

Java method declarations contain the return type, name, and input parameter list of the method. The declaration may also include modifying keywords and a `throws` clause. Java methods are more powerful and versatile than their C counterparts. For one thing, Java methods can be given an access modifier. This keyword defines how and when the method can be accessed by other code. Java methods can be declared to be `static`, `abstract`, `final`, `native`, and `synchronized`. As with C, the body of a Java method is enclosed in braces.

Input arguments are passed to a C function by value, meaning that a copy of the value of the variable is sent to the function. Any changes made to the variable inside the function will not be reflected in the original variable. To have a C function alter the value of the original variable, a pointer to the variable must be passed to the function.

Arguments to Java methods are also passed by value. For arguments representing primitive types, a copy of the argument value is sent to the method. Any changes made to the value inside the method will not be made to the original value. For arguments representing reference types (objects or arrays), a copy of the reference to the location in memory where the data for the object or array is stored is sent to the method. Any changes made to the object inside the method will also be made to the original object.

C functions are called by simply typing the function name and providing the appropriate arguments. The way that Java methods are called depends on where the method call occurs. Inside the class in which they are defined, Java methods can be called by typing the method name and providing the appropriate arguments. Outside of the class in which they are defined, Java methods are called relative to a class instance or the class name depending on whether it is an instance or static method.

Arrays

While Java and C both start array indices from zero, there is a fundamental difference in the way the two languages treat arrays. With C, an array of a given data type is treated as a sequence of members of that type stored in contiguous locations in memory. The declaration syntax is the data type, the array name, and the size of the array enclosed in brackets.

```
int data[5];
```

The members of a C array can be accessed using the array name and index or with a pointer to the array. C arrays can be given a fixed size when they are declared or you can create a dynamically allocated array using pointers and the `malloc()` function.

In Java, arrays are reference types just like class instances. Creating a Java array is a two-step process. You first declare an array variable by specifying its type and name followed by a pair of brackets—

```
int data[];
```

Declaring an array variable does not allocate any memory for it. The second step in the array creation process is to allocate memory for the array variable using the new keyword followed by the type and size of the array.

```
data = new int[5];
```

The two steps can be combined to a single line

```
int data[] = new int[5];
```

Elements of a C array can be accessed either through the array index or by using a pointer to the array. Because Java does not support pointers, Java array elements are accessed only through indexes. Both C and Java use a pair of brackets around the index of the element to be accessed. For example, to assign the value 45 to the third element of an array named `data` you would type—

```
data[2] = 45;
```

When looking at the above syntax, keep in mind that Java array indices start at 0. The first element of the `data` array would be `data[0]`.

Dynamic Memory Allocation

With C, you can define the size of an array when the array is declared. Using pointers, you can also determine the size and dynamically allocate memory for an array at runtime. This can be useful if the required size for the array may vary from run to run in that you don't have to worry about declaring a really large array to cover all possibilities. The downside to dynamic memory allocation is that it is up to the programmer to properly allocate and deallocate the dynamic memory. If memory is not properly deallocated, you can create the dreaded memory leak.

Java does not support explicit dynamic memory allocation and deallocation because a sophisticated memory management system is part of the JVM that executes Java programs. As part of the memory management system, Java uses a mechanism known as the garbage collector that periodically monitors a Java program while it is running. Whenever a variable goes out of scope it is eligible to be garbage collected, meaning that memory assigned to the variable is deallocated and made available for use by some other part of the program. A Java programmer never has to worry about manually deallocating memory.

Exception Handling

Exception handling allows you to recover from errors that might occur while your program is running. The C language has no built-in exception handling. If you want exception handling in a C program, you have to do it yourself. User-defined exception handling usually involves a potentially complicated series of `if-then` statements and user-defined error codes. The exception handling generally has to take place where the exception occurs. In a C program you cannot easily pass the exception handling off to another part of the code.

Exception handling is a part of the Java language. There are a series of classes and programming constructs that allow you to easily build exception handling capabilities into your Java program. You can define your own exception classes for any unique needs that your program might have. Blocks of code are used to catch and process exceptions. What's more, the exception handling can be passed on to another part of the program. The exception handling does not have to be performed where the exception occurs.

C Libraries and the Java APIs

Both C and Java have built-in libraries that you can access when writing your programs. The C libraries are somewhat limited in scope and consist mostly of functions and constants. You can import C libraries into your program using `#include` statements placed at the top of your program.

One of the great strengths of the Java language is the enormous collection of code libraries that you can utilize when developing your programs. The Java libraries are more commonly referred to as the Java Application Programming Interfaces (APIs). The Java APIs cover everything from I/O to GUI development to security and anything in between. The APIs consist of a collection of classes and interfaces organized in groups called *packages*. You can import part or all of a package into your program by placing `import` declarations at the top of the program. As well as providing a lot of useful methods and constants, the Java APIs include the class declarations that constitute a rich and sophisticated source of reusable code for your Java applications.

STRINGS

A string is a sequence of characters. Strings are very important when it comes to displaying, naming, and describing data. The C and Java languages represent strings in very different ways. In C, a string is represented by an array of characters. The end of the string is designated as such by the null character '/0'. The C libraries provide functions to manipulate strings such as the `strcpy()`, `strcat()`, and `strcmp()` functions. When dealing with these functions and with C strings in general you often use pointers.

In Java, strings are represented by the `String` class and as such are treated as any other reference type. The `String` class defines a large number of methods for creating, manipulating, and modifying strings. Java strings are immutable. Once a `String` object is initialized it cannot be changed. If a method is used to modify a string, a new `String` object is created containing the modified string. Both Java and C support the concept of a string literal. Any text surrounded by double quotes is a string literal.

BUILT-IN MATH FUNCTIONS

Both the Java and C libraries provide built-in functions to compute absolute value, power, square root, transcendental, trigonometric, rounding, and other mathematical functions. The built-in math capability of the two languages is quite similar, even some of the function/method names are identical. C has some built-in functions that Java does not—the hyperbolic trigonometric and base 10 logarithm functions, for example. Java has some math methods that C does not, the `toRadians()`, `min()`, and `max()` methods for instance. Java takes advantage of method overloading to streamline its math methods. While C has to define three absolute value methods, one for each of three data types, Java only has to define one absolute value method that can take integer or floating point arguments.

Basic Printing

Basic printing in C is performed using the `printf()` and `fprintf()` functions. These functions print a string to either the console or to a file using format specifiers (`%lf`, `%s`, etc.) to convert variable values to strings. The basic print functions in Java are the `print()` and `println()` methods. Every Java object has a handy method called `toString()` that returns a string representation of it.

Input/Output Capability

The I/O functionality in C is rudimentary at best. You spend a lot of time using nonintuitive functions such as `scanf()`, `sscanf()`, and `gets()`. Some of the functions will read a newline character at the end of a line and some will not. These functions also tend to be quite format-specific. You have to specify exactly what variable type is to be read and returned from these functions. It is easy to run into conversion problems between, say, a `float` and a `double`. Reading and parsing an input file can be an intricate and error-prone process.

Java has a much improved I/O functionality over that offered by C. Like C, Java uses a stream-based I/O system. A data stream is simply an abstraction that represents a data connection between a source and a destination. Java provides a wide array of specialized I/O stream classes in two general categories. Character streams are designed to read and write character data. The characters can be read in one at a time or an entire line of data can be read in as a `String`. Byte streams are intended to read and write binary data. The data can be read in one byte at a time or an entire buffer of byte data can be read.

GUIs and Web-Based Applications

The standard C libraries do not contain any GUI or web-based application capability. Java has entire libraries devoted to GUI development. You can also develop your own custom GUI components. With Java you can write a sophisticated GUI front-end for your scientific and engineering application without having to learn or use another programming language. A brief introduction to Java GUI development is provided in Chapter 26. Java also allows you to develop powerful web-based applications with an extraordinarily powerful set of facilities such as servlets, JavaServer Pages (JSP), and Enterprise JavaBeans (EJBs). An introduction to web-based applications can be found in Chapter 27.

MOVING FROM C++ TO JAVA

If you are moving from C++ to Java there is good news. The transition from C++ to Java is easier than the transition from C or Fortran to Java. The developers of Java based their language in part on C++. Much of the basic syntax is the same. Java is also an object-oriented language. You will still be defining classes, constructors, and so on. One way to think about Java is that it is a streamlined, expanded, purely object-oriented version of C++.

The language is streamlined because the developers of Java sought to include many of the more useful features of C++ while eliminating things that were of marginal value and/or could lead you into trouble. One of the key goals of the developers of Java was to eliminate the redundancies that exist in both C++ and C. For example, there is no need to support structures and unions in addition to classes. Anything you would do with a structure or union, you can do with a class. Java is expanded with respect to C++ because Java can do a lot of things that C++ cannot. For example, Java has a built-in capability for multithreaded programming. You can add GUI frontends to your programs using Java. The Java language is also designed to access and make use of the Internet. You can create Web-based scientific or engineering applications that can be accessed over the Internet via a web browser.

In this chapter we will look at some of the main differences between C++ and Java. We will also examine some of the things that a C++ programmer will have to change about her way of doing things when she moves over to Java. The specific topics we will cover in this chapter are—

- Basic syntax
- Preprocessor directives
- Data types
- Pointers
- Structures, unions, enumerations
- Inheritance and interfaces
- Built-in math functions
- Standard I/O streams
- Strings
- Memory management

Basic Syntax

Much of the basic syntax between Java and C++ is the same. Both languages do things like end executable statements in a semicolon, start array indices from 0, and so on. But there are some important differences. For example, other than the + operator that is used to add numbers and concatenate strings, Java does not support operator overloading. Eliminating operator overloading was done to simplify the language. In Java, the functionality of operator overloading can be achieved by defining appropriate methods. Java does not define the `delete` operator.

Java does not have a `goto` statement. This construct was probably the most hated and misused programming syntax of all time, so Java simply eliminated it. What's more, Java made `goto` a reserved word so it couldn't be used at all. To exit from a block of code, Java uses the `break` and `continue` statements. The `break` and `continue` statements can be labeled to exit a labeled block of code. This feature can be used to break out of an outer block of code from an inner block.

Preprocessor Directives

Java does not use preprocessor directives. As it is, preproccessor directives are more commonly used in C than in C++. Indeed many C++ programmers consider it bad form to use preprocessor directives. The Java developers decided to eliminate them entirely. The elimination of preprocessor directives makes a Java program more readable. You don't have to wind your way through all the `#define` and `typedef` statements to see what is actually going on with a Java program. Because there are no preproccessor directives there is also no need for header files. Java uses constants defined in classes to partly take the place of `#define` statements.

Data Types

The C++ and Java languages define many of the same types—`int`, `short`, `long`, `float`, `double`, to name a few. Java does not support structures or unions so there are no `struct` or `union` types in Java. Java also does not support unsigned integer types. All Java integral types (including `char`) are signed. Both Java and C++ define a boolean type. Java calls it `boolean`. C++ calls it `bool`. Other types not included in the Java language are `pointer` and `void` types. Java provides the `byte` type, representing a single byte of data, that C++ does not.

Pointers

One of the major differences between Java and C++ is that Java does not support publicly accessible pointers. A pointer, as any C++ programmer knows, is a powerful tool that lets you directly access locations in memory. Pointers are also dangerous for the same reason, because they let you directly access locations in memory. More programming bugs are caused by misuse of pointers than any other reason.

Beyond increasing the likelihood of introducing bugs into your programs, pointers also pose a security risk in that a pointer can be used to access memory locations outside of those used by the program. A malicious programmer can use pointers to corrupt memory, damage system files, or do other heinous things.

The way the Java language is constructed makes pointers of marginal value anyway. Arrays are objects. You can access array elements using an index. Strings are likewise objects, so there is no reason to define a pointer to a string. There aren't any structures, so there is no need for pointers there. You don't need to use pointers as method arguments, because when a method argument is an object Java will automatically pass to the method a reference to the object.

Structures, Unions, Enumerations

Java does not support the structure, union, or enumeration programming constructs. Structures and unions are redundant with respect to classes. Anything you can do with a structure or union you can do within a class. A similar redundancy exists between enumerations and classes. You can represent what an enumeration does by simply creating a class that defines a series of constants.

Inheritance and Interfaces

Both C++ and Java support the powerful object-oriented programming concept known as inheritance that allows a class to build upon the capabilities of another class. Java and C++ differ with respect to inheritance in that Java does not support multiple inheritance. A Java class can have only one direct superclass that itself can have only one direct superclass and so on.

Java partially compensates for its lack of multiple inheritance through a programming construct known as an interface. An interface declares one or more methods that must be implemented by any class that implements the interface. In this way, interfaces are somewhat similar to abstract classes. The interface only specifies the method name, return type, and input parameter list while providing no limitations on what the body of the method will be. How the method is implemented is up to the class that implements the interfaces. Two classes may implement a method declared in an interface in completely different ways. A given class can implement any number of interfaces.

Built-In Math Functions

Both the Java and C++ libraries provide standard functions to compute absolute value, power, square root, transcendental, trigonometric, rounding, and other mathematical functions. The built-in math capability of the two languages is quite similar and many of the function/method names are identical. The C++ language has some built-in math capability that Java does not, specifically the hyperbolic trigonometric and base 10 logarithmic functions. Java has some math methods that C++ does not— the `toRadians()`, `min()`, and `max()` methods for instance. Both Java and C++ make use of method overloading to define multiple versions of some mathematical functions that take different types of input arguments.

STANDARD I/O

C++ makes use of the `cin` identifier and the >> operator to read keyboard input. Java uses a static instance of the `InputStream` class named `System.in` to do the same thing. C++ uses the `cout` identifier with the << operator to write data to the console. Java uses a static instance of the `PrintStream` class named `System.out` to represent the standard output stream. Java does not use either the << or >> operators for I/O functions but does use these symbols to represent bitwise shift operators.

STRINGS

C++ supports strings in two ways. The first way is the C convention of using a null-terminated character array. The second is by using the `String` class. Java defines a `String` class that encapsulates a sequence of Unicode characters. The `String` class defines a wide variety of methods that can be used to create, modify, and manipulate strings. A Java `String` is by definition an object rather than an array of characters. Both Java and C++ use the + operator to concatenate two strings. The C++ language does not fully support all Unicode characters. A `char` in C++ is 1 byte. In Java, a `char` is 2 bytes, meaning that a Java `char` can represent any Unicode character.

MEMORY MANAGEMENT

With C++, the programmer is responsible for memory management for a given program. Memory that is allocated for an object using the `new` operator must be explicitly deallocated using the `delete` operator. The `delete` operation is often performed in a specialized method called a *destructor*. If you don't properly deallocate memory, you can get the dreaded memory leak.

You don't have to worry about managing memory with Java. A built-in system thread, the garbage collector, is automatically run every so often by the Java runtime. The garbage collector checks all existing objects and releases the resources allocated to any object if there are no longer any references to it. This feature eliminates the possibility of memory leaks that can happen with a C++ program. There are no destructors in Java although a class can declare a `finalize()` method that can perform some application-specific clean-up operations when it is called.

An Overview of Object-Oriented Programming Concepts

Moving into the object-oriented programming world can be a bit confusing. You are suddenly faced with a number of unfamiliar terms and concepts. You hear talk about objects, inheritance, and polymorphism and wonder what these mysterious terms really mean. This chapter is meant to take some of the mystery out of some general (and important) object-oriented programming concepts. Once you finish this chapter you should be comfortable with the following object-oriented topics—

- Objects
- Classes
- Encapsulation
- Inheritance
- Polymorphism

Objects

We have talked about Java being an object-oriented programming language. But what exactly is an object? To put it simply, an object is an abstraction that represents something. The "something" might be a gas mixture, a supporting beam, a charged particle, or any other element of your scientific or engineering analysis. An object has two general characteristics—state and behavior. An object's state represents what the object knows. The state is maintained in one or more variables associated with the object. An object's behavior represents what the object can do. The behavior is implemented by defining methods that the object can access. Simply put, a method is a named block of code that does something.

In Java, an object is an instance of a class. Java arrays are also objects, but their class is internally defined. An object contains its own copy of the nonstatic fields declared by the class. A class can declare variables that are reference types (objects and arrays) as well as primitive types such as the `char`, `int`, and `double`. In your Java programs you will likely create one or more objects and manipulate the state of the objects by calling methods on them.

Classes

A class provides the blueprint for an object. A class is a named block of code that defines the state (fields) and behavior (methods) for objects that are instances of the class. The fields and methods are called the *members* of the class. The fields can be either primitive (`int`, `double`, etc) or reference (objects, arrays) types. The class members can be *instance,* meaning they are associated with an instance of the class, or *static,* meaning there is one copy shared by all instances of the class. Members can be given access modifiers that determine how and if the member can be accessed outside of the class in which it is declared. While a class declares the data structure for an object, each object is free to assign its own values to that data structure. Every object will have its own copies of the nonstatic fields of its class.

Every Java program will have at least one class. All executable statements in a Java program must be placed inside a class. An abstract class is one that provides the blueprint for other classes. A subclass is one that extends the capabilities of another class. A class can be declared to be `final`, in which case it cannot be extended.

Encapsulation

Encapsulation is a concept that relates to how classes are defined. It states that a class should be self-contained, meaning that it should declare all of the fields and methods to do whatever it has to do. There is one school of thought that interprets encapsulation to mean that all access to an object's variables should be performed using methods provided by the object. Encapsulation facilitates modularity. A class that contains everything it needs can be easily incorporated into larger Java programs.

Encapsulation gives the class developer complete control over how the class is used. If the access to data is explicitly defined and controlled, it ensures that data can't be misused. Encapsulation is also a way to hide complexity. The user only has access to the publicly accessible members of a class. There may be a lot more complexity built in to the class that the user doesn't need to know about and, more importantly, shouldn't mess around with. This complexity can be hidden from outside interaction.

Encapsulation allows you to modify classes without breaking any existing applications that use the classes. As long as the public interface is unchanged, other elements of the class can be modified or added without impacting applications that use the older version. Older programs that use the class would still have to be recompiled, but their interface to the class would remain unchanged.

Inheritance

Inheritance is a very powerful and useful functionality that allows you to define a class that extends the capabilities of another class. You can build upon something that already exists. Inheritance provides a mechanism for creating hierarchies of related classes. Java allows only single inheritance. A class can have only one direct superclass, which itself can have only one superclass, and so on. This is in contrast to a language such as C++ that allows a class to inherit from multiple superclasses.

A subclass has access to all the nonprivate members of its superclass. The subclass also has access to the nonprivate members of the superclass of its superclass and so on up the inheritance hierarchy. Inheritance facilitates code reuse and reduces duplication of effort. You can declare a member used by multiple classes inside a superclass higher up the class hierarchy. All descendant classes can then access the member.

Inheritance also enables the concept of polymorphism.. An abstract superclass can declare the methods that must be implemented by subclasses without specifying the details of the implementation. More details on inheritance and how to use it are provided in Chapter 7.

Polymorphism

Polymorphism is described as "One interface, many implementations." It is a way of imposing a generic structure onto a group of related code elements. Java implements polymorphism by defining code structures that serve as blueprints for a wide range of classes and interfaces while giving the classes and interfaces the freedom to implement the blueprint as they see fit.

An abstract class is an example of polymorphism. An abstract class can define abstract methods by declaring a method's *signature,* including the return type, method name, and parameter list. The abstract methods provide no implementation. A subclass of the abstract class then implements the abstract class methods providing whatever functionality is required by the subclass. Different subclasses can implement the methods in different ways as long as the signature and accessibility are the same.

Interfaces are another example of polymorphism. They are similar to abstract classes in that they define method signatures without giving any implementation for the methods. It is up to a class that implements the interface to provide the method implementations, and the class has complete freedom in how it does this.

Polymorphism can also be seen in the fact that Java allows method overloading, letting you create different versions of a method. Each version will have the same function but will take different input arguments. An example of an overloaded method is the `abs()` method from the `java.lang.Math` class. There are four versions of the `abs()` method, each taking a different input argument type, but the four methods share a common name and function.

6

BASIC SYNTAX

J ava is a powerful, versatile, object-oriented programming language with a variety of structured elements. As a Java programmer you will be working with classes, methods, interfaces, constructors, variables, exception handling, and more. But before we cover those elements, we need to discuss the basic syntax that is common to all Java programming constructs. This chapter will cover the important elements of basic Java syntax. Specifically we will discuss—

- General Java syntax and a simple Java program
- Comments
- Operators
- Loops and other flow of control structures
- Transfer of control statements
- Basic printing and keyboard I/O

GENERAL SYNTAX AND A SIMPLE JAVA PROGRAM

Java is based on C and C++ and much of its basic syntax is similar to those languages. This is why the transition from a language like C or C++ to Java is easier than the transition from a language like Fortran to Java. For example, every executable statement in a Java program is terminated with a semicolon just as in a C or C++ program. Java array indices start at 0 and the array access expression uses brackets—[ ]— rather than parentheses—( ).

Lines of code can be indented any way you like. You can start a line in the first column or the 20th if you desire. In Java, indenting is primarily used to make certain sections of a code listing stand out, making it easier to read. It is customary, for instance, to indent the body of a method from the method declaration.

Braces—{ }—denote blocks of code in Java. You can define blocks of code anywhere in your program. Typically blocks of code are used to designate class definitions, method bodies, and loop and control structure elements.

Before we go any further, let's look at a simple Java program that will contain many of the elements we discussed in the previous paragraphs.

Example: A Simple Java Program

This is the simplest type of Java program. It consists of one class named `SimpleProgram` that defines one method called `main()`. Your programs will eventually have a lot more to them. You may import packages, extend the capabilities of existing classes, define constructors and methods, and so on. But every Java application you will write will consist of at least one class and will define a `main()` method.

The program defines two blocks of code. The first encloses the definition of the `SimpleProgram` class. The second surrounds the body of the `main()` method. Note the indentation. There are two levels of indentation. The first distinguishes the `main()` method from the `SimpleProgram` class. The second helps the body of the `main()` method stand out from the method declaration syntax.

Inside the `main()` method, two variables are declared and one is given an initial value. A mathematical operation is performed and the value of the `area` variable is assigned to the result. The `println()` method is called to write a `String` of text to an output stream. In this case the `main()` method calls the `println()` method of the standard output stream, and the `String` is written to the console. Basic printing is described at the end of this chapter, and the Java I/O classes are described in detail in Chapter 25.

```
public class SimpleProgram
{
  public static void main(String args[]) {
    double area, radius = 2.0;
    area = Math.PI*radius*radius;
```

```
      System.out.println("area of circle is " + area);
    }
}
```

Output—

```
area of circle is 12.566370614359172
```

COMMENTS

Every good computer program needs comments to help someone (even the developer) figure out what the code is doing. Java provides three types of comments. The first is the C-based multiline comment. The comment begins with the token /* and ends with the token */. Everything between these characters is considered a comment and is ignored by the compiler. As the name suggests, multiline comments can span more than one line.

The second type of comment is a single line comment. The token // is placed at the beginning of the comment. This comment cannot span multiple lines. The third type is a documentation comment. The syntax is similar to a multiline comment except it begins with /**. There is a utility that comes with the Java SDK called javadoc. By default, this utility creates HTML files that describe Java source code. (The Sun Java doc pages were created using the javadoc utility.) Documentation comments are incorporated into the HTML files created by javadoc.

Example: Using Comments

```
public class CommentDemo
{
  public static void main(String args[]) {
    //  This is a single line comment
    /* This is a comment
        that can span more
        than one line  */
    /**  @author Grant Palmer */
  }
}
```

This example shows the three types of comments in action. The @author syntax is one of the special javadoc tags that can be used with documentation comments. For more information on documentation comments and their associated tags, consult the Sun Java online documentation at http://java.sun.com/j2se/javadoc.

Operators

Every language defines operators for performing mathematical operations, making comparisons, or for creating logical expressions. In addition to the operators that perform these functions, Java defines other operators that create or evaluate objects, call methods, and access data members.

There are three general kinds of operators, based on the number of operands they act upon. *Unary* operators act upon one operand. The increment and decrement operators are examples. *Binary* operators are placed between a left-hand side and right-hand side operator. The addition operator (+) is an example. *Ternary* operators work with three operands. Java defines one ternary operator that provides a shorthand version of an `if-else` statement.

This section describes the operators supported by Java according to operator type. Specifically we will cover—

- Arithmetic operators
- Assignment operators
- Increment/Decrement operators
- Relational operators
- Boolean operators
- Bitwise operators
- Miscellaneous operators

Arithmetic Operators

The operators in Table 6.1 perform the basic math functions of addition, subtraction, multiplication, and division. They are binary operators, meaning that they are placed between two operands. The modulus operator returns the remainder of its left-hand operand divided by its right-hand operand. The - operator also has a unary form that changes the sign of its operand. A positive value becomes negative and vice versa. The + operator is also used for concatenating strings.

TABLE 6.1 Arithmetic Operators

Operator	Purpose
+	Addition
-	Subtraction
*	Multiplication
/	Division
%	Modulus (remainder)

The return value for the math operators depends on the data type of the operands. Floating point types (`float` and `double`) have precedence over integer types (`short`, `int`, and `long`). Higher precision types (`double`, `long`) have precedence over lower precision types (`float`, `int`). What this means is that a `float` added to a `long` will result in a `float`, a `double` multiplied by a `float` will result in a `double`, and so on.

Example: Using Arithmetic Operators

This example demonstrates some of the basic arithmetic operators in action. The output may look a little odd to you. There can be a small round-off error with floating point math. You have to be careful of this because, small though it may be, if you compared the value of the variable a to the value 15.28 (`if (a == 15.28)`) the comparison would be false. Note that the + operator is used in two contexts in this example. It is used as the addition operator and as a `String` concatenation operator with the `println()` method.

```
public class ArithOpDemo
{
  public static void main(String args[]) {
     double a = 2.3*8 - 4.12;
     System.out.println("answer is " + a);
     a = a + 1.0;
     System.out.println("answer is " + a);
  }
}
```

Output—

```
answer is 14.27999999998
answer is 15.27999999998
```

Assignment Operators

The assignment operators supported by Java are shown in Table 6.2. The = operator is the basic binary assignment operator. The value of the right-hand operand is assigned to the left-hand operand. The other operators are shorthand operators that combine an assignment with an arithmetic or bitwise operation. For example, a += b is equivalent to a = a + b. The other compound assignment operators work in the same manner.

Example: Using Assignment Operators

This example is the same as the "Using Arithmetic Operators" example except the += operator is used. In addition to being more compact, assignment operators can help prevent bugs in your code. Let's say you defined two variables named N202 and N02. You might accidentally type "N202 = N02 + 0.1"

Table 6.2 Assignment Operators

Operator	Purpose
=	Simple assignment
+=	a = a + b
-=	a = a − b
*=	a = a * b
/=	a = a / b
%=	a = a%b
&=	a = a & b
|=	a = a | b
^=	a = a ^ b
>>=	a = a >> b
>>>=	a = a >>> b
<<=	a = a << b

when you meant to type "N202 = N202 + 0.1." Using the += assignment operator would eliminate this possibility.

```
public class AssignOpDemo
{
  public static void main(String args[]) {
    double a = 2.3*8.0 - 4.12;
    System.out.println("answer is " + a);
    a += 1.0;
    System.out.println("answer is " + a);
  }
}
```

Output—

```
answer is 14.27999999998
answer is 15.27999999998
```

Increment/Decrement Operators

The unary operators in Table 6.3 are used to increment or decrement the value of their operands. The operand can be an integer or floating point type. The operator can perform the increment or decrement in either a prefix or postfix manner.

Table 6.3 Increment/Decrement Operators

Operator	Purpose
++	Increment value by 1
−−	Decrement value by 1

With a prefix operation, the operator is placed before the operand (++variable). The increment or decrement occurs before any other operations are performed. When the operand is placed after the variable (variable++), the increment or decrement is performed in a postfix manner, meaning it is done after any other operations take place. Because of this difference, you should be careful when combining an increment or decrement with other operations. To be safe, you can place the increment/decrement statement on a line by itself.

Example: Using the Increment Operator

The increment operator is used twice in this example—to cycle through the elements of an array and to increment the value of the integer variable j.

```
public class IncOpDemo
{
  public static void main(String args[]) {
    int j = 0;
    int[] intArray = new int[4];

    for(int k=0; k<intArray.length; ++k) {
      intArray[k] = ++j;
      System.out.println("intArray["+k+"] = " +
                      intArray[k]);
    }
  }
}
```

      Output—

```
intArray[0] = 1
intArray[1] = 2
intArray[2] = 3
intArray[3] = 4
```

The output of this program depends on whether the prefix or postfix version of the ++ operator is used. The way it is written, the increment happens and then the value is assigned to the array element. If the line were written as

```
intArray[k] = j++;
```

then the increment would have taken place after the assignment was performed. In this case, the output would have been

```
intArray[0] = 0
intArray[1] = 1
intArray[2] = 2
intArray[3] = 3
```

Relational Operators

The binary operators in Table 6-4 are used to compare one operand to another. They are commonly used in flow control structures such as if, while, and

TABLE 6.4 Relational Operators

OPERATOR	PURPOSE
==	Equal to
!=	Not equal to
>	Greater than
>=	Greater than or equal to
<	Less than
<=	Less than or equal to

do-while statements. The return value from these operators is a boolean true or false. Unlike C where you can get into trouble by mistakenly typing = instead of ==, Java will perform a type check of a conditional statement and won't allow syntax such as if (b = 2.0).

Example: Using Relational Operators

This is a typical use of a relational operator in a scientific or engineering application. A while loop is used to test whether a computation has converged. The current error is compared against a preset tolerance and the calculation continues until the error is less than or equal to the tolerance. In this simple case, the error is simply cut in half during every iteration.

```
public class RelationalOpDemo
{
  public static void main(String args[]) {
    double tol = 0.001;
    double error = 1.0;
    int iteration = 0;

    while (error >= tol) {
      error *= 0.5;
      ++iteration;
    }
    System.out.println("convergence achieved in " +
                       iteration + " steps");
  }
}
```

Output—

```
convergence achieved in 10 steps
```

Boolean Operators

The boolean operators shown in Table 6-5 are used with boolean operands. A boolean operand is one that evaluates to a true or false value. The first five

Table 6.5 Boolean Operators

Operator	Purpose
&	Logical AND
|	Logical OR
^	Exclusive OR
&&	Conditional AND
||	Conditional OR
!	NOT

are binary operators that are used to link two boolean expressions. The logical AND operator (&) returns true if both operands are true. The logical OR operator (|) returns true if either operand is true. The exclusive OR operator (^) returns true if either—but not both— operand is true. With these three operators, the right-hand operand will always be evaluated.

The conditional AND and OR operators work somewhat differently than their logical counterparts. With the conditional AND, the right-hand expression is only evaluated if the left-hand expression was true. With the conditional OR, the right-hand expression is only evaluated if the left-hand expression was false.

The NOT operator (!) is a unary operator. It is placed before a boolean operand and changes the value from true to false or vice versa. The return values for the binary boolean operators are summarized in Table 6.6.

Table 6.6 Results from Boolean Operators

	A&B A&&B	A|B A||B	A^B
a=true, b=true	true	true	false
a=true, b=false	false	true	true
a=false, b=true	false	true	true
a=false, b=false	false	false	false

Example: Using Boolean Operators

In this example, the `&&` operator is used to connect two boolean operands. If both operands are true, the statement following the `if` statement is executed. This is a situation where you need to use the conditional AND (`&&`) operator rather than the logical AND (`&`) operator. If you used the `&` operator both expressions are evaluated regardless of whether the first is true and you can get a divide by zero exception. With the && operator, the second expression is not evaluated if j=0.

```
public class BooleanOpDemo
{
  public static void main(String args[]) {
    int j = 0;
    if ( j != 0 && 1/j < 10 ) {
        System.out.println("Conditions met");
    } else {
        System.out.println("Conditions not met");
    }
  }
}
```

Output—

```
Conditions not met
```

Bitwise Operators

The bitwise operators shown in Table 6.7 accept only integral operands (byte, short, int, long, char). These operators act on the bits of their operands. The bitwise AND, OR, and exclusive OR operators are binary operators that evaluate each parallel pair of bits in each operand and return the appropriate value. For example, the bitwise OR returns 1 if either of the bits it is evaluating is 1.

The right and left bit shift operators (>> and <<) shift the bits of the left-hand operand right or left by the number of bits specified by the right-hand operand. The unsigned right shift operator (>>>) shifts the bits of the left-hand operand to the right by the number of bits specified by the right-hand operand and then places zeros in the vacated high order bit. The ~ operator is the bitwise complement. It is a unary operator that flips the bits of the operand it acts upon. Zeros become ones and vice versa. If you do use these operators in your

TABLE 6.7 Bitwise Operators

OPERATOR	PURPOSE
&	Bitwise AND
|	Bitwise OR
^	Bitwise exclusive OR
>>	Right bit shift
>>>	Unsigned right shift
<<	Left bit shift
~	Bitwise complement

scientific and engineering programming, you have to be careful. It is easy to think you are doing one thing when you are actually doing something else.

Example: Using Bitwise Operators

In this example, the bitwise OR operator is used between two integers. The binary representation of the number 12 is 1100. The binary representation of 13 is 1101. The statement 12 | 13 would return the value 1101 or 13.

```
public class BitwiseOpDemo
{
  public static void main(String args[]) {
    int j=12, k=13;
    int i = j|k;
    System.out.println("i is "+i);
  }
}
```

Output—

```
i is 13
```

Miscellaneous Operators

Table 6.8 lists miscellaneous operators that don't fall into the other general categories. The ternary operator (?:) is shorthand for an if-else statement. As its name implies, it acts upon three operands. The general usage of the ternary operator is

```
variable = condition ? value1 : value2;
```

This is equivalent to the syntax

```
if ( condition ) {
    variable = value1;
} else  {
    variable = value2;
}
```

TABLE 6.8 Miscellaneous Operators

OPERATOR	PURPOSE
?:	Ternary operator
(variable_type)	Cast operator
[ ]	Array index
.	Member call/access operator
new	Class instance creator
instanceof	Type comparison

The cast operator is used to temporarily convert or cast a variable of one type into another type. See Chapter 7 for more information on casting. Parentheses are also used to define method parameter lists and to designate operator precedence. The array indexer operator ([])is used to access the elements of an array. It is also used to declare and size arrays. See Chapter 13 for more information on this operator.

A period is used in the syntax to call methods and to access data members of a class. The new operator is used to create an object, allocating memory for it on the part of memory known as the heap. The instanceof operator is a binary operator that returns true if the left-hand operand is an instance of (part of the same class or interface hierarchy as) the right-hand operand.

Example: Miscellaneous Operators

This example shows three of the miscellaneous operators in action. The new keyword is used to create a Stack object. The instanceof operator is used to determine if the variable is an instance of the Vector class. The operator will also return true if the variable is a subclass of Vector. In this case, the Stack class is a subclass of Vector so the operator returns true. For more information on what a subclass is, consult Chapter 7. The Stack and Vector classes are contained in the java.util package of the Java API. To access these classes, we must import that package into our program. That is the reason for the import statement at the top of the program. For more information on packages, see Chapter 11. In the second part of the example, the ternary operator is used to implement an absolute value evaluation.

```
import java.util.*;

public class MiscOpDemo
{
  public static void main(String args[]) {
    Stack myStack = new Stack();
    double deltaT = -12.3;

    if (myStack instanceof Vector) {
       System.out.println("Variable is a Vector");
    }

    double temp = deltaT<0.0?-deltaT:deltaT;
    System.out.println("temp is "+temp);
  }
}
```

Output—

```
Variable is a Vector
temp is 12.3
```

The ternary syntax in the program is equivalent to

```
if (deltaT < 0.0) {
   temp = -deltaT;
} else {
   temp = deltaT;
}
```

Operator Precedence

If you use more than one operator in a given statement, how do you know which operation will be performed first? In many situations, the order in which things are done will make a difference. Fortunately, Java has a well-defined system of operator precedence to resolve these issues. The general hierarchy from highest to lowest precedence is —

1. Increment/Decrement
2. Casting
3. Arithmetic
4. Bitwise shift
5. Relational
6. Boolean
7. Ternary
8. Assignment

When binary operators of the same precedence appear in an expression, they are evaluated left-to-right except for assignment operators that are evaluated right-to-left. You can manually specify precedence by placing parentheses around the operation you want performed first.

Example: Operator Precedence Example

This example should be nothing new to anyone with programming experience. The basic rules are the same for most languages. Without the parentheses, the multiplication is performed before the addition. If you want the addition to be performed first, place parentheses around the operation.

```
public class OpPrecedence
{
  public static void main(String args[]) {
    int j;
    j = 8*4 + 2;
    System.out.println("j is " + j);
    j = 8*(4 + 2);
    System.out.println("j is " + j);
  }
}
```

Output—
```
j is 34
j is 48
```

Loops and Other Flow of Control Structures

A common programming need is to perform a given operation or computation over and over, either a set number of times or until a certain condition is met. You may also want to execute different sections of code depending on the evaluation of a condition. Java provides a wide variety of loops and flow of control structures to satisfy these programming requirements. This section will describe and demonstrate these structures.

`if-else` Statements

The `if-else` statement is a basic conditional branch statement. It allows you to selectively execute blocks of code according to whether a condition is satisfied. More than one condition can be tested and a default block of code can be provided if none of the conditions are met. The general syntax of the `if-else` statement is as follows—

```
if ( condition1 ) {
   //   execute this code
} else if ( condition2 ) {
   //   execute some other code
} else {
   //   default code
}
```

The conditions are expressions that evaluate to `true` or `false` values. The first condition to be tested is placed inside parentheses after the `if` keyword. You can nest `if-else` statements to test more than one condition. The block of code after the final `else` statement is a default block of code that is executed if none of the conditions are met. The `else` block is optional.

The conditions are evaluated in sequential order. If a condition is met, the block of code following the condition is executed and the `if-else` structure is exited. You can have compound conditions; for example, `if (a == 2 && b < 0)`. If only one executable statement follows the condition, the braces can be omitted, but this practice can be dangerous. If additional code is added at a later time you will have to remember to put the braces in. The safe way is to always use braces.

Example: Using `if-else` *Statements*

This is a typical example of using an `if-else` statement to evaluate an expression according to the value of a certain variable. In this case, we are computing a temperature-dependent property named `gamma`. Below a temperature of 500 K (Kelvin), `gamma` is a constant. Above 500 K, `gamma` is a function of temperature. Let us assume that the database for `gamma` only goes up to 2000 K. At temperatures above 2000 K, we can either extrapolate the value of `gamma` or set it to a fixed value.

A nested `if-else` statement is used to determine which expression for `gamma` should be used based on an input temperature. Another `if-else` statement decides what to do if the temperature exceeds the database range. Braces were used after every `if` and `else` statement. In some cases the braces aren't strictly necessary, but it is a safe way to program.

```
public class IfDemo
{
  public static void main(String args[]) {
    double temperature = 2340.0;
    double gamma;
    boolean extrapolate = false;

    if (temperature < 500.0 ) {
       gamma = 17.0;
    } else if (temperature < 2000.0 ) {
       gamma = 2.5 + 0.0295*temperature;
    } else {
       System.out.println(
            "temperature exceeds database range");
       if (extrapolate) {
          gamma = 2.5 + 0.0295*temperature;
       } else {
          gamma = 61.5;
       }
    }
    System.out.println("gamma is " + gamma);
  }
}
```

Output—

```
temperature exceeds database range
gamma is 61.5
```

`while` Loops

A `while` loop is a construct that executes a block of code as long as a condition is met. The condition can either be the value of a boolean variable or a boolean expression. The general syntax of a `while` loop is as follows—

```
while (condition) {
   // code to execute
}
```

The block of code after the condition will only execute if the condition is true. If the condition is never true, the block of code will never execute. Conversely, the syntax `while (true)` will create an infinite loop. Unlike C, the integers 1 and 0 cannot be used to represent true and false. You cannot, for instance, use the following syntax in a Java program—

```
while (1) {
   // code to execute
}
```

You could, however, use the following syntax, which, in this case, would create an infinite loop—

```
while (true) {
   // code to execute
}
```

Example: Using `while` Loops

Look at the "Using Relational Operators" example earlier in this chapter where a `while` loop is used to test for convergence.

`do-while` Loops

The `do-while` loop is similar to the `while` loop in that it will execute a block of code until a condition is met. With a `do-while` loop, the block of code is executed before the condition is evaluated. Therefore, the block of code is guaranteed to execute at least once. The general syntax for a `do-while` loop is as follows—

```
do {
   // code to execute
} while (boolean expression);
```

A `do-while` loop is useful for mathematical iterations and for creating console menus that redisplay themselves until the user types a certain keystroke.

Example: Using `do-while` Loops

In this example, a `do-while` loop is used to solve a fourth-order equation. The equation is solved using a Newton-Raphson iteration process. An initial guess is made of the dependent variable. An update to the dependent variable is found by computing the ratio of the current value of the function divided by the slope of the function. The iteration is placed inside a `do-while` loop and proceeds until the desired level of convergence is achieved. A `do-while` loop is used instead of a `while` loop because the evaluation of `deltaT` has to be performed at least once to compare it with the convergence criteria.

```
public class DoWhileDemo
{
  public static void main(String args[]) {
    double T = 0.0, deltaT, f, dfdT, tolerance = 0.001;
    int iteration = 0;

    //  The 4th-order equation T^4 - 2.5T = 1.5 is
    //  solved using a do-while loop
    do {
        f = Math.pow(T,4.0) - 2.5*T - 1.5;
        dfdT = 4.0*Math.pow(T,3.0) - 2.5;
        deltaT = -f/dfdT;
        T += deltaT;
        ++iteration;
    } while ( Math.abs(deltaT) > tolerance );

    f = Math.pow(T,4.0) - 2.5*T;

    System.out.println("convergence achieved in " +
                      iteration+" steps");
    System.out.println("T = " + T + "  f = " + f);
  }
}
```

Output—
```
convergence achieved in 3 steps
T = -0.56051718541    f = 1.5000173128
```

`for` Loops

The `for` loop is similar to the `while` loop in that it can be used to execute a block of code a number of times. A `for` loop is commonly used to iterate through the elements of an array. The general syntax of the `for` loop is as follows—

```
for (initialization; expression; update) {
   // code to execute
}
```

There are three parts to the syntax following the `for` keyword. There is an `initialization` statement that usually initializes the value of a loop control variable. This variable is typically part of the condition to be evaluated. The `expression` is a boolean that is evaluated every iteration. As long as the expression is true, the subsequent block of code is executed. The `update` part of the `for` loop usually increments or decrements the control variable. The `update` gets invoked after each iteration of the loop.

The `initialization`, `expression`, and `update` parts of the `for` loop are separated by semicolons. More than one statement can be placed inside the `initialization` and `update` sections, in which case commas separate the statements. You can nest `for` loops. Any or all of the three parts of the `for` loop can be omitted. For example, the following syntax creates an infinite loop—

```
for (;;) {
}
```

Example: Using `for` *Loops*

A typical use of `for` loops in scientific or engineering programming is to cycle through the elements of an array. In this example, elements of a 2-D array are assigned values using a pair of `for` loops, one for the rows of the array and one for the columns. The loop control variables (`i` and `j`) are defined in, and are local to, their respective `for` loops. More information about arrays can be found in Chapter 13.

```
public class ForDemo
{
  public static void main(String args[]) {
     int numSpecies = 3;
     double moleFr[] = { 0.1, 0.4, 0.5 };
     double dataArray[][] =
              new double[numSpecies][numSpecies];

     for (int i=0; i<numSpecies; ++i) {
       for (int j=0; j<numSpecies; ++j) {
          dataArray[i][j] = moleFr[i]*moleFr[j];
          System.out.println(
                   "dataArray[" + i + "][" + j +
                   "] = " + dataArray[i][j]);
       }
     }
  }
}
```

Output—

```
dataArray[0][0] = 0.01
dataArray[0][1] = 0.04
dataArray[0][2] = 0.05
dataArray[1][0] = 0.04
dataArray[1][1] = 0.16
dataArray[1][2] = 0.2
dataArray[2][0] = 0.05
dataArray[2][1] = 0.2
dataArray[2][2] = 0.25
```

`switch` Statements

A `switch` statement provides an alternative way to conditionally execute blocks of code as compared to an `if-else` statement. The result of an expression is compared against a number of values defined by `case` labels. If a match is found, the code following the `case` label is executed. An optional `default` label can be included that defines code to be executed if none of the `case` label values match the expression. The general syntax of a `switch` statement is —

```
switch (expression) {
   case value1:
       // execute some code
      break;
   case value2:
      // execute this code
      break;
   default:
     //  execute default code
}
```

The expression following the `switch` keyword must evaluate to a `byte`, `short`, `int`, or `char`. The values in the `case` labels must either be a constant expression or a `static final` variable. The `case` labels are terminated with colons rather than semicolons. You can nest `switch` statements.

The `break` statement causes the execution to exit the `switch` statement. The `break` statements are optional, but most of the time you will want to use them. If a `break` statement is omitted, the execution will continue to the next `case` label. This can sometimes be useful if you want to execute the same code after more than one `case`.

One difference between `switch` statements and `if-else` statements is that a `case` label only compares a single value. You can't build intricate boolean expressions (`if a << b && b==4`) into a `switch` statement.

Example: Using a `switch` *Statement*

In this example, a `switch` statement is used to allow the selection and execution of different physical models, depending on the value of a variable. Blottner, Gupta, and Sutherland are some of the models used for computing transport property coefficients. The value of the `model` variable is compared against the value of three `case` statements. The values that `model` is compared against are defined as `static final` variables. This makes the code easier to read and understand than if numbers were used in the `case` statements.

If a match is found, the code following the `case` statement is executed. In this simple example the name of the model selected is printed. In a real-life application, the transport property coefficients would be computed according to the selected model. The `break` statements exit the `switch` structure once the appropriate code is executed.

The Sutherland model is the default. There is no `break` statement after the `case SUTHERLAND:` syntax. If the value of `model` is 0 the code flows through to the `default` statement that indicates the Sutherland model was selected. Any model value other than 0, 1, or 2 will go to the `default` label as well.

```java
public class SwitchDemo
{
  static final int SUTHERLAND = 0;
  static final int BLOTTNER = 1;
  static final int GUPTA = 2;

  public static void main(String args[]) {
    int model = 0;

    switch (model) {
      case BLOTTNER:
        System.out.println("Blottner selected");
        break;
      case GUPTA:
        System.out.println("Gupta selected");
        break;
      case SUTHERLAND:
      default:
        System.out.println("Sutherland selected");
    }
  }
}
```

Output—

```
Sutherland selected
```

Transfer of Control Statements

Transfer of control statements moves the point of execution in your program to another location. They are used to exit from loops and other control structures, to return to the top of a loop, or to return from a method.

break Statements

We encountered the `break` statement in our discussion of `switch` statements. A `break` statement is used to exit the current loop or other flow control structure. The program execution is sent to the next statement following the control structure. By default, a `break` statement inside a nested loop will exit only the current loop, not the entire loop structure. You can add a label after a `break` statement to break out of a specified labeled block of code.

Example: Breaking Out of an Outer Loop

In this example, two `for` loops are used to search a 2-D array of data for a negative value. If a negative value is found, its location is noted and the loop exits. We want to exit both the inner and outer loops if a negative value is found. To do this, we label the outer `for` loop "outer" and use a labeled `break` statement. If a simple `break` statement had been used (without the label) only the inner loop would have been exited. The outer loop would continue normally.

```java
public class BreakDemo
{
  public static void main(String args[]) {
    double data[][] = { {4.1, 3.2, 1.1},
                        {-1.3, 2.4, 6.7},
                        {7.7, 0.3, 9.8} };

    outer: for(int i=0; i<3; ++i) {
      for(int j=0; j<3; ++j) {
        System.out.println("i= " + i + " j= " + j);
        if (data[i][j] < 0.0) {
          System.out.println("negative value at" +
              " [" + i + "][" + j + "]");
          break outer;
        }
      }
    }
  }
}
```

     Output—

```
i=0 j=0
i=0 j=1
i=0 j=2
i=1 j=0
negative value at [1][0]
```

`continue` Statements

A `continue` statement causes program execution to return to the top of the current loop, bypassing any code that may be defined below the `continue` statement. Similar to the `break` statement, a `continue` statement can provide a label to return to the top of a labeled loop. The `continue` statement is an example of a redundancy within Java. Anything you can do with a `continue` statement you can also do with an `if-else` statement. Because of this, you will rarely see or use `continue` statements.

`return` Statements

The `return` statement is used to return from a method. It transfers program control to the executable statement following the method call. The `return` keyword can be used by itself or it can precede a value that will be returned. More details on `return` statements are provided in Chapter 9.

BASIC PRINTING AND KEYBOARD I/O

Java has a powerful and sophisticated I/O capability, but sometimes you only want to read keyboard input and/or write things to the console. To facilitate this, Java provides three built-in data streams to handle standard input, output, and error. Standard input defaults to keyboard input. Standard output defaults to printing to the console. Standard error is an unbuffered output stream that writes to the console. In this section we'll focus on the standard input and output streams.

The standard input and output data streams are implemented as `public static` fields defined in the `System` class. A discussion on what a `static` field is can be found in Chapter 8. The names of the fields are `System.in` and `System.out`. Let's first discuss the standard output stream.

`System.out` is an instance of the `PrintStream` class, one of the Java I/O classes. `System.out` has two basic printing methods—`print()` and `println()`. We've already seen the `println()` method in action in many of the examples in this chapter. The `print()` and `println()` methods write a `String` (a collection of characters) to the invoking output stream. For instance, the syntax

```
System.out.println("Hello there everybody");
```

will display the text "Hello there everybody" on your console. If the value passed to the `print()` or `println()` methods is a primitive data type or non-`String` object the value is converted into a `String` representation. The difference between the `print()` and `println()` methods is that `println()` adds a newline character to the end of the `String` whereas `print()` does not.

TABLE 6.9 Commonly Used Escape Sequences

ESCAPE SEQUENCE	MEANING
\'	Single quote
\"	Double quote
\\	Backslash
\n	Newline
\t	Tab

Both methods take a `String` as their argument. You can pass the methods a simple `String` or a concatenated `String` made up from two or more pieces. An easy way to concatenate `Strings` is by using the + operator.

```
String name = "Jackson";
int age = 7;
System.out.println("Student name: "+name+" Age = "+age);
```

As we see in the example code snippet, a primitive datatype can also be concatenated to a `String`. The value of the integer variable is converted to a `String` representation before it is concatenated to the `String`.

Because double quotes surround a `String` literal definition, you might ask yourself how to represent a `String` that contains a double quote character. Java defines a number of escape sequences that represent special characters. Some of the commonly used escape sequences are shown in Table 6.9.

Now, let's discuss the standard input stream. The standard input stream defaults to keyboard input. The standard input stream is represented by an instance of the `InputStream` class named `System.in`. The `InputStream` class is designed to read byte data (as compared to character data). `System.in` can read keyboard input by invoking the `read()` method. This method reads one or more bytes from an input stream.

Reading console data as bytes, then converting the bytes into characters can be tedious. It is more convenient to wrap a character input stream around the standard input stream. The wrapped stream can then read the keyboard input either as individual characters or as a `String`. An example is shown in the next section. More information on the Java I/O classes can be found in Chapter 25.

Example: Reading Console Input

As we discussed previously, the standard input stream is a byte stream. It reads data as bytes. When reading console input, it is more convenient to read the data as characters. An `InputStreamReader` is a character input stream. If we wrap an `InputStreamReader` around the standard input stream, we can read console input as characters.

We also wrap a `BufferedReader` around the `InputStreamReader` because a `BufferedReader` can read an entire line of data at once. An `InputStreamReader` will read the data character by character. The `BufferedReader` object calls the `readLine()` method that waits until the Enter or Return key is clicked. It then returns the characters that were typed in previously as a `String`.

I/O operations can throw exceptions. Because of this we place the read operation inside a `try` block. Java exception handling is discussed in detail in Chapter 12. Note also the use of the standard output stream in this example calling both the `print()` and `println()` methods.

```java
import java.io.*;

public class StdIODemo
{
  public static void main(String args[]) {
    String name;

    System.out.print("Enter name:  ");

    try {
      BufferedReader reader =
        new BufferedReader(
            new InputStreamReader(System.in));

      name = reader.readLine();
      System.out.println("name was "+name);
    } catch (IOException ioe) {}
  }
}
```

Output (will vary)—

```
name was Lisa
```

7

CLASSES

If you are unfamiliar with object-oriented programming, you might find talk about classes and objects rather mysterious. In reality classes are not all that complicated to understand. A class is a named block of code that defines a reference type. The class is the basic building block of all Java programs. The class provides the structure or blueprint for objects. An object is an instance of a class.

Classes will, in general, consist of *members* (fields, methods, and nested classes and interfaces), *initializers* (both instance and static), and *constructors*. The fields define the data structure of the class. The methods will generally be used to access and manipulate the fields. Initializers and constructors are normally used to provide initial values for the fields. None of these elements is required although most classes will define fields and methods. A well-written class should satisfy the object-oriented concept of encapsulation in that it should define all of the methods and fields that it needs.

Languages like C and Fortran are function-based. The basic building block of a C or Fortran program is the function (or subroutine). Java programs are class-based. Every statement will be contained inside a class (or in some cases an interface). When a Java program runs, the execution will largely consist of creating and manipulating objects.

You might still be wondering what sort of classes you will write. The answer is any kind and every kind. If you are a structural engineer, you might write a `Beam` class that would define variables that describe the properties of a beam and methods to manipulate the variables. A chemist might write a `Species` class that represents a chemical species. If you are going to perform a finite-difference analysis, you might write a `Grid` class that would encapsulate a computational grid.

In this chapter will we look at classes, how to declare them, what their features are, and how to create instances of them. Specifically, we will discuss—

- Class declaration syntax
- Access privileges
- Objects
- Declaring fields
- Declaring methods
- Constructors
- Static initialization blocks
- Making copies of objects
- Nested classes
- Encapsulation
- Inheritance
- The `super` keyword
- The `this` keyword
- Abstract classes
- Final classes
- The garbage collector

Class Declaration Syntax

As we noted earlier, a class is simply a named block of code. It's a little more complicated than that because a class declaration can include a number of modifiers and keywords. The general syntax of a class declaration is as follows—

```
[modifiers] class <class_name> [extends superclass]
            [implements interface1, interface2, ...] {
   // field declarations
   // constructor declarations
   // method declarations
   // other declarations
}
```

The only required parts of a class declaration statement are the `class` keyword and a class name. The naming convention for a class is that the first letter is capitalized. Other standard naming restrictions apply. You cannot use a Java keyword as the name of a class. You cannot define two classes with the same name in the same package. A class declaration can also optionally include modifying keywords, information about inheritance, and a list of interfaces the class implements. The modifying keywords define the access and other special characteristics of the class. The body of the class is enclosed with braces and consists of field, constructor, method, and other declarations.

One of the powerful features of object-oriented programming is that you can define a class that extends the capabilities of another class. This concept is called *inheritance* and is described in detail later in this chapter. A class can also implement one or more interfaces. An *interface* is a blueprint that defines the methods a class must implement. More details on interfaces can be found in Chapter 10.

Collections of classes (and interfaces for that matter) can be stored in *packages*. Packages introduce certain access restrictions on the classes they contain. See Chapter 11 for more details on packages.

ACCESS PRIVILEGES

One of the powerful features of Java is the ability to specify the access to fields and methods. For instance, let's say you develop a scientific application that has proprietary data used as part of the analysis. For obvious reasons you do not want this data freely accessible by anyone who uses the classes that make up the application. With Java, you can specify the access to this data so it is available by the application internally but not to any external entity.

There are four types of access, `public`, `protected`, `private`, and default. A top-level class can have `public` or default access. A `public` class is accessible anywhere inside or outside of the package in which it is defined. The default access is assigned if no other access modifier is specified. If no access modifier is specified, the class and its members are accessible only from the package in which the class is defined.

In addition to `public` and default access, an inner class can also have `private` or `protected` access. A `private` inner class is available only to the class in which it is defined. A `protected` inner class is accessible to the class in which it is defined and to subclasses. Table 7.1 summarizes the access types.

TABLE 7.1   Class Member Accessibility

Member access type	Same class	Same package	Subclass, different package	Non-subclass, different package
public	Yes	Yes	Yes	Yes
protected	Yes	Yes	Yes	No
private	Yes	No	No	No
default	Yes	Yes	No	No

A source file can contain any number of class declarations, but only one class in each file can be declared `public`. The name of the `public` class must be the same as the file name. For example, a `public` class named `Foo` would be contained in a source file named `Foo.java`.

Objects

As we previously noted, Java is an object-oriented language. An object is simply an instance of a class. From now on in this book we will use the term *object* but keep in mind that an object is a class instance. Every object will have its own copy of the fields declared by its class and can access the methods declared in the class. There are two steps to creating an object. You must first declare a reference type variable of the desired type. Writing the class name followed by the variable name performs this declaration.

`class_name variable_name;`

After the variable is declared, you then allocate memory for the object on the heap using the `new` operator and create the object by calling one of the class constructors.

`variable_name = new class_name(input_arguments);`

The `new` operator dynamically allocates memory for the object on the heap at runtime. The two steps for creating an object can be combined into a single executable statement—

`class_name variable_name =`
`        new class_name(input_arguments);`

You can create an object without associating it with a variable by just using the allocation and initialization syntax. For instance, to add an unnamed

Integer object to a collection stored in a Vector, you might type the following—

```
Vector numPoints = new Vector();
numPoints.addElement(new Integer(5));
```

In this code snippet, a Vector object is created using the full declaration-initialization syntax. The addElement() method of the numPoints Vector object is called to load an Integer object into the first storage position of the Vector (Integer objects are used to represent an integer as a reference type variable). We don't need to save a reference to the Integer object, so we simply create one as an argument to the addElement() method using the new Integer(5) syntax.

The Java API also defines many methods that will return an instance of a class. This is another way in which you can create objects.

Example: Creating Objects

This example demonstrates two ways to create an object. A Date object is created using the new keyword and calling a Date class constructor. A String object is obtained by declaring a String variable and assigning to it the return value of the toString() method, which is the reference to the String created by the method.

```
import java.util.*;

public class CreateDemo
{
   public static void main(String args[]) {
      Date today = new Date();
      String time = today.toString();

      System.out.println("The time is "+time);
   }
}
```

Output (will vary)—

```
The time is Fri Aug 02 10:00:38 GMT-07:00 2002
```

DECLARING FIELDS

A class can declare any number of fields that are used to store data for a class. Fields can be of primitive or reference type, they can be instance or static, and so on. A static field is also called a *class variable*. A nonstatic field is also known as an *instance variable.* Variables are discussed in much more detail in Chapter 8, but a brief example is provided here.

Example: Defining a Simple Class

The `SimpleGas` class encapsulates in a very simplistic way a gas mixture. The thermodynamic state of a gas mixture can be characterized by specifying two state variables. In this case, we are specifying the pressure and temperature. To represent this, the `SimpleGas` class declares two primitive-type instance variables named `pressure` and `temperature`. The variables are given `private` access and are initialized when they are declared. For more information about declaring variables and about variables in general, consult Chapter 8.

```
public class SimpleGas
{
  private double pressure = 101325.0;
  private double temperature = 273.0;
}
```

Declaring Methods

Classes can also declare methods. Methods are generally used to access and manipulate the fields declared in a class. Methods may also perform such functions as mathematical operations, printing messages, and so on. As with the "Declaring Fields" section, this section will only give a broad overview of methods. More detail about methods is provided in Chapter 9.

There are two general types of methods—instance and static. Instance methods are associated with an object and called by referencing an object. Instance methods are commonly used to access and manipulate the instance variables of the class. For example, a class representing a gas mixture might define an instance method to compute the mixture enthalpy of the gas.

A static or class method is associated with a class rather than with an instance of a class. You can call a static method without first having to create an instance of the class in which the method is defined. Static methods are usually used for generic operations that are applicable to a wide range of classes. The mathematical square root and power methods in the `java.lang.Math` class, for example, are implemented as static methods.

Example: Adding Methods to a Class

One problem with the `SimpleGas` class from the previous example is that because the fields are given `private` access (which is the preferred access for fields) there is no way to directly access their values outside of the `SimpleGas` class. To rectify this situation, we will rewrite the class adding instance methods that access the current value of the `pressure` and `temperature` variables.

```
public class SimpleGas2
{
  private double pressure=101325.0;
  private double temperature=273.0;

  public double getPressure() {
    return pressure;
  }

  public double getTemperature() {
    return temperature;
  }
}
```

The `getPressure()` and `getTemperature()` methods return the current value of the `pressure` and `temperature` variables. Since the methods have `public` access, they can be called anywhere inside or outside of the `SimpleGas2` class. To make use of the `SimpleGas2` class, we will write a driver program. The driver will define a `main()` method that will create a `SimpleGas2` object and call the `getPressure()` and `getTemperature()` methods on the object.

```
public class GasDriver
{
  public static void main(String args[]) {
      SimpleGas2 testGas = new SimpleGas2();

    //  The getPressure()and getTemperature() methods
    //  are called.
    System.out.println("pressure is " +
                    testGas.getPressure());
    System.out.println("temperature is " +
                    testGas.getTemperature());
  }
}
```

When the `GasDriver.java` code is compiled and run, the output is

```
pressure is 101325.0
temperature is 273.0
```

Constructors

Constructors are similar to methods but are not considered members of a class. They are used to initialize the data structure of objects. Constructors have the same name as the class in which they are declared. They have no return type. A constructor is automatically called when an object is created using the `new` keyword. The system will provide a default constructor that takes no parameters if no constructor is explicitly declared, but the default constructor is not available if any constructors are provided in the class definition. The general syntax for a constructor is shown here.

```
[access] class_name (input_parameters) {
   //  body of constructor
}
```

A constructor can be given `public`, `protected`, `private`, or default access. If a constructor is given `public` access, it can be called anywhere inside or outside of the class in which it is defined. A `protected` constructor is available anywhere in the package in which it is defined. Outside of the package in which it is defined, a `protected` constructor can only be called inside a subclass. A `private` constructor cannot be called outside of the class in which it is defined. If no access is specified, the constructor has default access and only classes in the same package can call it. Constructors are generally given `public` or `protected` access.

Constructors can be (and often are) overloaded, meaning that more than one version of the constructor is defined with different input parameter lists. The system decides which constructor to call based on the number and type of arguments provided. For more information on method overloading, see Chapter 9.

Later in this chapter we will discuss the concept of inheritance. One of the features of inheritance is that a class can inherit members defined in a superclass. When a subclass object is created, the superclass fields must be initialized. This is accomplished by having the subclass constructor invoke a superclass constructor using the `super` keyword followed by whatever arguments the superclass constructor might need.

```
super(arguments);
```

The superclass constructor call must be the first statement in the subclass constructor.

Example: Adding Constructors to a Class

Because the `SimpleGas2.java` program initializes its members when they are declared, every instance of `SimpleGas2` will have the same values of pressure and temperature. To allow each `SimpleGas2` instance to have a different pressure and temperature value, we can initialize those members using constructors. The `SimpleGas3` class defines two constructors. The first is a constructor that takes no arguments and initializes the members to default values. The second takes two `double` values as arguments and can be used to customize the pressure and temperature values of a `SimpleGas3` object.

```java
public class SimpleGas3
{
  private double pressure;
  private double temperature;

  public SimpleGas3() {
    pressure = 101325.0;
    temperature = 273.0;
  }

  public SimpleGas3(double p, double t) {
    pressure = p;
    temperature = t;
  }

  public double getPressure() {
    return pressure;
  }

  public double getTemperature() {
    return temperature;
  }
}
```

We will also rewrite the driver program. This time it will create two `SimpleGas3` objects using the two-argument constructor. The `pressure` variable of each instance is given a different value.

```java
public class GasDriver3
{
  public static void main(String args[]) {
    SimpleGas3 gas1 = new SimpleGas3(21.95, 207.8);
    SimpleGas3 gas2 = new SimpleGas3(1.56, 245.4);

    System.out.println("pressure of Gas 1 is " +
                       gas1.getPressure());
    System.out.println("pressure of Gas 2 is " +
                       gas2.getPressure());
  }
}
```

Output—

```
pressure of Gas 1 is 21.95
pressure of Gas 2 is 1.56
```

Static Initialization Blocks

We have just discussed how constructors are used to initialize the instance variables of a class. But how do you initialize class (static) variables? Class variables can be initialized either when they are declared or by using a static initialization block. This is simply a block of code preceded by the `static` keyword.

```
static {
   // body of static initialization block
}
```

A static initialization block is not explicitly called. It is executed one time by the system when the class is first loaded.

Example: Using Static Initialization Blocks

This simple example shows how a static initialization block provides an initial value for a class variable. The `main()` method never actually calls the static initialization block. The block is called by the system when the class is loaded.

```
public class StaticInitDemo
{
  public static int MAX_ITERATIONS;

  static {
    MAX_ITERATIONS = 50;
  }

  public static void main(String args[]) {
    System.out.println("MAX_ITERATIONS = "+
                       MAX_ITERATIONS);
  }
}
```

Output—

```
MAX_ITERATIONS = 50
```

Making Copies of Objects

As we mentioned in the "Objects" section, an object is an instance of a class. A variable that refers to an object will store a reference to the location in memory where the object is stored. To make a copy of an object, you might think to declare a new reference type variable and assign it to the original variable. For example, if you wrote a class named Gas and wanted to make a copy of a Gas object, you might think you should type —

```
Gas oldGas = new Gas("air");
Gas newGas = oldGas;
```

However, this does not create two independent objects. What this has done is create two references to the same Gas object. To create an independent copy of the original Gas object, you would need to create a distinct Gas object and then copy the values of the fields of the original Gas object into the copy.

Example: Copying Objects

To demonstrate how to correctly access objects, we are first going to modify the SimpleGas3.java program to add methods that can be used to change the values of the pressure and temperature variables.

```java
public class SimpleGas4
{
  private double pressure;
  private double temperature;

  public SimpleGas4() {
    pressure = 101325.0;
    temperature = 273.0;
  }

  public SimpleGas4(double p, double t) {
    pressure = p;
    temperature = t;
  }

  // These methods return the values of the
  // pressure and temperature variables

  public double getPressure() {
    return pressure;
  }

  public double getTemperature() {
    return temperature;
  }
```

```java
  // These methods change the values of the
  // pressure and temperature variables

  public void setPressure(double p) {
    pressure = p;
    return;
  }

  public void setTemperature(double t) {
    temperature = t;
    return;
  }
}
```

The `GasDriver4` class creates three variables that reference `SimpleGas4` objects. The second variable is made to reference the same object as the first. The first and second variables will share the same copies of the `pressure` and `temperature` fields. The `GasDriver4` class then makes a `SimpleGas4` object that is an independent copy of the first object. One way to make an independent copy is to pass the current values of the first object's fields to the `SimpleGas4` class constructor. The two variables, although they refer to objects with the same initial state, are completely independent.

```java
public class GasDriver4
{
  public static void main(String args[]) {

    //  Declare two SimpleGas4 variables. Create a
    //  SimpleGas4 object and assign it to the first
    //  variable. Make the second variable reference the
    //  same object.

    SimpleGas4 gas1 = new SimpleGas4(21.95, 207.8);
    SimpleGas4 gas2 = gas1;

    System.out.println("pressure of Gas 1 is " +
                       gas1.getPressure());
    System.out.println("pressure of Gas 2 is " +
                       gas2.getPressure());

    //  The two SimpleGas4 variables point to the same
    //  object. Either variable can be used to change
    //  the object's pressure field.

    gas2.setPressure(19.2);
    System.out.println("\npressure of Gas 2 is " +
                       gas1.getPressure());
    System.out.println("pressure of Gas 1 is " +
                       gas1.getPressure());
```

```
        // Another SimpleGas4 variable is declared.  The
        // values from gas1 object are copied into a new
        // SimpleGas4 object.

        SimpleGas4 gas3 = new SimpleGas4(
              gas1.getPressure(), gas1.getTemperature());
        System.out.println("\npressure of Gas 3 is " +
                           gas3.getPressure());

        // The objects referenced by gas1 and gas3 are
        // independent. Changing the pressure of the gas3
        // object does not affect the gas1 object.

        gas3.setPressure(23.4);
        System.out.println("pressure of Gas 3 is " +
                           gas3.getPressure());
        System.out.println("pressure of Gas 1 is " +
                           gas1.getPressure());
   }
}
```

Output—

```
pressure of Gas 1 is 21.95
pressure of Gas 2 is 21.95

pressure of Gas 2 is 19.2
pressure of Gas 1 is 19.2

pressure of Gas 3 is 19.2
pressure of Gas 3 is 23.4
pressure of Gas 1 is 19.2
```

NESTED CLASSES

So far we have declared top-level classes. It is also possible to declare a class inside another class. This is called a *nested* class. Nested classes can be defined inside any block of code including method definitions, they can be either static or instance (also known as an *inner* class), and they can be given `public`, `protected`, `private`, or default access.

Why would you define a nested class? One reason is to give a class direct access to the fields of another (outer) class without giving the outer class members `public` or `protected` access. Nested classes are commonly used in writing event handlers for GUI applications. There are three general types of nested classes—static, instance (inner), and anonymous inner.

Static Nested Classes

A static nested class is designated using the `static` keyword in the class declaration statement. It is associated with its outer class directly rather than with an instance of its outer class. A static nested class can define and access static fields, but does not have direct access to the instance members of its outer class.

A static inner class is the only way you can define a static class. You can't define a stand-alone class as static. Static nested classes can be defined inside other static nested classes. A static nested class can be referred to outside of the outer class using the syntax

```
OuterClass.InnerClass
```

Instance Nested Classes

A nonstatic nested class is called an inner class. It is associated with an instance of its outer class and can only exist within an instance of its outer class. In other words, you can't create an instance of an inner class without first creating an instance of the outer class. The outer class can create and manipulate an instance of an inner class. The inner class has direct access to the members defined in the outer class. An inner class cannot define `static` fields unless they are `static` and `final`.

Example: Using an Inner Class as an Event Listener

One situation where you will typically use inner classes is in developing GUI applications. When a user interacts with a GUI component, objects called *events* are generated. The events are sent to an event listener object that defines methods that respond to the event. The event listener often needs access to the fields from the GUI application. If the event listener class is defined as an inner class of the GUI application class, the event listener has direct access to the GUI application fields. Event listeners and Java GUI development in general are covered in more detail in Chapter 26.

In this example, a button is used to clear the contents of a text field. The button will generate an `ActionEvent` object when it is pressed. The button registers an `ActionListener` that responds to the event by clearing the text field. Because the `ActionListener` needs access to the text field, the `ActionListener` class is implemented as an inner class of the `EventDemo` class.

When you run this example, you will see a frame appear on your screen with a label, text field, and button. Type something into the text field. Now click the Clear button and any text inside the text field will disappear.

```java
import javax.swing.*;
import java.awt.event.*;

public class EventDemo extends JFrame
{
  JTextField pressureTF;
  JLabel pressureLabel;
  JButton clearButton;

  public EventDemo() {

    //  A label and text field are created

    pressureLabel = new JLabel("pressure");
    pressureTF = new JTextField(10);

    //  A button is created and registered with an event
    //  listener.  The event listener is an instance of
    //  an inner class.

    clearButton = new JButton("clear");
    clearButton.addActionListener(
                  new ActionHandler());

    //  The GUI components are added to the frame.
    //  The frame is sized and made visible.

    JPanel panel = new JPanel();
    panel.add(pressureLabel);
    panel.add(pressureTF);
    panel.add(clearButton);

    getContentPane().add(panel);

    setDefaultCloseOperation(JFrame.EXIT_ON_CLOSE);
    setBounds(100,100,300,150);
    setVisible(true);
  }

  //  The ActionHandler class is an event listener for
  //  ActionEvents.  Because it needs access to the
  //  pressureTF component, the class is implemented
  //  as an inner class.  When the "clear" button is
  //  clicked, the text in the textfield is cleared.

  class ActionHandler implements ActionListener {
    public void actionPerformed(ActionEvent event) {
      pressureTF.setText("");
```

```
      }
  }

  public static void main(String args[]) {
    EventDemo demo = new EventDemo();
  }
}
```

Anonymous Inner Classes

An anonymous inner class is a special type of inner class that provides a compact inner class definition. An anonymous inner class has no name or modifiers. The class declaration is incorporated into the syntax used to create an instance of it. Only one, unnamed instance of the class can be created. Anonymous inner classes result in more compact programs but they do make a code listing more difficult to read. They are intended for single-use applications such as GUI component event handlers.

Example: Using an Anonymous Inner Class

The `AnonDemo` class is the same as the `EventDemo` class seen in the previous example except that the event listener is implemented as an anonymous inner class. The inner class declaration is incorporated into the syntax used to register the button with the event listener. The code listing is somewhat shorter and somewhat more difficult to follow.

```
import javax.swing.*;
import java.awt.event.*;

public class AnonDemo extends JFrame
{
  JTextField pressureTF;
  JLabel pressureLabel;
  JButton clearButton;

  public AnonDemo() {

    //  A label and text field are created

    pressureLabel = new JLabel("pressure");
    pressureTF = new JTextField(10);

    //  A button is created and registered with an event
    //  listener.  The event listener is an instance of
    //  an anonymous inner class so the class definition
    //  is included in the syntax for creating an
    //  instance of it.
```

```
      clearButton = new JButton("clear");
      clearButton.addActionListener(
         new ActionListener() {
            public void actionPerformed(ActionEvent ae) {
               pressureTF.setText("");
            }
         });

      //  The GUI components are added to the frame.
      //  The frame is sized and made visible.

      JPanel panel = new JPanel();
      panel.add(pressureLabel);
      panel.add(pressureTF);
      panel.add(clearButton);

      getContentPane().add(panel);

      setDefaultCloseOperation(JFrame.EXIT_ON_CLOSE);
      setBounds(100,100,300,150);
      setVisible(true);
   }
   public static void main(String args[]) {
      AnonDemo demo = new AnonDemo();
   }
}
```

Output—

The GUI display will be the same as in the "Using an Inner Class as an Event Listener" example.

ENCAPSULATION

Encapsulation is an object-oriented concept that says a class should be self-contained, that it should define (or inherit) all the fields and methods it needs to do whatever it is it has to do. The flip side is that access to any field declared in a class should only be allowed through methods declared by the class. The reason is one of developer control. If you allow users unlimited access to your fields, they may do things that would change the nature of a program in a detrimental way such as changing the value of a variable that was intended to be read-only.

Encapsulation is fairly easy to put into practice. Simply give your fields `private` access. That way no one can access them directly outside of the class. Then define appropriate public methods to access and/or change the values of the private variables. You now have complete control over how the data in your class will be used.

INHERITANCE

We briefly touched on the concept of inheritance in the "Constructors" section earlier in this chapter. It is a powerful object-oriented capability that allows you to write one class that extends the capabilities of another. A subclass has access to the nonprivate members of its superclass. Inheritance facilitates code reuse and allows the creation of class hierarchies.

Inheritance is indicated by the `extends` keyword followed by the name of the superclass in a class declaration statement. A subclass can only inherit from one superclass. Unlike C++, Java does not support multiple inheritance. The general syntax for a subclass is shown below.

```
[modifiers] class <class_name> extends superclass
           [implements interface1, interface2, …] {
   //   field declarations
   //   constructor declarations
   //   method declarations
   //   other declarations
}
```

When you create an instance of a subclass, the fields defined in both the subclass and superclasses must be initialized. The superclass fields can be initialized by having the subclass constructor first invoke a superclass constructor using the `super` keyword. While the subclass inherits the nonprivate methods and constructors of the superclass, it can overload or override them as it sees fit. Details on method overloading and overriding are provided in Chapter 9.

You will work with inheritance whether you want to or not. Every Java class implicitly inherits from the `Object` class, meaning that the `Object` class is the superclass (or ancestor) of all other classes. The inheritance from `Object` is implicit, meaning that you don't have to write `extends Object` in your class declaration syntax. What this implicit inheritance from `Object` also means is that every class you write will have access to the methods defined in the `Object` class.

Example: Inheritance Basics

In this example, we will demonstrate some of the basic concepts of inheritance. We first define a class named `Species` that represents a simplified model of a chemical species. The fields declared by the `Species` class represent the species name and its molar mass. Two methods are defined to access the current value of the fields.

```java
public class Species
{
  private String name;
  private double molarMass;

  public Species(String nm, double mw) {
    name = nm;
    molarMass = mw;
  }

  public String getName() {
    return name;
  }

  public double getMolarMass() {
    return molarMass;
  }
}
```

We next write a simple driver program for the `Species` class. The driver creates a `Species` object and calls the `getName()` and `getMolarMass()` methods on the object.

```java
public class SpeciesDriver
{
  public static void main(String args[]) {
    Species o2 =
        new Species("diatomic oxygen", 0.0319988);
    System.out.println("Molar mass of " +
        o2.getName() + " is " + o2.getMolarMass());
  }
}
```

Output—

```
Molar mass of diatomic oxygen is 0.0319988
```

Now, let's say we want to model an ionized species. To perform calculations with our ionized species class we might need to know the ionization level (O+, O++, etc.). Our ionized species class will have to include an ionization level as a variable. We could write a separate `IonizedSpecies` class, but it would have many of the same features as our `Species` class. Code duplication is poor object-oriented programming practice and is time-consuming as well. Instead, we will use inheritance to write a subclass of `Species`.

The `IonizedSpecies` class is written as a subclass of `Species`. It defines a constructor that takes three arguments. The first two are used to initialize the superclass fields defined in the `Species` class. Since every class is responsible for initializing its own fields, the `Species` class constructor is called using the `super` keyword. This operation must be performed first. After the `Species` class constructor is called, the `chargeLevel` variable is initialized. The `IonizedSpecies` class also declares an instance method that returns the value of the `chargeLevel` field.

```
public class IonizedSpecies extends Species
{
  private int chargeLevel;

  public IonizedSpecies(String nm, double mw,
                                      int charge) {
    super(nm, mw);
    chargeLevel = charge;
  }

  public int getChargeLevel() {
    return chargeLevel;
  }
}
```

Next, we'll write a new driver program that will create and manipulate an `IonizedSpecies` object. In addition to the `getChargeLevel()` method defined in its own class, the `IonizedSpecies` object can also access the `getName()` and `getMolarMass()` methods from the `Species` class.

```
public class SpeciesDriver2
{
  public static void main(String args[]) {
    IonizedSpecies o2p = new IonizedSpecies(
              "diatomic oxygen ion", 0.03199825, 1);

    System.out.println("molar mass of " +
        o2p.getName() + " is " + o2p.getMolarMass());
    System.out.println("charge level of " +
        o2p.getName() + " is " + o2p.getChargeLevel());
  }
}
```

Output—

```
molar mass of diatomic oxygen ion is 0.03199825
charge level of diatomic oxygen ion is 1
```

Inheritance and Access Modifiers

Inheritance is governed by the access modifiers applied to the superclass members. If you do not want a subclass to access a superclass member, give that member `private` access. A member that has `public` access is freely accessible inside or outside of the class in which it is defined. The `protected` access is more restrictive than `public`. Outside of the package in which it is defined, a `protected` member is only available to subclasses. If no access is specified for a member it will have `public` access inside its package and `private` access outside its package.

Table 7.1 summarizes the access types.

Inheritance and Method Arguments

When one class inherits from another, it becomes part of a class hierarchy. This has implications when passing reference type variables to methods. When a method defines a reference type as one of its input parameters, it is perfectly acceptable to pass a subclass of the specified type as an argument to the method. For example, the `setListData()` method from the `JList` class takes a `Vector` as an argument. You can call this method with a `Stack` variable as an argument because `Stack` is a subclass of `Vector`.

Example: Sending a Subclass Object to a Method

The `MethodArgDemo` class defines a method named `capName()` that takes a `Species` object as an input parameter. Any `Species` subclass object can also be passed to the method. In the `main()` method, an `IonizedSpecies` object is created and sent to the `capName()` method.

```
public class MethodArgDemo
{
  //  This method takes a Species argument

  public void capName(Species spc) {
    System.out.println("Name is " +
          spc.getName().toUpperCase());
  }

  public static void main(String args[]) {
    MethodArgDemo demo = new MethodArgDemo();

    IonizedSpecies o2p = new IonizedSpecies(
            "diatomic oxygen ion", 0.03199825, 1);

    //  Call the capName() method passing it an
    //  IonizedSpecies argument

    demo.capName(o2p);

  }
}
```

Output—

```
Name is DIATOMIC OXYGEN ION
```

Member Hiding and Member Overriding

If a subclass defines a field with the same name as one defined by a superclass, the subclass field will hide its superclass counterpart. The subclass can access the hidden superclass field using the `super` keyword. If a subclass defines a method with the same return type, name, and parameter list as a superclass, the subclass method is said to override the superclass method. A subclass object that calls the method will invoke the subclass version of it. The superclass method can be invoked inside a subclass using the `super` keyword. Method overriding is covered in more detail in Chapter 9.

The `super` Keyword

In addition to its own nonstatic fields, a subclass must also ensure that any inherited nonstatic fields are initialized. This can be achieved by having a subclass constructor first call a superclass constructor using the `super` keyword, followed by any arguments needed for the superclass constructor—

```
super(arguments);
```

The superclass constructor call must be the first executable statement in the subclass constructor. If a superclass constructor is not explicitly called, the system will call the no-argument (default) superclass constructor. The `super` keyword can also be used to access superclass data or function members.

Example: Using the *super* Keyword

For an example of calling a superclass constructor, look at the `IonizedSpecies` class from the "Inheritance Basics" example earlier in this chapter. For an example of calling a superclass method, see the "Method Overriding" section of Chapter 9.

The `this` Keyword

The `this` keyword is a reference to the current object and is implicitly passed to every nonstatic method. The `this` keyword can be used to clear up any ambiguities that might exist due to naming conflicts and so forth.

Example: Using the `this` Keyword

The `this` keyword is typically used when writing constructors, but can be applied to any situation where ambiguity is present. There is a school of thought in Java programming that the variable names in a constructor input parameter list should match the names of the fields of the class. Since you are now dealing with two variables with the same name, you need to use the `this` keyword to differentiate between the input parameter variable and the field.

As an example, let's rewrite the `Species` class so the input parameter names in the `Species` class constructor are the same as the field names. The `this` keyword tells the compiler that the `name` and `molarMass` variables to the left of the equals sign refer to the class fields.

```
public class Species2
{
  private String name;
  private double molarMass;

  public Species2(String name, double molarMass) {
    this.name = name;
    this.molarMass = molarMass;
  }

  public String getName() {
    return name;
  }

  public double getMolarMass() {
    return molarMass;
  }

  public static void main(String args[]) {
    Species2 ob = new Species2("unobtainium", 0.99);
    System.out.println("Molar mass of " +
            ob.getName() + " is "+ob.getMolarMass());
  }
}
```

Output—

```
Molar mass of unobtainium is 0.99
```

ABSTRACT CLASSES

An abstract class can be used to define the common structure for a family of related classes. An abstract class is designated as such by including the `abstract` keyword in the class declaration syntax. An abstract class is merely a blueprint. You cannot create an instance of an abstract class. Abstract classes can define both abstract and concrete methods.

When a concrete (i.e., nonabstract) class is written as a subclass of an abstract class, the subclass must provide an implementation of all abstract methods defined in the abstract superclass. If you don't do this, you will get a compiler error. An abstract class can be written as a subclass of another abstract class.

Example: Using Abstract Classes

To demonstrate how abstract classes are defined and used we will write an abstract Shape class that will serve as the blueprint for 2-D geometric shapes. All 2-D shapes will have an area and circumference associated with them. The Shape class declares the getArea() and getCircumference() methods for returning these properties. Note that the method declarations are terminated with semicolons.

```
public abstract class Shape
{
  abstract double getArea();
  abstract double getCircumference();
}
```

Next, we will write a subclass of the Shape class named Rectangle. The Rectangle class encapsulates a rectangular shape as you might have guessed. Because Rectangle is a subclass of Shape, the Rectangle class must provide an implementation of the getArea() and getCircumference() methods. The way it implements those methods is not specified. If you defined a Circle class, the Circle class implementation of getArea() and getCircumference() would be different than the Rectangle class implementation.

```
public class Rectangle extends Shape
{
  private double width, height;

  public Rectangle(double w, double h) {
    width = w;
    height = h;
  }

  //  The Rectangle class must implement the
  //  abstract methods from the Shape class

  public double getArea() {
    return width*height;
  }
```

```
  public double getCircumference() {
    return 2.0*(width+height);
  }

  public static void main(String args[]) {
    Rectangle rect = new Rectangle(2.0,3.0);
    System.out.println("area is " + rect.getArea());
    System.out.println("circumference is " +
                       rect.getCircumference());
  }
}
```

Output—

```
area is 6.0
circumference is 10.0
```

Final Classes

A final class is one that cannot be subclassed. A final class is designated by the final keyword in the class definition syntax. There are two general reasons for creating a final class.

1. As a security mechanism. Because of inheritance, a method that takes an object as an input parameter can be called using a subclass argument instead. Using subclasses is one technique hackers use to subvert systems. The subclass may share the common features of its parent but also be written to do something nasty like altering or accessing sensitive information. Code that contains a subclass of a final class will not compile.

2. You may wish to shut off the possibility of inheritance for a class. An example of a final class in the Java API is the String class. Because strings are so pervasive and so important to Java's operation, it's important that the function of the String class not be altered from the language specifications.

The Garbage Collector

Memory for Java objects is dynamically allocated at runtime. Other languages also support dynamic memory allocation. In C you can dynamically allocate memory to variables, structs, and arrays, but you must take care of deallocating memory when the field is no longer needed. If you don't do it properly, you get the dreaded memory leak.

Java has a very nice built-in system that takes care of memory management for you. The Java runtime environment uses what is called the garbage collector to deallocate resources assigned to objects that are no longer being used. An object is eligible for garbage collection when the system determines there are no longer any references to it. This generally happens when the variable goes out of scope or when the last reference to the variable is set to `null`. The garbage collector runs automatically in a background execution thread. You can manually invoke the garbage collector by calling the static `gc()` method from the `System` class.

8

VARIABLES

In Chapter 7 we discussed how classes could define fields as members of the class. You may be more familiar with the term *variable*. A variable is a storage location. A variable always has a type associated with it. A variable of primitive type holds the value of a primitive type. A reference type variable holds either a null reference or a reference to an object of the same type as the variable. There are seven kinds of Java variables. Fields, depending on how they are declared, represent two of them. Fields that are declared as static are called *class variables*. Fields not declared as static are called *instance variables*. The other Java variable types are array components, method parameters, constructor parameters, exception handler parameters, and local variables. Class and instance variables are the only variable types that can be inherited.

Java is a strongly typed language in that the type of a variable must be declared when the variable is declared. Among other things, this tells the compiler how much memory must be allocated for the variable. Variables can be declared anywhere in your program as long as they are declared before they are used. You can initialize a variable when it is declared or assign a value to it later in the program. The Java compiler will check to make sure that a value assigned to a variable is appropriate for that type. You cannot assign a `String` literal to an integer variable, for example.

Every variable will have a scope that defines where a variable exists and can be accessed. Generally speaking, a variable will only have scope in the block of code in which it is declared. There are two general types of scope. A variable defined at class scope is declared outside of any constructor or method definitions and is available to all constructors and methods in the program. A local variable is one that is declared inside a method, constructor, or other block of code. A local variable disappears once the block of code in which it is declared exits.

In this chapter we will cover the different types of variables, how to create variables, and how to access the values associated with them. Specifically, we will cover—

- Primitive and reference type variables
- Instance and class variables
- Creating variables
- Naming conventions and restrictions
- Access modifiers
- Accessing variable values
- Final variables
- Transient and volatile variables
- Casting
- Variable scope

Primitive and Reference Type Variables

There are two general classes of variables in Java—primitive and reference. Primitive variables, also referred to as value types, are memory locations that hold the value of a primitive type. The primitive types in Java are `boolean`, `byte`, `char`, `double`, `float`, `int`, `short`, and `long`. Their general characteristics are shown in Table 8.1.

We can see from Table 8.1 that primitive variables store one value. The value can be a byte, a Unicode character, a number, or a boolean (true or false). The `boolean` type is very useful in that you can define logical variables that can control the flow of execution. You can code statements like "If the variable is true, do one thing. If it is false, do something else." Boolean variables are not available in Fortran or C.

Java defines three types of integer primitives of varying memory requirements and range. Java does not support unsigned integer types. There are two types of floating point primitives. The mostly commonly used numerical primitive types are `int` and `double`. Java uses the Unicode encoding scheme to

TABLE 8.1 Primitive Types

DATA TYPE	DESCRIPTION	STORAGE REQUIREMENTS
boolean	Logical value that is either true or false	1 bit
byte	One byte of data	1 byte
char	A Unicode character	2 bytes
short	An integer value between $-32{,}768$ and $32{,}767$	2 bytes
int	An integer value between $-2{,}147{,}483{,}648$ and $2{,}147{,}483{,}647$	4 bytes
long	An integer value between $-9{,}223{,}372{,}036{,}854{,}775{,}808$ and $-9{,}223{,}372{,}036{,}854{,}775{,}807$	8 bytes
float	A single-precision floating point value between 3.4e-38 and 3.4e+38	4 bytes
double	A double-precision floating point value between 1.7e−308 and 1.7e+308	8 bytes

represent character data. The Unicode encoding scheme represents each character as a 16-bit integer value and can represent all international character sets.

We can also see from Table 8.1 why the type must be specified when the variable is declared. The primitive types require different amounts of memory and the compiler must know how much memory to allocate. Memory for primitive types is allocated on the part of memory known as the stack.

The second major variable type is the reference type. A reference type variable is a storage location that holds either a null reference or a reference to an object of the same type as the variable. Java arrays are also reference types. The value of a reference variable is the memory address at which the data associated with the object is stored. A reference is comparable to a pointer in C or C++. Unlike C or C++, you cannot use a Java reference type variable to directly access memory. You manipulate a reference variable by using the variable name rather than the reference itself.

Reference variables are different from primitive variables in that instance methods can be called on them. Indeed, instance methods can only be called outside of the class in which they are defined by using an object reference. The syntax for an instance method call is the reference variable name, a period, the method name, and the argument list. This process is dependent on the access available for the method. See Chapter 9 for further discussion on instance methods.

Reference variables can be used to access an object's fields. The syntax is the same as for calling methods: the variable name, a period, and the field name. This type of access is dependent on the access modifier given to the field. See the "Access Modifiers" section of this chapter for more details.

Java passes arguments to methods by value. What this means for primitive variables is that the value of the variable is passed to the method rather than a reference to the variable itself. Any changes made to the value inside the method are not reflected in the value stored by the variable. A primitive variable is not an object and cannot be passed to a method that takes an object as an input parameter. There are numerical wrapper classes that can be wrapped around a primitive variable. These are discussed in more detail in Chapter 15.

When a reference variable is passed to a method a copy of the reference to the object is passed to the method. This value is a pointer to the original object, so any changes made to the object through its reference in the method will be reflected in the original object.

Example: Using Primitive and Reference Variables

This example demonstrates how to declare, initialize, and manipulate both primitive and reference variables. The concepts shown in this example are explained in more detail later in this chapter. The `SimpleGas5` class declares three primitive (`pressure`, `temperature`, `perfectGas`) and one reference (`name`) variable. Two constructors are provided to initialize the variables. The first constructor takes no arguments and gives the variables default values. The second constructor initializes the variables by assigning them the same value as the arguments passed to the method.

```java
public class SimpleGas5
{
  private double pressure, temperature;
  private String name;
  private boolean perfectGas;

  public SimpleGas5() {
    pressure = 101325.0;
    temperature = 207.4;
    name = "air";
    perfectGas = true;
  }

  public SimpleGas5(double p, double t, String nm,
                    boolean pg) {
    pressure = p;
    temperature = t;
    name = nm;
    perfectGas = pg;
  }
```

```
    // These methods return the values of the variables

  public double getPressure() {
    return pressure;
  }

  public double getTemperature() {
    return temperature;
  }

  public String getName() {
    return name;
  }

  public boolean isPerfectGas() {
    return perfectGas;
  }
}
```

To use the `SimpleGas5` class, we will write a driver program. The driver creates a `SimpleGas5` variable and calls two of the methods defined in the `SimpleGas5` class. The data members of the `SimpleGas5` object are initialized by calling the four-argument constructor.

```
public class GasDriver5
{
  public static void main(String args[]) {

    //  Create a SimpleGas5 object.  Initialize its
    //  data members by calling a constructor

    SimpleGas5 air =
           new SimpleGas5(21.95, 207.8, "air", true);

    System.out.println("gas name is " + air.getName());
    System.out.println("pressure is " +
                         air.getPressure());
  }
}
```

Output—

```
gas name is air
pressure is 21.95
```

INSTANCE AND CLASS VARIABLES

In the previous section we discussed the difference between primitive and reference type variables. There are two other fundamental classifications for variables. A class variable is a field declared to be `static` within a class declaration. An instance variable is a field that is not declared to be `static` within a class declaration.

Let's first discuss instance variables. An instance variable is associated with an instance of a class rather than with the class itself. Instance is the default type. Every object will have its own copy of an instance variable. Outside of the class in which they are defined, instance variables can only be accessed by a reference to an instance of the class in which they are defined, or by a subclass object that inherits the variable. Instance variables (like all variables) will have an access associated with them that defines how the variable can be accessed. Generally speaking, it is considered bad form to give instance variables `public` access. More information on variable access is provided later in this chapter.

A class variable is associated with a class rather than with an instance of a class. One copy of the class variable is shared by all instances of the class in which it is defined. The system allocates memory for a class variable when the class in which it is defined is first loaded into the Java runtime environment.

A class variable must be declared as such by including the `static` keyword in the variable declaration. Class variables can be accessed directly without having to use an object. Class variables are typically given `public` access because they are generally meant to be accessible outside of the class in which they are defined. A typical use for a class variable is to define a mathematical constant such as π.

Example: Using Instance and Class Variables

A black body is any object that emits a radiative heat flux according to the expression $q = \sigma \varepsilon T^4$. The ε parameter is the emissivity, a material property that characterizes the efficiency of the radiative process and will vary from 0 to 1. The `T` parameter is the temperature of the body in K. The σ parameter is the Stefan-Boltzmann constant and has a value of $5.6697e-12$ $W/cm^2 K^4$ The resulting heat flux will have units of W/cm^2.

The `BlackBody` class represents a black body. It defines instance variables that represent the temperature and emissivity. Because we might want to use the Stefan-Boltzmann constant outside of the `BlackBody` class, we define it as a class variable with `public` access. We don't want users to have direct access to the `temperature` and `emissivity` variables so we assign those variables `private` access. A complete discussion of variable access modifiers is presented later in this chapter. The `BlackBody` class also defines the `getHeating()` method that returns the black body radiative heating.

Instance and Class Variables

```
public class BlackBody
{
  public static double SIGMA = 5.6697e-12;
  private double temperature, emissivity;

  public BlackBody(double emiss, double t) {
    emissivity = emiss;
    temperature = t;
  }

  public double getTemperature() {
    return temperature;
  }

  public double getHeating() {
    return SIGMA*emissivity*
              Math.pow(temperature,4.0);
  }

  public static void main(String args[]) {
    BlackBody body = new BlackBody(0.85, 1000.0);

    System.out.println("T is " +
                        body.getTemperature());

    double qDot = body.getHeating();
    System.out.println("heating rate is " + qDot);
  }
}
```

Output—

```
T is 1000.0
heating rate is 4.81924500000
```

Now let's define another class that will access the SIGMA variable from the BlackBody class. Because it is `public` and `static`, SIGMA can be accessed outside of the BlackBody class by typing the syntax BlackBody.SIGMA.

```
public class GetSigma
{
  public static void main(String args[]) {
    System.out.println("SIGMA is "+BlackBody.SIGMA);
  }
}
```

Output—

```
SIGMA is 5.6697e-12
```

You may have noticed there is one problem with the BlackBody class. Since the SIGMA variable has `public` access the value associated with it can be changed. You obviously don't want to let users change the value of the Stefan-Boltzmann constant. This deficiency can be corrected by declaring the SIGMA variable to be final as will be explained in the "Final Variables" section later in this chapter.

Creating Variables

Creating a usable variable is a two-step process. You must declare the variable and then initialize it. Unlike in C and Fortran, a Java variable can be declared anywhere in the code as long as it is declared before it is used. As we previously mentioned, Java is a strongly typed language (unlike, say, Microsoft Visual Basic) in that the type of the variable must be included in the variable declaration. The general syntax for declaring a primitive variable consists of the variable type followed by the variable name.

```
variable_type variable_name;
```

You can declare more than one instance of a variable of a given type on the same line. Commas separate the variable names.

```
variable_type variable1_name, variable2_name;
```

Primitive variables can be initialized when they are declared, but don't have to be. Initialization is different for primitive and reference type variables. Primitive variables are either assigned a value as a primitive literal or by the variable is assigned to another primitive variable. For example, the following are valid declaration-initialization statements.

```
int j = 4;
int k = j;
```

Creating a reference type variable is a two-step process. This first step is to declare a variable of the desired type by writing the variable type followed by the variable name.

```
variable_type variable_name;
```

This creates a null reference to an object of the specified type. The second step of the process is to allocate memory for the reference variable using the new keyword and to initialize the nonstatic data members of the class by calling one of the class constructors.

```
variable_name = new variable_type(arguments);
```

The new keyword is a unary operator that takes as its operand the name of a constructor to call. Constructors are described in more detail in Chapter 7.

The new operator returns a reference to the object that was created. The object reference is assigned to the variable name that was previously declared. The two parts of the reference variable creation syntax can be combined into one statement. For example, you could type the following—

```
StringBuilder name = new StringBuilder("Scott");
```

A `String` is a special reference variable type in that a `String` object can be given a value by assigning it to a `String` literal. For instance, instead of using a constructor, you can declare and initialize a `String` variable using the syntax

```
String name = "Diana";
```

Class variables are also treated differently; they must be initialized when they are either declared or inside a static initialization block. Static initialization blocks are described in Chapter 7.

Example: Declaring Variables

Java provides a random number generator in the `Random` class from the `java.util` package. The `Random` class really defines a random number sequence so in that sense it is not a true random number generator. The starting point of the sequence can be specified by providing a `Random` object with a seed. Random number generation is important in probabilistic analysis techniques such as Monte Carlo methods.

The `DeclareDemo` class demonstrates some of the ways in which variables can be declared. The `DeclareDemo` class defines two instance variables—a variable of type `long` that represents the seed and a `Random` object. The `getSum()` method defines two local variables. The `sum` variable contains the sum of a certain number of random numbers. The `for` loop defines an integer variable that serves as the loop control variable. Another integer variable is defined in the input parameter list of the `getSum()` method.

The one thing this example does not do is to declare a class variable, but you can see how this is done by looking at the "Using Instance and Class Variables" example earlier in this chapter.

```
import java.util.*;

public class DeclareDemo
{
  private long seed;
  private Random random;

  public DeclareDemo() {
    seed = System.currentTimeMillis();
```

```
    random = new Random(seed);
  }

  public double getSum(int number) {
    double sum = 0;

    for(int i=0; i<number; ++i) {
      sum += random.nextDouble();
    }
    return sum;
  }

  public static void main(String args[]) {
    DeclareDemo demo = new DeclareDemo();
    System.out.println("sum is " + demo.getSum(2));
  }
}
```

Output (will vary)—

```
sum is 1.72326567814789
```

Example: Initializing Variables

To demonstrate the different ways that variables can be given initial values, we will once again modify the `SimpleGas` class first seen in Chapter 7. The `SimpleGas6` class defines six variables. Two of them are initialized when they are declared. The others are initialized in constructors. If the no-argument constructor is called, the variables are initialized using literal values. If the four-argument constructor is used, the variables are initialized by assigning them to the values of the arguments passed to the constructor.

```
public class SimpleGas6
{
  public static int MAX_SPECIES = 20;

  private double pressure, temperature;
  private int numSpecies;
  private String name;
  private String units = "MKS";

  public SimpleGas6() {
    numSpecies = 1;
    pressure = 101325.0;
    temperature = 207.4;
    name = "air";
  }

  public SimpleGas6(int n, double p, double t,
                              String nm) {
    numSpecies = n;
    pressure = p;
```

```
    temperature = t;
    name = nm;
  }

  // These methods return the values of the variables

  public String getName() {
    return name;
  }

  public static void main(String args[]) {
    SimpleGas6 gas =
           new SimpleGas6(5, 21.95, 207.0, "air");
    System.out.println("name of gas is " +
                                gas.getName());
  }
}
```

Output—

```
name of gas is air
```

NAMING CONVENTIONS AND RESTRICTIONS

Java gives you a lot of freedom in the names you give to your variables, but there are some conventions and restrictions to keep in mind. A variable name must be a series of Unicode characters that begins with a letter. The name cannot be one of the Java keywords. A list and description of the Java keywords can be found in Appendix A. A variable cannot have the same name as another variable defined in the same scope. Scope is discussed later in this section. All variable names should be as descriptive as possible within reasonable character count limitations. Try to avoid abbreviations where possible except where the abbreviation is commonly used (using t for time is okay for instance).

According to the Java Language Specification, Java variable names should use the camel capitalization style. The first letter of the variable name is lower case. The first letter of subsequent words in the variable name is upper case. The underscore character is permitted but by convention is reserved for constant variable names. An example of a variable name that follows the standard convention would be isVisible rather than isvisible or is_visible.

The names of constant variables (usually just called constants) are by convention written in all capital letters. Distinct words in a constant name are separated by the underscore character (_). An example of a constant name that follows the conventions is GAS_CONSTANT.

Access Modifiers

We discussed access modifiers in Chapter 7. The purpose of an access modifier is the same for variables as it is for classes. An access modifier applied to a variable defines how the variable can be accessed outside of the class in which it is defined. There are four types of access applicable to a variable: `public`, `protected`, `private`, and default.

- `public`—accessible anywhere inside or outside of the class in which the variable is defined.
- `protected`—accessible to any class defined in the same package as the variable. Outside of the package it is available only to subclasses of its class. This can be useful if you want to give subclasses direct access to a variable defined in a superclass, but don't want the variable accessible to the world at large.
- `private`—accessible only to the class in which the variable is defined. There is one school of thought that contends that all data members should be given `private` access. This ensures that the only access to them will be through methods.
- default—if no access modifier is provided, a variable is available to any class defined in the same package as the variable (i.e., `public`). Outside of the package it is not available (i.e., `private`).

The access types and ramifications are summarized in Table 8.2. Note that variables are always available inside the class in which they are defined regardless of their access modifiers. It is only for access outside of the variable's class that access modifiers come into play.

It is generally considered bad form to declare instance variables as `public`. By doing so you lose some control over your class. Someone who uses the class for another application might do things with your data members that

TABLE 8.2 Variable Accessibility

Variable Access Type	Same Class	Same Package	Subclass, Different Package	Non-subclass, Different Package
`public`	Yes	Yes	Yes	Yes
`protected`	Yes	Yes	Yes	No
`private`	Yes	No	No	No
default	Yes	Yes	No	No

you never intended, such as change the value of a variable that was intended to be read-only. Or someone could inadvertently set a length or weight to be negative.

The proper way to access variables outside the class in which they are defined is by using methods. The methods can make sure that the variables are not set to inappropriate values. This goes back to satisfying the object-oriented concept of encapsulation.

ACCESSING VARIABLE VALUES

The way that you access the value of a variable depends on whether you are inside or outside the class in which the variable is defined and whether the variable is instance or static. The value of a variable can always be accessed directly inside the class where it is defined by using the simple name of the variable. The value of a variable can be directly accessed outside the class in which the variable is defined only if the variable is given `public` (and, in some cases, `protected`) access.

If it has the proper access, the value of an instance variable can be accessed outside of its class through an instance of the class. The syntax to access the value of the variable is the reference to the object, a period, and the variable name. For example, if you had a reference variable named `body` that was accessing a `public` variable named `pressure`, you would type the syntax

```
body.pressure
```

The syntax for accessing the value of a class variable outside of the class in which the variable is defined is the name of the class in which the variable is defined, a period, and the name of the variable. For instance, to access the static `PI` variable defined in the `java.lang.Math` class, you would type

```
Math.PI
```

As we said before, you generally should not give instance variables `public` access. The preferred way of doing things is to give instance variables `private` access and provide methods to access and/or change their value.

Example: Accessing Variables

Let us modify the `BlackBody` class from the "Using Instance and Class Variables" example earlier in this chapter, so the class doesn't define a `main()` method. We will make use of the `BlackBody2` class through a driver class. The `BlackBody2` class still defines one static and two instance variables. The instance variables are given `private` access, meaning they are available inside the `BlackBody2` class but inaccessible outside of the class.

```
public class BlackBody2
{
  public static double SIGMA = 5.6697e-12;
  private double temperature, emissivity;

  public BlackBody2(double emiss, double t) {
    emissivity = emiss;
    temperature = t;
  }

  public double getTemperature() {
    return temperature;
  }

  public double getHeating() {
    return SIGMA*emissivity*Math.pow(temperature,4.0);
  }
}
```

The `BlackBody2Driver` class simply creates a `BlackBody2` object and tries to access its data members. The `temperature` variable has `private` access, so an attempt to directly access the variable with the syntax `body.temperature` will fail to compile. To access the `temperature` variable, you must call the `getTemperature()` method on the `BlackBody2` object.

Inside the `BlackBody2` class, the class variable `SIGMA` can be accessed using only its simple name. Since the variable `SIGMA` has `public` access it can be freely accessed outside of the `BlackBody2` class. To access the `SIGMA` variable outside of the `BlackBody2` class, you have to use its fully qualified name, `BlackBody2.SIGMA`.

```
public class BlackBody2Driver
{
  public static void main(String args[]) {
    BlackBody2 body = new BlackBody2(0.85, 1000.0);

    //   This won't work
    //     System.out.println("T is "+body.temperature);

    // This is the proper way to access the temperature
    System.out.println("T is " +
                       body.getTemperature());

    // You can access the class variable directly
    System.out.println("Stefan-Boltzmann constant is " +
                       BlackBody2.SIGMA);
  }
}
```

Output—
```
T is 1000.0
Stefan-Boltzmann constant is 5.6697e-12
```

FINAL VARIABLES

A final variable is one whose value, once it is set, cannot be changed. Final variables are designated as such by using the `final` keyword in the variable declaration. Both instance and class variables can be declared `final`. Final variables are useful for defining constants that have `public` access but whose values aren't meant to be changed.

Example: Using Final Variables

One problem with the `BlackBody` class from the "Using Instance and Class Variables" example earlier in this chapter is that since the class variable `SIGMA` has `public` access the value of it can be changed. If a user were to change the value of the Stefan-Boltzmann constant, it would have an adverse effect on the accuracy of a radiative heating calculation. To prevent this, the variable `SIGMA` can be declared to be `final`.

```java
public class BlackBody3
{
  public static final double SIGMA = 5.6697e-12;
  private double temperature, emissivity;

  public BlackBody3(double emiss, double t) {
    emissivity = emiss;
    temperature = t;
  }

  public double getTemperature() {
    return temperature;
  }

  public double getHeating() {
    return SIGMA*emissivity*Math.pow(temperature,4.0);
  }
}
```
The BlackBody3Driver class creates a BlackBody3 object. Because the variable SIGMA is now final, any attempts to change its value will cause a compiler error.
```java
public class BlackBody3Driver
{
   public static void main(String args[]) {
      BlackBody3 body = new BlackBody3(0.85, 1000.0);
```

```
//  This statement won't compile
//      BlackBody3.SIGMA = 4.0e-12;

    double qDot = body.getHeating();
    System.out.println("heating rate is "+qDot);
  }
}
```

Output—

```
heating rate is 4.819245000000
```

Transient and Volatile Variables

There are two other modifiers that can be applied to variable declarations. The transient keyword indicates that a member variable should not be serialized. A serializable entity is one that can be persistently stored (to disk for instance) and recovered. If a variable is declared to be volatile, the compiler will not perform certain synchronization optimizations. These modifiers are not widely used in Java programming. They are briefly discussed here for completeness.

Casting

As we have seen, there are many variable types in the Java language. There may be times when you need to temporarily convert a variable of one type into another type. This operation is called *casting*. A common use of casting is to convert the return type of a method into a more specific type. For example, methods that are designed to work with all kinds of objects might have a return type of Object. You may need to cast the Object into a String for instance.

The cast operator is a pair of parentheses surrounding the type to which the variable will be cast. The cast operator precedes the variable to be cast.

```
(variable_type)variable_name;
```

Casting can be performed on both primitive and reference types. With primitive types, widening conversions (e.g., float to double) are performed automatically. No cast is needed. Narrowing conversions (e.g., double to float) that might involve a loss of precision require an explicit cast. When it comes to integers and floating point numbers, an integer type will automatically be cast into a floating point type, but a floating point type must be explicitly cast into an integer type. A reference type object can only be cast to a subclass object. Primitive types cannot be cast to reference types.

Example: Casting

Many of the methods in the Java API are designed to work with a wide variety of types. A method may have a return type of `Object`, meaning it can return any reference type. When you use such a method, you can cast the returned `Object` into the reference type you want.

The `CastDemo` class defines a `Vector` that stores three `BlackBody3` objects. The `BlackBody3` class was presented in the "Using Final Variables" example earlier in this chapter. The `getElement()` method is written to return the `BlackBody3` object at a specified index. The method does this by calling the `Vector` data member's `get()` method. This method returns an `Object`. Since we know the `Vector` stores `BlackBody3` objects, we cast the return value to a `BlackBody3` object and return the result of the cast.

The `get()` method from the `Vector` class can throw an exception. As such, the `get()` call is placed in a `try` block. Exception handling is described in more detail in Chapter 12. The second half of the `main()` method demonstrates how to cast integral to floating-point types and vice versa.

```
import java.util.*;

public class CastDemo
{
  private Vector data;

  // Create a Vector object and load it with
  // some BlackBody3 objects.

  public CastDemo() {
    data = new Vector();
    data.add(new BlackBody3(0.85, 2000.0));
    data.add(new BlackBody3(0.9, 4536.0));
    data.add(new BlackBody3(0.7, 1789.0));
  }

  // The get() method from the Vector returns
  // an Object.  It is cast into a BlackBody3
  // object

  public BlackBody3 getElement(int index) {
    BlackBody3 body;

    try {
      body = (BlackBody3)data.get(index);
```

```
      }
      catch (ArrayIndexOutOfBoundsException e) {
        body = (BlackBody3)data.get(0);
      }

      return body;
   }

   public static void main(String args[]) {
     CastDemo demo = new CastDemo();

     BlackBody3 first = demo.getElement(0);
     System.out.println("heating is "+
                         first.getHeating());

     //  This demonstrates integer-floating point casts

     float f = 12.34F;
//       int i = f;    This won't work

     int i = (int)f;
     System.out.println("i is " + i);
     f = i;
     System.out.println("f is " + f);
   }
}
```

Output—

```
heating is 77.10792
i is 12
f is 12.0
```

VARIABLE SCOPE

Every variable that you define will have a scope associated with it. A variable's scope is the region of the program where a variable can be accessed by its simple name. Scope is different from visibility. A variable is *visible* when it is not *shadowed* (hidden) by another variable of the same name. A variable is out of scope once the block of code in which it is defined exits or the object with which it is associated is no longer referenced.

Example: Dealing with Scope

As was previously explained, a variable only has scope in the block of code in which it is declared. This can sometimes become an issue when working with operations that can throw exceptions. Such operations are usually placed in a `try` block. Any variables declared inside the block go out of scope when the block exits.

The `ScopeDemo` class declares a `String` variable named `fileName` at class scope. This variable is available to the `getText()` method. The `getText()` method reads a line of text from a file and returns the text as a `String`. Because I/O processes can throw exceptions, the I/O stream object creation and read operation is placed inside a `try` block.

```java
import java.io.*;

public class ScopeDemo
{
  private String fileName = "scope.txt";

  //  The getText() method reads a line of text
  //  from a file.  The method has access to the
  //  fileName variable declared at class scope

  public String getText() {
    try {
      BufferedReader reader =
          new BufferedReader(new FileReader(fileName));
      String text = reader.readLine();
    }
    catch (FileNotFoundException fnfe) {
       System.out.println("file not found");
       return "";
    }

    return text;
  }

  public static void main(String args[]) {
    ScopeDemo demo = new ScopeDemo();
    System.out.println(demo.getText());
  }
}
```

This program will not compile because the `String` variable named `text` is declared within the `try` block. Once the `try` block exits, the variable is out of scope and disappears. When we try to `return text` a compiler error occurs because a reference to the `text` variable no longer exists. One solution to this problem is to declare the variable outside of the `try` block and initialize it to a default value. The modified `getText()` method now looks like this—

```java
  public String getText() {
    String text = "";
```

```
    try {
      BufferedReader reader =
         new BufferedReader(new FileReader(fileName));
      text = reader.readLine();
    }
    catch (IOException ioe) {
      System.out.println("IO Exception occurred");
      return text;
    }

    return text;
}
```

To run the modified program, create a text file named scope.txt and place it in the same directory as the program. If the file contained the line "This is the contents of scope.txt," the output from the program would be—

```
This is the contents of scope.txt
```

9

METHODS

In Chapter 8 we learned that a class can declare variables. A class can also declare methods. A method, in the simplest way of looking at it, is a named block of code that can be called from another part of a program. In non-object-oriented programming languages, such as C or Fortran, the method (or function or subroutine) is the basic building block of the program. Methods are used to divide the program into functional units. There are no access restrictions associated with a C or Fortran method. It can be called directly from anywhere in the program.

In Java, methods are an integral part of the object-oriented framework, but they are not the basic building block of a Java program—the class serves that function. Java methods are members of a class. Among other things, methods are used to access, change, and manipulate the fields of a class. Java methods have an access associated with them that defines how and when the method can be accessed outside of its class. You can define instance methods that are associated with an instance of a class or static (class) methods that are associated with the class itself. You can also define a method to be abstract, final, synchronized, or native.

Methods play a key role in the object-oriented concepts of encapsulation, inheritance, and polymorphism. According to the idea of encapsulation, you should not give direct access to the fields declared in a class. These should be given private access and access to them provided through methods. A subclass inherits the nonprivate methods from its superclasses. The subclass can use the inherited methods as they are or it can overload or override the methods as it sees fit, to implement polymorphism.

The topics we will cover in this chapter are—

- Declaring methods
- Naming conventions
- Access modifiers
- Instance methods
- Static methods
- The `main()` method
- Input parameters
- Abstract methods
- Final methods
- The `native` and `synchronized` keywords
- Method chaining
- Method overloading
- Method overriding
- The `return` statement

Declaring Methods

The general syntax for a method declaration is—

```
[modifiers] return_type method_name(parameter_list)
           [throws exception1, exception2, ...] {
   //  body of method
}
```

The first part of a method declaration is called the *header*. The header tells the compiler the method name, its return type, any special keywords applied to the method, and the method's parameter list. The header must include the method name and return type. The other parts are optional. Following the header, a method declaration must include a pair of parentheses and a body. For abstract methods the body must be an *empty statement,* represented by the semicolon. For all other types of methods, the body is a block of code, which may be just an empty pair of braces, {}. The modifiers that can be applied to a method include access modifiers and other keywords (`abstract`, `final`, `static`, `synchronized`, `native`) that define any special characteristics of the method. The header may include a `throws` clause that declares the exceptions that the method can throw. Exception handling is discussed in more detail in Chapter 12.

A method can return one and only one value. The return type specified in the method declaration defines the type of value that will be returned. The return type can be any primitive or reference type defined in the Java language. If a method does not return a value, the return type is `void`. When a method specifies a reference type as its return type, the return value can either be an instance of that type or an instance of a subclass of that type. For example, a method with a return type of `Object` could return any reference type since `Object` is the ancestor of all other Java classes.

The parameter list defines the number and type of arguments that will be passed to the method. The input parameters are given names that the method will use when referring to them. A method that takes multiple parameters separates them with commas in the parameter list.

Example: Declaring Methods

The `DeclareDemo` class declares two methods. The `getHeight()` method is an instance method that returns the value of a variable named `height`. The `getDateTime()` method is a static method that returns the date and time that the method was invoked. Note that the instance and static methods are called in different ways. This is explained in more detail in the "Instance Methods" and "Static Methods" sections later in this chapter. The `DeclareDemo` class also defines a constructor. Constructors are discussed in Chapter 7.

```java
import java.util.*;

public class DeclareDemo
{
  private double height;

  // The DeclareDemo constructor initializes the height
  // field

  public DeclareDemo(double h) {
    height = h;
  }

  // Three methods are declared.

  public double getHeight() {
    return height;
  }

  public static String getDateTime() {
    Date date = new Date();
    return date.toString();
  }
```

```
    public static void main(String args[]) {
      DeclareDemo demo = new DeclareDemo(2.3);

      System.out.println("height is "+
                         demo.getHeight());
      System.out.println("date and time are " +
                         DeclareDemo.getDateTime());
    }
}
```

Output—

```
height is 2.3
date and time are Sat Aug 10 19:09:41 GMT-7:00 2002
```

Naming Conventions

As was the case with variables, Java gives you a lot of flexibility in choosing names for your methods, although some restrictions and conventions do apply. A method name must consist of Unicode characters and must begin with a letter. The method name cannot be a Java keyword. According to the Java Language Specification, the naming convention for Java methods is to use the camel capitalization style. The first letter of a method name is lower case. The first letter of any subsequent word in a method name is capitalized.

The method name should describe what the method does. Methods that are used to access the value of a data member are, by convention, named "get" followed by the data member name. For example, a method used to retrieve the value of a variable named `pressure` would be called `getPressure()`. Methods that return the value of a boolean variable are named "is" followed by the variable name. For example, `isKinetic()` might be a method used to return the value of a boolean variable named `kinetic`. Methods used to change the value of a variable are named "set" followed by the variable name. A method used to change the value of a variable named `pressure` would be named `setPressure()`.

Access Modifiers

All methods will have an associated access that defines how and if the method can be called outside of the class in which it is defined. You can either specify the access explicitly with an access modifier or the method will be given default access if no access is specified. The four types of access a method can have are `public`, `protected`, `private`, and default.

- `public`—no access restrictions. A `public` method can be called anywhere. This is the most commonly used access modifier for methods.
- `protected`—can be called inside the class in which it is defined or inside a subclass of the class in which it is defined. Also available to any classes defined in the same package as the method.
- `private`—can only be called inside the class in which it is defined. Intended for methods that are used internally inside a class.
- default—if no access modifier is specified, a method has default access.

The method has `public` access to other members inside the same package that the method is defined. The method is not accessible outside of the package in which it is defined.

The method access types and what they mean are summarized in Table 9.1. All methods are freely accessible inside the class in which they are defined. It is only outside of their class that access modifiers come into play.

TABLE 9.1 Method Accessibility

Method Access Type	Same Class	Same Package	Subclass, Different Package	Non-subclass, Different Package
public	Yes	Yes	Yes	Yes
protected	Yes	Yes	Yes	No
private	Yes	No	No	No
default	Yes	Yes	No	No

Example: Method Access

The `AccessDemo` class defines two methods. The `getTotalCost()` method is meant to be accessed outside of the `AccessDemo` class and therefore is given `public` access. The `secretMethod()` method is intended for internal use only. To prevent outside access of this method, it is given `private` access.

```
public class AccessDemo
{
  private double totalCost, fixedCost;

  public AccessDemo(double fixed) {
    fixedCost = fixed;
  }

  // The getTotalCost() method is given public access.
  // The secretMethod() method is given private access.
```

```
  public double getTotalCost() {
    totalCost = fixedCost + secretMethod();
    return totalCost;
  }

  private double secretMethod() {
    return 1.4*fixedCost;
  }
}
```

We next write a driver program for the `AccessDemo` class. The `AccessDriver` class creates an `AccessDemo` object. You can't call the `secretMethod()` method outside of the `AccessDemo` class. Any attempt to do so will result in a compiler error. The `getTotalCost()` method is `public` and can be called outside of the `AccessDemo` class.

```
public class AccessDriver {
  public static void main(String args[]) {
    AccessDemo demo = new AccessDemo(1234.56);

    //  Can't access the private method
    //     demo.secretMethod();

    //  Can access the public method

    System.out.println("cost is " +
                       demo.getTotalCost());
  }
}
```

Output—

```
cost is 2962.944
```

INSTANCE METHODS

There are two basic types of methods—instance and static. An instance method is associated with an object. Instance is the default type for methods. Every object will share the same implementation of the method, but the method will act upon the data specific to its associated object. As a matter or semantics, objects do not call instance methods. Instance methods are called on objects.

Inside the class in which it is defined, an instance method can be called by simply typing the method name and providing the appropriate number of arguments. Outside of the class in which it is defined, an instance method can only be called by referencing an instance of the class. The syntax for calling an instance method outside of its class is the instance variable name, a period, the method name, and any input arguments.

```
instance_name.method_name(arguments);
```

Example: Writing Instance Methods

This example shows a typical use of instance methods—to retrieve or change the value of a data member. The `InstanceDemo` class declares one instance variable named `pressure`. We do not want to allow direct access to the variable outside of the `InstanceDemo` class so the variable is given `private` access. The `InstanceDemo` class provides access to the `pressure` variable through two methods—`getPressure()` returns the current value of the variable, `setPressure()` changes the value of the variable. The names `get` and `set` are the conventional beginnings for names of data member access methods.

```java
public class InstanceDemo
{
  private double pressure;

  //  The InstanceDemo constructor initializes the
  //  pressure field.

  public InstanceDemo(double p) {
    pressure = p;
  }

  //  Define methods to access or change
  //  the value of the pressure variable

  public double getPressure() {
    return pressure;
  }

  public void setPressure(double p) {
    pressure = p;
  }

  public static void main(String args[]) {
    InstanceDemo demo = new InstanceDemo(21.95);

    //  Call two methods of the InstanceDemo class

    demo.setPressure(54.3);
    System.out.println("pressure is " +
                       demo.getPressure());
  }
}
```

Output—

```
pressure is 54.3
```

STATIC METHODS

The second general category of methods is static, or class, methods. A static method is associated with a class rather than with an individual object. A static method is designated as such by including the `static` keyword in the method declaration. Static methods are often used to implement generic functionality that can be used by a wide variety of classes. As such, static methods are often given `public` access.

A static method can be called inside the class in which it is defined simply by typing the method name followed by any input arguments. To call a static method outside of the class in which it is defined, you must type the class name, a period, the method name, and any input arguments.

```
class_name.method_name(arguments);
```

You can also call a static method through an object reference, but this is never necessary and is considered a bad practice.

Static methods can only access other static members. You must use an object to call an instance method from within a static method. Static methods can only act upon static variables. A static method will not have access to any instance variables since these are associated with an object rather than with the class itself. Static methods cannot reference the `this` or `super` keywords since these refer to objects as well.

Example: Defining Static Methods

Static methods are often used for implementing mathematical functions that can be used in a variety of applications. The `StaticDemo` class defines a static method named `hypotenuse()` that returns the hypotenuse of a right triangle. The method is given `public` access so it can be called directly outside of the `StaticDemo` class. Note that the `hypotenuse()` method itself calls a static method, `sqrt()` from the `Math` class.

```
public class StaticDemo
{
  public static double hypotenuse(double height,
                                  double width) {
    return Math.sqrt( height*height + width*width );
  }
}
```

To access the hypotenuse method outside of the `StaticDemo` class, you must type `StaticDemo.hypotenuse` along with the method arguments. The `CallStatic` class demonstrates how this can be done.

```
public class CallStatic {
  public static void main(String args[]) {

    //  Call the hypotenuse method

    System.out.println("hypotenuse is " +
         StaticDemo.hypotenuse(3.0, 4.0));
  }
}
```

Output—

```
hypotenuse is 5.0
```

The main() Method

The `main()` method is a special static method that serves as the entry point for Java applications. It is declared as `static` because the `main()` method is called by the Java runtime before any objects are created. The `main()` method can call static methods, declare local variables, create objects, and manipulate them. The general syntax of the `main()` method is—

```
public static void main(String args[]) {
   //  body of method
}
```

An alternative, and perfectly acceptable, syntax for the `main()` method is—

```
public static void main(String[] args) {
   //  body of method
}
```

The `main()` method must be declared in the class whose name is invoked to start the program. If you wanted to run a program using the syntax `java BlackBody`, the `BlackBody` class would have to declare a `main()` method.

The `main()` method can take command line arguments. These are included in the syntax to run the Java program and are passed to the `main()` method as a `String` array. For example, the following syntax would run the program `MyProgram.class` with two command line arguments named `arg1` and `arg2`—

```
java MyProgram arg1 arg2
```

The command line argument `arg1` would be placed into `args[0]`. The command line argument `arg2` would be placed into `args[1]`. Command line arguments are always passed to `main()` as `String` objects. If a command line argument is intended to be a number, you can convert it from a `String` to the desired primitive type. Command line argument delimiters are white space. If an argument has white space in it, surround it with double quotes. For example, the text "Bobby McGee" (with the double quotes) would be treated as a single command line argument.

Example: Using Command Line Arguments in `main()`

The `main()` method of the `CommandLine` class calls the static `hypotenuse()` method described in the "Defining Static Methods" example but the inputs for the method are obtained from command line arguments. The command line arguments are passed to `main()` as `String` objects. The `String` objects must be converted to type `double` before being passed to the `hypotenuse()` method. This is done using the static method `parseDouble()` from the `Double` class.

```
public class CommandLine {
  public static void main(String args[]) {

    //  Convert the command line arguments from
    //  Strings to doubles.

    double height = Double.parseDouble(args[0]);
    double width = Double.parseDouble(args[1]);

    //  Call the hypotenuse method

    System.out.println("hypotenuse is "+
          StaticDemo.hypotenuse(height, width));
  }
}
```

Output—

Your output will vary according to the command line arguments you provide. If you run this program by typing

```
java CommandLine 3.0 4.0
```

you will get the output

```
hypotenuse is 5.0.
```

Input Parameters

Methods are often not meant to be self-contained entities. They are intended to act upon arguments that are passed to the method when it is called. The number and type of arguments a method requires are declared in a parameter list that is part of the method declaration. Each element in the list consists of the type of the parameter and a parameter name that will be used by the method to access the parameter. Commas separate each type-name pair in the list. Parameters can be primitive or reference types. A method that has no inputs will have an empty pair of parentheses as its parameter list.

The parameter names only exist within the scope of the method. A parameter name can be the same as the name of one of the class members. Inside the method, such a parameter will temporarily *shadow,* or hide, the class member variable. You cannot pass a method into a Java method (unlike C which supports the concept of a function pointer). However, you can pass an object to a method and call the object's methods. This topic becomes important when we discuss "Generic Class Libraries" in Chapter 23.

Passing Arguments to Methods

Before we explore how arguments are passed to methods, let's discuss an issue of semantics. Parameters are declared in the method declaration. When a method is called, arguments are sent to the method. When you call a method, the number and type of arguments you pass to the method must match its parameter list. The arguments can be the names of variables, primitive or `String` literals, or any expression that is compatible with the parameter type.

Arguments to Java methods are passed by value. When an argument is sent to a method, the value of the argument is sent to the method rather than the argument itself. For arguments that are primitive types, a copy of the value of the argument is sent to the method. For example, if you wanted to call a method named `blah()` that takes an `int` type as an argument, the syntax

```
int j=4;
blah(j);
```

is functionally equivalent to the syntax

```
blah(4);
```

When an argument value reaches the method, it is assigned to the corresponding variable in the method's parameter list. The value and the original argument are disconnected. Any changes made to the value inside the method are not made to the value of the argument.

Reference type arguments are also passed by value to methods. The value that is passed is a copy of the reference to the object or array referenced by the argument. When the reference is assigned to the corresponding variable from the method's parameter list, the variable points to the same object as the argument. This means that any changes made through a reference type parameter inside a method will also change the original object. This is handy if you want a method to modify more than one object. A method can only return one value, but it can modify any number of objects if references to them are passed to the method as arguments.

Example: Primitive and Reference Type Input Arguments

This example demonstrates the difference between primitive and reference type variables when they are passed to methods. The `doubleThem()` method takes two arguments—an integer variable and an integer array. The method doubles the value of the input arguments. In the `main()` method of the `InputDemo` class, an integer variable and an integer array are created, initialized, and passed to the `doubleThem()` method.

When the method returns, the values of the variables are printed. The elements of the integer array have doubled in value but the integer variable has not. This is because the integer variable is a primitive type. Its value was passed to the method rather than the variable itself. When the value of the parameter variable was doubled inside the method, the original variable was unaffected. An array is a reference type and a copy of the reference to the array was passed to the method. Any changes made through the reference copy in the method are also made to the original object.

```
public class InputDemo
{
  // This method doubles the value of its input
  // parameters

  public void doubleThem(int j, int array[]) {
    j*=2;

    for(int i=0; i<array.length; ++i) {
      array[i]*=2;
    }
  }

  public static void main(String args[]) {

    // create and initialize a primitive and
    // reference type variable.
```

```
        int j = 4;
        int array[] = { 1,2,3 };
        InputDemo demo = new InputDemo();

        //  Call the doubleThem() method

        demo.doubleThem(j,array);

        //  Print the new values of the variables

        System.out.println("j is "+j);

        for(int i=0; i<array.length; ++i) {
          System.out.println("array[" + i +
                            "] is " + array[i]);
        }
      }
    }
```

Output—

```
j is 4
array[0] = 2
array[1] = 4
array[2] = 6
```

Abstract Methods

In Chapter 7, we introduced abstract classes as a way to define the framework for a collection of related classes. Among other things, an abstract class can declare abstract methods. An abstract method is designated by the `abstract` keyword in the method declaration. Abstract methods can only be defined in abstract classes. An abstract method declaration consists of the method name, return type, parameter list, `throws` clause (if any), and a semicolon. There are no braces and no method body.

Abstract methods are used to impose a certain structure on subclasses of an abstract class. The abstract method provides the basic method syntax to which subclasses must adhere. Nonabstract subclasses must provide an implementation of any abstract methods defined in superclasses. How the methods are implemented is up to the subclass. The only restriction is that the method name, return type, and input parameter list must match the abstract method declaration.

Example: Abstract Methods

To see abstract methods in action, look at the example in the "Abstract Classes" section of Chapter 7 where the `Shape` class defines two abstract methods intended to compute the area and circumference of a 2-D geometric shape.

FINAL METHODS

Final methods, like final classes and variables, cannot be overridden. A final method is designated as such by using the `final` keyword in the method declaration. Final methods are used to protect certain functionality from being altered by subclasses. An example of a final method is the `wait()` method from the `Thread` class. This method notifies a thread in a waiting state that the condition it is waiting for has been met. You don't want people messing around with threading functionality, so this method is declared `final`.

THE `native` AND `synchronized` KEYWORDS

Methods can also be declared to be `native` or `synchronized`. A `native` method is one that is written in a programming language other than Java. This book focuses on Java code development, but you may very well have legacy code that you would like to incorporate into your Java programs. For more information on utilizing native code, see *Essential JNI: Java Native Interface* by Rob Gordon.

A `synchronized` method is one that ensures thread-safe data access. In other words, two threads would not be able to simultaneously change the value of a variable in a `synchronized` method. Synchronization becomes a concern when developing multithreaded programs. As that is not a focus of this book, we won't spend any significant time on `synchronized` methods. For an informative chapter on synchronization, consult *Java How-to Program* by Harvey M. Deitel and Paul J. Deitel.

METHOD CHAINING

As we discussed earlier in this chapter, an instance method is called on an object. Methods can also have a reference type as their return type. It is possible to use the return value of one method as the reference on which another is called. What's more, this operation can be performed in a single executable statement. This is called *method chaining* or *cascading* and is a way to call multiple methods successively.

Method chaining is provided as a convenience. While it can make your Java code more compact, it doesn't add any functionality and can make a code listing somewhat more difficult to follow. You don't have to chain methods, but the capability is there for you if you want it.

Example: Using Method Chaining

One way to convert a `String` to a primitive `double` type is to first convert the `String` to a `Double` object and then convert the `Double` object to a primitive `double`. The `Double` class provides the following two methods to achieve this goal—

```
public static Double valueOf(String str)
public double doubleValue()
```

The `valueOf()` method returns a `Double` object corresponding to the specified `String`. The `doubleValue()` method can then be called on the `Double` object returning a `double` value. Because the return value of `valueOf()` is the calling type of `doubleValue()` the method calls can be chained.

```
public class ChainDemo
{
  public static void main(String args[]) {

    //  You can convert the type in two steps

    Double d = Double.valueOf("45.3");
    double value = d.doubleValue();

    value = value*3.0;
    System.out.println("value is " + value);

    //  Or you can chain the two steps together

    value = Double.valueOf("45.3").doubleValue();

    value = value*3.0;
    System.out.println("value is " + value);
  }
}
```

Output—

```
value is 135.9
value is 135.9
```

Method Overloading

Method overloading is one of the ways Java implements polymorphism. It allows a number of methods that perform the same general functionality to be given the same name. The C programming language does not support method overloading. That is why the C libraries define the `abs()`, `fabs()`, and `labs()` methods for computing the absolute value of `int`, `double`, and `long` data types. Java defines a single method, `Math.abs()`, that is overloaded such that it can compute the absolute value of `int`, `long`, `float`, and `double` data types. Constructors and methods that perform mathematical functions are often overloaded.

Overloading also allows you to extend the capability of inherited methods. A subclass may need additional functionality above what is provided by a method inherited from its superclass. Instead of the subclass defining a new method with a distinct name, the subclass can define an overloaded version of the inherited method.

Overloaded methods share the same name, but must have a different parameter list. The compiler decides which method to call, based on the arguments passed to the method. A method call must be unambiguous. The compiler must be able to decide which overloaded method to call. Return types do not play a role in overloaded method resolution. If an exact match is not found, the compiler will try to call the method that best matches the provided input arguments using whatever type conversions are allowed (`int` to `float`, for instance).

Example: Overloading Methods

The `Math2` class implements three overloaded versions of the `average()` method. The first version returns the average value of two arguments. The second overloaded version returns the average value of three arguments. The third version returns the average value of an array of `double` values.

```
public class Math2
{
  public static double average(double a, double b) {
    return (a + b)/2.0;
  }

  public static double average(double a, double b,
                               double c) {
    return (a + b + c)/3.0;
  }
```

```
    public static double average(double values[]) {
      double sum = 0.0;

      for(int i=0; i<values.length; ++i) {
        sum += values[i];
      }

      return sum/values.length;
    }
}
```

The `main()` method of the `OverloadDemo` class calls each of the three `average()` methods. The compiler knows which one to call based on the number and type of arguments passed to the method.

```
public class OverloadDemo
{
  public static void main(String args[]) {

    double answer;

    answer = Math2.average(5.0, 6.8);
    System.out.println("average is "+answer);

    answer = Math2.average(5.0, 6.8, 9.5);
    System.out.println("average is "+answer);

    double values[] = {1.2, 2.4, 3.0, 10.2};
    answer = Math2.average(values);
    System.out.println("average is "+answer);
  }
}
```

Output—

```
average is 5.9
average is 7.1
average is 4.2
```

METHOD OVERRIDING

Method overriding is when a subclass implements a method with the same name, return type, and parameter list as a method it inherits from a superclass. This differs from method overloading where methods of the same name but different parameter lists are defined. Method overriding is used when a subclass wants to define a method with the same parameters as a superclass method but with a different functionality.

An example of a commonly overridden method is the `toString()` method defined in the `Object` class. This method returns a `String` representation of an object. The default implementation as defined in the `Object` class simply returns the name of the class and its hash code. The `toString()` method is overridden by other classes in the Java API to provide a more meaningful description of an instance of the class.

You can call a superclass method that has been overridden using the `super` keyword.

```
super.methodName(arguments);
```

This is useful if you don't want to reinvent a method but instead want to augment its functionality.

Example: Overriding Methods

To demonstrate method overriding we will rewrite the `BlackBody3` class from Chapter 8. The `BlackBody3` class has access to the default `toString()` method it inherited from the `Object` class. The default version from the `Object` class returns the class name followed by its hash code, which is not very informative. The `BlackBody4` class overrides the `toString()` method to return the values of the `temperature` and `emissivity` variables for invoking the `BlackBody4` object.

```
public class BlackBody4
{
  public static final double SIGMA = 5.6697e-12;
  private double temperature, emissivity;

  public BlackBody4(double emiss, double t) {
    emissivity = emiss;
    temperature = t;
  }

  public double getTemperature() {
    return temperature;
  }

  public double getHeating() {
     return SIGMA*emissivity*Math.pow(temperature,4.0);
  }

  public String toString() {
    String str = "Black Body4: temperature=" +
            temperature + " emissivity=" + emissivity;
    return str;
  }
}
```

Next we will write a driver program that will create a `BlackBody4` object and call its `toString()` method. When an object is concatenated to a `String` using the + operator, the object's `toString()` method is automatically called.

```
public class OverrideDemo
{
  public static void main(String args[]) {

    BlackBody4 body = new BlackBody4(0.85, 2000.0);

    // Concatenating an object to a String calls the
    // toString() method associated with the object.

    System.out.println("object is " + body);
  }
}
```

Output—

```
object is BlackBody4: temperature=2000.0 emissivity=0.85
```

If the `toString()` method was not overridden, the output would be—

```
object is BlackBody4@ea2dfe
```

THE return STATEMENT

The `return` statement is a transfer of control statement that is used to exit a method. The `return` statement can return a value from a method. The type of the value that is returned must match the return type from the method declaration. A method that has a return type of `void` would simply use the `return` statement by itself. The following are all valid `return` statements—

```
return;
return Math.PI;
return 2.3;
```

A method can contain any number of `return` statements. A method can return reference as well as primitive type variables. When the return type is an object, the return value must be an instance of the return type class or a subclass of that class. For example, the `Stack` class is a subclass of the `Vector` class. A method with a return type of `Vector` could return a `Stack` object as well as a `Vector` object.

Example: Using `return` *Statements*

The `ReturnDemo` class defines the `nonNegative()` method that defines two `return` statements. If the value of the input argument is less than zero, the first `return` statement returns the numeric literal value `0.0`. If the argument is greater than zero, the second `return` statement returns the input argument variable.

```
public class ReturnDemo
{
  //  The nonNegative() method defines two return
  //  statements.  One returns a literal value,
  //  the other returns a variable

  public double nonNegative(double value) {
    if ( value < 0 ) {
      return 0.0;
    } else {
      return value;
    }
  }

  public static void main(String args[]) {
    double d;
    ReturnDemo demo = new ReturnDemo();

    d = demo.nonNegative(-2.0);
    System.out.println("value is "+d);

    d = demo.nonNegative(4.3);
    System.out.println("value is "+d);
  }
}
```

Output—

```
value is 0.0
value is 4.3
```

Many other examples of `return` statements can be found throughout this book.

10

INTERFACES

An interface is another general programming construct provided by the Java language. An interface, in essence, is a named block of code that contains method definitions and constant variable declarations. An interface declares abstract methods that must be implemented by any class that implements the interface. The interface does not implement the methods, it defines the method name, return type, and input parameter list. An interface can also define constants that can be accessed by classes that implement the interface.

In some ways the function of an interface is similar to that of an abstract class. An interface specifies the methods a class must implement, but not how to implement them. A class that implements an interface can implement the interface methods any way it likes as long as the method name, return type, and input parameter list are the same. In this way, an interface is another example of polymorphism. Interfaces can give you clues about the nature of the classes that implement them. For instance, you can infer with confidence that an instance of a class that implements the `IComparable` interface is an object that is meant to be compared against something else.

In this chapter we will discuss—

- Differences between interfaces and abstract classes
- Declaring an interface
- Interface members

- Implementing an interface
- Interfaces and inheritance
- Interface instances as input parameters and return types

Differences Between Interfaces and Abstract Classes

In many ways an interface is similar to an abstract class. Both are used to provide a blueprint for class functionality, but there are differences. Because Java does not permit multiple class inheritance, Java class hierarchies are linear. A class can have only one direct superclass that itself can have only one direct superclass and so on. If you want an abstract class to define certain functionality for two unrelated classes, the abstract class would have to be placed in a location common to both class hierarchies. You would end up with a lot of abstract classes placed right below the `Object` class.

You can avoid this situation by imposing the functionality using interfaces. A class can implement any number of interfaces. The interfaces do not have to be part of a class hierarchy (which should be obvious since they aren't classes). Unrelated classes can implement the same interface.

Another difference between abstract classes and interfaces is that abstract classes can implement some of the methods that they define. Interface methods are always abstract.

Declaring an Interface

An interface declaration consists of the `interface` keyword and interface name. The declaration can also optionally include modifiers and can indicate if the interface extends (inherits from) a superinterface.

```
[modifiers] interface interface_name
           [extends superinterface(s)]
{
   //  method declarations
   //  constant declarations
}
```

The body of the interface, usually consisting of method and constant declarations, is surrounded by braces. Interfaces can have `public` or default access. A `public` interface is available to any other code. An interface with default (unspecified) access is only available to other members of the package in which it is declared. Only one `public` interface can exist in a given file.

Example: Declaring Interfaces

See the example in the "Interface Members" section where the `Electrostatic` interface is declared.

INTERFACE MEMBERS

The body of an interface will usually consist of abstract method and/or constant declarations. These elements are called the interface members. An interface can also declare classes and interfaces as its members although this is not commonly the case. Variables declared inside interfaces are implicitly `public`, `static`, and `final`; i.e., they are *constants*. The naming convention for interface constants is that the names are in all capital letters. When a class implements an interface that declares constants, it has direct access to them. You do not need to write the interface name to access them.

Methods declared within interfaces are implicitly `abstract`. Method declarations consist of the method return type, method name, input parameter list, and a semicolon. All interface members are implicitly public and cannot be modified with the `transient`, `volatile`, or `synchronized` keywords.

Example: Defining Interface Members

A body that carries an electric charge will generate an electric field. The `Electrostatic` interface is designed to be implemented by classes that represent charged bodies. The interface declares a method named `getElectricField()` that returns the electric field of the body. The interface also defines a constant named `EPS0` that represents the permittivity of free space. This constant is used in electric field calculations.

```
public interface Electrostatic {

  //  permittivity of free space, C^2/(N-m^2)

  double EPS0 = 8.85e-12;

  double getElectricField();
}
```

Implementing an Interface

A class indicates that it will implement an interface by including the interface name after the `implements` keyword in the class declaration. If the class will implement more than one interface, the interface names are separated by commas.

```
[modifiers] class class_name
            implements interface1, interface2, …
```

To implement an interface, a class must provide an implementation of all the methods declared by the interface. If a class does not provide implementation for all of the interface methods, the class must be declared `abstract` and you cannot create an instance of this class.

A class that implements an interface has direct access to all constants defined in the interface. The constants can be accessed using only their simple name (`EPS0` rather than `Electrostatic.EPS0`). A class that does not implement the interface can still access the constants defined in the interface by using the qualified name (`Electrostatic.EPS0`).

Example: Implementing an Interface

Let us define two classes that will implement the `Electrostatic` interface described in the previous section. The `InfiniteChargedPlate` class represents an infinite charged plate. The electric field normal to an infinite flat plate is given by this expression—

$$E = \frac{\sigma}{2\varepsilon_0} \quad (10.1)$$

The electric field, *E*, in Eq. (10.1) is the force per unit charge and has units of *N/C*. The parameter σ is the surface charge density in C/m^2. The constant ε_0 is the permittivity of free space. Because the `InfiniteCharged-Plate` class implements the `Electrostatic` interface, it must implement `getElectricField()`. The class can implement this method any way it likes and does so according to Eq. (10.1).

```
public class InfiniteChargedPlate
                implements Electrostatic
{
  private double chargeDensity;

  public InfiniteChargedPlate(double chargeDensity) {
     this.chargeDensity = chargeDensity;
  }

  // Implement the Electrostatic interface method
```

```
    public double getElectricField() {
       return chargeDensity/(2.0*EPS0);
    }
}
```

The second class is named `ParallelPlate` and it represents two infinite, parallel, oppositely charged plates. Outside the plates, the electric fields cancel each other and the net field is zero. Between the plates the fields combine and the total electric field is given by the expression

$$E = \frac{\sigma}{\varepsilon_0} \qquad (10.2)$$

The `ParallelPlate` class must implement `getElectricField()` and does so according to Eq. (10.2). Note that both classes have direct access to the `EPS0` variable defined in the `Electrostatic` interface. There is no need to type `Electrostatic.EPS0`.

```
public class ParallelPlate implements Electrostatic
{
  private double chargeDensity;

  public ParallelPlate(double chargeDensity) {
    this.chargeDensity = chargeDensity;
  }

  //  Implement the Electrostatic interface method

  public double getElectricField() {
    return chargeDensity/EPS0;
  }
}
```

Finally, we will write a simple driver program that will create `ParallelPlate` and `InfiniteChargedPlate` objects and call the `getElectricField()` methods.

```
public class ImplementDemo
{
  public static void main(String args[]) {

    // Create InfiniteChargedPlate and ParallelPlate
    // objects

    InfiniteChargedPlate plate =
                 new InfiniteChargedPlate(1.0e-6);
    ParallelPlate plate2 = new ParallelPlate(1.0e-6);

    //  Write out their electric field intensities

    System.out.println("infinite plate field is " +
                       plate.getElectricField());
```

```
        System.out.println("parallel plate field is " +
                           plate2.getElectricField());
   }
}
```

Output—

```
infinite plate field is 56497.175 .
parallel plate field is 112994.350
```

Interfaces and Inheritance

An interface can inherit the members of another interface. Unlike classes, multiple inheritance is allowed with interfaces. Interface inheritance is indicated by the `extends` keyword in the interface declaration.

```
[modifiers] interface interface_name
       extends superinterface1, superinterface2,…]
{
   //   method declarations
   //   constant declarations
}
```

One reason to use interface inheritance is to extend the declarations and definitions of an existing interface. If you simply added a method declaration to an existing interface, you would break any program that had been compiled using the older version. Creating a new interface that builds upon an existing one avoids this problem.

A class that implements an interface that inherits other interfaces must provide implementations for all of the methods defined in all interfaces in the inheritance hierarchy. For example, let's say an interface named `Ionized` declares a method named `getField()`. Let's also suppose that the `Ionized` interface extends the `Gas` interface that declares two methods, `getEnthalpy()` and `getEntropy()`. A class that implemented the `Ionized` interface would have to provide implementation for the `getField()`, `getEnthalpy()`, and `getEntropy()` methods.

Interface Instances as Input Parameters and Return Types

Interfaces are different from classes in that you cannot create an instance of an interface. Interface reference types can be used, however, both as input arguments and return types. This may sound odd, but it provides a lot of functionality and flexibility when creating your methods. An instance of a class is also considered an instance of any interface it implements. A method that lists an interface type as an input parameter can take as an argument any object that implements the interface.

This is commonly used for methods that are applicable to a variety of classes in different class hierarchies. Because there may not be a single parent class for all the applicable classes, a method can define an interface type as an input parameter instead. The method can then accept a variety of object types as an argument rather than just members of a given class hierarchy. The same is true when a method defines an interface type as its return type. The method can return an instance of any class that implements the interface.

Example: Using Interfaces to Reference Disparate Classes

Java defines a variety of collection classes in the `java.util` package, many of which can work together because they all implement a set of common interfaces. In this example, `Vector` and `ArrayList` objects are created and loaded with data. We next want to put the contents of these objects into a `LinkedList`. We can do this with the following method from the `LinkedList` class—

```
public boolean addAll(Collection c)
```

The `Collection` interface is defined in the `java.util` package. Because the `Vector` and `ArrayList` classes both implement the `Collection` interface, instances of the `Vector` and `ArrayList` classes can be passed to this method.

Interface instances can also be used as the return type from methods. The `LinkedList` object calls the `listIterator()` method that returns an instance of the `ListIterator` interface. This instance can be used to iterate through the elements of the `LinkedList`.

```
import java.util.*;

public class ArgDemo
{
  public static void main(String args[]) {

    // A Vector and ArrayList object are created and
    // filled with some elements.

    Vector vector = new Vector();
    vector.add("Jackson");
    vector.add("Zachary");
```

```
      ArrayList arrayList = new ArrayList();
      arrayList.add("Mark");
      arrayList.add("Maria");

      //  A LinkedList object is created

      LinkedList linkedList = new LinkedList();

      //  The contents of the Vector and ArrayList are
      //  added to the LinkedList using the addAll()
      //  method. Because the method takes a Collection
      //  instance as an argument, it can accommodate many
      //  different types of input arguments.

      linkedList.addAll(vector);
      linkedList.addAll(arrayList);

      //  The listIterator() method returns an object that
      //  implements the ListIterator interface. This
      //  object can be used to iterate through the linked
      //  list.

      ListIterator iterator = linkedList.listIterator();

      while( iterator.hasNext() ) {
        System.out.println( iterator.next() );
      }
    }
}
```

Output—

```
Jackson
Zachary
Mark
Maria
```

11

PACKAGES AND JAR FILES

When you start to develop more complicated Java applications, you may end up with a large number of source code, bytecode, and support files. Java provides packages and Java Archive (JAR) files to help you organize and store your work. Packages are used to separate and organize a collection of classes and interfaces. One reason to place your files in a package is to avoid naming conflicts. Two classes can't share the same name unless they are placed in different packages. If you write a class with an obvious name such as Beam, you don't have to worry about whether that name is being used by some other library if you place the Beam class in a user-defined package.

Packages allow you to bundle collections of classes and interfaces with similar functions. It would be convenient, for instance, to bundle classes that deal with gas mixtures into a Gas package. If you needed a class that encapsulated a gas mixture, you would look for it in the Gas package. Packages also have access control implications. See Chapters 7, 8, and 9 for an explanation of how packages affect class, variable, and method access.

We've been using packages in this book although you probably weren't aware of it. If you don't specify a package in your source code, your program will be placed in an unnamed package that originates from your current working directory.

JAR files are a way to store and compress a collection of Java files. The files can be source code, bytecode, image files, or anything else that a Java program might require. JAR files can be very useful when dealing with complicated applications or large libraries that may contain dozens of files. You can run applications directly from a JAR file.

In this chapter we will cover—

- Defining a package
- `import` declarations
- CLASSPATH environment variable
- Packages and access control
- JAR files

Defining a Package

Assigning the contents of a source file (called a *compilation unit* in Java) to a package is easy. You simply include a package declaration at the top of the source file. The declaration consists of the package keyword followed by the package name.

```
package package_name;
```

The classes and interfaces contained in the source file will be associated with the specified package. Subpackages may also be used and follow a hierarchical naming structure, where the package levels are separated by periods.

```
package package1.package2.package3;
```

The `java.awt.event` and `javax.swing.table` packages are examples of package hierarchies in the Java API.

Packages are typically mapped to a directory hierarchy. The files corresponding to a given package must be placed in a directory hierarchy that has the same name as the package. For example, the files that make up the `ThermoData.AirSpecies` package would be placed in an AirSpecies directory that would be a subdirectory of a ThermoData directory.

The bytecode files of a package must be compiled in their appropriate directories from the package root directory. For example, if an O2 class was defined in the `ThermoData.AirSpecies` package and the root directory of the package was named MyData, you would place the O2 class source code in the ThermoData\AirSpecies directory and compile it from the MyData directory using the syntax

```
javac ThermoData\AirSpecies\O2.java
```

Example: Including Classes in Packages

Let's create a package named `Fluids.Gas`. We will define a `Species` class and an `IonizedSpecies` class as members of the `Fluids.Gas` package. The classes are assigned to a package by placing a package declaration at the beginning of the source file. The `Species.java` code listing follows—

```
package Fluids.Gas;

public class Species
{
  private String name;
  private double molarMass;

  public Species(String name, double molarMass) {
    this.name = name;
    this.molarMass = molarMass;
  }

  public String getName() {
    return name;
  }

  public double getMolarMass() {
    return molarMass;
  }
}
```

Here is the `IonizedSpecies.java` code listing—

```
package Fluids.Gas;

public class IonizedSpecies extends Species
{
  private int chargeLevel;

  public IonizedSpecies(String nm, double mw,
                        int charge) {
    super(nm, mw);
    chargeLevel = charge;
  }

  public int getChargeLevel() {
    return chargeLevel;
  }
}
```

To physically associate the .class files with the package, the `Species.java` and `IonizedSpecies.java` source codes should be placed in the Fluids\Gas (or Fluids/Gas or Fluids:Gas) directory below the current working directory. The files should be compiled from the current working directory using the syntax

```
javac Fluids\Gas\Species.java
javac Fluids\Gas\IonizedSpecies.java
```

import Declarations

When a class or interface has been placed in a package, it is identified by its fully qualified name, the package and class names together. For instance, the Species class described in the previous section would be referred to as the Fluids.Gas.Species class. You can well imagine that this situation becomes quite cumbersome if intricate package hierarchies are involved.

You can avoid having to use the fully qualified name of a package member by placing an import declaration at the beginning of your source code, below any package declarations. The import declaration does not load anything into the code. It simply allows you to use the unqualified or simple name for one or more package members. There are two ways to use the import declaration—to access a single class or interface type and to refer to any member of a single package by its unique name.

To access a single class or interface type, enter the fully qualified name of the member after the import keyword. For example, to import the Species class from the Fluids.Gas package you would type

```
import Fluids.Gas.Species;
```

To refer to any member of a single package by its unqualified name, place an asterisk after the package name. To import the contents of the Fluids.Gas package you would type

```
import Fluids.Gas.*;
```

One thing to be aware of is that the wildcard character * will only import all the types defined in a single package, not an entire package hierarchy.

Example: Importing a User-Defined Package

The SpeciesDriver class creates a Species object and an IonizedSpecies object. To refer to these classes by their simple names, an import declaration is placed at the beginning of the source code. To get this example to work, the Fluids.Gas package path will need to be part of the CLASSPATH environment variable described in the next section.

```
import Fluids.Gas.*;

public class SpeciesDriver
{
  public static void main(String args[]) {

    // Create Species and IonizedSpecies objects

    Species n = new Species("atomic nitrogen", 0.0140067);
    IonizedSpecies o2p =
           new IonizedSpecies(
              "diatomic oxygen ion", 0.03199825, 1);

    // Print out some information about the objects

    System.out.println("molar mass of " +
          n.getName() + " is " + n.getMolarMass());
    System.out.println("molar mass of " +
          o2p.getName() + " is " + o2p.getMolarMass());
    System.out.println("charge level of " +
          o2p.getName() + " is " + o2p.getChargeLevel());
  }
}
```

Output—

```
molar mass of atomic nitrogen is 0.0140067
molar mass of diatomic oxygen ion is 0.03199825
charge level of diatomic oxygen ion is 1
```

CLASSPATH ENVIRONMENT VARIABLE

The Java runtime has to know where to locate the .class files associated with an `import` declaration. The search paths are defined in the CLASSPATH environment variable. Don't worry about setting the CLASSPATH variable if you are using the unnamed package; the system will know to search your current working directory for the required files. You also don't have to worry about setting the CLASSPATH variable when working with the built-in libraries that come with the Java SDK.

You do have to change the CLASSPATH variable if you want to freely access the contents of user-defined packages. If you add the root directory of your package library to the CLASSPATH variable, you can freely access your libraries anywhere on your computer. If you don't add the package root directory to CLASSPATH, you will need to place your code development directory directly above the package directories.

Setting the CLASSPATH environment variable is system-dependent. On computers running Windows, you can modify the variable by editing the AUTOEXEC.BAT file. For example, if the C:/Books/Technical_Java directory were the root directory of the previously described `Fluids.Gas` package, you would set your CLASSPATH definition to the following—

```
SET CLASSPATH = .;C:/Books/Technical_Java
```

The period in the CLASSPATH indicates that the system will search the current working directory for .class files. If you are running on a Unix system in csh you can change the CLASSPATH environment variable using the `setenv` command.

```
setenv CLASSPATH .;C:/Books/Technical_Java
```

In sh, the CLASSPATH variable can be changed with the following command—

```
CLASSPATH = .;C:/Books/Technical_Java
export CLASSPATH
```

Another way to set the search path for .class files (and the one recommended at the Sun Java website) is by using the `-classpath` compiler and JVM options. This approach allows you to customize the CLASSPATH for a given application without affecting other applications, although it can be somewhat tedious if you have to specify a large number of paths.

Example: Using CLASSPATH to Locate .class Files

Add the directory containing the `SpeciesDriver.java` program and the Fluids directory to your CLASSPATH environment variable list. You can now compile the `SpeciesDriver.java` program anywhere on your system.

PACKAGES AND ACCESS CONTROL

Packages are part of Java's access control mechanism. A member with `protected` access is accessible to all members of the same package. Outside of the package in which it is defined, a `protected` member is only accessible to subclasses of the class in which it is defined. A member with default access is accessible to all members in the same package but is not accessible outside of the package.

JAR FILES

JAR files are commonly used to store a collection of Java files. The files can be source code, bytecode, image files, or anything else a Java program might require. JAR files make it easier to store and deploy the files required by a complicated application. A JAR file can be compressed using the Zip format. Components can be accessed (e.g., Java applications can be executed) directly from JAR files.

JAR files are maintained by the `jar` utility that is part of the Java SDK. This utility can be used to create, examine, or extract files from a JAR file. The general syntax of the `jar` utility is

```
jar [options] [manifest_name] jar_name [file1,file2,...]
```

The manifest name is required only if certain options are used. The files at the end of the `jar` command syntax are the files that will be stored in the JAR file. The available `jar` utility options are listed in Table 11.1.

The c, t, and x options are mutually exclusive. You would only use one of them in a given `jar` command. Using the f option means that the operation will be performed on a file. You would then provide the name of a JAR file. The convention is for JAR file names to end with the .jar extension although

TABLE 11.1 jar Utility Options

COMMAND	DESCRIPTION
c	Creates a JAR file.
-C	Allows you to change directories during a JAR creation.
f	Specifies a file to be created, listed, or extracted from. Without this option, the standard input and output streams will be used.
i	Generates index information for the specified JAR file.
m	Includes information from an existing manifest file into the manifest file generated for this JAR file.
M	Indicates that a manifest file will not be included with the JAR file.
t	Lists the contents of an existing JAR file.
u	Updates an existing archive.
v	Generates verbose output.
x	Extracts a specified file from the JAR file. If no files are specified after this command, all the files are extracted.
0	Do not use Zip compression.

this is not mandatory. If you don't use the `f` option, the files will be read from or written to the standard I/O streams.

A JAR file will commonly contain a manifest file describing the contents of the JAR file. The manifest file can be user-specified or can be generated automatically. The manifest file will consist of a series of attribute-value pairs containing information about the JAR file contents. If a manifest file name is specified as part of the `jar` command, the information in that file will be used to create the manifest file. The system will fill in the blanks of any necessary information not provided in the user-specified manifest file. By default, the manifest file will be placed in a directory named META-INF inside the JAR file.

Be careful when you extract files from a JAR file, because any existing files and directories with the same name or path as the contents of the JAR file will be overwritten. When specifying multiple options, the order of the options generally doesn't matter, but there can't be any spaces between them. The -C option will temporarily change the directory. Immediately after the file following the -C option is accessed, the point of execution will return to the working directory.

To help clear up any lingering confusion about JAR files, let's demonstrate the basic concepts of creating and manipulating JAR files in a series of examples.

Example: Creating a JAR File

Let's create a JAR file using the classes defined in the examples from this chapter. Starting from the working directory that is the root of the `Fluids.Gas` package hierarchy, we will create the JAR file using the command

```
jar cvf species.jar .
```

Output—

```
added manifest
adding Fluids/(in = 0) (out=0) (deflated 0%)
adding Fluids/Gas/(in = 0) (out=0) (deflated 0%)
adding Fluids/Gas/IonizedSpecies.class(in=378) (out=268) (deflated 29%)
adding Fluids/Gas/IonizedSpecies.java(in=293) (out=165) (deflated 43%)
adding Fluids/Gas/Species.class(in=466) (out=303) (deflated 34%)
adding Fluids/Gas/Species.java(in=352) (out=159) (deflated 54%)
adding SpeciesDriver.class(in=1133) (out=652) (deflated 42%)
adding SpeciesDriver.java(in=615) (out=275) (deflated 55%)
```

The period at the end of the `jar` command indicates that all of the files and subdirectories of the current working directory are to be placed in the JAR file. We get the output because we specified `v`, the verbose option. The output indicates that a manifest was included in the JAR file and lists the files that were added to the file. The size of the files before and after compression is listed.

Example: Viewing the Contents of a JAR File

To view the contents of the previously created `species.jar` file, we will use the command

```
jar tf species.jar
```

Output—

```
META-INF/
META-INF/MANIFEST.MF
Fluids/
Fluids/Gas/
Fluids/Gas/IonizedSpecies.class
Fluids/Gas/IonizedSpecies.java
Fluids/Gas/Species.class
Fluids/Gas/Species.java
SpeciesDriver.class
SpeciesDriver.java
```

The `f` option is used to specify the JAR file to be examined. Without the `f` option you would have to supply the JAR file contents through standard input. We could have also used the `v` option for verbose output that would include the size of the uncompressed files and the date and time they were last modified.

Example: Extracting Files from a JAR File

To extract the SpeciesDriver.class file from the species.jar file, we would type

```
jar xf species.jar SpeciesDriver.class
```

When you do this you will see a SpeciesDriver.class file present in your working directory. To really make sure this worked, first delete the existing SpeciesDriver.class file. To extract a file that is stored in a directory, you need to specify the path to the file. For example, to extract the Species.class file, we would type

```
jar xf species.jar Fluids/Gas/Species.class
```

Note the use of forward slash characters in the expression. Even on Windows machines, you can use forward slashes (rather than the traditional backward slash) to indicate paths if you like. To extract all of the files from the species.jar file, we would type

```
jar xf species.jar
```

Once again, be careful when extracting files from a JAR file because the extracted files will overwrite any files of the same name and path.

Example: Running an Application from a JAR File

To run an application contained in a JAR file, the manifest file for the JAR must contain a header that tells the Java runtime which class in the JAR file defines the `main()` method for the application. This header takes the form

```
Main-Class: classname
```

If we want to run the `SpeciesDriver` program directly from the species.jar file, we will have to recreate the JAR file attaching a `Main-Class` header to the manifest file. We first create a text file named species.mf with one line of text, `Main-Class: SpeciesDriver`. We then recreate the JAR file using the syntax

```
jar cmvf species.mf species.jar .
```

The information in the species.mf file will be added to the manifest file generated by the system. In this case, the order of the options does matter. The `m` option must follow the `c` option and precede the `f` option. You can now run the `SpeciesDriver` application using the syntax

```
java -jar species.jar
```

Output—

```
molar mass of atomic nitrogen is 0.0140067
molar mass of diatomic oxygen ion is 0.03199825
charge level of diatomic oxygen ion is 1
```

12

EXCEPTION HANDLING

A lot can go wrong when a program runs. The user can provide inappropriate input data, a system or network error might occur, or there might simply be a bug in the code that you didn't know was there. Exception handling allows a program to continue running when an exception occurs. The exception is detected and processed in such a way that the program can keep going.

There is no built-in exception handling in Fortran or C. If you want exception handling in these languages, you have to do all the programming work yourself which usually involves a potentially complicated set of `if-then` statements and error codes. You also have to perform the exception handling where the exception will occur. You can't easily pass the exception handling to another part of your program.

Java has a sophisticated exception handling capability built into the language. When a problem occurs inside a Java program, an exception object is thrown. The Java runtime then will try to send the exception to an appropriate section of code that can handle the exception. The section of code can try to correct the problem or can gracefully terminate the program. Java exception handling lets you decide where the exception handling will occur. An exception thrown by one method can be passed back to a calling method. You can also define your own exception classes for any specific needs your program might have.

There are two general types of Java exceptions—checked and unchecked. Checked exceptions are those for which the Java compiler checks for the presence of exception handlers. An example of a checked exception is an `IOException` that can occur if there is a problem with an I/O operation. The compiler will make sure that all checked exceptions are either caught in a `catch` clause or declared in a `throws` clause. If you don't catch or declare a checked exception, the program won't compile.

Unchecked exceptions are more generic and can happen in a number of circumstances. Exceptions that occur at runtime, such as an `ArithmeticException`, are treated as unchecked exceptions. System errors that can't usually be recovered from by an application are also not checked. The compiler will not ensure that unchecked exceptions are caught or declared. If you don't handle an unchecked exception inside a `catch` clause, the default system handler will take care of it by terminating the program.

There are two basic ways of handling exceptions. You can process the exception where it happens by providing a `try` statement or you can pass the exception to another part of your program for processing by using the `throw` statement and `throws` clause.

In this chapter we will discuss—

- The `Exception` class hierarchy
- `try` statements
- The `throw` and `throws` keywords

THE EXCEPTION CLASS HIERARCHY

When an exception occurs, an exception object is created. When a system-generated exception occurs, the Java runtime will create an instance of the appropriate exception class containing the information pertinent to the exception. You can also define your own exception classes to suit any specialized needs.

The `Exception` class hierarchy is shown in Figure 12.1. The `Throwable` class is the superclass ancestor of all exception classes and is a direct subclass of `Object`. There are two main branches from `Throwable`. One is headed by the `Error` class and represents catastrophic exceptions such as stack overflows that are not checked and usually should not be caught. The `Exception` class is the parent of recoverable exceptions that your program can catch and process. User-defined exception classes are written as subclasses of `Exception` or of one of the existing `Exception` subclasses.

Runtime exceptions are subclasses of the `RuntimeException` class and represent exceptions that occur while the program is running. Examples of

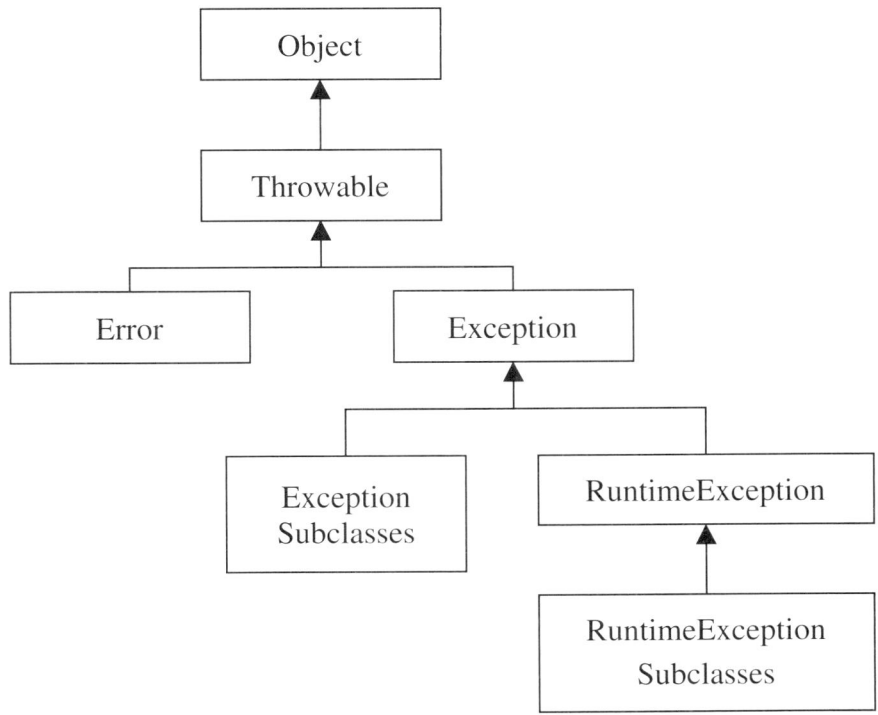

FIGURE 12.1 Exception Class Hierarchy

`RuntimeException` subclasses include the `ArithmeticException` and `ClassCastException` classes. Runtime exceptions can happen anywhere in a program. It would be unreasonable to catch or declare all possible occurrences of a runtime exception, so Java allows them to be uncaught and undeclared. You can catch or declare them if you want to, but it is not required.

Any subclass of `Exception` that is not a `RuntimeException` must be either caught or declared by the method that can cause the exception. Examples of this type of exception include the `IOException` and `ClassNotFoundException` classes.

try STATEMENTS

There are two ways to handle Java exceptions—you can handle an exception where it occurs using a `try` statement or you can throw the exception to another section of code and handle it there. With a `try` statement, the code that can throw the exception is placed inside a block of code after the `try` keyword. One or more `catch` clauses can be used to catch any thrown exceptions. The `finally` clause is for code that will run regardless of whether an exception is thrown or caught.

The general syntax of the `try` statement is—

```
try {
   // code that can throw an exception
} catch (exception_type exception_name) {
   // code to handle the exception
} finally {
   // code that will always be run
}
```

Every checked exception must ultimately be sent to a `catch` clause. Unchecked exceptions can be tested for and processed inside a `try` statement as well. You can write nested `try` statements.

Let's look at the different parts of the `try` statement in more detail.

The `try` Statement

A `try` statement is defined using the `try` keyword. Code that can generate an exception is placed inside a block of code after the `try` statement—

```
try {
   // code that can throw an exception
}
```

The block of code after a `try` statement acts like any other inner block of code. Any local variables declared inside the block of code will not be available outside of it. If an exception is thrown, the block of code exits. Any code following the point where the exception occurs is not executed. The system will then try to match the exception type with any `catch` clauses. A `try` statement must be followed by either one or more `catch` clauses or a `finally` clause.

The `catch` Clause

A `catch` clause catches and processes an exception of a specified type. A `catch` clause is defined by the `catch` keyword, an exception type and exception variable name in parentheses, followed by a block of code—

```
catch (exception_type exception_name) {
   // code to handle the exception
}
```

When an exception is thrown inside a `try` statement, the system will try to match the exception type against the types declared in any subsequent `catch` clauses. If a match is found, the block of code following the `catch` clause is executed. A superclass of the exception that is thrown is considered a match. For example, if a `catch` clause declares an exception of type `Exception` (the parent class of all catchable exceptions), the `catch` clause will catch all exceptions that can be generated.

There can be multiple `catch` clauses associated with a given `try` statement. Multiple `catch` clauses are useful if a section of code can generate more than one type of exception. If multiple `catch` clauses are used, only one of them will be called when an exception is thrown. You must place exception subclasses before superclasses in the `catch` clause sequence. For example, if you place an `IOException catch` clause before a `FileNotFoundException catch` clause, the `IOException catch` clause will be called if a `FileNotFoundException` exception occurs (because `FileNotFoundException` is a subclass of `IOException`). The `FileNotFoundException catch` clause will never be called. You can have zero `catch` clauses if you define a `finally` clause.

A `catch` clause will typically provide a detailed error message and/or try to correct the problem. You can provide a short description of the exception by concatenating the exception object onto a `String`. For example, the following code would concatenate a `String` representation of an `IOException` object with the string `"exception type: "`

```
catch (IOException ioe) {
   System.out.println("exception type: " + ioe);
}
```

The `finally` Clause

A `finally` clause can be optionally placed at the end of a `try` statement. However, if a `try` statement does not have one or more `catch` clauses following it, it must be followed by a `finally` clause. A `finally` clause consists of the `finally` keyword followed by a block of code:

```
finally {
   //  code that will always be run
}
```

The block of code after a `finally` clause will be executed whether or not an exception is thrown and whether or not a thrown exception is caught. A `finally` clause can be used to return data or to ensure that things such as closing I/O streams occur even if an exception is thrown.

*Example: Using **try** statements*

A lot of things can go wrong during I/O operations. You can try to read a file that doesn't exist, you can attempt to read past the end of a file, or a system interruption may occur during your read or write operation. Because of their tendency to throw exceptions, I/O operations are often placed in `try` statements.

The `TryDemo` class attempts to read the first line of a user-specified file and assign this text to a `String`. Inside a block of code following the `try` statement the user is prompted for a file name and a `BufferedReader` object is created according to the specified file name. Two `catch` clauses are provided. The first catches a `FileNotFoundException` that occurs if the specified file is not available. The second responds to any other `IOException` that might occur during the read or file open operations. A `finally` clause returns either the text that was read from the file or a default `String`.

```java
import java.io.*;

public class TryDemo
{
  public static void main(String args[]) {
    String fileName;
    String text = "bailey boy";

    //   Create two BufferedReader objects.
    //   The first reads keyboard input.

    BufferedReader reader =
        new BufferedReader(
            new InputStreamReader(System.in));

    //   The second BufferedReader will read data
    //   from a file.

    BufferedReader fileReader;

    //   The user is prompted for a file name

    System.out.print("Enter file name:   ");

    //   The program reads the keyboard input and
    //   attempts to open and read the specified file.
    //   These operations can throw an IOException and a
    //   FileNotFoundException and are placed in a try
    //   statement.

    try {
      fileName = reader.readLine();
```

```java
      fileReader =
        new BufferedReader(new FileReader(fileName));

  //  The first line of the file is read and assigned
  //  to the text variable

      text = fileReader.readLine();
    }

    // This clause catches a FileNotFoundException.

    catch (FileNotFoundException fnfe) {
      System.out.println("File not found. "+
                         "Default text used\n");
    }

    // This clause catches a generic IOException from
    // the input read, file open, or file read
    // operations

    catch (IOException ioe) {
      System.out.println("IO exception occurred");
    }

    //  The finally clause prints either the text read
    //  from the file or the default text.

    finally {
      System.out.println("\n"+text);
    }
  }
}
```

Output—

    The output will differ, depending on whether or not you enter a valid text file name. If you enter a valid file name, the first line of that file will be written to the console. If you don't enter a valid file name, the text "bailey boy," the author's dog's nickname, will appear on your screen.

THE throw AND throws KEYWORDS

One of the nice features about Java exception handling is that you don't have to handle an exception where it occurs. You can pass the exception to another method and let the second method take care of it. Being able to pass the exception handling to another piece of code is useful if you don't want to hard-code exception handling into a given method.

An exception is explicitly thrown using the `throw` statement followed by an instance of the exception class to be thrown. This is the mechanism used by all exception-throwing methods in the Java API. A thrown exception is either handled in a `catch` clause or sent to the calling method of the method that threw the exception. The method that receives a thrown exception can either process the exception or re-throw it to another method.

Most of the time, the system will generate and throw the necessary exceptions. If you like, you can manually throw an exception using the `throw` statement followed by the object to be thrown. The general syntax to manually throw an exception is

```
throw throwableObject;
```

The object thrown must be a subclass of `Throwable`. This syntax can also be used to rethrow a caught exception.

The `throws` clause is used to declare the exception types that a method can throw. Java requires that methods either catch or declare all checked exceptions that can be thrown within the scope of the method. If appropriate handlers are not provided inside the method, the `throws` keyword followed by the types of checked exceptions that can be thrown must be included in the method declaration.

```
[modifiers] return_type method_name (argument_list)
        throws exception_type1, exception_type2, ...
```

This declaration requirement only applies to checked exceptions. You do not have to declare the unchecked exceptions a method can throw.

Example: Passing Exceptions to Another Method

It is usually undesirable to hard-code exception handling into a method that is meant to be used by many different applications. A better solution is to leave the details of the exception handling up to the individual application by throwing any exceptions back to the calling method.

The `ArrayFunctions` class defines the static method `scaleArray()` that divides the elements of a one-dimensional array by a specified value. A floating point divided by zero will not cause the system to throw an exception, but will instead return a garbage value such as infinity or `NaN`. To avoid this possibility, we will have the method throw an `ArithmeticException` if the method argument `d` has the value `0.0`. Because an `ArithmethicException` is a `RuntimeException`, we do not have to declare it using the `throws` clause in the method declaration.

```
public class ArrayFunctions {
  public static void scaleArray(
              double[] array, double d)
  {
    if ( d == 0.0 ) throw new ArithmeticException();

    for(int i=0; i<array.length; ++i) {
      array[i] /= d;
    }
  }
}
```

The `ThrowDemo` class creates a 1-D area of `double` values and calls the `scaleArray()` method. Because the `scaleArray()` method can throw an `ArithmeticException`, the method call is placed inside a block of code after a `try` statement. Since we are passing the `scaleArray()` method the value `0.0`, an exception will be thrown and caught by the `catch` clause. Try running this code as it is listed and also try passing the `scaleArray()` method a non-zero input value.

```
public class ThrowDemo

  public static void main(String args[]) {
    double data[] = { 1.2, 2.3, 3.4 };

    try {
      ArrayFunctions.scaleArray(data, 0.0);
      printArray(data);
    } catch(ArithmeticException ae) {
       System.out.println("oops, divide by zero");
    }
  }

  public static void printArray(double array[]) {
    for(int i=0; i<array.length; ++i) {
      System.out.println("array[" + i +
                "] = " + array[i]);
    }
    System.out.println();
  }
}
```

Output—

```
oops, divide by zero
```

13

ARRAYS

If you have done any scientific or engineering programming you are familiar with using arrays. In Java, as in every other programming language, arrays are used for storing data. If you solve a system of equations or create a computational grid you will be using arrays. Since Java is a C-based language, there are some similarities between Java and C arrays. Java array indices start at 0. An element of a Java array can be accessed using the element index surrounded by brackets, [].

There are some notable differences between Java and C arrays. Java arrays are objects. Memory for an array is allocated on the heap using the `new` keyword. Arrays implicitly extend from the `Object` class and can use `Object` class methods. Unlike other languages, the Java runtime will make sure that you don't try to use an inappropriate (too large or negative) array index. If you do, an exception is thrown.

Elements stored in an array can be either reference or primitive type variables. Arrays can only hold variables of the same type. Java arrays have a fixed length, set when the array is created and afterwards cannot be changed. If you need a collection whose size can be changed and/or can store elements of different types, you can use one of the specialized collection classes from the `java.util` package. These classes are discussed briefly at the end of this chapter.

In this chapter we will cover—
- One-dimensional arrays
- Two-dimensional arrays
- Arrays of more than two dimensions
- Initializing array elements
- Accessing array elements
- Arrays as method arguments and return types
- Array length
- Collection classes in the Java API

ONE-DIMENSIONAL ARRAYS

There are two acceptable syntaxes for creating a 1-D array. In the first, square brackets are placed after the array name.
```
variable_type array_name[] = new variable_type[size];
```
The second acceptable syntax is to place the square brackets after the variable type.
```
variable_type[] array_name = new variable_type[size];
```
As with objects, the two parts of the array creation syntax may be placed on separate lines.
```
variable_type array_name[];
array_name = new variable_type[size];
```
When an array is created, its elements are given default values, 0 for primitive type elements and `null` for reference type elements. You can assign your own initial values to the array elements when the array is declared.

Example: Creating a 1-D array

In this example, we will write an `Air` class that encapsulates a gas mixture of air. The `Air` class declares two `double` type variables that represent the pressure and temperature of the gas. The class also declares a 1-D array of `Species` objects that represent the primary species in low temperature air (O2 and N2).

When you create an array of reference type variables, of type `Species` in this example, the array elements are initially `null` references. You have to initialize each element of the array, in this case by invoking a constructor.

```
public class Air
{
  private double pressure, temperature;
  private Species species[] = new Species[2];
```

```java
  //  The constructor initializes each element
  //  of the species[] array

  public Species(double p, double t) {
    pressure = p;
    temperature = t;
    species[0] = new Species("N2",0.0280134);
    species[1] = new Species("O2",0.0319988);
  }

  public double getPressure() {
    return pressure;
  }

  public double getTemperature() {
    return Temperature;
  }

  public Species getSpecies(int i) {
    return species[i];
  }
}
```

The code listing for the `Species` class is—

```java
public class Species
{
  private String name;
  private double molarMass;

  public Species(String name, double molarMass) {
    this.name = name;
    this.molarMass = molarMass;
  }

  public String getName() {
    return name;
  }

  public double getMolarMass() {
    return molarMass;
  }
}
```

Two-Dimensional Arrays

Java treats two-dimensional arrays as nested one-dimensional arrays. Each row of a 2-D array is a 1-D array. There are two acceptable syntaxes for creating a 2-D array. You can place two sets of square brackets either after the variable type or after the variable name.

```
    variable_type array_name[][] =
    new  variable_type[num_rows][num_columns];

    variable_type[][] array_name =
  new  variable_type[num_rows][num_columns];
```

You can create a 2-D array with a variable number of columns for each row by omitting the `num_columns` argument. In this case you have to specify the number of columns for each row.

```
variable_type[][] array_name =
              new variable_type[num_rows][];
array_name[0] = new variable_type[num_columns0];
array_name[1] = new variable_type[num_columns1];
...
array_name[num_rows-1] =
              new variable_type[num_columnsX];
```

Example: A 2-D Numerical Grid

Finite-difference or finite-element techniques are often used to solve complex physical problems. The domain of the problem is divided into discrete units called *cells* and the governing equations for whatever physical model is being solved are applied to each cell. A collection of cells is called a *grid*. For a 2-D analysis, the *x*- and *y*-coordinates of each cell vertex are usually stored in 2-D arrays.

The `CircCylGrid` class creates a 90-degree, equispaced, circular grid with an inner radius of 1.0. This is a grid that you might use if you were performing an analysis on a 2-D circular cylinder configuration. The `CircCyl-Grid` class defines two 2-D arrays of `double` values representing the *x*- and *y*-values of each point of the grid. The size of the arrays is set according to integer values passed to the constructor. The `generateGrid()` method assigns values to the elements of the array. The `writeLine()` method writes the *x*- and *y*-values along one radial line of the grid.

```
public class CircCylGrid
{
  private double x[][];
  private double y[][];
  private double angle, R;
  private int idim, jdim;

  public CircCylGrid(int idim, int jdim) {
     this.idim = idim;
     this.jdim = jdim;
     x = new double[idim][jdim];
     y = new double[idim][jdim];
     generateGrid();
  }
```

```
//   The grid points are computed and stored in
//   the 2-D arrays.  The grid is an equispaced
//   90 degree circular grid of inner radius 1.0

private void generateGrid() {
  for(int i=0; i<idim; ++i) {
    angle = 0.5*Math.PI*i/(idim-1);
    for(int j=0; j<x[0].length; ++j) {
      R = 1.0 + 1.0*j/(jdim-1);
      x[i][j] = R*Math.cos(angle);
      y[i][j] = R*Math.sin(angle);
    }
  }
}

//   This method writes the x and y values along
//   one radial line of the grid.

public void writeLine(int i) {
  System.out.println("i="+i);
  for(int j=0; j<jdim; ++j) {
    System.out.println("j=" + j +
              " x=" + x[i][j] + " y=" + y[i][j]);
  }
}
}
```

The `TwoDimDemo` class is a driver program that creates a `CircCyl-Grid` object and writes out the *x*- and *y*-values along the 0 and 45 degree radial lines of the grid.

```
public class TwoDimDemo
{
  public static void main(String args[]) {
    CircCylGrid grid = new CircCylGrid(11,11);

    //  Write out the x- and y-values along the 0
    //  and 45 degree radial lines of the grid

    grid.writeLine(0);
    System.out.println();
    grid.writeLine(5);
  }
}
```

Output—

```
i=0
j=0    x=1.0   y=0.0
j=1    x=1.1   y=0.0
j=2    x=1.2   y=0.0
j=3    x=1.3   y=0.0
j=4    x=1.4   y=0.0
```

```
j=5    x=1.5      y=0.0
j=6    x=1.6      y=0.0
j=7    x=1.7      y=0.0
j=8    x=1.8      y=0.0
j=9    x=1.9      y=0.0
j=10   x=2.0      y=0.0

i=5
j=0    x=0.707106 y=0.707106
j=1    x=0.777817 y=0.777817
j=2    x=0.848528 y=0.848528
j=3    x=0.919238 y=0.919238
j=4    x=0.989949 y=0.989949
j=5    x=1.060660 y=1.060660
j=6    x=1.131370 y=1.131370
j=7    x=1.202081 y=1.202081
j=8    x=1.272792 y=1.272792
j=9    x=1.343502 y=1.343502
j=10   x=1.414213 y=1.414213
```

Arrays of More Than Two Dimensions

You can create arrays of any dimension you want (within reason) by using the proper number of square brackets in the array creation expression. For instance, to declare a 3-D integer array you might type

```
int myArray[][][] = new int[3][4][5];
```

A 3-D array is treated as an array of 2-D arrays, a 4-D array is treated as an array of 3-D arrays, and so on.

Initializing Array Elements

When an array is created, its elements are given default initial values of 0 for primitive types and `null` for reference types. Array elements can be given user-defined initial values when the array is declared. The initial values, separated by commas, are placed in braces in place of the `new variable_type[size]` syntax. The number of initial values provided determines the size of the array. For example, to create and initialize a four-element 1-D integer array, you might use

```
int[] intArray = {11, 18, 3, 42};
```

The zeroth (first) element of the array will have an initial value of 11 and so on. The elements of a 2-D array can be initialized with a similar convention except that an extra set of braces is used to denote each row of the array. For instance, to create and initialize a 2-D array of double values, you might use this syntax—

```
double[][] doubleArray = { {1.0, 5.6, 3.2},
                          {5.2, 11.2, 0.8} };
```

This syntax would create a 2-D array with two rows and three columns. The initial value of the [0][0] element would be 1.0 and so on. Floating point literals default to type `double`. Arrays that store reference type elements can initialize their elements inside braces as well.

Example: Initializing Array Elements

Let us add an array of type `double` to the `Air` class first described in the "Creating a 1-D Array" example. The `moleFr[]` array represents the mole fraction of each species in the gas mixture. The sum of the mole fractions for any gas mixture will equal 1. The elements of the `moleFr[]` array are initialized when the array is declared by placing the initial values inside curly braces. The elements of the `species[]` array are initially set to null references. They are then assigned values using the `Air2` constructor.

```
public class Air2
{
  private double pressure, temperature;
  private Species species[] = new Species[2];
  private double moleFr[] = { 0.7885, 0.2115 };

  public Air2(double p, double t) {
    pressure = p;
    temperature = t;
    species[0] = new Species("N2",0.0280134);
    species[1] = new Species("O2",0.0319988);
  }

  public double getPressure() {
    return pressure;
  }

  public double getTemperature() {
    return temperature;
  }
}
```

Accessing Array Elements

Java array elements are accessed using indices within brackets. For example, to retrieve the value of an element of a 1-D array at a given index, you would use this general syntax—

```
value = array_name[index];
```

Keep in mind that Java array indices start from 0. Similarly, to set the value of an element of a 1-D array at a given index, you would use this general syntax—

```
array_name[index] = value;
```

Multidimensional array elements are accessed in the same manner using indices for each dimension of the array. For instance, to access the value of an element of a 2-D array, you would type

```
value = array_name[index1][index2];
```

Example: Accessing Array Elements

Let's modify the `Air` class once again by adding a new variable that represents the molar mass of the gas mixture. The molar mass of a gas mixture is the sum of the mole fraction of each species multiplied by the species molar mass. In the `Air3` class, the value of the `molarMass` variable is computed in the constructor by accessing the appropriate elements of the `moleFr[]` and `species[]` arrays.

The `Air3` class also includes methods to return the mole fraction value or `Species` object at a specified index in the array.

```java
public class Air3
{
  private double pressure, temperature, molarMass;
  private Species species[] = new Species[2];
  private double moleFr[] = { 0.7885, 0.2115 };

  // The value for the molarMass variable is computed
  // inside the constructor by accessing the elements
  // in the moleFr[] and species[] arrays.

  public Air3(double p, double t) {
    pressure = p;
    temperature = t;
    species[0] = new Species("N2",0.0280134);
    species[1] = new Species("O2",0.0319988);
    for(int i=0; i<species.length; ++i) {
      molarMass +=
            moleFr[i]*species[i].getMolarMass();
    }
  }
```

```
//  The element of the species[] array at index i
//  is obtained using the indexer operator, []

public Species getSpecies(int i) {
  return species[i];
}

//  The value of the moleFr[] array at index i
//  is obtained using the indexer operator, []

public double getMoleFraction(int i) {
  return moleFr[i];
}

public double getPressure() {
  return pressure;
}

public double getTemperature() {
  return temperature;
}

public double getMolarMass() {
  return molarMass;
}
}
```

Just to be sure everything works, here is a simple driver program that creates an `Air3` object and retrieves the value of the `molarMass` variable.

```
public class AccessDemo
{
  public static void main(String args[]) {
    Air3 gas = new Air3(101325.0, 300.0);

    System.out.println("molar mass is " +
                       gas.getMolarMass());
  }
}
```

Output—

```
molar mass is 0.0288563121
```

For an example of accessing the elements of a 2-D array, see "A 2-D Numerical Grid" example earlier in this chapter.

ARRAYS AS METHOD ARGUMENTS AND RETURN TYPES

Since arrays are so widely used in scientific and engineering programs, there will be times when you want to define an array as an input parameter to a method, pass an array as an argument to a method, or define an array as the return type for a method. Fortunately, all of these things are possible. To define an array as an input parameter, simply include the array type, an array name, and the appropriate number of bracket pairs in the input argument list. For example, a method named `blah()` that declares a 1-D array of `double` values named `data[]` as an input parameter might have a declaration statement like

```
public void blah(double data[])
```

To pass an array as an argument to a method, simply type the array name by itself without any square brackets. For example, to pass a 1-D array named `pressure[]` to the `blah()` method, you might type

```
blah(pressure);
```

Arrays are objects, so a reference to the array is passed to the method. Any changes made to the array elements in the method will persist when the method exits. Once inside the method, the number of elements of each dimension of the array can be determined using the `length` property described later in this chapter.

A method can define an array to be its return type by using the array element type and the appropriate number of brackets. For example, a `public` method named `getArray()` that returns a 2-D integer array might have the following signature—

```
public int[][] getArray()
```

Example: Passing an Array as a Method Argument

The `printArray()` method is a static method that prints the elements of a 2-D array. The array is passed to the method by providing the array name as an argument. Inside the `printArray()` method, the number of rows and columns of the array to be printed is obtained using the `length` field described in the next section.

```
public class ArgDemo
{
  public static void main(String args[]) {
    double data[][] = { {1.2, 2.3, 3.4, 4.5},
                        {0.1, 7.8, 11.2, 0.1} };

    //  The printArray() method is called sending the
    //  data[][] array as an argument.

    printArray(data);
  }

  //  This method prints the elements of a 2-D array
  //  array.length gives the number of rows
```

```
//   array[j].length gives the number of columns
//   in a given row.

public static void printArray(double array[][]) {
  for(int i=0; i<array.length; ++i) {
    for(int j=0; j<array[i].length; ++j) {
      System.out.println("[" + i + "][" + j + "] = " +
                         array[i][j]);
    }
  }
}
```

Output—

```
[0][0] = 1.2
[0][1] = 2.3
[0][2] = 3.4
[0][3] = 4.5
[1][0] = 0.1
[1][1] = 7.8
[1][2] = 11.2
[1][3] = 0.1
```

ARRAY LENGTH

Every array has a static field named length implicitly associated with it. For a 1-D array, the value of the length field is equal to the number of elements in the array. For multidimensional arrays, the value of length is equal to the number of nested subarrays. For example, the length field for a 2-D array will have a value equal to the number of nested 1-D arrays (i.e., rows) in the 2-D array. The length field is useful for cycling through the elements of an array or to determine the size of an array that was passed to a method.

To access the length property, type the array name, a period, and then length. For instance, to define a 1-D, five-element integer array—

```
int array[] = new int[5];
```

The value of array.length would be five, the number of elements in the array. Now let's consider the following 2-D array—

```
double data[][] = new double[2][3];
```

The syntax data.length would return the number 2, the number of rows in the array. The syntax data[0].length would return the number 3, the number of columns in the zeroth row of the array.

Example: Using length

To see the `length` field in action look at the "Passing an Array as a Method Argument" example in this chapter where the `length` field was used to determine the number of rows and columns in a 2-D array.

COLLECTION CLASSES IN THE JAVA API

So far in this chapter we have been discussing only how to create and manipulate arrays, but the `java.util` package of the Java API contains a variety of collection classes that you can use in your scientific or engineering applications. One difference between the `java.util` collection classes and arrays is that the `java.util` collection classes can store only objects. They cannot be used to store primitive types. This section is intended to give a snapshot of the collection classes available in the `java.util` package. For complete details on these classes, including the constructors and methods available to them, consult the Sun Java API documentation.

Here are some of the important collection classes—

`ArrayList`: A 1-D, resizable array of objects. The size of a traditional array cannot be changed once it is created. An `ArrayList` can grow or shrink as needed.

`HashMap`: A hash table implementation of the `Map` interface. The `Map` interface defines a collection that stores a series of key-value pairs. A `HashMap` stores its elements in "buckets." The size of the `HashMap` is automatically increased when the storage amount reaches a specified load factor. The elements of a `HashMap` are not sorted. There is no structure to the ordering of the elements of a `HashMap` and the element order may change over time.

`HashSet`: A hash table implementation of the `Set` interface. This interface defines a collection with no duplicate pairs. An attempt to add an element to the collection that already contains the element will fail. There is no ordering of the elements of a `HashSet`.

`Hashtable`: A hash table is a collection of key-value pairs. This is an older collection class. The Java 1.1 implementation of the `Hashtable` class was updated in Java 1.2 to implement the `Map` interface.

`LinkedHashMap`: A `HashMap` that maintains its elements in a doubly linked list. The order of the elements in the collection will remain constant.

`LinkedHashSet`: A `HashSet` that maintains its elements in a doubly linked list. The order of the elements in the collection will remain constant.

`LinkedList`: A collection of objects stored as a linked list.

`Stack`: A last-in-first-out collection of objects. The objects are added to and removed from the top of the stack using the `push()` and `pop()` methods. You can examine the element at the top of the stack using the `peek()` method.

`TreeMap`: A collection of key-value pairs stored in a tree structure.

`TreeSet`: A tree structure collection of key-value pairs with no duplicate elements. An attempt to add a value that already exists in the `TreeSet` will fail.

`Vector`: A collection of objects whose size can grow or shrink according to the number of elements in the collection.

14

THE JAVA CLASS LIBRARIES

In the preceding chapters, reference was made to the contents of the Java API. One of the things that makes Java such a powerful programming language is the enormous collection of predefined classes and interfaces that you can access. Java API refers to these libraries that you can download from the Sun website, from the *apache.org* website, and from other sources. You'll find that with Java a lot of the low-level programming work has already been done for you. You can leverage off of the built-in classes when you are writing your own.

The libraries are divided into packages according to the general function of the classes and interfaces that they contain. When you download and install the Java SDK, you are also downloading and installing the J2SE libraries. Also available for downloading are the J2EE and J2ME libraries (also from the Sun website) and the Extensible Markup Language (XML) libraries that can be found at *http://xml.apache.org*. To refer to the contents of the Java libraries by their simple name, you must import part or all of the desired package into your program. Importing packages is covered in Chapter 11.

This chapter will provide a brief description of the classes, interfaces, and methods that are contained in the J2SE libraries. We won't cover all the packages in the J2SE libraries, nor will we provide details on all the classes and interfaces in the packages we do discuss. We'll focus on the library elements most commonly used in scientific or engineering programming.

The topics discussed in this chapter are—

- Package naming conventions
- The core J2SE libraries
- The GUI libraries

Package Naming Conventions

When you look at the contents of the J2SE API you will notice three general groups of packages. Those whose names begin with "java" are typically (but not always) older APIs that have been in existence since Java 1.1. Package names that begin with "javax" indicate more recent additions to the Java API, added in version 1.2 or later. The packages whose names begin with "org" deal with topics such as the Common Object Request Broker Architecture (CORBA), naming contexts, and XML processing classes.

As the Java language has evolved, so has the Java API. An example of this can be found in the Java Database Connectivity (JDBC) classes. The original JDBC classes, called the core JDBC API, were introduced in Java 1.1 and can be found in the `java.sql` package. Additional JDBC functionality was added in Java 1.2 by way of the `javax.sql` package. With J2SE version 1.4, the distinction between the "core" and "later" JDBC facilities is no longer made. The packages are still distinct but collectively they are referred to as the JDBC 3.0 API.

The Core J2SE Libraries

The core libraries are things that can be used in any type of programming application. They include the basic I/O, math, system, `String`, and collection classes. Any reasonably sized Java program you write will make use of the core libraries. This section provides a snapshot view of four of the core packages most important to scientific and engineering programming.

java.io

The `java.io` package contains many of the classes and interfaces used for Java I/O operations. These are the elements you will use to read and write data. There are two main branches of the `java.io` package. The first defines classes and interfaces used to read or write byte data. The bytes can be read or written one at a time or an array of bytes can be processed. Byte I/O is useful for reading or writing things like images, objects, or sound files.

The second branch defines classes and interfaces used to read or write character data. The character I/O classes include `FileReader` and `FileWriter`, which are used to read or write character data to a file. The `BufferedReader` and `BufferedWriter` classes provide buffered I/O for more efficient reading and writing of character data. The `StreamTokenizer` class can be used to parse an input stream into tokens. This class can be used to parse the contents of an input file. The `java.io` package also defines many of the I/O exception classes. The Java I/O classes are covered in more detail in Chapter 25.

One of the significant additions under J2SE version 1.4 was the introduction of the `java.nio` packages to the Java API. These packages provide buffer classes for primitive data types to improve I/O performance, classes that define character set encoders and decoders to convert bytes to Unicode characters and vice versa, and a regular expression pattern matching capability. The `java.nio` packages are briefly discussed in Chapter 25.

java.lang

The `java.lang` class is unique in that it is implicitly imported into every Java program. You never have to write `import java.lang.*;` at the top of your program. This package contains the core classes that are used in a variety of Java programs. The contents of `java.lang` include the `Object` class, the superclass of all Java classes. The primitive variable wrapper classes can be found in `java.lang` as can the `String` class. The `Throwable` class is the superclass of all Java exceptions. The `Math` and `StrictMath` classes contain methods for the exponential, logarithm, square root, and trigonometric mathematical functions. The `System` class defines high-level functions that do things like terminate a program or invoke the system garbage collector. The `java.lang` package also contains some of the classes used in multithreaded programming applications.

java.math

The `java.math` package defines the `BigDecimal` and `BigInteger` classes for performing arbitrary-precision decimal and integer arithmetic. In addition to being able to specify the precision of mathematical operations using these classes, a user can specify what rounding procedures will be used.

java.util

The `java.util` package defines utility classes that are applicable to a wide range of programming applications. Included are the collections classes first discussed in Chapter 13. The `Calendar`, `Date`, and `GregorianCalendar` classes allow you to represent and manipulate dates and times. The `Random` class can be used to generate random numbers. The `Locale` class allows you to customize your applications for different countries and languages. The `StringTokenizer` class allows you to break up a `String` into substrings. This can be useful for parsing lines read from an input file.

The GUI Libraries

The second group of packages from the J2SE libraries we will discuss are the GUI libraries. Java provides a rich set of libraries for creating GUIs that can provide an alternative for command line input or reading input from a file. The ability to create GUIs is yet another nice feature of the Java language in that an application and its front-end GUI can be written in the same programming language. This avoids any integration issues that can arise if you are mixing and matching languages. An introduction to Java GUI development is provided in Chapter 26, but a snapshot of some of the important GUI packages is given here.

java.awt

The `java.awt` package contains the older (Java 1.1) GUI component and support classes. Java GUI application development as of Java 1.2 has largely moved to the more powerful and versatile Swing classes; however, some Swing components, particularly the high-level windows, inherit from Abstract Window Toolkit (AWT) superclasses. This package also contains the `Dimension` and `Rectangle` classes that are used to size GUI components. The `java.awt` package also contains the `Color` and `Font` classes.

java.awt.event

The `java.awt.event` package defines event classes and listeners. When a user interacts with a GUI component, the system creates event objects that contain information about the interaction. If an appropriate event listener is registered with the GUI component, the event object will be sent to the listener which will then process and respond to the event. Originally developed for AWT GUI components, the event capability defined in the `java.awt.event` package is also utilized by many of the Swing GUI components. For example, both `Button` and `JButton` components can generate instances of the `ActionEvent` class that is contained in the `java.awt.event` package.

javax.swing

The `javax.swing` package contains the Swing GUI component and support classes. Swing components are much more powerful and versatile than their AWT counterparts. For one thing, the Swing GUI containers have different panes or layers on which you can place your components. The `javax.swing` package contains interesting new container classes including `JSplitPane` and `JTabbedPane`.

The `javax.swing` package has a greatly expanded set of GUI components from which to choose. In the `java.awt` package there is only one class that represents a button and many of the style features, such as the component border, are hard-coded into the class. The `javax.swing` package defines many kinds of buttons including the `JButton`, `JToggleButton`, and `JRadioButton` classes. You have a lot more freedom to define the look and feel of Swing components. You can select or customize the border around the component, for example.

javax.swing.border

With Swing, you can be creative when it comes to assigning borders to your GUI components. The `javax.swing.border` class provides classes to generate raised, line, matte, etched, empty, titled, or compound borders.

javax.swing.event

Swing GUI components are more diverse, versatile, and powerful than their AWT counterparts. It is only natural that they would need additional event classes to support their enhanced functionality. Among other things, the `javax.swing.event` package defines events and event listeners for `JTable` and `JTree` components, internal frames, pop-up menus, documents, and cell editors. There are additional event classes and interfaces for menu and list components.

javax.swing.table

One of the powerful Swing components is the `JTable` class, defined in the `javax.swing` package, which allows you to represent data in a table-like format. The `javax.swing.table` package provides support classes and interfaces for `JTable` objects. Included are classes and interfaces to define the table and table column models, the table cell renderer, and the table cell editor.

javax.swing.text

The `javax.swing.text` package provides classes and interfaces for working with editable and noneditable text components. Included is the `Document` interface that defines the document model for Swing text components. The classes defined in this package include the editor kit, view, highlighter, and document filter classes.

javax.swing.tree

Another powerful Swing component is the `JTree` class that allows you to represent data in a tree-like structure. The `javax.swing.tree` package contains interfaces and classes that define the nodes, model, selection model, cell editor, and cell renderer of a `JTree`.

15

Primitive Variable Wrapper and String Classes

The previous chapter provided an overview of some of the classes and interfaces in the Java APIs. In this chapter we will explore in more detail some of the classes from the `java.lang` package that you are likely to use in your scientific or engineering programming work. In Chapter 8 we discussed that there are two general types of Java variables—primitive variables that store a single value and reference type variables that contain references to arrays or to objects.

The two variable types are treated differently by Java. You usually cannot mix and match. For instance, you cannot pass a primitive variable to a method that expects a reference type argument. There may be times when you want to use a primitive type variable with a class or method that takes reference type arguments. For example, you might want to use one of the `java.util` collections classes to store a collection of integer variables.

Java provides a number of primitive variable wrapper classes that provide a reference type representation of a primitive type. These classes, in effect, are a bridge between the primitive and reference type worlds. They are referred to as wrapper classes, because they are used to wrap a class around a primitive type value. In addition to methods that convert their underlying value to any primitive type, the primitive variable wrapper classes define methods for converting a `String` representation of a value into a primitive value. One of the handy uses of the primitive variable wrapper classes is for parsing and converting character input data.

We will also discuss the `String` class in more detail in this chapter. We have already used `String` objects in many examples in the preceding chapters. A `String` is an object that represents a sequence of characters. You will use `String`s when you read data from a file, display output to the screen, store the names of things as data members of a class, and countless other uses. We will outline the various ways to create a `String`, some of the important `String` methods, and how to convert `String`s to and from other types.

The specific topics this chapter will cover are—

- Primitive variable wrapper classes
- Creating primitive variable wrapper class objects
- Converting a wrapper class object to a primitive value
- The `parse()` methods
- The `String` class
- Obtaining `String` objects
- Concatenating `String`s
- Other important `String` class methods
- Converting primitive and reference types to `String`s
- Converting `String`s to primitive values

PRIMITIVE VARIABLE WRAPPER CLASSES

Primitive variable wrapper classes are aptly named because they are used to wrap a class around a primitive data type value. They are contained in the `java.lang` package so they are accessible to any program. The importance of primitive variable wrapper classes is evident when you want to pass a primitive value to a method or constructor that takes an `Object` argument. You cannot, for example, store primitive values in a `TreeSet` collection, but if you place a wrapper class around the primitive value the wrapper class object can be stored in a `TreeSet`.

The primitive variable wrapper classes define methods that can be used to convert `String` objects into wrapper class objects or into primitive values. This can be very useful when reading character data from input files or when a Web-based application such as a Java servlet receives `String` input arguments from a client request. The input `String` is parsed into substring elements, and a primitive variable wrapper class method converts the appropriate

TABLE 15.1 Primitive Variable Wrapper Classes
public final class Boolean extends Object implements Serializable
public final class Byte extends Number implements Serializable
public final class Character extends Object implements Serializable
public final class Double extends Number implements Serializable
public final class Float extends Number implements Serializable
public final class Integer extends Number implements Serializable
public final class Long extends Number implements Serializable
public final class Short extends Number implements Serializable

substring into a primitive value. More details on this process are provided later in this chapter.

There is a primitive variable wrapper class for every primitive data type. Table 15.1 lists the declarations for the wrapper classes.

When a class implements the `Serializable` interface it indicates that an instance of the class can be persistently stored. Usually this means an object can be written to or restored from disk. The `Number` class is the abstract parent class for the numerical primitive variable wrapper classes.

Creating Primitive Variable Wrapper Class Objects

There are several ways to create an instance of a primitive variable wrapper class. The first way is to use one of the constructors provided by the classes. The constructors for each class are shown in Table 15.2. Each class provides a constructor that takes its corresponding primitive type as an input parameter. This is the value that the wrapper class wraps. Every class except `Character` also defines a constructor that takes a `String` representation of a primitive data type value as its input parameter. If the `String` passed to the `Boolean` constructor is not `true` (ignoring case) the resulting `Boolean` object will represent the value `false`. The numerical wrapper class constructors will throw a `NumberFormatException` if the `String` does not represent a parsable numerical value. The `Float` class defines a third constructor that takes a primitive `double` value as an argument.

TABLE 15.2 Primitive Variable Wrapper Class Constructors

Class	Constructor
Boolean	public Boolean(boolean value)
	public Boolean(String value)
Byte	public Byte(byte value)
	public Byte(String value)
Character	public Character(char value)
Double	public Double(double value)
	public Double(String value)
Float	public Float(float value)
	public Float(double value)
	public Float(String value)
Integer	public Integer(int value)
	public Integer(String value)
Long	public Long(long value)
	public Long(String value)
Short	public Short(short value)
	public Short(String value)

Another way to obtain a primitive variable wrapper class object is by using one of the `valueOf()` methods defined in each class. These are static methods so you don't need to create a wrapper class object to use them. Similar to the constructors, the `valueOf()` methods can take either a primitive value or a `String` representation of a primitive value as an argument. The declarations for these methods are shown in Table 15.3.

An important difference between the `valueOf()` methods and the constructors is that other than one version defined in the `Boolean` class, the `valueOf()` methods do not take a primitive value as an input argument. The methods require a `String` representation of a primitive value. The `Byte`, `Integer`, `Long`, and `Short` classes provide versions of `valueOf()` that let you specify the base of the number system being used by setting the `radix` value. The default value of `radix` is 10, which corresponds to the decimal system. The `valueOf()` methods in the numerical wrapper classes will throw a `NumberFormatException` if the `String` is not a proper representation of a number.

TABLE 15.3 Static Instance Creation Methods

CLASS	METHOD
Boolean	public static Boolean valueOf(boolean value)
	public static Boolean valueOf(String value)
Byte	public static Byte valueOf(String value)
	public static Byte valueOf(String value, int radix)
Double	public static Double valueOf(String value)
Float	public static Float valueOf(String value)
Integer	public static Integer valueOf(String value)
	public static Integer valueOf(String value, int radix)
Long	public static Long valueOf(String value)
	public static Long valueOf(String value, int radix)
Short	public static Short valueOf(String value)
	public static Short valueOf(String value, int radix)

One final note about primitive variable wrapper class objects— they are immutable. Once a primitive variable wrapper class object is created, the primitive value associated with it cannot be changed.

Example: Using Primitive Variable Wrapper Classes

In the `CreateWrapper` class, we want to store some information about a rocket engine configuration in a `HashMap`. The data includes `int` and `double` primitive type values and a `String`. A `HashMap` can only store objects, so the primitive variable wrapper classes `Integer` and `Double` are used to wrap the primitive values

In the second part of the example, the `get()` method is used to retrieve the value of the fuel density key in the `HashMap`. The `get()` method returns an `Object` that is cast into a `Double`. The `Double` object's `doubleValue()` method can then be called that returns the primitive value associated with the `Double`. The `doubleValue()` method is described in the next section.

```
import java.util.HashMap;

public class CreateWrapper
{
  public static void main(String args[]) {

    //  Some data about an engine configuration is
    //  created as well as a HashMap object.
```

```
        String name = "SSME";
        int numberOfEngines = 4;
        double fuelDensity = 4.43;
        double oxidizerDensity = 71.3;

        HashMap engineData = new HashMap();

        //  Data is added to the HashMap. A HashMap can only
        //  store Objects, so primitive variable wrapper
        //  classes are used to wrap the integer and
        //  floating point values.

        engineData.put("engine type", name);
        engineData.put("engine number",
                    new Integer(numberOfEngines));
        engineData.put("fuel density",
                    new Double(fuelDensity));
        engineData.put("oxidizer density",
                    new Double(oxidizerDensity));

        //  The get() method returns the value associated
        //  with a specified key in the HashMap.  The return
        //  value is an Object which is cast into a Double,
        //  on which the doubleValue() method is called to
        //  convert it to the corresponding primitive value

        double value =
  ((Double)engineData.get("fuel density")).doubleValue();

        System.out.println("fuel density is "+value);
    }
}
```

Output—

```
fuel density is 4.43
```

Converting a Wrapper Class Object to a Primitive Value

The primitive variable wrapper classes are used to wrap a class around a primitive value, but sometimes you need to access the primitive value that was wrapped. Every primitive variable wrapper class defines methods to convert an instance of itself back into a primitive data type value. These methods are shown in Table 15.4.

The numerical wrapper classes Byte, Double, Float, Integer, Long, and Short define a common set of methods. They can be used to con-

TABLE 15.4	Primitive Variable Conversion Methods
CLASS	METHOD
Byte, Double, Float, Integer, Long, Short	public byte byteValue()
	public double doubleValue()
	public float floatValue()
	public int intValue()
	public long longValue()
	public short shortValue()
Boolean	public boolean booleanValue()
Character	public char charValue()

vert the primitive value represented by the object into any numerical primitive type. In effect these methods allow you to cast the value contained by a numerical wrapper class object.

The `Boolean` and `Character` classes are a bit more exclusive. The `Boolean` class only defines the `booleanValue()` method for extracting the `boolean` value wrapped by the class. Similarly, the `Character` class only defines the `charValue()` method to return the `char` value wrapped by the class.

Example: Extracting Primitive Values from Wrapper Class Objects

Look at the "Using Primitive Variable Wrapper Classes" example in the previous section where the `doubleValue()` method is used to retrieve the primitive double value associated with a `Double` object.

THE parse() METHODS

We've talked about the need to convert a `String` representation of a primitive value into a primitive value. There are two general ways to do this. The first way involves a combination of the `valueOf()` and `<primitive>Value()` methods previously described. As an example, consider the following syntax—

```
double width = Double.valueOf("4.3").doubleValue();
```

The above statement calls the static method `valueOf()` of the `Double` class. This method parses the `String` "4.3" and creates a `Double` object that wraps the value 4.3. The `doubleValue()` method is called on this ob-

Table 15.5	String Parsing Methods
Class	Method
Byte	public static byte parseByte(String value)
	public static byte parseByte(String value, int radix)
Double	public static double parseDouble(String value)
Float	public static float parseFloat(String value)
Integer	public static int parseInt(String value)
	public static int parseInt(String value, int radix)
Long	public static long parseLong(String value)
	public static long parseLong(String value, int radix)
Short	public static short parseShort(String value)
	public static short parseShort(String value, int radix)

ject and returns the primitive `double` value `4.3`. This value is assigned to the `double` variable named `width`.

Converting a `String` to a primitive value in this manner is a little convoluted. You must create an intermediate wrapper class object that you don't use for any other purpose. The second way to convert a `String` representation of a primitive value into a primitive value is easier. Some of the primitive variable wrapper classes define `parse()` methods that convert a `String` directly into a primitive value. A list of the `parse()` methods for each wrapper class is shown in Table 15.5.

You can see from Table 15.5 that all of the `parse()` methods take a `String` argument to represent the number to be parsed. The methods defined in each class will only return the primitive type wrapped by the class. These methods can all throw a `NumberFormatException` if the argument passed to the method is not a parsable `String`.

Example: Using `String` Parsing Methods

To see the `parse()` methods in action, look at the "Parsing an Input File" example at the end of this chapter.

The String Class

Almost every example in this book will make use of `String` objects. A `String` object represents a sequence of Unicode characters. It is the basic mechanism that you will use to read, transmit, display, and name data. For example, a class that represents a metal object might define the following field as one of its members.

```
private String elementName = "copper";
```

The `String` class is defined in the `java.lang` package. The class declaration is:

> public final class String extends Object implements Serializable, Comparable, CharSequence

The `String` class is a direct subclass of the `Object` class. It belongs to the `java.lang` package. Remember that `java.lang` is implicitly imported into every Java program so you always have access to the `String` class. The `String` class is `final`, meaning you can't override it or change its implementation in any way. `Strings` are so important to the implementation of Java that the developers of the language didn't want anyone to mess with the class.

`Strings` are immutable objects. This is done for performance reasons since a constant object requires less system overhead than one that can be modified. Once initialized, a `String` object cannot change the sequence of characters that it represents. Methods used to modify a `String` object actually create a new `String` object.

Obtaining String Objects

There are three basic ways to obtain a `String` object. You can create one with a `String` class constructor, you can create one using a `String` literal, or you can acquire one from a method that returns a `String`. The constructors defined in the `String` class are shown in Table 15.6.

TABLE 15.6 String Class Constructors
public String()
public String(byte[] bytes)
public String(byte[] bytes, int offset, int length)
public String(byte[] bytes, int offset, int length, String charSetName)
public String(byte[] bytes, String charSetName)
public String(char[] chars)
public String(char[] chars, int offset, int length)
public String(String original)
public String(StringBuffer stringBuffer)

As you can see, most of the `String` constructors define byte or character arrays as their input arguments. Creating these arrays can be a bit inconvenient. The more commonly used method of creating a `String` object is to assign a `String` literal to a `String` reference. A `String` literal is a series of characters surrounded by double quotes. For example, you could create a `String` object named `model` using the syntax

```
String model = "Mars Pathfinder";
```

You can also acquire a `String` from a method that returns a `String`. One commonly used method that does this is `toString()`, defined in the `Object` class (and typically overridden in subclasses). This method returns a `String` representation of the object on which it is invoked.

Example: Creating `Strings`

The `CreateString` class shows the three primary ways to obtain a `String` object. A `String` object is created using a `String` constructor. The character sequence stored by the `String` is obtained from a `char` array. An easier way to get a `String` object is by using a `String` literal. The `String` variable `string2` is initialized in this way. You can also get a `String` object from a method that returns a `String`. A `Date` object is created, and the `toString()` method is called on it to return a `String` representation of the object on which it is invoked.

```java
import java.util.Date;

public class CreateString
{
  public static void main(String args[]) {

    // There are three ways to obtain a String
    // object. Using a constructor

    char array[] = { 'R', 'i', 'g', 'h', 't',
                     ' ', 'n', 'o', 'w' };
    String string1 = new String(array);

    // Using a String literal

    String string2 = "the time is\n";

    // From a method that returns a String

    Date date = new Date();
    String string3 = date.toString();

    System.out.println(string1+string2+string3);
  }
}
```

Output (will vary)—

```
Right now the time is
Tue Aug 27 22:14:31 GMT-07:00 2002
```

CONCATENATING Strings

One of the common manipulations you will perform on `Strings` is to concatenate two or more `String` objects together. One way to do this is by using the concatenation operator, +.

```
String name = "Jackson";
System.out.println("My boy is "+name);
```

The argument to the left of the + operator must be a `String` or the compiler will think you are using the arithmetic addition operator instead. The argument to the right of the operator can be any type. When you concatenate a non-`String` reference type to a `String`, the system uses the `toString()` method to return a `String` representation of the non-`String` type and then concatenates the result. For primitives, the primitive value is converted to a `String`.

Another way to concatenate `Strings` is by using the `concat()` method of the `String` class.

```
public String concat(String str)
```

When the `concat()` method is used, the argument `String` is concatenated onto the `String` on which the method is called. A `NullPointerException` is thrown if the input argument is `null`.

Example: Concatenating *Strings*

This example demonstrates the different ways of concatenating `String` objects. The literal " molar mass is " is concatenated to a `String` variable named `gas` using the `concat()` method. The + operator is then used to concatenate the `String` representation of the value of a `double` value onto the `String`.

```
public class ConcatDemo
{
  public static void main(String args[]) {

    String gas = "air";
    double molarMass = 0.02885;

    //  The concat() method concatenates two Strings
```

```
    String label = gas.concat(" molar mass is ");

    // The + operator concatenates the String
    // representation of the value of the molarMass
    // variable onto the label String.

    System.out.println(label + molarMass);
  }
}
```

Output—

```
air molar mass is 0.02885
```

OTHER IMPORTANT String CLASS METHODS

The `String` class has other methods that will be useful to you in your scientific and engineering programming. These methods can be used to compare, split, trim, or determine the length of `Strings`. The syntax of some of the more important methods is—

> public int compareTo(String str)
> public int compareToIgnoreCase(String str)
> public boolean equals(Object obj)
> public boolean equalsIgnoreCase(String str)
> public int length()
> public String[] split(String regex)
> public String[] split(String regex, int limit)
> public String substring(int beginIndex)
> public String substring(int beginIndex, int endIndex)
> public String trim()

`compareTo()` compares two `Strings` lexicographically based on the Unicode value of each character. The method returns a negative integer if the `String` on which the method is invoked lexicographically precedes the argument, a positive integer if it follows the argument `String`, and zero if the `Strings` are equal. This method can be used to sort a collection of `Strings` and throws a `NullPointerException` if the argument is `null`.

`compareToIgnoreCase()` does the same thing as `compareTo()` but case is ignored.

`equals()` returns `true` if the `Object` argument is a `String` and has the same character sequence as the `String` on which the method is invoked.

`equalsIgnoreCase()` does the same thing as `equals()` but case is ignored.

`length()` returns the number of 16-bit Unicode characters in a `String`.

`split()` splits a `String` into substrings around matches of the specified regular expression. The regular expression can be a single character or a series of characters. If a `limit` argument is specified, this is the maximum number of times the regular expression will be applied. A negative `limit` value means the regular expression will be matched as many times as possible. A `limit` value of 0 matches the regular expression as many times as possible and any empty substrings are discarded. This method can throw a `PatternSyntaxException` if the `regex` syntax is invalid or a `NullPointerException` if `regex` is null.

`substring()` returns a substring of a `String`. The substring is extracted between `beginIndex` and `endIndex` of the original `String`. If `endIndex` is not specified, the substring will continue to the end of the original `String`. This method can throw an `IndexOutOfBoundsException` if a bad index value is passed to the method.

`trim()` returns a `String` with leading and trailing white space removed.

Example: Using `String` *Class Methods*

A *comparator* is a class that implements the `Comparator` interface. A comparator class overrides the `compare()` method to provide a comparison of two objects. In this example, the `LexComparator` class will implement the `compare()` method to lexicographically compare two `String` objects using the `compareTo()` method from the `String` class. The `compareTo()` method returns a positive integer if `str1` is lexicographically greater than `str2`, a negative integer if it is lexicographically less, and zero if the two `Strings` are the same.

```
import java.util.Comparator;

public class LexComparator implements Comparator
{
  public int compare(Object obj1, Object obj2) {
    String str1 = (String)obj1;
    String str2 = (String)obj2;

    return str1.compareTo(str2);
  }
}
```

The `MethodsDemo` class creates a `TreeSet` object that will be used to store the names of planets. One of the `TreeSet` constructors allows you to specify a `Comparator` that will be used to sort the elements of the `TreeSet`. We will use a `LexComparator` that will sort the elements lexicographically. The elements of the `TreeSet` are automatically placed in alphabetical order. Every time an element is added to the collection, the elements are resorted by the `Comparator`.

```java
import java.util.TreeSet;

public class MethodsDemo
{
  public static void main(String args[]) {

    // Create a TreeSet using a LexComparator object
    // to sort the elements

    TreeSet planets =
            new TreeSet(new LexComparator());

    //  When elements are added they are automatically
    //  placed in alphabetical order.

    planets.add("Jupiter");
    planets.add("Mercury");
    planets.add("Earth");
    System.out.println("contents = " + planets);

    //  Every time you add an element the
    //  collection is resorted.

    planets.add("Mars");
    System.out.println("contents = " + planets);
  }
}
```

Output—

```
contents = [Earth, Jupiter, Mercury]
contents = [Earth, Jupiter, Mars, Mercury]
```

For more examples of using the `String` class methods, see the "Parsing an Input File" example at the end of this chapter where the `equals()`, `trim()`, and `split()` methods are used to parse `String` objects read from an input file.

Converting Primitive and Reference Types to Strings

Let's now discuss how to convert a primitive value or class object into a String. The easiest way to convert a reference type to a String is to use the toString() method. Because this method is defined in the Object class, all Java classes have access to it. The default (i.e., Object class) implementation of toString() returns the class name and its hash code. The toString() method is typically overridden in subclasses to provide a more meaningful description.

An object can also be converted into a String representation by concatenating the object to a String using the + operator. In this case, the toString() method is called by the system to return a String representation of the object. For example—

```
Date date = new Date();
System.out.println("The date and time are: " + date);
```

In this code snippet, a Date object containing the current date and time values is converted to a String using the + operator.

The toString() method can only be called on a reference type. A primitive variable cannot invoke toString(). The most convenient way to convert a primitive value to a String is once again to use the + operator. When a primitive variable is concatenated to a String using the + operator, the system will generate a String representation of the primitive value. For instance, the following syntax will assign the character sequence "4" to the String object named value—

```
int j = 4;
String value = "" + j;
```

Example: Converting Primitive and Reference Types to *Strings*

See the "Concatenating Strings" example earlier in this chapter where a double variable is converted to a String. Also see the "Creating Strings" example where the toString() method is used to return a String representation of a Date object.

Converting Strings to Primitive Values

We previously explored how other types can be converted into a String. It is sometimes necessary to go the other way, to convert a String into a primitive value. The input data that you use in your programs will be read one of two ways—as a series of bytes or as character data. If you use character stream I/O you need to convert the input character data into the appropriate type. For example, you may need to convert the `String` "14" into the primitive integer value 14.

To accomplish `String`-to-primitive type conversions, we turn again to the primitive variable wrapper classes. As was discussed in the "The `parse()` Methods" section earlier in this chapter, there are basically two ways to convert `String` objects to primitive values. The first way is to use a combination of the `valueOf()` and `<primitive>Value()` methods. For example, to convert the `String` "14" to an integer primitive value and assign that value to an integer variable you might type

```
int k = Integer.valueOf("14").intValue();
```

The example is really a compound version of two separate statements—

```
Integer temp = Integer.valueOf("14");
int k = temp.intValue();
```

The second, and more efficient, way to convert a `String` to a primitive value is by using one of the `parse()` methods. For example, you can use the `parseInt()` method to convert the `String` "14" to a primitive integer value.

```
int k = Integer.parseInt("14");
```

Input file data will often be read as a `String` that contains other characters besides the input data that you need. This is often done to make the input file more readable. For instance, an input file might contain the following—

```
Number of engines = 14
```

If you read this entire line into your program as a single `String`, using the `readLine()` method of the `BufferedReader` class for instance, you would need to extract the substring "14" from the remainder of the `String`. The `split()` method from the `String` class can be used to divide a `String` into substrings based on a regular expression that will serve as the delimiter. In this case, the regular expression would be set to = and the `String` 14 would be the last element of the resulting substring array.

Example: Parsing an Input File

This example shows how `String` objects and the primitive variable wrapper classes can work together to parse data read from an input file. The input file, parse.inp, contains the following three lines:

Converting Strings to Primitive Values

```
configuration = 2D
width = 2.0
height = 3.0
```

When we read the lines of this input file, we are only interested in the parts after the equals sign. The data will be read in line by line as `Strings`. We need to extract the part of each `String` after the equal sign, and we need to convert the `2.0` and `3.0` substrings into primitive values.

`BufferedReader` and `FileReader` objects are used to connect a character input stream to the input file. The first line of the input file describes the geometry type of the problem. A 2-D rectangle will have a width and a height. The `readLine()` method reads the first line of the input file in as a `String`. This `String` is then divided into substrings with the `split()` method using the = character as the delimiter. The last element of the resulting `String` array is the configuration data that we want.

The `equals()` method is used to check if the `String` assigned to the `config` variable is equal to the `String` "2D." If it is, then the program reads the next two lines of the input file and extracts the width and height data from the appropriate `Strings`. Once again, the `split()` method is used to split the `Strings` into substrings using = as the regular expression to search for. The `String` representation of the numerical values we want will be the last element of the `strings[]` array. The `parseDouble()` method from the `Double` class is used to return the primitive `double` value associated with the last substring. Just to check that everything worked out properly, the product of the `width` and `height` values is printed.

```java
import java.io.*;

public class ParseDemo
{
  public static void main(String args[]) {

    String data;
    String strings[];
    String config;
    double width=0.0, height=0.0;

    // Connect an input stream with an input file

    try{
      BufferedReader reader =
          new BufferedReader(
              new FileReader("parse.inp"));

      // Read the first line of the input file.  This
      // will have the configuration information.  The
      // String is split into substrings.  The last
```

```
      //  substring is the one we want to keep after any
      //  leading and trailing white space is trimmed.

      data = reader.readLine();
      strings = data.split("=");
      config = strings[strings.length-1].trim();

      //  If the config String equals "2D", read the
      //  next two lines from the input file, split the
      //  resulting Strings into substrings, and use the
      //  parseDouble() method to extract the desired
      //  double value. Note that "length" is the array
      //  length field not the length() method of the
      //  String class.

      if ( config.equals("2D") ) {
        data = reader.readLine();
        strings = data.split("=");
        width =
          Double.parseDouble(strings[strings.length-1]);

        data = reader.readLine();
        strings = data.split("=");
        height =
          Double.parseDouble(strings[strings.length-1]);
      } else {
        System.out.println("not 2D");
      }
      reader.close();
    } catch (IOException ioe) {
      System.out.println("IOException: "+ioe);
    }

    System.out.println("area is "+width*height);
  }
}
```

Output—

```
area is 6.0
```

16

BUILT-IN MATH FUNCTIONS

Despite some ill-informed opinions to the contrary, Java is a programming language that is well suited to perform mathematical computations. The `Math` and `StrictMath` classes from the `java.lang` package offer a wide variety of built-in math methods. The capability includes methods to perform absolute value, power, square root, exponential, logarithmic, trigonometric, minimum, maximum, and rounding operations. The Java math methods are based on Institute of Electrical and Electronics Engineers (IEEE) mathematical algorithms.

The `java.math` package contains two classes that encapsulate variable precision integer and decimal values. These classes allow you to specify how numbers are rounded. The `BigDecimal` and `BigInteger` classes are not widely used in scientific and engineering calculations, but a brief discussion of them is presented. At the end of this chapter we will do a one-to-one comparison of the built-in math capabilities of Java, C, C++, and Fortran.

The specific topics we will cover in this chapter are—

- `Math` and `StrictMath` classes
- Mathematical constants
- Absolute value methods
- Power and square root methods
- Transcendental math functions
- Trigonometric methods

- Conversion methods
- Minimum and maximum methods
- Rounding and remainder methods
- Random number generator methods
- The `java.math` package
- Comparing the built-in math capability of C, C++, Fortran, and Java

Math and StrictMath Classes

Much of the built-in math capability of Java can be found in the `Math` and `StrictMath` classes from the `java.lang` package. These two classes define a parallel set of methods that encompass absolute value, power, square root, exponential, logarithmic, trigonometric, minimum, maximum, and rounding operations as well as random number generation. They also define the constants e and π.

As you might guess from the class name, the methods in the `StrictMath` class, introduced in Java 1.3, are stricter in that they are required to produce the same results as certain published algorithms. These algorithms are found in the Freely Distributable Math Library (`fdlibm`) package and are written in C. The Java math libraries are defined according to the 1995 version of `fdlibm`. When the `fdlibm` defines more than one version of a function, Java uses the IEEE 754 core function version

The `Math` class defines higher performance versions of the methods found in the `StrictMath` class. The `Math` class methods do not guarantee bit-for-bit comparison with the `fdlibm` algorithms, but many of the `Math` class methods are implemented so they simply call the corresponding `StrictMath` version. One gauge of accuracy for floating point methods is a measure called units of last place (ulps). A method that is accurate to 0.5 ulps will always return the floating point number that is nearest to the exact result. Because they are written for higher performance, some of the `Math` class methods are accurate to 1 or 2 ulps. The `Math` class methods are sufficiently accurate for most applications.

The methods and constants in the `Math` and `StrictMath` classes are all `public` and `static`. They can be accessed by typing the class name, a period, and the constant or method name. Because they reside in the `java.lang` package, the `Math` and `StrictMath` members are available to every Java program. In the next several sections, we will look in more detail at the constants and methods in the `Math` and `StrictMath` classes.

Mathematical Constants

The `Math` and `StrictMath` classes provide the two transcendental number constants. The first is Euler's number, e; that is, the base for natural logarithms. The second constant is the fundamental trigonometric constant π that is the ratio of the circumference of a circle to its diameter.

> public static final double E
> public static final double PI

E is Euler's number, the base of natural logarithms

PI is the ratio of the circumference of a circle to its diameter.

Absolute Value Methods

> public static double abs(double value)
> public static float abs(float value)
> public static int abs(int value)
> public static long abs(long value)

`abs()` returns the absolute value of the input argument. This method is overloaded to accept `double`, `float`, `int`, and `long` arguments. If the argument is infinite, the return value is positive infinity. If the argument is the value `NaN`, the return value will be `NaN`.

Example: Using the abs() Method

A typical use for the `abs()` method is to check the convergence level of a computation. When an equation is being iterated, updates to the dependent variable or variables may be either positive or negative. When the absolute value of the updates reaches a specified tolerance, the result is assumed to be converged and the computation can stop.

As an example, we will compute the surface temperature of a body exposed to a gas flow by performing a heat balance on the body surface. If the body is nonconducting, the heat coming in to the body due to a thermal gradient in the gas flow around the body is equal to the heat radiating back from the body. Eq. (16.1) shows a simplified governing equation for this situation.

$$\kappa \left.\frac{\partial T}{\partial x}\right|_{wall} = \sigma \varepsilon T_{wall}^4 \qquad (16.1)$$

In Eq. (16.1), κ is the thermal conductivity of the gas, $\partial T/\partial x$ is the temperature gradient at the wall, σ is the Stefan-Boltzmann constant with a value of 5.67e-12, ε is the emissivity of the surface, and T_{wall} is the wall temperature. If we assume that the temperature gradient can be recast as a finite-difference expression (Eq. (16.2)),

$$\left.\frac{\partial T}{\partial x}\right|_{wall} = \frac{T_2 - T_{wall}}{\Delta x} \qquad (16.2)$$

then finding the wall temperature according to the surface heat balance comes down to solving a fourth-order equation.

$$f = \frac{\sigma \varepsilon \Delta x}{\kappa} T_{wall}^4 + T_{wall} - T_2 = 0 \qquad (16.3)$$

Eq. (16.3) cannot be solved directly so a solution must be found by iteration. A standard solution technique for this type of problem is the Newton-Raphson iteration. Starting with an initial guess for the value of T_{wall}, updates to the value are obtained from the expression

$$\Delta T_{wall} = -\frac{f}{\partial f / \partial T_{wall}} \qquad (16.4)$$

The iteration in Eq. (16.4) is continued until the absolute value for the updates to the wall temperature is less than a specified tolerance. The `AbsDemo` class demonstrates a Newton-Raphson solution of the heat balance problem. It follows the preceding discussion with some slight simplifications along the way. For one thing the thermal conductivity is assumed to be a constant when in fact it will be a function of temperature. The `abs()` method is used inside the iteration loop to determine if the calculation has reached convergence.

```
public class AbsDemo
{
  public static void main(String args[]) {

    // Define some variables and some constants

    double sigma = 5.67e-12;
    double emissivity = 0.85;
    double kappa = 0.05;
    double T2 = 1000.0;
    double deltaX = 1.0e-2;
    double tolerance = 0.01;
    double T, A, f, dfdT, deltaT;
```

```
        A = sigma*emissivity*deltaX/kappa;

        //  Make an initial guess for wall temperature and
        //  iterate the heat balance equation.  When the
        //  absolute value of deltaT is below a specified
        //  tolerance, the iteration is complete.

        T = 500.0;
        System.out.println("Wall temperature is "+T+" K");

        do {
          f = A*Math.pow(T,4.0) + T - T2;
          dfdT = 4.0*A*Math.pow(T,3.0) + 1.0;
          deltaT = -f/dfdT;
          T += deltaT;
          System.out.println("Wall temperature is "+T+" K");
        } while ( Math.abs(deltaT) > tolerance );
    }
}
```

Output—

```
Wall temperature is 500.0 K
Wall temperature is 999.6989263524445 K
Wall temperature is 999.0397993308752 K
Wall temperature is 999.0397968305151 K
```

Power and Square Root Methods

The power and square root methods are used to raise the value of one argument to the power of a second. The `sqrt(double a)` method described later in this chapter is equivalent to the method `pow(double a, 0.5)`.

> public static double pow(double a, double b)
> public static double sqrt(double value)

`pow()` returns the first argument raised to the power of the second argument, a^b. There are some special cases if one or both of the arguments is infinity or NaN. In these cases, the return value will be either infinity or NaN. You can also pass integer arguments to this method, as the integers will be automatically cast into `double` values.

`sqrt()` returns the square root of the input argument. If the argument is less than zero, NaN is returned. You can pass integer values to the `sqrt()` method as they will be automatically cast into `double` values.

Example: Using the `pow()` and `sqrt()` Methods

The coefficient of viscosity relates a velocity gradient to the shear stress the velocity gradient will generate. It is an important quantity when performing viscous flow calculations. For a pure gas species, the coefficient of viscosity is given by Eq. (16.5).

$$\eta = 2.6693 x 10^{-5} \frac{\sqrt{MT}}{\sigma^2 \Omega_{ii}^{(2,2)*}} \quad \frac{gm}{cm - sec} \quad (16.5)$$

In Eq. (16.5), M is the molar mass of the gas species in *gm/mole* and T is the temperature in K. The $\sigma^2 \Omega_{ii}^{(2,2)*}$ quantity is the reduced collision integral for the gas species. There are many ways to obtain values for the collision integral. For diatomic nitrogen, you can use the curve fit relation in Eq. (16.6).[1]

$$\sigma^2 \Omega_{ii}^{(2,2)*} = 19.0158 * T^{[-0.0203T + 0.0683]} \quad (16.6)$$

The `PowDemo` class uses the `pow()` and `abs()` methods to compute the coefficient of viscosity for diatomic nitrogen at a temperature of 1000 K using Eq. (16.5) and Eq. (16.6). It also makes use of the `log()` method that will be described later in this chapter.

```
public class PowDemo
{
  public static void main(String args[]) {

    // Define some variables and some constants

    double M = 28.0134;
    double T = 1000.0;
    double Omega22, eta, grp;

    // Use the pow() and sqrt() methods to compute
    // the coefficient of viscosity for diatomic
    // nitrogen at 1000 K.

    grp = -0.0203*Math.log(T) + 0.0683;
    Omega22 = 19.0158*Math.pow(T,grp);
    eta = 2.6693e-5*Math.sqrt(M*T)/Omega22;

    System.out.println("Viscosity is " + eta +
                " gm/cm-sec");   }
}
```

Output—

```
Viscosity is 3.86142846e-4 gm/cm-sec
```

TRANSCENDENTAL MATH FUNCTIONS

Java provides two transcendental math functions. The first raises Euler's constant to the power of the value of an argument. The second returns the natural logarithm of an argument.

> public static double exp(double a)
> public static double log(double a)

`exp()` returns the value e^a, Euler's number raised to the power of the input argument. If the input argument is NaN, the return value is NaN. If the input argument is negative infinity, zero is returned. If the input argument is positive infinity, positive infinity is returned.

`log()` returns the natural logarithm of the input argument. If the argument is less than zero or NaN, the return value is NaN.

Example: Using `log()` and `exp()`

Another way to compute the coefficient of viscosity for a pure gas species is by using the Blottner curve fit expression.[2] The general form of the expression is shown in Eq. (16.7).

$$\eta = e^{[A(\ln T)^2 + B\ln T + C]} \quad \frac{gm}{cm - sec} \qquad (16.7)$$

Eq. (16.7) is also a good way to demonstrate the use of the `log()` and `exp()` methods. The LogDemo class uses `log()` and `exp()` to compute the coefficient of viscosity of diatomic nitrogen at a temperature of 1000 K using the Blottner relation. Compare the result using this method with the result from the "Using `pow()` and `sqrt()` Methods" example.

```
public class LogDemo
{
  public static void main(String args[]) {

    // Define some variables and some constants

    double A = 0.0268142;
    double B = 0.3177838;
    double C = -11.3155513;
    double T = 1000.0;
    double eta, grp;

    // Use the log() and exp() methods to compute
    // the coefficient of viscosity for diatomic
    // nitrogen at 1000 K.
```

```
    grp = A*Math.log(T)*Math.log(T) + B*Math.log(T) + C;

    eta = Math.exp(grp);

    System.out.println("Viscosity is "+eta+
                       " gm/cm-sec");
  }
}
```

Output—

```
Viscosity is 3.93321517e-04 gm/cm-sec
```

TRIGONOMETRIC METHODS

The Math and StrictMath classes define a number of methods for computing trigonometric and inverse trigonometric functions. A general note about all of the trigonometric methods is that the angles used as arguments or return values are in radians. The Math and StrictMath classes provide the toRadians() and toDegrees() methods to convert from degrees to radians and vice versa.

> public static double acos(double value)
> public static double asin(double value)
> public static double atan(double value)
> public static double cos(double angle)
> public static double sin(double angle)
> public static double tan(double angle)

acos() returns the angle whose cosine is the argument value. The return values will range from 0.0 to π. If the argument is NaN or if its absolute value is greater than 1, the return value will be NaN.

asin() returns the angle whose sine is the argument value. The return values will range from $-\pi/2$ to $\pi/2$. If the argument is NaN or if its absolute value is greater than 1, the return value will be NaN.

atan() returns the angle whose tangent is the argument value. The return values will range from $-\pi/2$ to $\pi/2$. If the argument is NaN, the return value will be NaN.

cos() returns the cosine of the specified angle. If the argument is NaN or infinity, the return value will be NaN.

`sin()` returns the sine of the specified angle. If the argument is NaN or infinity, the return value will be NaN.

`tan()` returns the tangent of the specified angle.

Example: Using the Trigonometric Methods

The `TrigDemo` class uses the `sin()` and `cos()` methods to uniformly distribute points around a circle. This might be useful, for instance, if you were building a finite-difference grid around a circular shape. This example also makes use of the `PI` constant defined in the `java.Math` package.

```
public class TrigDemo
{
  public static void main(String args[]) {

    int numPoints = 9;
    double x[] = new double[numPoints];
    double y[] = new double[numPoints];
    double angle;

    // Use sin() and cos() methods to uniformly
    // distribute points around a circle of
    // radius 1.0

    for(int i=0; i<numPoints; ++i) {
      angle = i*2.0*Math.PI/(numPoints-1);
      x[i] = Math.cos(angle);
      y[i] = Math.sin(angle);

      System.out.println("x[" + i + "] = " + x[i] +
                         "  y[" + i + "] = " + y[i]);
    }
  }
}
```

Output—

```
x[0] = 1.0              y[0] = 0.0
x[1] = 0.7071067        y[1] = 0.7071067
x[2] = 6.123233e-17     y[2] = 1.0
x[3] = -0.7071067       y[3] = 0.7071067
x[4] = -1.0             y[4] = 1.224625e-16
x[5] = -0.7071067       y[5] = -0.7071067
x[6] = -1.82145e-16     y[6] = -1.0
x[7] = 0.7071067        y[7] = -0.7071067
x[8] = 1.0              y[8] = -2.442487e-16
```

Figure 16.1 shows the circle grid we created. Of course, if you were really creating a grid over a circular geometry you would most likely use more than nine points.

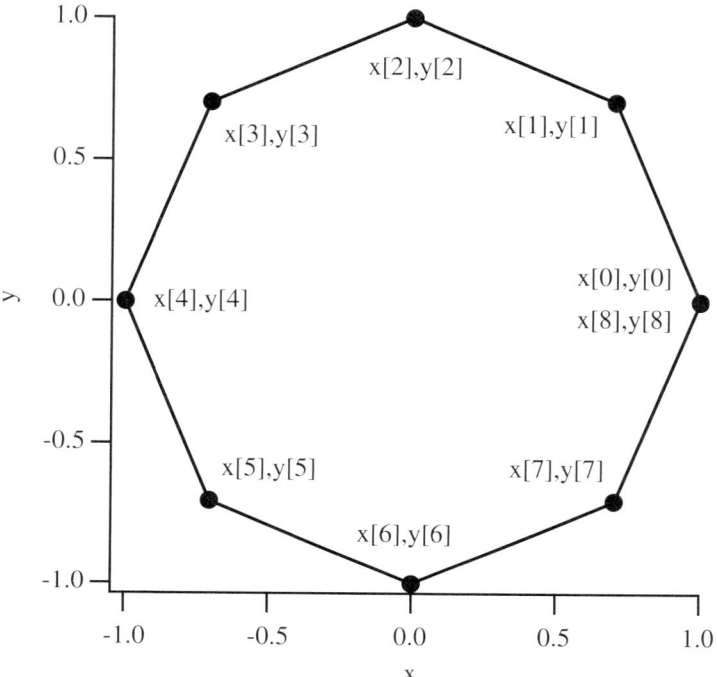

FIGURE 16.1 Circle grid

Conversion Methods

The Math and StrictMath classes provide three convenience methods for converting degrees to radians, radians to degrees, and rectangular coordinates to polar coordinates.

```
public static double toDegrees(double angle)
public static double toRadians(double angle)
public static double atan2(double y, double x)
```

toDegrees() converts the specified input angle from radians to degrees.

toRadians() converts the specified input angle from degrees to radians.

atan2() converts rectangular coordinates (x, y) to polar coordinates (r,θ). The return value is the θ angle, which is calculated by taking the arctangent of the ratio y/x. The value of r can be computed from the expression $r = \sqrt{x^2 + y^2}$.

Example: Converting Angles

The trigonometric functions in the `Math` and `StrictMath` classes use angles in units of radians. Most people find it easier to think of angles in terms of degrees. In the `ConvertDemo` class, the `toRadians()` method is used to convert a user specified angle in degrees to a radian value that can be used by the `sin()` and `cos()` methods.

```java
import java.io.*;

public class ConvertDemo
{
  public static void main(String args[]) {

    double angleDeg, angleRad;

    System.out.print("Enter angle in degrees:  ");

    //  A BufferedReader reads the user specified
    //  angle as a String.  The String is converted
    //  into a double value and this value is
    //  converted from degrees to radians using the
    //  toRadians() method

    try {
      BufferedReader reader =
          new BufferedReader(
             new InputStreamReader(System.in));

      angleDeg =
          Double.parseDouble(reader.readLine());

      angleRad = Math.toRadians(angleDeg);

      System.out.println("cos("+angleDeg+") = " +
                    Math.cos(angleRad));
      System.out.println("sin("+angleDeg+") = " +
                    Math.sin(angleRad));
    } catch (IOException ioe) {}
  }
}
```

Output—

The output will vary. If you type in "60" as the input angle the output is—

```
cos(60) = 0.5
sin(60) = 0.86602540378
```

Minimum and Maximum Methods

The Java math libraries contain two overloaded methods for computing the maximum or minimum of two input arguments. The return type of each method version is the same as the data type of the input arguments.

> public static double max(double a, double b)
> public static float max(float a, float b)
> public static int max(int a, int b)
> public static long max(long a, long b)

`max()` returns the greater of the input argument values. The method is overloaded to take `double`, `float`, `int`, and `long` arguments. If either value is NaN, the result is NaN.

> public static double min(double a, double b)
> public static float min(float a, float b)
> public static int min(int a, int b)
> public static long min(long a, long b)

`min()` returns the smaller of the input argument values. The method is overloaded to take `double`, `float`, `int`, and `long` arguments. If either value is NaN, the result is NaN.

Example: Finding the Maximum of a Collection of Data

In this example, an array of type `double` contains a collection of width values. The `max()` method is used to determine the maximum width in the collection.

```
public class MaxDemo
{
  public static void main(String args[]) {

    double width[] = { 1.2, 2.3, 0.8, 1.7 };
    double maxWidth;

    maxWidth = 0.0;
    for(int i=0; i<width.length; ++i) {
      maxWidth = Math.max(maxWidth, width[i]);
    }
    System.out.println("maximum width = "+maxWidth);
  }
}
```

Output—

```
maximum width = 2.3
```

ROUNDING AND REMAINDER METHODS

The `Math` and `StrictMath` classes contain a number of methods for rounding a value according to various schemes. Some will simply round a double value to the next higher or lower integer value. Others perform the rounding according to a slightly more complicated algorithm. There is also a method to return the IEEE remainder of two numbers.

> public static double ceil(double a)
> public static double floor(double a)
> public static double IEEEremainder(double f1, double f2)
> public static double rint(double a)
> public static long round(double a)
> public static int round(float a)

`ceil()` returns the smallest `double` value that is not less than the argument and is equal to a mathematical integer. If the input argument is equal to an integer value, then the input value is returned.

`floor()` returns the largest `double` value that is not greater than the argument and is equal to a mathematical integer. If the input argument is equal to an integer value, then the input value is returned.

`IEEEremainder()` returns the value $f_1 - nf_2$ where n is the integer closest to the ratio f_1/f_2. If the ratio f_1/f_2 is equally close to two integers, then n is set to the even integer.

`rint()` returns the `double` value equal to a mathematical integer that is closest to the input argument. If the input argument is equally close to two integer values, the even integer value is returned.

`round()` returns the closest integer to the input argument. There are two versions of this method. The first takes a `double` argument and returns a `long` value. The second version takes a `float` argument and returns an `int` value. In either case the return value is obtained by adding $1/2$ to the argument and taking the floor of the result.

Example: Using Rounding and Remainder Methods

The `RoundDemo` class demonstrates the output for each of the rounding methods. The first value tested is 12.5, a floating point number exactly between two integer values. The `ceil()` and `floor()` methods return the value 13.0 and 12.0 respectively. The `rint()` method will return 12.0 because 12.0 and 13.0 are equally close to 12.5 and 12.0 is the even number. The `round()` method will return 13.0 because when you add 0.5 to 12.5 you get 13.0.

The same group of methods is called using the value 4.67. The `ceil()` and `floor()` methods return 5.0 and 4.0. The `rint()` and `round()` methods in this case return the same value, 5.0. The output of the `IEEEremainder()` method using 12.5 and 4.67 as inputs is shown. One thing to remember about the `IEEEremainder()` method is that the return value can be positive or negative.

```
public class RoundDemo
{
  public static void main(String args[]) {

    double value1 = 12.5;
      System.out.println("initial value = " + value1);
      System.out.println("ceiling = " +
                         Math.ceil(value1));
    System.out.println("floor = "+Math.floor(value1));
    System.out.println("rint = "+Math.rint(value1));
    System.out.println("round = "+Math.ceil(value1));
    System.out.println();

    double value2 = 4.67;
    System.out.println("initial value = "+value2);
    System.out.println("ceiling = " +
                       Math.ceil(value2));
    System.out.println("floor = "+Math.floor(value2));
    System.out.println("rint = "+Math.rint(value2));
    System.out.println("round = "+Math.ceil(value2));
    System.out.println("IEEE remainder = " +
                   Math.IEEEremainder(value1,value2));
  }
}
```

Output—

```
initial value = 12.5
ceiling = 13.0
floor = 12.0
rint = 12.0
round = 13.0

initial value = 4.67
ceiling = 5.0
```

```
floor = 4.0
rint = 5.0
round = 5.0
IEEE remainder = -1.5099999999
```

RANDOM NUMBER GENERATOR METHODS

There are two ways to generate pseudorandom numbers in Java. The first way is using the `random()` function defined in the `Math` and `StrictMath` classes.

> public static double random()

The `random()` method returns a positive `double` value between 0.0 and 1.0. The numbers generated are psuedorandom in that they are actually a set sequence of numbers. The starting point in the sequence is dictated by a seed that by default is set to the current time in milliseconds.

The second way to generate pseudorandom numbers is to use the `Random` class from the `java.util` package. With the `Random` class you can use a `long` value as the initial seed to make the number sequence more random. With the `Random` class you can pick your own seed value. You don't have to accept the current time in milliseconds as the seed. The `Math.random()` method is implemented in such a way that it simply calls the default `Random` class constructor.

Example: Using Random Number Generators

The `RandomDemo` class demonstrates two ways of creating a pseudorandom number sequence. The `random()` method will create a random number sequence using the current time in milliseconds as the seed. If a `Random` object is used, you can specify a different seed value. Two random number sequences that start with the same seed will produce the same sequence of numbers.

```
import java.util.Random;

public class RandomDemo
{
  public static void main(String args[]) {

    //  Generating a psuedorandom number using the
    //  random() method.
```

```
      double value1 = Math.random();
      System.out.println("value1 = "+value1);

      // Generating a psuedorandom number using a
      // Random object.  The Random object is seeded
      // with the current time in milliseconds + 1000
      // to produce a more random number.

      try {
        Thread.sleep(500);
      } catch (InterruptedException ie ) {}

      long seed = System.currentTimeMillis()+1000L;
      Random rand = new Random(seed);

      double value2 = rand.nextDouble();
      System.out.println("value2 = "+value2);
   }
}
```

Output (will vary)—

```
value1 = 0.4126443695
value2 = 0.7111293714
```

The java.math Package

The `java.math` package contains two classes, `BigInteger` and `BigDecimal`, which allow arbitrary precision integer and decimal arithmetic. In addition to arithmetic methods, the `BigInteger` class provides functionality for such things as modular arithmetic, prime generation, and bit manipulation. The `BigDecimal` class provides arbitrary-precision signed decimal numbers for currency calculations and a customizable rounding capability. The examples in this book won't make use of either of the `java.math` classes. For more information on them, consult the Sun Java docs.

Comparing the Built-in Math Capability of C, C++, Fortran, and Java

There are some in the non-Java programming world who sniff that Java is only good for creating applets or perhaps business-related programs. They point to the supposedly superior math libraries of a language like C, C++, or Fortran.

Let's do a one-to-one comparison of the math capabilities between Java and each of the other languages to see what the truth really is.

First let's compare the built-in math capabilities of Java and C, shown in Table 16.1.

Looking at Table 16.1 we can see that there is a lot of similarity between the C and Java math libraries. Java has the same absolute value, power, square root, exponential, natural logarithm, trigonometric, and inverse trigonometric capability. Many of the method names are the same too. In some ways the Java math libraries are more compact. C has three absolute value functions, one each for `int`, `long`, and `double` data types. Because Java supports method overloading, Java only needs one absolute value method that can accept `int`, `long`, `float`, and `double` type arguments.

It's true that the C libraries have some functionality that is not available with Java. Java does not have base 10 logarithm or the hyperbolic trigonometry methods in its math libraries. Nor does Java have the fractional splitting methods defined in the C libraries. On the other hand, the C libraries do not contain the `min()` or `max()` functions. The degrees-to-radians, radians-to-degrees, and rectangular-to-polar conversion methods are not available in C.

TABLE 16.1 Comparing C and Java Math Capabilities

C	JAVA	DESCRIPTION
abs(), fabs(), labs()	abs()	Absolute value
pow()	pow()	Power
sqrt()	sqrt()	Square root
exp()	exp()	Exponential
log()	log()	Natural logarithm
log10()	N/A	Base 10 logarithm
acos(), asin(), atan()	acos(), asin(), atan()	Inverse trigonometric
cos(), sin(), tan()	cos(), sin(), tan()	Trigonometric
cosh(), sinh(), tanh()	N/A	Hyperbolic trig
N/A	min(), max()	Minimum/Maximum
atan2()	toDegrees(), toRadians(), atan2()	Unit conversion
ceil(), floor(), fmod()	ceil(), floor(), rint(), round()	Rounding
frexp(), ldexp(), modf()	N/A	Fractional splitting
div(), ldiv()	IEEERemainder()	Remainder
rand(), srand()	random()	Random number

The built-in C++ math capability closely mirrors that of C including the hyperbolic trigonometric and base 10 logarithm functions. The C++ math libraries use method overloading to remove the need for separate functions to handle different argument types. The intrinsic math capability of Fortran is not markedly different from that offered by the other three languages, but over the years a number of commercially available libraries have been developed that substantially increase the Fortran math capability. The Numerical Algorithms Group (NAG) Fortran 90 Library, for example, offers functions that compute gamma functions, Bessel functions, error functions, Fresnel integrals, and elliptic integrals, to name a few.

All in all, Java math libraries hold their own when compared to the capabilities offered by C and C++ and for most standard mathematical computations also compare well against the Fortran math capability. In the next chapter, we will learn how you can define your own math methods to extend the built-in capabilities of the core Java libraries.

References

1. Gupta, R. N., J. M. Yos, R. A. Thompson, and K-P Lee, "A Review of Reaction Rates and Thermodynamic and Transport Properties for an 11-species Air Model for Chemical and Thermal Nonequilibrium Calculations to 30000 K," NASA RP-1232, Aug. 1990.

2. Blottner, F. G., M. Johnson, and M. Ellis, "Chemically Reacting Viscous Flow Program for Multi-Component Gas Mixtures," Report SC-RR-70-754, Sandia Labs, Albuquerque, NM, Dec. 1971.

17

USER-DEFINED MATH FUNCTIONS

In the previous chapter, we covered the built-in math capability of Java. The intrinsic math capability of Java is similar to that provided by C and C++. Among the methods Java defines are those that compute trigonometric, natural logarithm, power, square root, and exponential functions. There are some holes in the intrinsic Java math functionality—there are no hyperbolic trigonometric functions for instance, and there is nothing exotic such as methods to compute gamma or Bessel functions.

One of the great strengths of Java is that it is easily expandable. If the Java libraries don't provide certain functionality, it is a relatively simple matter to add that yourself. In this chapter, we will show you how to create user-defined math methods and how to package the methods so they are freely accessible anywhere on your computer. The basic process can be applied to any mathematical function. The examples in this chapter include creating logarithmic and hyperbolic trigonometric functions, but we will also write a method to compute a higher transcendental function, the gamma function.

The specific topics covered in this chapter are—

- Basic plan of attack
- The `Math2` class
- Logarithm methods
- Hyperbolic trigonometric methods
- The gamma function

- The final version of the Math2 class
- Compiling the Math2 class
- Using Math2 class methods
- Comparing Java, C, and Fortran values

Basic Plan of Attack

Let us use what we have learned in the first half of this book to design our user-defined math methods. Our methods will have to be defined inside a class, which we will call Math2. We want the methods to be freely accessible to other programs, so the methods will be declared to be public and static. We will organize the user-defined math capability by placing the Math2 class in a package named TechJava.MathLib. If at some point we develop more user-defined math classes, they can be placed in the TechJava.MathLib package as well.

The general approach for writing mathematical methods is to first find an approximate form for the function we wish to model. Generally speaking, the approximate form will involve a series or summation expression. For example, the sine function can be modeled using the Maclaurin series (Eq. (17.1)).

$$\sin(x) = \sum_{k=0}^{\infty} \frac{(-1)^k x^{2k+1}}{(2k+1)!} \qquad (17.1)$$

It is usually a good idea to build upon what already exists, so whenever possible we will leverage off of the existing Java math capability by incorporating Math class methods into our user-defined math methods.

The Math2 Class

Let's begin the development process by defining a skeleton version of the Math2 class. At the top of the class goes the declaration to place the Math2 class in the TechJava.MathLib package. We are going to define six methods in the class. The log10() method will compute the base 10, or common, logarithm. The logX() method will compute the logarithm of a number according to a user-specified base. The next three methods will calculate hyperbolic trigonometric values. The final method will compute a higher transcendental function known as the gamma function.

```
package TechJava.MathLib;

public class Math2
{
  public static double log10(double a) {
  }

  public static double logX(double a, double b) {
  }

  public static double sinh(double a) {
  }

  public static double cosh(double a) {
  }

  public static double tanh(double a) {
  }

  public static double gamma(double a) {
  }
}
```

In the following sections we will implement each method in the `Math2` class.

Logarithm Methods

The `Math` class from the `java.lang` package provides the `log()` method that returns the natural logarithm of the input argument. The natural logarithm is a very important mathematical function, but it is not the only useful logarithm. The base 10, or common, logarithm is used for things like computing the acid/alkaline balance of a liquid or converting sound intensities to decibels. You may come across uses for logarithms of other base numbers as well.

The `Math2` class defines two additional logarithm methods. The first, `log10()`, returns the base 10 logarithm of an input argument. The second, `logX()`, computes a logarithm using a user-specified base number. To determine an expression for an arbitrary base logarithm, we make use of the formula for converting logarithms from one base to another.

$$\log_b(a) = \frac{\log_z(a)}{\log_z(b)} \qquad (17.2)$$

Eq. (17.2) shows a very interesting relation. It says that the logarithm of a number a to the base b is equal to the logarithm of a to the base z divided by the logarithm of b to the base z. The number z is arbitrary. If we set z equal to Euler's constant, $z = e$, we can make use of the built-in `Math.log()` method. The logarithm conversion expression now becomes

$$\log_b(a) = \frac{\ln(a)}{\ln(b)} \tag{17.3}$$

Eq. (17.3) will be used by the `logX()` method. The common logarithm uses a specific version of Eq. (17.3) where $b = 10$. In this case, the conversion expression becomes that shown in Eq. (17.4).

$$\log_{10}(a) = \frac{\ln(a)}{\ln(10)} \tag{17.4}$$

The code listings for the `log10()` and `logX()` methods are shown next. Both make use of the `Math.log()` method. A static constant named `LN10` will be declared at the top of the `Math2` class to be equal to ln(10). You will notice that the two logarithm methods are very simple. They consist of only one line, a `return` statement.

```
public static double log10(double a) {
  return Math.log(a)/LN10;
}

public static double logX(double a, double b) {
  return Math.log(a)/Math.log(b);
}
```

HYPERBOLIC TRIGONOMETRIC METHODS

Another useful set of mathematical functions that are provided by the C, C++, and Fortran—but not the Java—libraries are the hyperbolic sine, cosine, and tangent functions. These can be used to solve certain types of second-order differential expressions, for example. We will define methods to compute the sinh, cosh, and tanh functions in the `Math2` class.

The hyperbolic sine and cosine functions are defined as combinations of e^x and e^{-x} shown in Eq. (17.5).

$$\sinh(x) = \frac{e^x - e^{-x}}{2} \quad \cosh(x) = \frac{e^x + e^{-x}}{2} \tag{17.5}$$

As you would probably expect, the hyperbolic tangent function is the ratio of the hyperbolic sine and cosine functions (Eq. (17.6)).

$$\tanh(x) = \frac{\sinh(x)}{\cosh(x)} = \frac{e^x - e^{-x}}{e^x + e^{-x}} \tag{17.6}$$

You can see from Eq. (17.5) and Eq. (17.6), the hyperbolic trigonometric functions are easily implemented using the `Math.exp()` method. The code listings for these methods are—

```
public static double sinh(double a) {
  return 0.5*(Math.exp(a) - Math.exp(-a));
}

public static double cosh(double a) {
  return 0.5*(Math.exp(a) + Math.exp(-a));
}

public static double tanh(double a) {
  double e1 = Math.exp(a);
  double e2 = Math.exp(-a);
  return (e1-e2)/(e1+e2);
}
```

As with the logarithmic methods, the `sinh()` and `cosh()` hyperbolic trigonometric methods consist of one executable statement. The `tanh()` method requires three lines of code.

THE GAMMA FUNCTION

The techniques used to create logarithm and hyperbolic trig methods can be applied to model more complicated mathematical functions as well. As an example, let's write a method that will compute the gamma function. The gamma function is one of the higher transcendental functions and can be used to solve certain types of second-order differential equations. It is defined by the integral expression in Eq. (17.7).

$$\Gamma(z) = \int_0^\infty t^{z-1} e^{-t} dt \tag{17.7}$$

An interesting quality of the gamma function is it satisfies the following recurrence expression (Eq. (17.8)).

$$\Gamma(z) = \frac{\Gamma(z+1)}{z} \tag{17.8}$$

To numerically solve for the gamma function, an approximate form must be derived for Eq. (17.7). A number of methods to approximate the gamma function have been developed over the years. The approximate form we will use was derived by Lanczos[1] and approximates the gamma function according to Eq. (17.9).

$$\Gamma(z + 1) = \sqrt{2\pi}\left(z + \gamma + \frac{1}{2}\right)^{z+\frac{1}{2}} e^{-\left(z + \gamma + \frac{1}{2}\right)} \left[c_0 + \sum_{i=1}^{N} \frac{C_i}{z + i}\right] \quad (17.9)$$

Lanczos found that the error of this approximation was minimized when $\gamma = 5$ and $N = 6$. The implementation of this method is actually quite simple. The c_i coefficients and the constant $\sqrt{2\pi}$ are defined as static members of the Math2 class. The gamma() method only requires one call each to the Math.pow() and Math.exp() methods. The code listing for the gamma() method is—

```
public static double gamma(double z) {
  double grp1, grp2, grp3;
  int j;

  grp1 = z + 0.5;
  grp2 = z + 5.5;

  grp3 = c[0];
  for(j=1; j<7; ++j) {
    grp3 += c[j]/(z+j);
  }

  return Math.pow(grp2,grp1)*
         Math.exp(-grp2)*TwoPi*grp3/z;
}
```

Despite the complicated look of Eq. (17.9), the gamma() function requires relatively few lines of code. Since the gamma() function increases as a function of $(z - 1)!$ most computers will experience an arithmetic overflow at $z > 140$ or so. For this reason, gamma functions are sometimes written to return the logarithm of the gamma function rather than the gamma function itself.

THE FINAL VERSION OF THE Math2 CLASS

This is what the Math2.java source code looks like after we are finished implementing the methods. The LN10 constant is used in the log10() method. The TWOPI constant and c[] coefficients are used in the gamma() method.

The Final Version of the Math2 Class

```
package TechJava.MathLib;

public class Math2
{
  private static final double LN10 = Math.log(10.0);
  private static final double TWOPI =
                  Math.sqrt(2.0*Math.PI);
  private static double c[] = {1.000000000190015,
           76.18009172947146, -86.50532032941677,
           24.01409824083091, -1.231739572450155,
          0.1208650973866179, -0.5395239384953e-5};

  public static double log10(double a) {
    return Math.log(a)/LN10;
  }

  public static double logX(double a, double b) {
    return Math.log(a)/Math.log(b);
  }

  public static double sinh(double a) {
    return 0.5*(Math.exp(a) - Math.exp(-a));
  }

  public static double cosh(double a) {
    return 0.5*(Math.exp(a) + Math.exp(-a));
  }

  public static double tanh(double a) {
    double e1 = Math.exp(a);
    double e2 = Math.exp(-a);
    return (e1-e2)/(e1+e2);
  }

  public static double gamma(double z) {
    double grp1, grp2, grp3;
    int j;

    grp1 = z + 0.5;
    grp2 = z + 5.5;

    grp3 = c[0];
    for(j=1; j<7; ++j) {
      grp3 += c[j]/(z+j);
    }

    return Math.pow(grp2,grp1)*
           Math.exp(-grp2)*TWOPI*grp3/z;
  }
}
```

With the built-in math capability of Java and the logarithm and hyperbolic trigonometric methods defined in the Math2 class, we have exceeded the intrinsic math capability of C and C++. It took about 20 lines of code to do that. Even complicated formulas such as the gamma function can be included in your user-defined math libraries with relatively little effort.

COMPILING THE Math2 CLASS

This section is a review of material first presented in Chapter 11, but it is useful to go over it again. The `Math2` class was placed in the `TechJava.MathLib` package so we must be careful how we compile the `Math2.java` source code. Choose a root directory for the `TechJava.MathLib` package on your system. Create TechJava and TechJava\MathLib directories below the package root directory. Place the `Math2.java` source code in the `TechJava\MathLib` directory. Compile the `Math2.java` program from the package root directory using the command

```
javac TechJava\MathLib Math2.java
```

Once this is done, add the package root directory to your CLASSPATH environment variable. You can now access the `Math2` class methods from anywhere on your computer.

USING Math2 CLASS METHODS

Let's write a program named `UserMathDemo.java` that makes use of some of the methods defined in the `Math2` class. A typical use of the common logarithm function is to compute the pH of a liquid. The pH is defined as the negative of the natural logarithm of the concentration of hydrogen ion in the liquid.

$$pH = -\log_{10}[H^+] \tag{17.10}$$

The hydrogen ion concentration in Eq. (17.10) is in units of moles per liter. The `UserMathDemo` class defines the `getPH()` method that returns the pH value based on a specified hydrogen ion concentration. The `getPH()` method makes use of the `log10()` method defined in the `Math2` class.

A *catenary* is the curve a uniform flexible cable will assume when supported at its ends and acted upon by a uniform gravitational force. The shape of the curve follows that of the hyperbolic cosine function shown in Eq. (17.11).

$$y = a \cosh\left(\frac{x}{a}\right) \qquad (17.11)$$

The *x*-direction is parallel to the ground and the *y*-direction is perpendicular to the ground. The point (0,*a*), where *a* is a positive number, is the lowest point of the curve. The `UserMathDemo` class defines the `getCatenaryY()` method that returns the value of *y* for a catenary curve based on specified values of *x* and *a*. It makes use of the `cosh()` method from the `Math2` class. The source code for the `UserMathDemo` class is shown here.

```
import TechJava.MathLib.Math2;

public class UserMathDemo
{
  // This method returns the pH of a liquid.
  // It tests for zero or negative numbers.

  public static double getPH(double concH) {
    concH = Math.max(concH,1.0e-30);
    return -Math2.log10(concH);
  }

  // This method returns the y-location of a flexible
  // cable

  public static double getCatenaryY(double x,double a) {
    return a*Math2.cosh(x/a);
  }

  public static void main(String args[]) {

    System.out.println("pH = "+getPH(3.4e-6));

    System.out.println("catenary y = " +
                      getCatenaryY(3.4,2.0));
  }
}
```

Output—

```
pH = 5.46852108295
catenary y = 5.6566309157
```

COMPARING JAVA, C, AND FORTRAN VALUES

In this section we'll compare the results generated by our user-defined logarithm and hyperbolic trigonometric math functions against values obtained using the intrinsic C and Fortran functions. The C++ math functions will mir-

TABLE 17.1	Result Comparison		
METHOD	JAVA	C	FORTRAN
log10(4.3)	0.6334684555748	0.6334684555795	0.633468449
log3(4.3)	1.3276886102082	N/A	N/A
sinh(1.3)	1.6983824372926	1.6983824372926	1.69838238
cosh(1.3)	1.9709142303266	1.9709142303266	1.97091413
tanh(1.3)	0.8617231593133	0.8617231593133	0.861723125

ror the results of C so we won't include them in the table. Neither C nor Fortran offers a gamma function as an intrinsic function, although the gamma function is available in one of the commercially available Fortran libraries (IMSL or NAG, for instance).

The value "4.3" was passed to each of the Java, C, and Fortran logarithm methods and "1.3" was passed to the hyperbolic trig methods. The results from the various methods are shown in Table 17.1.

The Java and C results are very close. The values from our user-defined hyperbolic trigonometric methods match the C library function values exactly. The common logarithm values match to 11 decimal places. There is a slight difference in the C/Java and Fortran results, but this is something intrinsic to the way the functions are implemented in each language. Neither C nor Fortran offers an arbitrary base logarithm function as an intrinsic function.

REFERENCES

1. Lanczos, C., *SIAM Journal on Numerical Analysis*, ser. B, vol. 1, 1964, pp. 86-96.

18

BUILDING CLASS HIERARCHIES

In Chapter 1, "Introduction to Java," we mentioned that one of the strengths of Java is that it allows you to develop class hierarchies. Hierarchies help you to organize your code and they facilitate code reuse. Because of inheritance, you can place common methods higher in the class hierarchy so they can be accessed by any number of classes lower in the hierarchy. In this chapter, we will go through the process of designing and implementing a class hierarchy to model a gas mixture, but the concepts and design strategies demonstrated here are applicable to all class hierarchies.

Developing class hierarchies is as much a design problem as it is one of programming. You must first think about the best way to create your hierarchy and there are many different approaches. For instance, should the root of your class hierarchy be a concrete class or an abstract class, or should an interface define the blueprint for the classes? Oftentimes, there will be no "right" answer. If you don't like the way the class hierarchy is created in this chapter and can think of a better way, more power to you! For a more detailed reference on object-oriented programming concepts, consult *Thinking in Java* by Bruce Eckel.

The specific topics we will discuss in this chapter are—

- Defining the state and behavior of a gas mixture
- The general class hierarchy structure
- `AbstractGas` class

- `PerfectGas` class
- `Air` class
- `RealGas` class
- `Species` class
- `N2` class
- `N` class
- `NitrogenGas` class

Defining the State and Behavior of a Gas Mixture

Before we begin to create our class hierarchy we must think about the state and behavior of what we are modeling—in this case, a gas mixture. We need to consider what things are common to all gas mixtures and what things are specific to certain types of gas mixtures. The common elements will be placed higher in the class hierarchy so the specific subclasses can share them.

Every gas mixture will have certain state variables associated with it, including pressure, density, molar mass, and temperature. These quantities are related according to an equation of state. For thermally perfect gases, the equation of state is shown in Eq. (18.1).

$$p = \rho \frac{R}{M} T \qquad (18.1)$$

In Eq. (18.1), p is the pressure, ρ is the density, M is the molar mass, and T is the temperature. We will use MKS units for the gas mixture example presented in this chapter. The quantity R is the Universal Gas Constant and has a value of 8.31441 $J/(mole - K)$.

There are other state variables associated with a gas mixture to consider as well—transport coefficients of viscosity and thermal conductivity and thermodynamic properties of enthalpy, internal energy, and entropy. These quantities are functions of pressure, density, and/or temperature. We need to consider whether to include them as separate fields or simply provide methods to compute and return their value.

We also must decide on which methods we need in our gas classes to model the gas mixture's behavior. At the very least, we will want to include methods that change or return the value of our state variables. More complicated gas classes may implement methods to do things like determine the equilibrium composition of the gas. We also must decide where to implement the methods. Methods that will be shared by more than one class should be placed higher in the hierarchy. Subclasses may override methods that are declared in a superclass.

Gas mixtures can be divided into two main categories. A perfect gas is one that is nonreacting and can be considered to be composed of a single gas species with a constant specific heat. A real gas is one that can undergo chemical reactions. Its composition can change with changes in temperature and pressure. The thermodynamic properties of a real gas are not constant but instead vary with temperature and, to a lesser extent, pressure. We may want to have different branches in our class hierarchy, one for perfect gases and one for real gases.

The General Class Hierarchy Structure

Now it is time to map out the general structure of our gas mixture class hierarchy starting with the topmost or root class. The hierarchy root should declare methods that will (or must) be implemented by all gas classes. The root defines the blueprint that all subclasses must follow.

The question becomes, what kind of programming construct should this be? Should we use a concrete class, an abstract class, or an interface? In this situation it makes sense to use an abstract class as the root of the class hierarchy. All of our gas classes will be related, so there is no need to use an interface to define the generic class structure. We also don't want to get too specific at our hierarchy root but instead give ourselves flexibility in the ways in which we can implement subclasses. We will call the abstract superclass of our gas mixture class hierarchy `AbstractGas`. This class will declare a static variable representing the Universal Gas Constant and declare a number of abstract methods.

The simplest type of gas mixture is a perfect gas, so we'll make the `PerfectGas` class a subclass of `AbstractGas`. The `PerfectGas` class will define `pressure`, `molarMass`, and `temperature` fields. It will also declare methods that will be used to compute the density, viscosity, enthalpy, and entropy of the gas mixture. (To simplify things, we'll omit thermal conductivity and internal energy from our gas data model.) The `PerfectGas` class will implement the abstract methods of the `AbstractGas` class.

A real gas is a more general case of a perfect gas, so we will define `RealGas` as a subclass of `PerfectGas`. The `RealGas` class will inherit the methods declared in the `PerfectGas` class and will define additional fields to compute real gas viscosity, and other real gas properties. The `RealGas` class will use some of the `PerfectGas` class methods as is and will override others to provide a real gas calculation of enthalpy, entropy, specific heat, and viscosity.

Specific perfect gas classes will be written as subclasses of the `PerfectGas` class. We will create an `Air` class that represents a perfect gas mixture of air. Specific real gas classes will be written as subclasses of the `RealGas` class. We will create a `RealGas` subclass named `NitrogenGas` that will represent a mixture of atomic and diatomic nitrogen.

It may sound confusing but it really isn't too complicated. The gas class hierarchy that we will create is shown schematically in Figure 18.1.

This example will make use of two class hierarchies. The `RealGas` class will declare an array of `Species` objects as one of its fields. The `Species` class has fields and methods that model a generic gas species. We will create two subclasses of `Species` named `N2` and `N`. These classes will model diatomic and atomic nitrogen. The `Species` class hierarchy is shown in Figure 18.2.

Now that we have mapped out what our class hierarchy will look like, it is time to code the classes starting with the `AbstractGas` class.

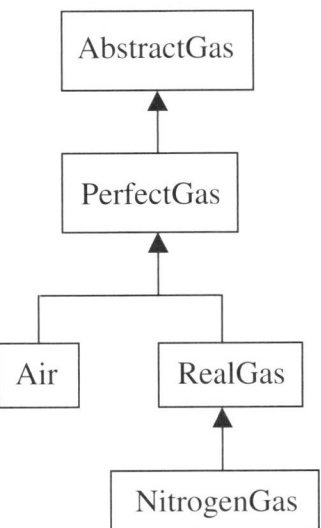

FIGURE 18.1 Gas class hierarchy

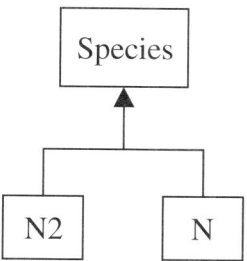

FIGURE 18.2 Species class hierarchy

AbstractGas Class

The `AbstractGas` class is at the top of the gas class hierarchy and is a direct subclass of `Object`. An abstract class declares methods that all of its concrete (i.e., nonabstract) subclasses must implement. It can also be used to declare constants useful to its subclasses. The `AbstractGas` class declares seven abstract methods that, when implemented by subclasses, will return the value of state variables associated with a gas mixture. The `AbstractGas` class also defines a constant representing the Universal Gas Constant. This constant is used in the gas equation of state, Eq. (18.1), and in many other thermodynamic computations as well. The `AbstractGas` class source code is shown here.

```
package TechJava.Gas;

public abstract class AbstractGas
{
  public static final double R = 8.31441;

  public abstract double getPressure();
  public abstract double getDensity();
  public abstract double getMolarMass();
  public abstract double getTemperature();
  public abstract double getViscosity();
  public abstract double getEnthalpy();
  public abstract double getEntropy();
}
```

The `AbstractGas` class and all other classes in this example are members of a package called `TechJava.Gas`. Packages are useful for organizing related classes and interfaces. If we were to develop another gas-related class hierarchy at some future date, we could also include it in the `TechJava.Gas` package.

PerfectGas Class

The `PerfectGas` class is a nonabstract subclass of `AbstractGas`. It represents a perfect gas, one that does not chemically react and that has a constant specific heat. Every gas mixture will have an associated pressure, temperature, and molar mass. The `PerfectGas` class declares fields that represent these quantities. Other fields include the gas mixture name, the constant specific heat, and the reference entropy at a temperature of 100 K.

The `PerfectGas` class declares constructors to initialize its fields. The first constructor is used to create a `PerfectGas` object. The second constructor will be used by subclasses of `PerfectGas` that represent real gases. We will discuss the `RealGas` class in a subsequent section. The second constructor does not initialize the `molarMass`, `cp`, and `Sref` fields, so they are given default values. The `cp` and `Sref` fields are not used by the `RealGas` class, and the `RealGas` constructor initializes the `molarMass` field. After the constructors, the `PerfectGas` class declares methods to get or set the values of its fields.

One of the design considerations for the `PerfectGas` class is whether to include the density, viscosity, enthalpy, and entropy as fields. Since these quantities are all functions of pressure and temperature, including them as fields would result in an overspecified system. Rather than including them as fields, `get()` methods are provided to compute and return the value of these quantities. The `getDensity()` method computes the density according to Eq. (18.1). The `getEnthalpy()` and `getEntropy()` methods calculate the enthalpy and entropy according to the perfect gas relations in Eq. (18.2) and Eq. (18.3).

$$h = c_p RT \quad \frac{J}{mole} \qquad (18.2)$$

$$s = c_p R \ln\left(\frac{T}{T_0}\right) + S_{ref} - R \ln\left(\frac{p}{p_0}\right) \quad \frac{J}{mole - K} \qquad (18.3)$$

The specific heat, c_p, in Eq. (18.2) and Eq. (18.3) is normalized by the Universal Gas Constant and has a value of 3.5 for diatomic gases. The T_0 and p_0 parameters in Eq. (18.3) are the reference temperature and pressure for the calculation. We will use values of 100 K and 1.0e+5 Pa for these quantities. The S_{ref} parameter is the entropy at the reference temperature of 100 K.

The `getViscosity()` method returns the viscosity coefficient of the gas mixture using a relation known as Sutherland's law, shown in Eq. (18.4).

$$\eta = 1.458 x 10^{-6} \frac{T^{\frac{3}{2}}}{(T + 110.4)} \quad \frac{kg}{m-s} \tag{18.4}$$

The source code for the `PerfectGas` class is shown next. Keep in mind the principles of state and behavior. The `PerfectGas` class has a number of variables to represent state and methods to get or set the value of these variables.

```
package TechJava.Gas;

public class PerfectGas extends AbstractGas
{
  //  The PerfectGas class declares fields for the gas
  //  mixture name, temperature, molar mass, and
  //  pressure. The cp variable is the specific heat at
  //  constant pressure and Sref is the reference
  //  entropy at 100 K

  private String name;
  private double temperature, molarMass, pressure;
  private double cp, Sref;

  //  The PerfectGas class defines two constructors

  public PerfectGas(String name, double temperature,
                    double molarMass, double pressure,
                    double cp, double Sref) {
    this.name = name;
    this.temperature = temperature;
    this.molarMass = molarMass;
    this.pressure = pressure;
    this.cp = cp;
    this.Sref = Sref;
  }

  //  The second constructor is used by the RealGas
  //  class. Default values are assigned to the
  //  molarMass, cp, and Sref fields

  public PerfectGas(String name, double temperature,
                    double pressure) {
    this.name = name;
    this.temperature = temperature;
    this.pressure = pressure;
  }

  //  These methods set the values of pressure,
  //  molar mass, or temperature.

  public void setPressure(double p) {
    pressure = p;
  }
```

```java
  public void setMolarMass(double m) {
    molarMass = m;
  }

  public void setTemperature(double t) {
    temperature = t;
  }

  //  These methods return the gas mixture name
  //  and the current value of the pressure,
  //  temperature, and molarMass variables.

  public String getName() {
    return name;
  }

  public double getPressure() {
    return pressure;
  }

  public double getMolarMass() {
    return molarMass;
  }

  public double getTemperature() {
    return temperature;
  }

  //  Compute and return density in units of kg/m^3

  public double getDensity() {
    return pressure*molarMass/(R*temperature);
  }

  //  Viscosity is computed using Sutherland's law.
  //  The units are kg/m-s

  public double getViscosity() {
    return 1.458e-06*
       Math.pow(temperature,1.5)/(temperature+110.4);
  }

  //  Compute enthalpy in units of J/mole

  public double getEnthalpy() {
    return cp*R*temperature;
  }

  //  Compute entropy in units of J/mole-K

  public double getEntropy() {
    return Sref +
```

```
              cp*R*Math.log(temperature/100.0) -
              R*Math.log(pressure/100000.0);
  }
}
```

Air Class

Since a lot of the functionality needed to model perfect gas mixtures has been built into the `PerfectGas` class it is a very simple matter to create classes for specific perfect gas mixtures. The `Air` class represents an air gas mixture. The only thing the `Air` class does is to define a constructor that accepts temperature and pressure values as arguments. It then adds in the name, molar mass, specific heat, and reference entropy data for air and calls the `PerfectGas` constructor. The `Air` class inherits all of the methods declared in the `PerfectGas` class.

```
package TechJava.Gas;

public class Air extends PerfectGas
{
  //  The Air class declares one constructor that calls
  //  the PerfectGas constructor passing it the
  //  specified temperature and pressure and the
  //  molarMass, specific heat and reference entropy
  //  values for air.

  public Air(double temperature, double pressure) {
    super("Air",temperature, 0.02885,
              pressure, 3.5, 162.665);
  }
}
```

To make sure everything is working properly, let's write a driver program that will create an `Air` object and access the data associated with the object. The `AirDriver` class source code is shown next. Remember, that because the `AbstractGas`, `PerfectGas`, and `Air` classes have been placed in the `TechJava.Gas` package, you will have to place the source code for those classes in a \TechJava\Gas directory, compile them from the package root directory, and add the package root directory to your `CLASS-PATH` environment variable.

```
import TechJava.Gas.*;

public class AirDriver
{
  public static void main(String args[]) {
    Air air = new Air(500.0, 100000.0);
```

```
                  System.out.println("gas mixture name = " +
                                     air.getName());
                  System.out.println("pressure = " +
                                     air.getPressure() + " N/m^2");
                  System.out.println("temperature = " +
                                     air.getTemperature() + " K");
                  System.out.println("density = " +
                                     air.getDensity() + " kg/m^3");
                  System.out.println("molar mass = " +
                                     air.getMolarMass() + " kg/mole");
                  System.out.println("viscosity = " +
                                     air.getViscosity() + " kg/m-s");
                  System.out.println("enthalpy = " +
                                     air.getEnthalpy() + " J/mole");
                  System.out.println("entropy = " +
                                     air.getEntropy() + " J/mole-K");
            }
      }
```

Output—

```
gas mixture name = Air
pressure = 100000.0 N/m^2
temperature = 500.0 K
density = 0.6939758804292788 kg/m^3
molar mass = 0.02885 kg/mole
viscosity = 2.6705333479641985E-5 kg/m-s
enthalpy = 14550.2175 J/mole
entropy = 209.50034335732423 J/mole-K
```

RealGas Class

The `PerfectGas` class defines the state and behavior of a perfect gas. A real gas is more complicated. For instance, it cannot be treated as a homogenous gas mixture, but instead must be considered as a collection of individual gas species. The gas species interact with each other and the chemical composition of the gas can change. The specific heat of the gas mixture and of each individual species in the gas mixture is no longer constant but instead is a function of temperature. The transport properties of the gas, including the mixture viscosity, depend on the interaction of the individual gas species.

We will define the `RealGas` class to represent a generic real gas mixture. We will build upon the capabilities of the `PerfectGas` class, so the `RealGas` class will be written as a subclass of `PerfectGas`. The `RealGas` class will have to define some new fields to represent the more complicated state of a real gas. For one thing it needs an array of `Species` objects for data relating to the species that make up the gas mixture. Other fields will represent the number of species in the gas mixture, the number of elements, the species mole fractions, and arrays containing coefficient data used to compute the transport properties of the gas. A mole fraction is the number of molecules of a given species divided by the total number of molecules in the gas mixture. The sum of the species mole fractions will, by definition, be 1. Because RealGas is a subclass of PerfectGas which itself is a subclass of AbstractGas, the R constant declared in the AbstractctGas class can be accessed inside the RealGas class using the constant's simple name, R.

The RealGas class declares one constructor. The first thing the Real-Gas constructor does is to call a PerfectGas constructor to initialize the temperature, molarMass, and pressure instance variables. The Real-Gas members include arrays containing coefficient data. These arrays would be somewhat tedious to load manually, but in the next section we will define a RealGas subclass that will automatically load this data.

The next section of the RealGas class declares get() methods for returning the value of some of its variables. The RealGas class inherits the getTemperature(), getDensity(), and getPressure() methods from the PerfectGas class and these methods are used to return the temperature, density, and pressure of the gas. The computeMolarMass() method is written to compute the molar mass of a real gas mixture by summing the product of the species mole fractions and the species molecular weights (Eq. (18.5)).

$$M = \sum_i x_i M_i \tag{18.5}$$

One big difference between perfect and real gases is the way the thermodynamic functions of enthalpy and entropy are computed. Perfect gases have a constant specific heat and the equations to compute enthalpy and entropy are relatively simple. With a real gas, specific heat is a function of temperature. To calculate species enthalpy or entropy requires integrating the specific heat with respect to temperature over the desired temperature range. Methods to compute the species enthalpy and entropy will be defined in the Species class. The mixture enthalpy and entropy can be expressed as a summation of the species mole fractions multiplied by the species enthalpy or entropy (Eq. (18.6) and Eq. (18.7)).

$$h = \sum_i x_i h_i \tag{18.6}$$

$$s = \sum_i x_i s_i \tag{18.7}$$

You may have noted that we haven't discussed how to implement the `getViscosity()` method for a real gas. That question will be deferred to the next chapter where we discuss solving systems of equations. The RealGas class source code is shown next.

```
package TechJava.Gas;

public class RealGas extends PerfectGas
{
  //  The RealGas class defines some additional data
  //  members. The A11, B11, etc. contain
  //  coefficients used to calculate viscosity and
  //  thermal conductivity.

  private int numSpecies, numElements;
  private Species spc[];
  private double moleFr[];
  private double A11[][], B11[][], C11[][], E11[][];
  private double A22[][], B22[][], C22[][], E22[][];

  //  The RealGas class defines one constructor

  public RealGas(String name, int numSpecies,
    int numElements, double temperature,
    double pressure, Species spc[],
    double moleFr[], double A11[][], double B11[][],
    double C11[][], double E11[][], double A22[][],
    double B22[][], double C22[][], double E22[][]) {

    //  A PerfectGas constructor is called to initialize
    //  the name, temperature, and pressure values.

    super(name, temperature, pressure);

    //  Initialize the rest of the RealGas variables.

    this.numSpecies = numSpecies;
    this.numElements = numElements;
    this.spc = spc;
    this.moleFr = moleFr;
    this.A11 = A11;
    this.B11 = B11;
    this.C11 = C11;
    this.E11 = E11;
    this.A22 = A22;
    this.B22 = B22;
    this.C22 = C22;
    this.E22 = E22;

    //  Compute the molar mass based on mole fractions.

    setMolarMass(computeMolarMass());
  }
```

```
//   These methods return the number of species and
//   elements in the gas mixture, the mole fraction
//   of a specified species, or a Species object.

public int getNumSpecies() {
  return numSpecies;
}

public int getNumElements() {
  return numElements;
}

public double getMoleFraction(int i) {
  return moleFr[i];
}

public Species getSpecies(int i) {
  return spc[i];
}

//   This method can be used to change the species
//   mole fractions

public void setMoleFraction(int i, double value) {
  moleFr[i] = value;
}

//   Compute molar mass from mole fractions

public double computeMolarMass() {
  double molarMass = 0.0;
  for(int i=0; i<numSpecies; ++i) {
    molarMass += moleFr[i]*spc[i].getMolarMass();
  }
  return molarMass;
}

//   The mixture enthalpy is the sum of the species
//   mole fractions times the species enthalpy.

public double getEnthalpy() {
  double enthalpy = 0.0;
  for(int i=0; i<numSpecies; ++i) {
    enthalpy += moleFr[i]*
                spc[i].getEnthalpy(getTemperature());
  }
  return enthalpy;
}

//   The mixture entropy is the sum of the species
//   mole fractions times the species entropy.

public double getEntropy() {
  double entropy = 0.0;
```

```
        for(int i=0; i<numSpecies; ++i) {
          entropy += moleFr[i]*
            spc[i].getEntropy(
               getTemperature(), getPressure(), moleFr[i]);
        }
        return entropy;
    }
}
```

Species Class

A real gas mixture can be thought of as a collection of individual gas species. The `RealGas` class declares as one of its fields an array of `Species` objects. The `Species` class declares three fields—the species name, the species molecular weight in kg/mole, and an array of coefficients used to compute the species enthalpy and entropy.

The specific heat of a real gas species is not constant but is a function of temperature. (It is also to a lesser extent a function or pressure, but we will ignore that here.) There are several ways to obtain the real gas specific heat. One way is to use statistical mechanics to partition the specific heat according to different energy modes. There have also been a number of curve fit relations developed over the years to approximate specific heat over a certain temperature range. For the `Species` class, we will use the Lewis curve fits,[1] developed at NASA, that are valid for temperatures ranging from 200 K to 20,000 K. There are three sets of nine coefficients for each gas species. We will refer to each set of nine coefficients as a_0 through a_8. The specific heat for arbitrary gas species can be computed using the expression in Eq. (18.8).

$$c_p = \frac{a_0}{T^2} + \frac{a_1}{T} + a_2 + a_3 T + a_4 T^2 + a_5 T^3 + a_6 T^4 \qquad (18.8)$$

The species enthalpy and entropy are found using the expressions in Eq. (18.9) and Eq. (18.10).

$$h = -\frac{a_0}{T} + a_1 \ln(t) + a_2 T + \frac{a_3 T^2}{2} + \frac{a_4 T^3}{3} + \frac{a_5 T^4}{4} + \frac{a_6 T^5}{5} + a_7 \qquad (18.9)$$

$$\begin{aligned} s = &-\frac{a_0}{2T^2} - \frac{a_1}{T} + a_2 \ln(t) + a_3 T + \frac{a_4 T^2}{2} + \frac{a_5 T^3}{3} + \frac{a_6 T^4}{4} \\ &+ a_8 - \ln\left(\frac{p}{p_0}\right) - \ln(x_j) \end{aligned} \qquad (18.10)$$

The values computed by Eq. (18.8) through Eq. (18.10) are normalized by the Universal Gas Constant, R. The quantity p_0 is the reference pressure for the entropy computation and x_j is the species mole fraction. In addition to methods that return the species name and molar mass, the Species class defines methods to compute and return the species enthalpy and entropy according to Eq. (18.9) and Eq. (18.10). The Species class source code is—

```
package TechJava.Gas;

public class Species
{
  // The a[][] array contains Lewis curve fit
  // coefficients used to compute species enthalpy
  // and entropy.

  private String name;
  private double molarMass;
  private double a[][];

  // The Species class has one constructor

  public Species(String name, double molarMass,
                 double a[][]) {
    this.name = name;
    this.molarMass = molarMass;
    this.a = a;
  }

  // These methods return the current value of the
  // name and molarMass variables.

  public String getName() {
    return name;
  }

  public double getMolarMass() {
    return molarMass;
  }

  // Compute species enthalpy in units of J/mole using
  // Lewis curve fits. The Lewis curve fit coefficients
  // come in three temperature bands, T<1000 K, 1000<T
  // <6000 K, and T>6000 K and have the heat of
  // formation already built into them. They are based
  // on a reference temperature of 298 K.

  public double getEnthalpy(double T) {
    double enthalpy;
    int i = 2;

    if (T <= 6000.0) i=1;
    if (T <= 1000.0) i=0;
```

```
      enthalpy = -a[0][i]/T +
                 a[1][i]*Math.log(T) +
                 a[2][i]*T +
                 a[3][i]*Math.pow(T,2.0)/2.0 +
                 a[4][i]*Math.pow(T,3.0)/3.0 +
                 a[5][i]*Math.pow(T,4.0)/4.0 +
                 a[6][i]*Math.pow(T,5.0)/5.0 +
                 a[7][i];

    return enthalpy*AbstractGas.R;
  }

  //  Compute entropy in units of J/mole-K using
  //  Lewis curve fits

  public double getEntropy(double T, double p,
                           double moleFr) {
    double entropy;
    double eps = 1.234e-10;

    int i = 2;
    if (T <= 6000.0) i=1;
    if (T <= 1000.0) i=0;

    entropy = -a[0][i]/(Math.pow(T,2.0)*2.0) -
               a[1][i]/T +
               a[2][i]*Math.log(T) +
               a[3][i]*T +
               a[4][i]*Math.pow(T,2.0)/2.0 +
               a[5][i]*Math.pow(T,3.0)/3.0 +
               a[6][i]*Math.pow(T,4.0)/4.0 +
               a[8][i] - Math.log(p/100000.0) -
               Math.log(moleFr+eps);

    return entropy*AbstractGas.R;
  }
}
```

N2 Class

As we saw with the PerfectGas class, writing a specific gas species subclass of the Species class is a simple and straightforward effort. All the subclass will do is load the data for a given gas species and call the Species constructor. All other functionality the subclass needs it inherits from the Species class. We will define two Species subclasses. The first, N2, represents diatomic nitrogen. The a[][] array contains the Lewis coefficient data used to compute the species' specific heat, enthalpy, and entropy.

Here is the source code for the N2 class.

```
package TechJava.Gas;

public class N2 extends Species
{
  // Fill the Lewis curve fit coefficient
  //   array with data for N2

  private static double a[][] = {
    { 2.21037122e+04, 5.87709908e+05, 8.30971200e+08},
    {-3.81846145e+02,-2.23924255e+03,-6.42048187e+05},
    { 6.08273815e+00, 6.06694267e+00, 2.02020507e+02},
    {-8.53091381e-03,-6.13965296e-04,-3.06501961e-02},
    { 1.38464610e-05, 1.49179819e-07, 2.48685558e-06},
    {-9.62579293e-09,-1.92309442e-11,-9.70579208e-11},
    { 2.51970560e-12, 1.06194871e-15, 1.43751673e-15},
    { 7.10845911e+02, 1.28320618e+04, 4.93850663e+06},
    {-1.07600320e+01,-1.58663484e+01,-1.67204791e+03} };

  //  The N2 constructor calls the Species constructor
  //   with the appropriate data for N2

  public N2() {
    super("N2", 0.0280134, a);
  }
}
```

N Class

The second gas species class we will use in this chapter is the N class that represents atomic nitrogen. Here is its source code.

```
package TechJava.Gas;

public class N extends Species
{
  // Fill the Lewis curve fit coefficient
  //   array with data for N

  private static double a[][] = {
    {0.0          , 8.876501380e+04, 5.475181050e+08},
    {0.0          ,-1.071231500e+02,-3.107574980e+05},
    {2.5          , 2.362188287e+00, 6.916782740e+01},
    {0.0          , 2.916720081e-04,-6.847988130e-03},
    {0.0          ,-1.729515100e-07, 3.827572400e-07},
    {0.0          , 4.012657880e-11,-1.098367709e-11},
    {0.0          ,-2.677227571e-15, 1.277986024e-16},
    {5.61046378e+04, 5.697351330e+04, 2.550585618e+06},
    {4.19390932e+00, 4.865235790e+00,-5.848769710e+02} };
```

```
   // The N constructor calls the Species class
   // constructor with data for atomic nitrogen

   public N() {
     super("N", 0.0140067, a);
   }
}
```

It is always good to check our work, so we will write a driver program that will create an N object and access its fields. The class is called SpeciesDriver and its source code is—

```
import TechJava.Gas.*;

public class SpeciesDriver
{
  public static void main(String args[]) {
    N spc = new N();

    System.out.println("species name = " +
                      spc.getName());
    System.out.println("molar mass = " +
                      spc.getMolarMass() + " kg/mole");
    System.out.println("\ntemperature = 600.0");
    System.out.println("enthalpy = " +
                  spc.getEnthalpy(600.0) + " J/mole");
    System.out.println("entropy = " +
      spc.getEntropy(600.0,100000.0,1.0) + " J/mole-K");
  }
}
```

Output—

```
species name = N
molar mass = 0.0140067 kg/mole

temperature = 600.0
enthalpy = 478948.576570698 J/mole
entropy = 167.83662132483943 J/mole-K
```

NitrogenGas Class

Now that we have defined the Species, N2, and N classes we are ready to create a specific real gas mixture class. The class we will write will encapsulate a nitrogen gas mixture containing two species—atomic and diatomic nitrogen. The class will be called NitrogenGas and will be a subclass of the RealGas class.

Similar to all the other specific subclasses we have looked at so far, the main function of the `NitrogenGas` class will be to send data for a nitrogen gas to the `RealGas` constructor. All of the other functionality the `NitrogenGas` class needs will be inherited from the `RealGas` class. The mole fraction and collision integral coefficient data is loaded into arrays. The `NitrogenGas` constructor sends this data and a specified pressure and temperature to the `RealGas` constructor. The source code for the `NitrogenGas` class is shown here.

```
package TechJava.Gas;

public class NitrogenGas extends RealGas
{
  // Load data for a nitrogen gas with species
  // [N2,N] into arrays.

  private static Species spc[] = {new N2(), new N()};

  // mole fractions

  private static double moleFr[] = {1.0, 1.0e-10};

  // Collision integral coefficients

  private static double A11[][] = {
      {-6.0614558E-03,-1.0796249E-02},
      {-1.0796249E-02,-8.4619226E-03} };

  private static double B11[][] = {
      {1.2689102E-01,2.2656509E-01},
      {2.2656509E-01,1.8327232E-01} };

  private static double C11[][] = {
      {-1.0616948E+00,-1.7910602E+00},
      {-1.7910602E+00,-1.5439009E+00} };

  private static double E11[][] = {
      {2.5768925E+02,1.2877295E+03},
      {1.2877295E+03,6.6477619E+02} };

  private static double A22[][] = {
      {-7.6303990E-03,-8.3493693E-03},
      {-8.3493693E-03,-7.0254351E-03} };

  private static double B22[][] = {
      {1.6878089E-01,1.7808911E-01},
      {1.7808911E-01,1.5491560E-01} };

  private static double C22[][] = {
      {-1.4004234E+00,-1.4466155E+00},
      {-1.4466155E+00,-1.3587248E+00} };
```

```
    private static double E22[][] = {
        {6.8206512E+02,6.1510870E+02},
        {6.1510870E+02,5.0280608E+02} };

    // The NitrogenGas constructor calls the RealGas
    // constructor passing it data for a nitrogen
    // gas mixture.

    public NitrogenGas(double temperature,
                       double pressure) {

      super("Nitrogen Gas", 2, 1, temperature,
            pressure, spc, moleFr, A11, B11,
            C11, E11, A22, B22, C22, E22);
    }
}
```

To make sure everything works properly, let's write another driver program that will create a `NitrogenGas` object and access the data associated with the object. The driver program is named `RealGasDriver` and its source code is displayed next.

```
import TechJava.Gas.*;

public class RealGasDriver
{
  public static void main(String args[]) {
    NitrogenGas gas =
           new NitrogenGas(5000.0, 100000.0);

    System.out.println("gas mixture name = " +
                       gas.getName());
    System.out.println("number of species = " +
                       gas.getNumSpecies());
    System.out.println("number of elements = " +
                       gas.getNumElements());

    for(int i=0; i<gas.getNumSpecies(); ++i) {
      System.out.println("mole fraction[" + i +
                "] = " + gas.getMoleFraction(i));
    }

    for(int i=0; i<gas.getNumSpecies(); ++i) {
      System.out.println("molar mass[" + i + "] = " +
                  gas.getSpecies(i).getMolarMass());
    }

    System.out.println("pressure = " +
            gas.getPressure() + " N/m^2");
    System.out.println("temperature = " +
            gas.getTemperature() + " K");
    System.out.println("density = " +
```

```
                    gas.getDensity() + " kg/m^3");
        System.out.println("molar mass = " +
                    gas.getMolarMass() + " kg/mole");
        System.out.println("viscosity = "+
                    gas.getViscosity() + " kg/m-s");
        System.out.println("enthalpy = " +
                    gas.getEnthalpy() + " J/mole");
        System.out.println("entropy = " +
                    gas.getEntropy() + " J/mole-K");  }
}
```

Output—

```
gas mixture name = Nitrogen Gas
number of species = 2
number of elements = 1
mole fraction[0] = 1.0
mole fraction[1] = 1.0E-10
molar mass[0] = 0.0280134
molar mass[1] = 0.0140067
pressure = 100000.0 N/m^2
temperature = 5000.0 K
density = 0.06738517826616842 kg/m^3
molar mass = 0.028013400001400672 kg/mole
viscosity = 1.191101312472402E-4 kg/m-s
enthalpy = 167762.46361168486 J/mole
entropy = 286.03757189521207 J/mole-K
```

In addition to the `NitrogenGas` class, a class representing a five species air mixture named `FiveSpeciesAir` can be downloaded from the FTP site associated with this book. You should also download the NO, O2, and O class source files. Try to modify the `RealGasDriver.java` program to create a `FiveSpeciesAir` object and see what happens.

Summary

In this chapter we went through the process of developing a class hierarchy. The example we chose was to create a hierarchy of classes that model a gas mixture. The first step was to think about what we were modeling, about the state and behavior of a gas mixture. Then we mapped out the general structure of our class hierarchy determining which classes would be subclasses of which other classes and so on. We then implemented the classes in the hierarchy and tested our work with three driver programs.

The class hierarchies we developed are easily expandable. A new gas mixture or species class only needs to load the required data for the gas mixture or species and call the appropriate superclass constructor. The subclasses inherit all other functionality that they need from their superclasses.

Now that we have developed gas mixture classes, what can we do with them? There are many applications in science and engineering, from modeling chemical processes to computing heat transfer on the surface of a spacecraft entering a planetary atmosphere to performing aerodynamic analyses. A well-designed Java class will often be useful for a wide variety of applications, and this quality is one of the powerful advantages of object-oriented programming.

References

1. Gordon, S., and B. J., McBride, "Computer Program for Calculation of Complex Chemical and Equilibrium Compositions and Applications," NASA RP-1311, Oct. 1994.

19

SOLVING SYSTEMS OF EQUATIONS

When performing a scientific or engineering analysis, things aren't always as easy as solving a single equation for a single unknown. There will be many times when you will need to solve a coupled system of equations for a vector of unknowns. There are different types of systems of equations. There are underspecified systems with more unknowns than equations. There are also overspecified systems with more equations than unknowns. In this chapter we will concern ourselves with solving systems, where the number of equations and unknowns are equal. Specifically, we will create a family of methods that solve a system of equations of the form shown in Eq. (19.1).

$$
\begin{aligned}
a_{00}x_0 + a_{01}x_1 + \cdots + a_{0N}x_N &= b_0 \\
a_{10}x_0 + a_{11}x_1 + \cdots + a_{1N}x_N &= b_1 \\
&\vdots \\
a_{N0}x_0 + a_{N1}x_1 + \cdots + a_{NN}x_N &= b_N
\end{aligned}
\tag{19.1}
$$

The system of equations shown in Eq. (19.1) can be expressed in a more compact form as

$$Ax = b \tag{19.2}$$

In both Eq. (19.1) and Eq. (19.2), the *x* vector contains the unknowns we want to solve. A number of algorithms have been developed over the years to solve systems of equations. We will look at three of them—Gauss-Jordan elimination, Gaussian elimination, and Lower-Upper decomposition. The specific topics we will cover in this chapter are—

- General considerations
- The `EqnSolver` class
- Test case
- Pivoting
- Gauss-Jordan elimination
- Gaussian elimination
- Lower-Upper decomposition
- Matrix inversion
- Testing the `EqnSolver` class methods
- Real gas viscosity method

General Considerations

Unless the *A* matrix is very sparse, you will not be able to solve the initial system of equations directly. Methods to solve a system of equations for the vector of unknowns involve changing the *A* matrix into a form such that the unknowns can be solved for directly. The process of converting the *A* matrix makes use of three linear algebra relations—

1. You can add a multiple of any row of the *A* matrix to any other row without altering the solution. Whatever is done to the *A* matrix must also be done to the *b* vector. If you add two times the third row of the *A* matrix to the fourth row of the *A* matrix, you must also add two times the third *b* element to the fourth *b* element.

2. You can interchange two rows of the *A* matrix and *b* vector without changing the solution. This is equivalent to writing the system of equations in a different order.

3. You can switch two columns of the *A* matrix if you also switch the corresponding rows of the *b* vector.

All of the methods discussed in this chapter overwrite the original *A* matrix during the solution process. If you want to retain the original *A* matrix, you will have to make a copy of it before solving the system of equations.

The EqnSolver Class

Before we dive into implementing algorithms to solve systems of equations, let us think about the structure of the methods and of the class that will define the methods. The thought process and design strategy will be similar to what was used in Chapter 17, "User-Defined Math Functions." We will define the methods in a class called EqnSolver. This class will be placed in the TechJava.MathLib package, the same package we used to store our user-defined math methods.

The methods in the EqnSolver class are intended to be used by a variety of applications; therefore, we will define the methods to be public and static. The original *b* vector and/or *A* matrix will be passed as input arguments to the methods. Any changes made to the *A* matrix and *b* vector will persist after the methods return. The *b* vector will be overwritten to contain the unknown quantities. The *A* matrix will be modified in a method-specific manner.

We will define five methods in the EqnSolver class, three will solve a system of equations, one will compute the inverse of a matrix, and one will be used to perform something known as partial pivoting. The skeleton form of the EqnSolver class is shown here.

```
package TechJava.MathLib;

public class EqnSolver
{
  public static void gaussJordan(double a[][],
                                 double b[]) {}

  public static void gaussian(double a[][],
                              double b[]) {}

  public static void luDecomp(double a[][],
                              double b[]) {}

  public static void invertMatrix(double a[][]) {}

  private static void partialPivot(double a[][],
              double b[], int index[][]) {}
}
```

Test Case

Each of the solution methods we will define in the EqnSolver class will be tested using the following 4x4 system of equations.

$$\begin{bmatrix} 0 & 1 & 5 & -2 \\ 7 & -6 & 3 & 1 \\ 1 & 4 & 2 & -3 \\ 5 & -2 & 1 & 4 \end{bmatrix} \begin{bmatrix} x_0 \\ x_1 \\ x_2 \\ x_3 \end{bmatrix} = \begin{bmatrix} 9 \\ 8 \\ 3 \\ 20 \end{bmatrix} \quad (19.3)$$

During the development of this chapter, the solution methods were tested over a wide variety of systems of equations, but only results for the system of equations shown in Eq. (19.3) will be presented in this chapter. Eq. (19.4) shows the solution vector for this system of equations.

$$x = \begin{bmatrix} 1 \\ 2 \\ 3 \\ 4 \end{bmatrix} \quad (19.4)$$

There is a problem with the system of equations shown in Eq. (19.3). The three methods we will use, Gauss-Jordan elimination, Gaussian elimination, and Lower-Upper (LU) decomposition, are unstable under certain circumstances. One of those circumstances is when the top-left diagonal element is zero, as it is (intentionally) for our test problem. Round-off error is another way in which the system can become unstable. One of the ways that stability can be restored to the solution process is by using a technique called *pivoting*.

PIVOTING

Pivoting is a technique to rearrange the *A* matrix such that more desirable (as in more stable) elements are placed along the diagonal. If you recall from the "General Considerations" section, we can interchange rows and columns of the *A* matrix and *b* vector without changing the final solution. It can be shown mathematically that a "desirable" element to place on the diagonal is one with the largest magnitude among the available choices. The row or column containing the largest magnitude element among those considered is swapped with the row or column containing the current diagonal element. The rearrangement of the rows and columns is known as pivoting.

There are two types of pivoting. With partial pivoting, only rows are exchanged. With full pivoting, rows and/or columns can be exchanged. It turns out partial pivoting yields almost the same stability enhancements as full pivoting at a reduced computational cost. We will use partial pivoting in the methods declared in the `EqnSolver` class.

In the partial pivoting process, start with the first diagonal element (the first element of the first row of the *A* matrix). The elements in the first column below the first diagonal element are examined. If the element with the largest magnitude is greater than the magnitude of the first diagonal element, those rows are switched. You then proceed to the second diagonal element (the second element of the second row of the *A* matrix). The elements in the second column below the second diagonal element are searched. If the element with the largest magnitude is greater than the magnitude of the second diagonal element, those rows are switched.

The process continues all the way down the diagonal of the *A* matrix. Remember that the search is only conducted below the diagonal element being considered. As an example, if we perform a partial pivoting on the *A* matrix for our test case we would obtain the matrix in Eq. (19.5).

$$\begin{bmatrix} 7 & -6 & 3 & 1 \\ 1 & 4 & 2 & -3 \\ 0 & 1 & 5 & -2 \\ 5 & -2 & 1 & 4 \end{bmatrix} \quad (19.5)$$

You can see that the zero has been moved off of the first diagonal element, meaning that the solution process has been made more stable.

One final note about pivoting concerns scaling effects. We can multiply any row of the *A* matrix and *b* vector by any number and preserve the solution vector. Such scaling will affect the pivoting process as the scaled row might be moved to a position to which it would not normally be moved. A way to avoid this is to use something called *implicit pivoting*. With implicit pivoting you evaluate each element in the array as if it had been scaled by the largest magnitude element in its row. For the purposes of pivoting, each element will have a magnitude between 0 and 1.

Four of the methods in the `EqnSolver` class make use of partial pivoting. Because it is a common function, we will write a `partialPivot()` method that the other classes can call. The code listing for the `partialPivot()` method is shown next. The `index[][]` matrix stores the history of the row swaps. This information is needed by the Gauss-Jordan method to unscramble the inverse *A* matrix. The `scale[]` array contains the largest magnitude element for each row.

```
private static void partialPivot(
        double a[][], double b[], int index[][]) {
  double temp;
  double tempRow[];
  int i,j,m;
  int numRows = a.length;
  int numCols = a[0].length;
  double scale[] = new double[numRows];

  //  Determine the scale factor (the largest element)
  //  for each row to use with implicit pivoting.
  //  Initialize the index[][] array for an unmodified
  //  array.

  for(i=0; i<numRows; ++i) {
    index[i][0] = i;
    index[i][1] = i;
    for(j=0; j<numCols; ++j) {
      scale[i] = Math.max(scale[i],Math.abs(a[i][j]));
    }
  }

  //  Determine the pivot element for each column and
  //  rearrange the rows accordingly. The m variable
  //  stores the row number that has the maximum
  //  scaled value below the diagonal for each column.
  //  The index[][] array stores the history of the row
  //  swaps and is used by the Gauss-Jordan method to
  //  unscramble the inverse a[][] matrix

  for(j=0; j<numCols-1; ++j) {
    m=j;
    for(i=j+1; i<numRows; ++i) {
      if ( Math.abs(a[i][j])/scale[i] >
           Math.abs(a[m][j])/scale[m] ){
        m=i;
      }
    }
    if ( m != j ) {
      index[j][0] = j;
      index[j][1] = m;

      tempRow = a[j];
      a[j] = a[m];
      a[m] = tempRow;

      temp = b[j];
      b[j] = b[m];
      b[m] = temp;

      temp = scale[j];
      scale[j] = scale[m];
```

Standard

Order Details:

Quantity	SKU	Listing ID	Product Title and Description
1	u0131018159	1017T719530	Technical Java: Applications for Science and Engineering by Palmer, Grant *Condition:*Used - Very good Pages clean! Cover/spine/binding intact. Minimal wear. Usually ships the same day! Expedited orders shipped via UPS!

Thanks for buying on Amazon Marketplace.
Please be sure to rate your experience with this seller by visiting www.amazon.com/marketplace.

about:blank

11/4/2007

```
      scale[m] = temp;
   }
 }
 return;
}
```

Gauss-Jordan Elimination

The first method we will look at to solve a system of equations is Gauss-Jordan elimination. As we stated previously, the general solution process is to reduce the A matrix to a form such that the system of equations can be solved directly. With Gauss-Jordan elimination, the A matrix is reduced to the identity matrix. One advantage of Gauss-Jordan is that it will also give you the inverse of the A matrix. Gauss-Jordan, when pivoted, is a very stable algorithm. One disadvantage is that it requires about three times the number of operations of Gaussian elimination or LU decomposition and thus is slower than those methods. For this reason, Gauss-Jordan elimination is less frequently used than Gaussian elimination or LU decomposition.

In addition to solving the system of equations from Eq. (19.2), Gauss-Jordan elimination can be used to simultaneously solve for the inverse of the A matrix starting from Eq. (19.6).

$$AA^{-1} = I \tag{19.6}$$

In Eq. (19.6), A^{-1} is the inverse of the A matrix and I is the identity matrix.

$$\begin{pmatrix} 1 & 0 & 0 & 0 \\ 0 & 1 & 0 & 0 \\ 0 & 0 & \ddots & \vdots \\ 0 & 0 & \cdots & 1 \end{pmatrix} \tag{19.7}$$

What Gauss-Jordan elimination does is to convert the original A matrix in both Eq. (19.2) and (19.6) to the identity matrix by adding multiples of one row to another. When this is done, we are left with the equations in Eq. (19.8).

$$\begin{aligned} Ix &= A^{-1}b \\ IA^{-1} &= A^{-1} \end{aligned} \tag{19.8}$$

The original *b* vector of Eq. (19.2) is overwritten to contain the vector of unknowns. The identity matrix on the right-hand side of Eq. (19.6) becomes the inverse *A* matrix. You don't have to allocate memory to store the identity (and later inverse *A*) matrix on the right-hand side of Eq. (19.6). The *A* matrix is reduced column by column, and while this is going on the inverse *A* matrix is being formed column by column. The Gauss-Jordan algorithm is written such that the columns of the A^{-1} matrix replace the columns of the *A* matrix one by one. When the solution process is complete, the original *A* matrix now contains its inverse.

The Gauss-Jordan method is unstable unless pivoting is used. When you pivot the original *A* matrix (and perform the same operations on the *b* vector), the resulting A^{-1} matrix will be scrambled. If the *A* matrix were partially pivoted, the inverse matrix can be unscrambled by swapping its columns in the opposite order that you swapped the rows of the original *A* matrix.

We will implement the Gauss-Jordan elimination solution process in a method named `gaussJordan()`. There are three parts to the method. First, the `partialPivot()` method is called to perform partial pivoting on the *A* matrix. Next, the pivoted *A* matrix is reduced to the identity matrix. The same operations are performed on the *b* vector. Finally, the *A* matrix, which now contains the inverse *A* matrix, is unscrambled. The code listing for the `gaussJordan()` method is shown here.

```
public static void gaussJordan(double a[][], double b[]) {
  int i,j,k,m;
  double temp;

  int numRows = a.length;
  int numCols = a[0].length;
  int index[][] = new int[numRows][2];

  //  Perform an implicit partial pivoting of the
  //  a[][] array and b[]  array.

  partialPivot(a, b, index);

  //  Perform the elimination row by row. First dividing
  //  the current row and b element by a[i][i]

  for(i=0; i<numRows; ++i) {
    temp = a[i][i];
    for(j=0; j<numCols; ++j) {
      a[i][j] /= temp;
    }
    b[i] /= temp;
    a[i][i] = 1.0/temp;
```

```
//   Reduce the other rows by subtracting a multiple
//   of the current row from them. Don't reduce the
//   current row. As each column of the a[][] matrix
//   is reduced its elements are replaced with the
//   inverse a[][] matrix.

     for(k=0; k<numRows; ++k) {
       if ( k != i ) {
         temp = a[k][i];
         for(j=0; j<numCols; ++j) {
           a[k][j] -= temp*a[i][j];
         }
         b[k] -= temp*b[i];
         a[k][i] = -temp*a[i][i];
       }
     }
   }

//   Unscramble the inverse a[][] matrix.
//   The columns are swapped in the opposite order
//   that the rows were during the pivoting.

   for(j=numCols-1; j>=0; —j) {
     k = index[j][0];
     m = index[j][1];
     if ( k != m ) {
       for(i=0; i<numRows; ++i) {
         temp = a[i][m];
         a[i][m] = a[i][k];
         a[i][k] = temp;
       }
     }
   }

   return;
}
```

The `gaussJordan()` method is tested in the "Testing the `EqnSolver` Class Methods" section later in this chapter.

GAUSSIAN ELIMINATION

A lot of times when solving a system of equations you don't need or don't care about the inverse *A* matrix. You only want the vector of unknowns. In this situation, there is no need to reduce the *A* matrix all the way down to the identity matrix. The Gaussian elimination algorithm reduces the *A* matrix to an upper (or lower if you wish) diagonal matrix, as in Eq. (19.9).

$$\begin{pmatrix} u_{00} & u_{01} & \cdots & u_{0N} \\ 0 & u_{11} & \cdots & u_{1N} \\ \vdots & \vdots & \ddots & \vdots \\ 0 & 0 & \cdots & u_{NN} \end{pmatrix} \begin{bmatrix} x_0 \\ x_1 \\ \vdots \\ x_N \end{bmatrix} = \begin{bmatrix} b'_0 \\ b'_1 \\ \vdots \\ b'_N \end{bmatrix} \qquad (19.9)$$

The reduction of the A matrix to upper diagonal form is performed column-by-column from left to right. Whatever multiplications and additions are done to the A matrix to place it into upper diagonal form are also performed on the b vector (the primes indicate that the b vector elements have changed). Once the A matrix is reduced to upper diagonal form, the solution vector can be computed using back substitution, as shown in Eq. (19.10).

$$x_N = \frac{b'_N}{u_{NN}}$$

$$x_i = \frac{1}{u_{ii}} \left[b'_i - \sum_{j=i+1}^{N} u_{ij} x_j \right] \quad i = N-1, N-2, \ldots, 0 \qquad (19.10)$$

Gaussian elimination uses approximately two-thirds fewer operations than Gauss-Jordan elimination and as such is a faster algorithm. Like Gauss-Jordan, the Gaussian elimination algorithm is unstable unless the original A matrix is pivoted. Gaussian elimination can be used to determine the inverse A matrix by solving for a series of b vectors equal to each column of the identity matrix. This process requires roughly the same number of operations as determining the inverse using Gauss-Jordan elimination.

The Gaussian elimination procedure is implemented by the `gaussian()` method of the `EqnSolver` class. The method is somewhat shorter and simpler than the `gaussJordan()` method previously described, but the basic process is similar. The A matrix is pivoted and then reduced to an upper diagonal form. The solution vector is then solved for using back substitution.

The source code for the `gaussian()` method is shown here.

```
public static void gaussian(double a[][], double b[]) {
  int numRows = a.length;
  int numCols = a[0].length;
  int index[][] = new int[numRows][2];

  //  Perform an implicit partial pivoting of the
  //  a[][] array and b[]  array.

  partialPivot(a, b, index);
```

```
    //  Turn the a[][] into an upper-diagonal by
    //  subtracting a multiple of the current row
    //  from those below it. Do the same to the
    //  b[]  array.

    for(int i=0; i<numRows; ++i) {
      b[i] /= a[i][i];
      for(int j=numCols-1; j>=i; -j) {
        a[i][j] /= a[i][i];
      }

      for(int k=i+1; k<numRows; ++k) {
        b[k] -= a[k][i]*b[i];
        for(int m=i+1; m<numCols; ++m) {
          a[k][m] -= a[k][i]*a[i][m];
        }
      }
    }

    //  Solve for b[]  array with back substitution
    //  The diagonal elements of the a[][] matrix
    //  were previously normalized to 1.

    for(int i=numRows-2; i>=0; -i) {
      for(int j=i+1; j<numRows; ++j) {
        b[i] -= a[i][j]*b[j];
      }
    }

    return;
}
```

A program to test the `gaussian()` method is presented in the "Testing the EqnSolver Class Methods" section later in this chapter.

LOWER-UPPER DECOMPOSITION

One disadvantage of the Gauss-Jordan and Gaussian elimination methods is that when you reduce the A matrix, you also modify the b vector. If you want to apply the original A matrix to a different b vector, either you need to keep track of every change made to the first b vector or you have to reduce the A matrix again. It is true that with Gauss-Jordan elimination you can multiply the inverse A matrix with the new b vector, but this approach is more prone to round-off error than if the new b vector is modified along with the A matrix.

The LU decomposition method is different from the Gauss-Jordan and Gaussian methods in that the reduction of the A matrix is performed independently of any *b* vector. This approach avoids the coupling problems we've just discussed. The reduced *A* matrix can be applied to any number of *b* vectors. It is for this reason and because it is as efficient as Gaussian elimination that LU decomposition is the most commonly used method for solving systems of equations.

The LU decomposition method is based on the fact that the *A* matrix can be decomposed into the product of upper and lower triangular matrices.

$$Ax = LUx = b \qquad (19.11)$$

Eq. (19.11) converts the original system of equations into two triangular systems of equations that can be more easily and rapidly solved. The lower and upper triangular matrices take the form of Eq. (19.12).

$$L = \begin{pmatrix} 1 & 0 & \cdots & 0 \\ l_{10} & 1 & \cdots & 0 \\ \vdots & \vdots & \ddots & \vdots \\ l_{N0} & l_{N1} & \cdots & 1 \end{pmatrix} \quad U = \begin{pmatrix} u_{00} & u_{01} & \cdots & u_{oN} \\ 0 & u_{11} & \cdots & u_{1N} \\ \vdots & \vdots & \ddots & \vdots \\ 0 & 0 & \cdots & u_{NN} \end{pmatrix} \qquad (19.12)$$

The l_{ij} and u_{ij} elements are computed column by column. For a given column number *j*, the u_{ij} and l_{ij} elements are computed according to the following equations—

$$u_{ij} = a_{ij} - \sum_{k=0}^{i-1} l_{ik}u_{kj} \quad i = 0, 1, 2, \ldots j \qquad (19.13)$$

$$l_{ij} = \frac{1}{u_{jj}} \left[a_{ij} - \sum_{k=0}^{j-1} l_{ik}u_{kj} \right] \quad i = j+1, j+2, \ldots, N \qquad (19.14)$$

The a_{ij} terms in Eq. (19.13) and Eq. (19.14) are elements of the original *A* matrix. Because the l_{ij} and u_{ij} elements reside in different regions of the matrix, it is not necessary to allocate memory for separate *L* and *U* matrices. As we did with the implementation of Gaussian and Gauss-Jordan elimination, we will implement LU decomposition such that the *A* matrix is overwritten column by column with the l_{ij} and u_{ij} elements. This process is known as Crout's algorithm and results in the modified *A* matrix in Eq. (19.5).

$$A' = \begin{pmatrix} u_{00} & u_{01} & \cdots & u_{0N} \\ l_{10} & u_{11} & \cdots & u_{1N} \\ \vdots & \vdots & \ddots & \vdots \\ l_{N0} & l_{N1} & \cdots & u_{NN} \end{pmatrix} \qquad (19.15)$$

Once the A matrix is placed into upper and lower diagonal form, the solution vector can be obtained by solving the systems of equations shown in Eq. (19.16) and Eq. (19.17).

$$Ly = b \qquad (19.16)$$

$$Ux = y \qquad (19.17)$$

Equation (19.16) is solved using forward substitution, Eq. (19.18).

$$y_0 = \frac{b_0}{l_{00}}$$
$$y_i = \frac{1}{l_{ii}}\left[b_i - \sum_{j=0}^{i-1} l_{ij} y_j\right] \quad i = 1, 2, ...N \qquad (19.18)$$

Once the y vector is known, the solution vector can be obtained by solving Eq. (19.17) using back substitution, Eq. (19.19).

$$x_N = \frac{y_N}{u_{NN}}$$
$$x_i = \frac{1}{u_{ii}}\left[y_i - \sum_{j=i+1}^{N} u_{ij} x_j\right] \quad i = N-1, N-2, ..., 0 \qquad (19.19)$$

One final consideration about implementing LU decomposition is pivoting. Pivoting is essential to maintain stability of the algorithm, to avoid zeros on the diagonal of the upper diagonal matrix, for instance. Pivoting is done differently for LU decomposition than for Gaussian or Gauss-Jordan elimination in that the original A matrix is not pivoted. What is pivoted is the combined LU matrix shown in Eq. (19.15). The pivoting is performed column by column as the matrix is formed. The l_{ij} elements are first computed without dividing them by the u_{jj} term. The magnitude of the initial u_{jj} diagonal element is then compared to the magnitude of the undivided l_{ij} elements. The row containing the largest magnitude element is placed on the diagonal and is then used to divide the l_{ij} elements.

The `luDecomp()` method implements the pivoted LU decomposition algorithm we have just described. Because the pivoting is done differently in this case, the pivoting code is built in to the `luDecomp()` method. The original A matrix is decomposed into lower and upper components with pivoting performed as each column of the LU matrix is formed. The solution vector is then computed using forward and backward substitution. The `luDecomp()` method source code is—

```
public static void luDecomp(double a[][], double b[]) {
  double temp;
  int i,j,k,m;
  double tempRow[];

  int numRows = a.length;
  int numCols = a[0].length;

  //  The a[][] matrix is overwritten into one that
  //  holds the lower and upper diagonal matrices

  for(j=0; j<numCols; ++j) {

    //  Upper diagonal elements

    for(i=0; i<=j; ++i) {
      for(k=0; k<i; ++k) {
        a[i][j] -= a[i][k]*a[k][j];
      }
    }

    //  Lower diagonal elements

    for(i=j+1; i<numRows; ++i) {
      for(k=0; k<j; ++k) {
        a[i][j] -= a[i][k]*a[k][j];
      }
    }

    //  Determine the pivot element for the current
    //  column and rearrange the rows accordingly

    m=j;
    for(i=j+1; i<numRows; ++i) {
      if ( Math.abs(a[i][j]) > Math.abs(a[m][j]) ){
        m=i;
      }
    }
    if ( m != j ) {
      tempRow = a[j];
      a[j] = a[m];
      a[m] = tempRow;
      temp = b[j];
      b[j] = b[m];
      b[m] = temp;
    }

    //  Divide lower diagonal elements by diagonal value
```

```
      for(i=j+1; i<numRows; ++i) {
        a[i][j] /= a[j][j];
      }

   } // end of LU matrix load

   // Use forward and backward substitution to solve for
   // the unknowns. First the forward substitution.

   for(i=1; i<numRows; ++i) {
     for(j=0; j<i; ++j) {
       b[i] -= a[i][j]*b[j];
     }
   }

   // And then the backward substitution.

   b[numRows-1] = b[numRows-1]/a[numRows-1][numRows-1];
   for(i=numRows-2; i>=0; —i) {
     for(j=i+1; j<numCols; ++j) {
       b[i] -= a[i][j]*b[j];
     }
     b[i] /= a[i][i];
   }

   return;
}
```

MATRIX INVERSION

Although it doesn't happen often, there may be times when you will need to determine the inverse of a matrix on its own rather than in the context of solving a system of equations. An example would be if you were using an implicit solution technique to perform a certain analysis. The gaussian() and luDecomp() methods we developed previously could be modified to compute a matrix inverse. Since the gaussJordan() method already calculates the matrix inverse, we will use it to create our matrix inverter method.

The modification is quite simple. All we do is remove the *b* vector as an input parameter and remove any operations performed on the *b* vector inside the method. The Gauss-Jordan elimination technique is used to convert the *A* matrix into its inverse. Remember that when the original *A* matrix is pivoted the computed inverse matrix will have its columns in the wrong order. We can unscramble the inverse matrix by interchanging its columns in the opposite order that the rows of the original *A* matrix were swapped. The resulting method is called invertMatrix() and its code listing is shown next.

```java
public static void invertMatrix(double a[][]) {
  int i,j,k,m;
  double temp;

  int numRows = a.length;
  int numCols = a[0].length;
  int index[][] = new int[numRows][2];

  //  Perform an implicit partial pivoting of the
  //  a[][] array. We will provide a dummy b  array
  //  to the partialPivot() method.

  partialPivot(a, new double[numRows], index);

  //  Perform the elimination row by row. First dividing
  //  the current row by a[i][i]

  for(i=0; i<numRows; ++i) {
    temp = a[i][i];
    for(j=0; j<numCols; ++j) {
      a[i][j] /= temp;
    }
    a[i][i] = 1.0/temp;

    //  Reduce the other rows by subtracting a multiple
    //  of the current row from them. Don't reduce the
    //  current row. As each column of the a[][] matrix
    //  is reduced its elements are replaced with the
    //  inverse a[][] matrix.

    for(k=0; k<numRows; ++k) {
      if ( k != i ) {
        temp = a[k][i];
        for(j=0; j<numCols; ++j) {
          a[k][j] -= temp*a[i][j];
        }
        a[k][i] = -temp*a[i][i];
      }
    }
  }

  //  Unscramble the inverse a[][] matrix.
  //  The columns are swapped in the opposite order
  //  that the rows were during the pivoting.

  for(j=numCols-1; j>=0; --j) {
    k = index[j][0];
    m = index[j][1];
    if ( k != m ) {
      for(i=0; i<numRows; ++i) {
        temp = a[i][m];
```

```
            a[i][m] = a[i][k];
            a[i][k] = temp;
         }
      }
   }

   return;
}
```

TESTING THE EqnSolver CLASS METHODS

The methods we wrote look very nice, but we need to test them to make sure everything is working properly. First we have to compile the `EqnSolver.java` source code. Because the `EqnSolver` class was placed in the `TechJava.MathLib` package, you will have to copy the `EqnSolver.java` source code to the TechJava\MathLib directory and compile the code from the package root directory as we have done previously. If you followed the examples in Chapter 17, your CLASSPATH should already include the package root directory.

We will then write a driver program named `SolverDemo.java`. This program simply loads the *A* matrix and *b* vector from our test case and calls the `gaussJordan()`, `gaussian()`, or `luDecomp()` method. The resulting solution vector is written out. The `SolverDemo` source code is shown here.

```
import TechJava.MathLib.EqnSolver;

public class SolverDemo
{
  public static void main(String args[]) {
    double a[][] = { {0.0, 1.0, 5.0, -2.0},
                     {7.0, -6.0, 3.0, 1.0},
                     {1.0, 4.0, 2.0, -3.0},
                     {5.0, -2.0, 1.0, 4.0} };
    double b[] = { 9.0, 8.0, 3.0, 20.0 };

    EqnSolver.gaussJordan(a,b);
//     EqnSolver.gaussian(a,b);
//     EqnSolver.luDecomp(a,b);

    for (int i=0; i<a.length; ++i) {
      System.out.println("b["+i+"] = "+b[i]);
    }
  }
}
```

Output—

```
b[0] = 1.000000000004
b[1] = 2.0
b[2] = 3.0
b[3] = 4.0
```

In this case the `gaussJordan()` method was called. There was a slight round-off error in the first unknown value, but the other three values came out cleanly. You will find that there is usually a small round-off error when using floating-point math. If you try calling the `gaussian()` and `luDecomp()` methods, you will see that they also return the correct solution vector.

To test the `invertMatrix()` method, we will create another driver program named `InvertDemo`. The `main()` method from this class computes the inverse of the *A* matrix from our test case using the `invertMatrix()` method. It then computes the product of the original *A* matrix with its computed inverse to see if it equals the identity matrix.

```
import TechJava.MathLib.EqnSolver;

public class InvertDemo
{
  public static void main(String args[]) {
    double a[][] = { {0.0, 1.0, 5.0, -2.0},
                     {7.0, -6.0, 3.0, 1.0},
                     {1.0, 4.0, 2.0, -3.0},
                     {5.0, -2.0, 1.0, 4.0} };
    int i,j,k;

    //  Compute the inverse of the A matrix.

    EqnSolver.invertMatrix(a);

    //  Re-create the original A matrix, compute
    //  the product of it and its inverse, and
    //  see if it equals the identity matrix.

    double A[][] = { {0.0, 1.0, 5.0, -2.0},
                     {7.0, -6.0, 3.0, 1.0},
                     {1.0, 4.0, 2.0, -3.0},
                     {5.0, -2.0, 1.0, 4.0} };
    double I[][] = { {0.0, 0.0, 0.0, 0.0},
                     {0.0, 0.0, 0.0, 0.0},
                     {0.0, 0.0, 0.0, 0.0},
                     {0.0, 0.0, 0.0, 0.0} };

    int numRows = A.length;
    int numCols = A[0].length;
```

```
      for(i=0; i<numRows; ++i) {
        for(j=0; j<numCols; ++j) {
          for(k=0; k<numRows; ++k) {
            I[i][j] += A[i][k]*a[k][j];
          }
        }
      }

      for(i=0; i<numRows; ++i) {
        for(j=0; j<numCols; ++j) {
          System.out.println("I["+i+"]["+j+"] = "+
                                    I[i][j]);
        }
      }
    }
}
```

Output—

```
I[0][0] = 0.9999999999
I[0][1] = 0.0
I[0][2] = 0.0
I[0][3] = 0.0
I[1][0] = 1.5356534878e-16
I[1][1] = 0.9999999999
I[1][2] = 0.0
I[1][3] = 1.1022334581e-16
I[2][0] = 0.0
I[2][1] = 0.0
I[2][2] = 1.0
I[2][3] = 1.1022334581e-16
I[3][0] = 2.2204460492e-16
I[3][1] = 0.0
I[3][2] = 1.1022334581e-16
I[3][3] = 1.0
```

While the `SolverDemo` and `InvertDemo` classes only test the `EqnSolver` class methods with one 4x4 system of equations, the three methods were extensively tested with a variety of A matrices and b vectors during the development of this chapter. You are encouraged to modify the `SolverDemo` class to perform your own testing of the `EqnSolver` class methods.

REAL GAS VISCOSITY METHOD

So far in this chapter, we have tested our equation solver methods on a simple test case. Now let's apply one of them to a realistic problem—computing the viscosity coefficient of a multicomponent gas mixture. If you remember from Chapter 18, "Building Class Hierarchies," we deferred implementation of the real gas viscosity method because it required the solution of a system of equations. We are now ready to implement that method. It is important to remember when reading this section to focus on the process. Even if you never need a real gas viscosity method, you can apply the process described in this section to set up and solve your own system of equations problems.

The viscosity coefficient of a multicomponent gas mixture can be obtained by solving Boltzmann's equation using a Sonine polynomial expansion. Because of the rapid convergence of the Sonine polynomials, an accurate representation of the mixture viscosity coefficient can be obtained by including only the first term in the expansion. The resulting equation is—

$$\eta = \sum_{j=1}^{N} x_j b_{j0}(1) \tag{19.20}$$

On the surface Eq. (19.20) looks very simple. The mixture viscosity coefficient (η) is equal to the sum of the species mole fractions (x_j) and the Sonine polynomial coefficients ($b_{j0}(1)$). The trick is to evaluate the coefficients. It turns out they can be obtained by solving a system of equations.

$$\sum_{j=1}^{N} H_{ij} b_{j0}(1) = x_i \quad i = 1, 2, \ldots N \tag{19.21}$$

The N parameter in Eq. (19.21) is the number of species in the gas mixture. The elements of the H matrix can be evaluated according to Eq. (19.22).

$$H_{ij} = 52979 \frac{x_i}{\sqrt{T}} \sum_{k=1}^{N} \frac{x_k \sqrt{\mu_{ik}}}{(m_i + m_k)} \left[\frac{5}{3} (\delta_{ij} - \delta_{jk}) \sigma^2 \Omega_{ik}^{(1,1)*} + \frac{m_k}{m_j} (\delta_{ij} + \delta_{jk}) \sigma^2 \Omega_{ik}^{(2,2)*} \right] \tag{19.22}$$

In Eq. (19.22), the x terms are the species mole fractions, the m terms are the species molar masses in $gm/mole$, T is the temperature, and $\Omega_{ik}^{(1,1)*}$ and $\Omega_{ik}^{(2,2)*}$ are reduced collision integrals. The Kronecker delta term, δ_{ij}, is equal to 1 if $i = j$ and 0 otherwise. The μ_{ik} term is the reduced mass of a species pair and is given by the expression in Eq. (19.23).

$$\mu_{ik} = \frac{m_i m_k}{m_i + m_k} \tag{19.23}$$

The process for computing the mixture viscosity coefficient is straightforward. We simply load up the H matrix and solve the system of equations $Hx = b$. The b vector will initially store the species mole fractions. Once the system of equations is solved, the *b* vector will be overwritten to contain the expansion coefficients. Once the expansion coefficients are obtained, we can compute the mixture viscosity coefficient according to Eq. (19.20).

We will augment the `RealGas` class, first described in Chapter 18, to include a `getViscosity()` method that will compute the real gas viscosity coefficient. The code listing for the method is shown next. The `getViscosity()` method uses the `gaussian()` method to solve the system of equations $Hx = b$.

```
public double getViscosity() {
  double viscosity, tmp, T, lnT, sqrtT;
  int i,j,k,n;
  double delta[][] =
        new double[numSpecies][numSpecies];
  double Omega11[][] =
        new double[numSpecies][numSpecies];
  double Omega22[][] =
        new double[numSpecies][numSpecies];
  double sqrtMu[][] =
        new double[numSpecies][numSpecies];
  double H[][] = new double[numSpecies][numSpecies];
  double m[] = new double[numSpecies];
  double b[] = new double[numSpecies];

  //  species molar mass is converted to gm/mole

  for (i=0; i<numSpecies; ++i) {
    m[i] = 1000.0*getSpecies(i).getMolarMass();
  }

  //  Compute the Kronecker delta, reduced mass,
  //  and define some local convenience variables

  T = getTemperature();
  lnT = Math.log(T);
  sqrtT = Math.sqrt(T);

  for (i=0; i<numSpecies; ++i) {
    for (j=0; j<numSpecies; ++j) {
      delta[i][j] = 0.0;
      sqrtMu[i][j] =
          Math.sqrt((m[i]*m[j])/(m[i]+m[j]));
    }
    delta[i][i] = 1.0;
  }

  // Compute the collision integrals

  for (i=0; i<numSpecies; ++i) {
    for (j=0; j<numSpecies; ++j) {
      tmp = A11[i][j]*lnT*lnT +
```

```
              B11[i][j]*lnT + C11[i][j];
    Omega11[i][j] = E11[i][j]*Math.pow(T,tmp);
    tmp = A22[i][j]*lnT*lnT +
              B22[i][j]*lnT + C22[i][j];
    Omega22[i][j] = E22[i][j]*Math.pow(T,tmp);
  }
}

// Load up the b vector and the diagonal
// H terms

for(i=0; i<numSpecies; ++i) {
  b[i] = moleFr[i];
  H[i][i] = 0.0;
  for(k=0; k<numSpecies; ++k) {
      H[i][i] += sqrtMu[i][k]*moleFr[k]*52979.0*
   ((5.0/3.0)*m[i]*(1.0 - delta[i][k])*Omega11[i][k] +
            m[k]*(1.0 + delta[i][k])*Omega22[i][k])/
            (m[i] + m[k]);
  }
  H[i][i] *= moleFr[i]/(m[i]*sqrtT);
}

// Load up the off-diagonal H terms

for(i=0; i<numSpecies; ++i) {
  for(j=i+1; j<numSpecies; ++j) {
    H[i][j] = sqrtMu[i][j]*moleFr[i]*moleFr[j]*
52979.0*(-(5.0/3.0)*Omega11[i][j] + Omega22[i][j])/
            ( sqrtT*(m[i] + m[j]) );
  }
  for(j=0; j<i; ++j) {
    H[i][j] = sqrtMu[i][j]*moleFr[i]*moleFr[j]*
52979.0*(-(5.0/3.0)*Omega11[i][j] + Omega22[i][j])/
            ( sqrtT*(m[i] + m[j]) );
  }
}

// Solve Hx=b and compute viscosity convert it
// to units of kg/m-s by multiplying value by 0.1

EqnSolver.gaussian(H,b);

viscosity = 0.0;
for(i=0; i<numSpecies; ++i) {
  viscosity += moleFr[i]*b[i];
}

return 0.1*viscosity;
}
```

Let's test our new viscosity method by writing a driver program named `ViscosityDemo.java`. The program creates a `FiveSpeciesAir` object corresponding to a five species air gas mixture at a temperature of 1000 K. The `getViscosity()` method is called to compute the viscosity coefficient of the gas mixture. Because we have modified the `RealGas.java` class, you will have to recompile the `RealGas.java` source code in the TechJava\Gas directory (compile it from the package root directory).

```
import TechJava.Gas.*;

public class ViscosityDemo
{
   public static void main(String args[]) {
      FiveSpeciesAir gas =
          new FiveSpeciesAir(1000.0, 100000.0);

      System.out.println("viscosity = " +
          gas.getViscosity() + " kg/m-s");
   }
}
```

Output—

```
viscosity = 4.56260372708E-5 kg/m-s
```

20

Solving Differential Equations

Differential equations, those that define how the value of one variable changes with respect to another, are used to model a wide range of physical processes. You will use differential equations in chemistry, dynamics, fluid dynamics, thermodynamics, and almost every other scientific or engineering endeavor. A differential equation that has one independent variable is called an *ordinary differential equation* or ODE. Examples of ODEs include the equations to model the motion of a spring or the boundary layer equations from fluid dynamics. A *partial differential equation* (PDE) has more than one independent variable. The Navier-Stokes equations are an example of a set of coupled partial differential equations used in fluid dynamic analysis to represent the conservation of mass, momentum, and energy.

This chapter will focus primarily on how to solve ordinary differential equations and will touch upon the more difficult to solve partial differential equations only briefly at the end of the chapter. We will discuss the difference between initial value and two-point boundary problems. We will write a class that represents a generic ODE and write two subclasses that represent the motion of a damped spring and a compressible boundary layer over a flat plate. We will develop a class named `ODESolver` that will define a number of methods used to solve ODEs and compare results generated by these methods with results from other sources.

The specific topics covered in this chapter are—

- Ordinary differential equations
- The ODE class
- Initial value problems
- Runge-Kutta schemes
- Example problem: damped spring motion
- Embedded Runge-Kutta solvers
- Other ODE solution techniques
- Two-point boundary problems
- Shooting methods
- Example problem: compressible boundary layer
- Other two-point boundary solution techniques
- Partial differential equations

ORDINARY DIFFERENTIAL EQUATIONS

An ODE is used to express the rate of change of one quantity with respect to another. You have probably been working with ODEs since you began your scientific or engineering course work. One defining characteristic of an ODE is that its derivatives are a function of one independent variable. A general form of a first-order ODE is shown in Eq. (20.1).

$$\frac{dy}{dx} + a(x)y + b(x) + c = 0 \tag{20.1}$$

The order of a differential is defined as the order of the highest derivative appearing in the equation. Ordinary differential equations can be of any order. A general form of a second-order ODE is shown in Eq. (20.2).

$$\frac{d^2y}{dx^2} + a(x)\frac{dy}{dx} + b(x)y + c(x) + d = 0 \tag{20.2}$$

Any higher-order ODE can be expressed as a coupled set of first-order differential equations. For example, the second-order ODE shown in Eq. (20.2) can be reduced to a coupled set of two first-order differential equations.

$$\frac{d}{dx}\left(\frac{dy}{dx}\right) = -a(x)\frac{dy}{dx} - b(x)y - c(x) - d$$
$$\frac{d}{dx}(y) = \frac{dy}{dx} \tag{20.3}$$

The second expression in Eq. (20.3) looks trivial in that the left-hand side is the same as the right-hand side, but the ODE solvers we will discuss later in this chapter use the coupled first-order form of the ODE in their solution process. The ODE solvers would integrate the first-order equations shown in Eq. (20.3) to obtain values for the dependent variables y and dy/dx as a function of the independent variable x.

THE ODE CLASS

As you certainly know by this time, everything in Java is defined within a class. If we are working with ODEs we need to define a class that will encapsulate an ODE. We will write the ODE class to represent a generic ODE. It will be the superclass for specific ODE subclasses. The ODE class will declare fields and methods used by all ODE classes. Since an ODE is a mathematical entity, we will place the ODE class in the TechJava.MathLib package.

When writing a class you must always consider the state and behavior of the item you are modeling. Let us first consider the fields that will define the state of an ODE. The ODE class will represent its associated ODE by one or more first-order differential equations. The ODE class will declare a field to store the number of first-order equations. Another field is needed to store the number of *free variables* in the ODE. Free variables are those that are not specified by boundary conditions at the beginning of the integration range. For initial value problems, the number of free variables will be zero. Two-point boundary problems will have one or more free variables.

The coupled set of first-order ODEs is solved by integrating each of the ODEs step-wise over a certain range. The values of the independent and dependent variables will have to be stored at every step in the integration. To facilitate this, the ODE class declares two arrays— x[] which stores the values of the independent variable at each step of the integration domain and y[][] which stores the dependent variable or variables. The y[][] array is 2-D because an ODE might represent a system of first-order differential equations and therefore have more than one dependent variable.

The ODE class constructor will take two input arguments that specify the number of first-order differential equations and number of free variables used by the ODE. Because the required number of steps along the integration path is not a fixed value, the x[] and y[][] arrays are allocated to a maximum number of steps. This approach may waste a little memory but is the simplest way to do things.

Now let's turn to the behavior of an ODE class. What does an ODE class have to do? It must declare a method to return the right-hand sides of the first-order differential equations that describe the ODE. The ODE class will declare methods to return the number or first-order equations and free variables as well as methods to return the values of the x[] and y[][] arrays. There will be one method to return the entire array and another to return a single element of the array.

The ODE class also declares methods to set the conditions at the start of the integration range and to compute the error at the end. These methods and the right-hand side method are ODE-specific. Since the ODE class represents a generic ODE, they are implemented as stubs. ODE subclasses will override these methods according to their needs.

The ODE class code listing is shown next.

```
package TechJava.MathLib;

public class ODE
{
  // This is used to allocate memory to the
  // x[] and y[][] arrays

  public static int MAX_STEPS = 999;

  // numEqns = number of 1st order ODEs to be solved
  // numFreeVariables = number of free variables
  //                    at domain boundaries
  // x[] = array of independent variables
  // y[][] = array of dependent variables

  private int numEqns, numFreeVariables;
  private double x[];
  private double y[][];

  public ODE(int numEqns, int numFreeVariables) {
    this.numEqns = numEqns;
    this.numFreeVariables = numFreeVariables;
    x = new double[MAX_STEPS];
    y = new double[MAX_STEPS][numEqns];
  }

  // These methods return the values of some of
  // the fields.

  public int getNumEqns() {
    return numEqns;
  }

  public int getNumFreeVariables() {
    return numFreeVariables;
  }
```

```
  public double[] getX() {
    return x;
  }

  public double[][] getY() {
    return y;
  }

  public double getOneX(int step) {
    return x[step];
  }

  public double getOneY(int step, int equation) {
    return y[step][equation];
  }

  //  This method lets you change one of the
  //  dependent or independent variables

  public void setOneX(int step, double value) {
    x[step] = value;
  }

  public void setOneY(int step, int equation,
                      double value) {
    y[step][equation] = value;
  }

  //  These methods are implemented as stubs.
  //  Subclasses of ODE will override them.

  public void getFunction(double x, double dy[],
                          double ytmp[]) {}

  public void getError(double E[], double endY[]) {}

  public void setInitialConditions(double V[]) {}
}
```

INITIAL VALUE PROBLEMS

Before we discuss how to solve them, let's explore a little bit about the nature of ODEs themselves. There are two basic types of boundary condition categories for ODEs—initial value problems and two-point boundary value problems. With an initial value problem, values for all of the dependent variables are specified at the beginning of the range of integration. The initial boundary serves as the "anchor" for the solution. The solution is marched outward from the initial boundary by integrating the ODE at discrete steps of the independent variable. The dependent variables are computed at every step.

Initial value problems are simpler to solve because you only have to integrate the ODE one time. The solution of a two-point boundary value problem usually involves iterating between the values at the beginning and end of the range of integration. The most commonly used techniques to solve initial value problem ODEs are called Runge-Kutta schemes and will be discussed in the next section.

Runge-Kutta Schemes

One of the oldest and still most widely used groups of ODE integration algorithms is the Runge-Kutta family of methods. These are step-wise integration algorithms. Starting from an initial condition, the ODE is solved at discrete steps over the desired integration range. Runge-Kutta techniques are robust and will give good results as long as very high accuracy is not required. Runge-Kutta methods are not the fastest ODE solver techniques but their efficiency can be markedly improved if adaptive step sizing is used.

Runge-Kutta methods are designed to solve first-order differential equations. They can be used on a single first-order ODE or on a coupled system of first-order ODEs. If a higher-order ODE can be expressed as a coupled system of first-order ODEs, Runge-Kutta methods can be used to solve it. To understand how Runge-Kutta methods work, consider a simple first-order differential equation.

$$\frac{dy}{dx} = f(x,y) \tag{20.4}$$

To solve for the dependent variable y, Eq. (20.4) can be integrated in a step-wise manner. The derivative is replaced by its delta-form and the Δx term is moved to the right-hand side.

$$\Delta y = y_{n+1} - y_n = \Delta x f(x,y) \tag{20.5}$$

Eq. (20.5) is the general form of the equation that is solved. Starting at an independent variable location x_n where the value of y_n is known, the value of the dependent variable at the next location, y_{n+1}, is equal to its value at the current location, y_n, added to the independent variable step size, Δx, times the right-hand side function.

There is one question left to be resolved—where should we evaluate the right-hand side function? With the Euler method, as shown in Eq. (20.6), the function is evaluated at the current location, x_n.

$$y_{n+1} = y_n + \Delta x f(x_n, y_n) \qquad (20.6)$$

The value of y at the next step is computed using the slope of the $f(x,y)$ function at the current step. If you perform a Taylor series expansion on Euler's method you will find that it is first-order accurate in Δx. The Euler method is really only useful for linear or nearly linear functions. What happens, for instance, if the slope of the $f(x,y)$ curve changes between x_n and x_{n+1}? The Euler method will compute an incorrect value for y_{n+1}.

This is where the Runge-Kutta methods come into play. The Runge-Kutta methods perform a successive approximation of y_{n+1} by evaluating the $f(x,y)$ function at different locations between x_n and x_{n+1}. The final computation of y_{n+1} is a linear combination of the successive approximations. For example, the second-order Runge-Kutta method evaluates $f(x,y)$ at two locations, shown in Eq. (20.7).

$$\Delta y_1 = \Delta x f(x_n, y_n)$$
$$y_{n+1} = y_n + \Delta x f\left(x_n + \frac{1}{2}\Delta x, y_n + \frac{1}{2}\Delta y_1\right) \qquad (20.7)$$

The first step of the second-order Runge-Kutta algorithm is the Euler method. A value for Δy is computed by evaluating $f(x,y)$ at x_n. The second step calculates the value of y_{n+1} by evaluating $f(x,y)$ midway between x_n and x_{n+1} using a y value halfway between y_n and $y_n + \Delta y_1$. The result is a second-order accurate approximation to y_{n+1}. The two-step Runge-Kutta scheme is more accurate than Euler's method because it does a better job of handling potential changes in slope of $f(x,y)$ between x_n and x_{n+1}.

There are numerous Runge-Kutta schemes of various orders of accuracy. The most commonly used scheme and the one we will implement in this chapter is the fourth-order Runge-Kutta algorithm. As the name implies, it is fourth-order accurate in Δx. The algorithm consists of five steps, four successive approximations of Δy and a fifth step that computes y_{n+1} based on a linear combination of the successive approximations. The fourth-order Runge-Kutta solution process is:

1. Find Δy_1 using Euler's method.
2. Compute Δy_2 by evaluating $f(x,y)$ at $\left(x_n + \frac{1}{2}\Delta x, y_n + \frac{1}{2}\Delta y_1\right)$.
3. Calculate Δy_3 by evaluating $f(x,y)$ at $\left(x_n + \frac{1}{2}\Delta x, y_n + \frac{1}{2}\Delta y_2\right)$.

4. Evaluate Δy_4 by evaluating $f(x,y)$ at $(x_n + \Delta x, y_n + \Delta y_3)$.
5. Compute y_{n+1} using a linear combination of Δy_1 through Δy_4.

The mathematical equations for the five steps are shown in Eq. 20.8.

$$\Delta y_1 = \Delta x f(x_n, y_n)$$
$$\Delta y_2 = \Delta x f\left(x_n + \frac{1}{2}\Delta x, y_n + \frac{1}{2}\Delta y_1\right)$$
$$\Delta y_3 = \Delta x f\left(x_n + \frac{1}{2}\Delta x, y_n + \frac{1}{2}\Delta y_2\right) \quad (20.8)$$
$$\Delta y_4 = \Delta x f(x_n + \Delta x, y_n + \Delta y_3)$$
$$y_{n+1} = y_n + \frac{\Delta y_1}{6} + \frac{\Delta y_2}{3} + \frac{\Delta y_3}{3} + \frac{\Delta y_4}{6}$$

Now that we have gone over the derivation of the fourth-order Runge-Kutta method, let's write a method to implement it. The method will be named `rungeKutta4()`. As Runge-Kutta solvers are used by a wide variety of applications, we will define the `rungeKutta4()` method to be `public` and `static`, so it can be universally accessed. We will define `rungeKutta4()` in a class named `ODESolver` and place the `ODESolver` class in the `TechJava.MathLib` package.

The `rungeKutta4()` method takes three arguments. The first argument is an `ODE` object (or an `ODE` subclass object). If you recall, the `ODE` class will define the number of coupled first-order equations that characterize the ODE and will provide arrays to store the dependent and independent variables. The `ODE` class also defines the `getFunction()` method that returns the $f(x,y)$ function for a given x and y.

The other two input arguments are the range over which the integration will take place and the increment to the independent variable. This increment will be held constant throughout the entire integration. The number of steps that will be performed is not a user-specified value but is computed based on the `range` and `dx` arguments. The integration will stop if the step number reaches the `MAX_STEPS` parameter defined in the `ODE` class.

The integration follows the steps shown in Eq. (20.8). When the integration is complete, the `x[]` and `y[][]` fields of the `ODE` object will contain the values of the integrated independent and dependent variables. The return value of the `rungeKutta4()` method is the number of steps computed. The `rungeKutta4()` code is shown next.

Runge-Kutta Schemes

```java
package TechJava.MathLib;

public class ODESolver
{
  public static int rungeKutta4(ODE ode,
                   double range, double dx) {

  //  Define some convenience variables to make the
  //  code more readable

    int numEqns = ode.getNumEqns();
    double x[] = ode.getX();
    double y[][] = ode.getY();

  //  Define some local variables and arrays

    int i,j,k;
    double scale[] = {1.0, 0.5, 0.5, 1.0};
    double dy[][] = new double[4][numEqns];
    double ytmp[] = new double[numEqns];

  //  Integrate the ODE over the desired range.
  //  Stop if you are going to overflow the matrices

    i=1;
    while( x[i-1] < range && i < ODE.MAX_STEPS-1) {

  //  Increment independent variable. Make sure it
  //  doesn't exceed the range.

      x[i] = x[i-1] + dx;
      if (x[i] > range) {
        x[i] = range;
        dx = x[i] - x[i-1];
      }

  //  First Runge-Kutta step

      ode.getFunction(x[i-1],dy[0],y[i-1]);

  //  Runge-Kutta steps 2-4

      for(k=1; k<4; ++k) {
        for(j=0; j<numEqns; ++j) {
          ytmp[j] = y[i-1][j] + scale[k]*dx*dy[k-1][j];
        }
        ode.getFunction(x[i-1]+scale[k]*dx,dy[k],ytmp);
      }

  //  Update the dependent variables

      for(j=0; j<numEqns; ++j) {
        y[i][j] = y[i-1][j] + dx*(dy[0][j] +
```

```
                                 2.0*dy[1][j] + 2.0*dy[2][j] +
                                 dy[3][j])/6.0;
        }

    //  Increment i

        ++i;

      }   //  end of while loop

    //  Return the number of steps computed

      return i;
    }
  }
```

EXAMPLE PROBLEM: DAMPED SPRING MOTION

To demonstrate how the `rungeKutta4()` method can be used to solve an initial value ODE problem, we will use as an example the motion of a damped spring. Consider the spring shown in Figure 20.1. The upper end of the spring is fastened to a solid object such that it can't move. The lower end of the spring is attached to a body of mass m.

When the spring is stretched a distance x from its equilibrium position, the force exerted on the mass by the spring is given by Hooke's law.

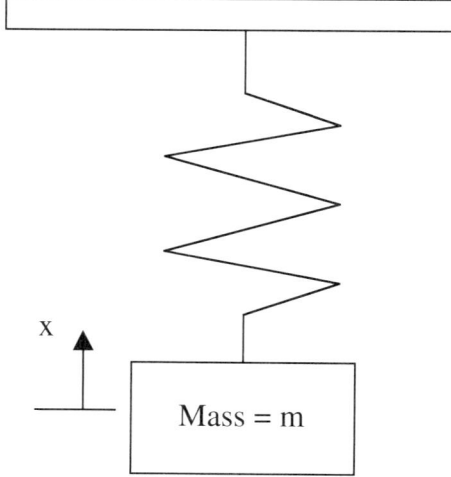

FIGURE 20.1 Spring configuration

$$F = -kx \tag{20.9}$$

The k parameter is the spring constant. The force on the body attached to the string can also be characterized by Newton's second law

$$F = ma = m\frac{d^2x}{dt^2} \tag{20.10}$$

Putting Eq. (20.9) and Eq. (20.10) together we obtain the general equation for the motion of an undamped spring.

$$m\frac{d^2x}{dt^2} + kx = 0 \tag{20.11}$$

Eq. (20.11) assumes that there are no other forces acting on the spring. In reality damping forces such as friction and air resistance will slow the spring's motion. Damping forces are a function of the velocity of the spring and a damping constant, μ. When damping forces are added to Eq. (20.11), we obtain the general equation of motion for a spring.

$$m\frac{d^2x}{dt^2} + \mu\frac{dx}{dt} + kx = 0 \tag{20.12}$$

You can see that the spring equation is a second-order ODE with time as its independent variable. What makes the spring motion example a good test case for our ODE solver development is that there is an exact solution to Eq. (20.12). If $\mu^2 > 4mk$, the spring system is overdamped. When the mass is moved from its equilibrium position and released it will simply return asymptotically to its equilibrium position. If $\mu^2 < 4mk$, the system is underdamped and the result will be damped harmonic motion. The mass oscillates about its equilibrium position with asymptotically declining minimum and maximum values. The general solution for the position of a mass connected to an underdamped spring is shown in Eq. (20.13).

$$x(t) = e^{-At}[C_1 \cos(Bt) + C_2 \sin(Bt)] \tag{20.13}$$

The A and B constants in Eq. (20.13) are defined by the expressions in Eq. (20.14).

$$A = \frac{\mu}{2m} \quad B = \frac{\sqrt{4mk - \mu^2}}{2m} \tag{20.14}$$

The constants C_1 and C_2 are derived from the initial conditions. Assume that initially the spring mass is extended a distance x_0 from its equilibrium position and the spring velocity is zero. Under these conditions the constants take the values in Eq. (20.15).

$$C_1 = x_0 \quad C_2 = \frac{C_1 A}{B} \tag{20.15}$$

Before we can use the `rungeKutta4()` method to numerically solve for underdamped spring motion, Eq. (20.12) is recast in terms of two first-order ODEs.

$$\frac{d}{dt}\left(\frac{dx}{dt}\right) = -\frac{\mu}{m}\frac{dx}{dt} - \frac{k}{m}x$$
$$\frac{d}{dt}(x) = \frac{dx}{dt} \tag{20.16}$$

Equation (20.16) is integrated with respect to time to solve for x and dx/dt.

`SpringODE` class

To solve the damped spring initial value problem, we will write a `SpringODE` class that is a subclass of the `ODE` class. The `SpringODE` class will represent the equations of motion for a damped spring. In addition to the members it inherits from the `ODE` class, the `SpringODE` class defines three new fields representing the spring constant, damping constant, and mass. While reading through this section focus on the process. Even if you don't need to solve for the motion of a damped spring, you can apply the solution process described in this section to your own ODE problems.

The `SpringODE` class declares one constructor. The equations of motion for a damped spring consist of two first-order differential equations and zero free variables. The first thing the `SpringODE` constructor does is to call the `ODE` class constructor passing it values of 2 and 0 respectively. The `SpringODE` constructor then initializes the k, mu, and mass fields.

The `SpringODE` class overrides the `getFunction()` and `setInitialConditions()` methods of the `ODE` class. Since `SpringODE` represents an initial value problem there is no need to override the `getError()` method. The `getFunction()` method is overridden to return the right-hand side of Eq. (20.16). This evaluation will occur at various points along the range of integration. The `ytmp[]` array holds the value of the dependent variables at the point currently being evaluated. The `setInitialConditions()` method is overridden to provide the initial conditions for the spring motion. At time $t = 0$ the spring is at rest so $dx/dt = 0$. The `v[]` array holds the initial displacement of the spring from its equilibrium position.

The `SpringODE` class source code is shown next.

```
package TechJava.MathLib;

public class SpringODE extends ODE
{
  double k, mu, mass;

  //  The SpringODE constructor calls the ODE
  //  class constructor passing it data for
  //  a damped spring. There are two first
  //  order ODEs and no free variables.

  public SpringODE(double k, double mu, double mass) {
    super(2,0);
    this.k = k;
    this.mu = mu;
    this.mass = mass;
  }

  // The getFunction() method returns the right-hand
  // sides of the two first-order damped spring ODEs
  // y[0] = delta(dxdt) = delta(t)*(-k*x - mu*dxdt)/mass
  // y[1] = delta(x) = delta(t)*(dxdt)

  public void getFunction(double x, double dy[],
                          double ytmp[]) {
    dy[0] = -k*ytmp[1]/mass - mu*ytmp[0]/mass;
    dy[1] = ytmp[0];
  }

  // This method initializes the dependent variables
  // at the start of the integration range.

  public void setInitialConditions(double V[]) {
    setOneY(0, 0, 0.0);
    setOneY(0, 1, V[0]);
    setOneX(0, 0.0);
  }
}
```

Solving the Spring Motion ODE

Now let us apply the fourth-order Runge-Kutta solver to compute the motion of a damped spring. We will write a driver program named `RK4Spring .java` that will create a `SpringODE` object and call the `rungeKutta4()` method on that object. The `mass`, `mu`, and `k` parameters are given values representing an underdamped spring. The initial conditions are set such that the spring is extended 0.2 meters from its equilibrium position. The ODE is integrated from $t = 0$ to $t = 5.0$ seconds using a step size of 0.1 seconds. The `RK4Spring` class source code is shown next.

```
import TechJava.MathLib.*;

public class RK4Spring
{
  public static void main(String args[]) {

    //  Create a SpringODE object

    double mass = 1.0;
    double mu = 1.5;
    double k = 20.0;

    SpringODE ode = new SpringODE(k, mu, mass);

    //  load initial conditions.  The spring is
    //  initially stretched 0.2 meters from its
    //  equilibrium  position.

    double V[] = {-0.2};
    ode.setInitialConditions(V);

    //  Solve the ODE over the desired range using
    //  a constant step size.

    double dx = 0.1;
    double range = 5.0;

   int numSteps = ODESolver.rungeKutta4(ode, range, dx);

    //  Print out the results

    System.out.println("i    t    dxdt    x");
    for(int i=0; i<numSteps; ++i) {
      System.out.println(
         ""+i+" " + ode.getOneX(i) +
         " " + ode.getOneY(i,0) +" " + ode.getOneY(i,1));
    }
  }
}
```

Output—

 Rather than list a long table of output values, a plot was created that displays the spring position as a function of time as computed by the RK4Spring.java program. Also shown on the plot is the exact solution of the ODE. You can see from Figure 20.2 that the rungeKutta4() method did an excellent job of reproducing the exact solution of the spring equation. The spring oscillates around the position $x = 0$ with asymptotically diminishing maximum and minimum values.

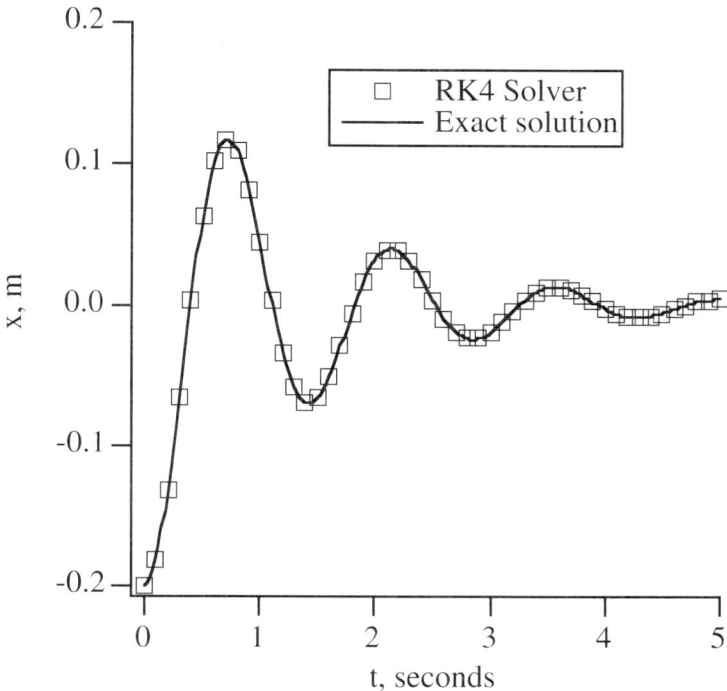

FIGURE 20.2 Spring position as a function of time

EMBEDDED RUNGE-KUTTA SOLVERS

One problem with the fourth-order Runge-Kutta method we developed in the previous section is that it uses a constant independent variable increment, Δx, over the entire integration range. In certain situations, regions of high gradients may require smaller step sizes while regions of lesser gradients can maintain solution accuracy with larger step sizes. Using the high-gradient step size over the entire integration range results in an inefficient algorithm. Using a low-gradient step size over the entire range may cause the solution to be inaccurate in certain regions of the domain.

A solution to this problem is to use what is known as an embedded Runge-Kutta technique with adaptive step size control. There are certain types of Runge-Kutta schemes that have embedded within them a lower-order Runge-Kutta scheme. These are called *embedded Runge-Kutta algorithms.* Why is this significant? Because the difference in solution between the higher- and lower-order schemes can provide an estimate of the truncation error of the solution.

The ability to estimate truncation error is what makes adaptive step size control possible. You can automatically adjust the local step size either up or down so the computed truncation error is within a certain range. There is no longer a need to estimate an appropriate step size for the entire domain. The step size can be quite large in smoothly varying regions of the ODE solution and can be reduced to smaller values in regions of strong gradients.

The embedded Runge-Kutta solver we will use implements the fifth-order Runge-Kutta algorithm in Eq. (20.17).

$$\Delta y_1 = \Delta x f(x_n, y_n)$$
$$\Delta y_2 = \Delta x f(x_n + a_2 \Delta x, y_n + b_{21} \Delta y_1)$$
$$\Delta y_3 = \Delta x f(x_n + a_3 \Delta x, y_n + b_{31} \Delta y_1 + b_{32} \Delta y_2)$$
$$\Delta y_4 = \Delta x f(x_n + a_4 \Delta x, y_n + b_{41} \Delta y_1 + b_{42} \Delta y_2 + b_{43} \Delta y_3) \quad (20.17)$$
$$\Delta y_5 = \Delta x f(x_n + a_5 \Delta x, y_n + b_{51} \Delta y_1 + b_{52} \Delta y_2 + b_{53} \Delta y_3 + b_{54} \Delta y_4)$$
$$\Delta y_6 = \Delta x f(x_n + a_6 \Delta x, y_n + b_{61} \Delta y_1 + b_{62} \Delta y_2 + b_{63} \Delta y_3 + b_{64} \Delta y_4 + b_{65} \Delta y_5)$$
$$y_{n+1} = y_n + c_1 \Delta y_1 + c_2 \Delta y_2 + c_3 \Delta y_3 + c_4 \Delta y_4 + c_5 \Delta y_5 + c_6 \Delta y_6$$

In Eq. (20.17), the a, b, c, and d values are constant coefficients. Using different coefficients, you can also write a fourth-order Runge-Kutta solver, shown in Eq. (20.18), using the same computed Δy values.

$$y_{n+1}^* = y_n + d_1 \Delta y_1 + d_2 \Delta y_2 + d_3 \Delta y_3 + d_4 \Delta y_4 + d_5 \Delta y_5 + d_6 \Delta y_6 \quad (20.18)$$

The truncation error at any step in the integration process can be estimated by Eq. (20.19).

$$E = y_{n+1} - y_{n+1}^* = \sum_{i=1}^{6} (c_i - d_i) \Delta y_i \quad (20.19)$$

The a, b, c, and d coefficients we will use were derived by Cash and Karp[1] and are shown in Table 20.1.

The only thing that remains to be done in the development of our embedded Runge-Kutta solver is to come up with a scheme to compute the value of Δx for a given step that will keep the truncation error below a specified maximum value. There are several ways to specify the maximum allowable error. You can use a constant value or evaluate the maximum allowable error as a function of the derivatives of the dependent variables. We're going to keep things simple in this example. Since the Runge-Kutta scheme is fifth-order accurate, the error should scale with Δx^5. The optimum step size can be determined from Eq. (20.20).

TABLE 20.1 Cash-Karp Coefficients

I	A_i	B_{i1}	B_{i2}	B_{i3}	B_{i4}	B_{i5}	C_i	D_i
1	0	0	0	0	0	0	$\dfrac{37}{378}$	$\dfrac{2825}{27648}$
2	$\dfrac{1}{5}$	$\dfrac{1}{5}$	0	0	0	0	0	0
3	$\dfrac{3}{10}$	$\dfrac{3}{40}$	$\dfrac{9}{40}$	0	0	0	$\dfrac{250}{621}$	$\dfrac{18575}{48384}$
4	$\dfrac{3}{5}$	$\dfrac{3}{10}$	$-\dfrac{9}{10}$	$\dfrac{6}{5}$	0	0	$\dfrac{125}{594}$	$\dfrac{13525}{55296}$
5	1	$-\dfrac{11}{54}$	$\dfrac{5}{2}$	$-\dfrac{70}{27}$	$\dfrac{35}{27}$	0	0	$\dfrac{277}{14336}$
6	$\dfrac{7}{8}$	$\dfrac{1631}{55296}$	$\dfrac{175}{512}$	$\dfrac{575}{13824}$	$\dfrac{44275}{110592}$	$\dfrac{253}{4096}$	$\dfrac{512}{1771}$	$\dfrac{1}{4}$

$$\frac{\Delta x_{optimum}}{\Delta x_{current}} = \left[\frac{E_{max}}{E_{current}}\right]^{0.2} \tag{20.20}$$

The E_{max} parameter is the maximum error or tolerance that you are willing to accept in your calculation. For a situation with more than one dependent variable, $E_{current}$ would be the maximum current error among the dependent variables.

We are now ready to write a method that implements an embedded Runge-Kutta solver. The method is called embeddedRK5() and is placed inside the ODESolver class previously described in this chapter. In many respects it is similar to the rungeKutta4() method. The embeddedRK5() method takes four arguments, an ODE object and three variables of type double defining the range, initial Δx, and error tolerance for the computation.

One principal difference between the embeddedRK5() and rungeKutta4() methods is that the embeddedRK5() method will estimate the maximum truncation error at each step in the integration. If the maximum error is greater than the tolerance, then Δx is decreased and the current step is integrated again. If the maximum error is less than the tolerance, the dependent variables are updated and Δx is increased to its optimum value.

The embeddedRK5() method source code follows.

```
public static int embeddedRK5(ODE ode, double range,
                    double dx, double tolerance) {
  double maxError;
  int i,j,k,m;

  //  Define some convenience variables to make
  //  the code more readable.
```

```java
        int numEqns = ode.getNumEqns();
        double x[] = ode.getX();
          double y[][] = ode.getY();

        // Create some local arrays

        double dy[][] = new double[6][numEqns];
        double dyTotal[] = new double[numEqns];
        double ytmp[] = new double[numEqns];
        double error[][] =
              new double[ODE.MAX_STEPS][numEqns];

        // load the Cash-Karp parameters

        double a[] = {0.0, 0.2, 0.3, 0.6, 1.0, 0.875};
        double c[] = {37.0/378.0, 0.0, 250.0/621.0,
                    125.0/594.0, 0.0, 512.0/1771.0};
        double d[] = new double[6];
        d[0] = c[0] - 2825.0/27648.0;
        d[1] = 0.0;
        d[2] = c[2] - 18575.0/48384.0;
        d[3] = c[3] - 13525.0/55296.0;
        d[4] = c[4] - 277.0/14336.0;
        d[5] = c[5] - 0.25;
        double b[][] = { {0.0, 0.0, 0.0, 0.0, 0.0},
                         {0.2, 0.0, 0.0, 0.0, 0.0},
                         {0.075, 0.225, 0.0, 0.0, 0.0},
                         {0.3, -0.9, 1.2, 0.0, 0.0},
              {-11.0/54.0, 2.5, -70.0/27.0, 35.0/27.0, 0.0},
              {1631.0/55296.0, 175.0/512.0, 575.0/13824.0,
                 44275.0/110592.0, 253.0/4096.0} };

        // Integrate the ODE over the desired range.
        // Stop if you are going to overflow the matrices

        i=1;
        while( x[i-1] < range && i < ODE.MAX_STEPS-1) {

          // Set up an iteration loop to optimize dx

          while (true) {

            // First Runge-Kutta step

            ode.getFunction(x[i-1],dy[0],y[i-1]);

            for(j=0; j<numEqns; ++j) {
              dy[0][j] *= dx;
              dyTotal[j] = c[0]*dy[0][j];
              error[i][j] = d[0]*dy[0][j];
            }

            // Runge-Kutta steps 2-6
```

```
      for(k=1; k<6; ++k) {
        for(j=0; j<numEqns; ++j) {
          ytmp[j] = y[i-1][j];
          for(m=0; m<k; ++m) {
            ytmp[j] += b[k][m]*dy[m][j];
          }
        }
        ode.getFunction(x[i-1]+a[k]*dx,dy[k],ytmp);

        for(j=0; j<numEqns; ++j) {
          dy[k][j] *= dx;
          dyTotal[j] += c[k]*dy[k][j];
          error[i][j] += d[k]*dy[k][j];
        }
      }

      //   Compute maximum error

      maxError = 0.0;
      for(j=0; j<numEqns; ++j) {
        maxError =
            Math.max(maxError, Math.abs(error[i][j]));
      }

      //   If the maximum error is greater than the
      //   tolerance, decrease delta-x and try again.
      //   Otherwise, update the variables and move on to
      //   the next point.

      if ( maxError > tolerance ) {
        dx *= Math.pow(tolerance/maxError,0.2);
      } else {
        break;
      }
    }

    //   Update the dependent variables

    for(j=0; j<numEqns; ++j) {
      y[i][j] = y[i-1][j] + dyTotal[j];
    }

    //   Increment independent variable, reset dx, and
    //   move on to the next point. Make sure you don't
    //   go past the specified range.

    x[i] = x[i-1] + dx;
    dx *= Math.pow(tolerance/maxError,0.2);
    if ( x[i]+dx > range ) {
      dx = range - x[i];
    }

    //   Go to the next dependent variable location
```

```
    ++i;
  }  //  end of outer while loop

  //  Return the number of steps computed

  return i;
}
```

Let's use the `embeddedRK5()` method to solve the same spring problem that was solved by the `rungeKutta4()` method in the earlier example. The `EmbedSpring.java` program is a driver program that creates a `SpringODE` object with the same initial values as the one from the `rungeKutta4()` method example. The ODE is solved by calling the `embeddedRK5()` method. The truncation error tolerance is set to be 1.0e-6.

```
import TechJava.MathLib.*;

public class EmbedSpring
{
  public static void main(String args[]) {

    //  Create a SpringODE object

    double mass = 1.0;
    double mu = 1.5;
    double k = 20.0;

    SpringODE ode = new SpringODE(k, mu, mass);

    //  load initial conditions.  The spring is
    //  initially stretched 0.1 meters from its
    //  equilibrium  position.

    double V[] = {-0.2};
    ode.setInitialConditions(V);

    //  Solve the ODE over the desired range with the
    //  specified tolerance and initial step size

    double dx = 0.1;
    double range = 5.0;
    double tolerance = 1.0e-6;

    int numSteps =
       ODESolver.embeddedRK5(ode, range, dx, tolerance);

    //  Print out the results

    System.out.println("i    t    dxdt    x");
    for(int i=0; i<numSteps; ++i) {
      System.out.println(
          ""+i+"  "+ode.getOneX(i)+
```

```
                    " "+ode.getOneY(i,0)+ " "+ode.getOneY(i,1));
        }
    }
}
```

The output of the `EmbedSpring` program is shown in Figure 20.3. At first glance it seems quite similar to the results generated by the `rungeKutta4()` method. The output from the `embeddedRK5()` method tracks the exact solution very closely. If you look at the distribution of points you will notice that the embedded Runge-Kutta algorithm placed more points in regions of high gradients (around the maximum and minimum amplitudes) and fewer points in the smoother regions of the curve.

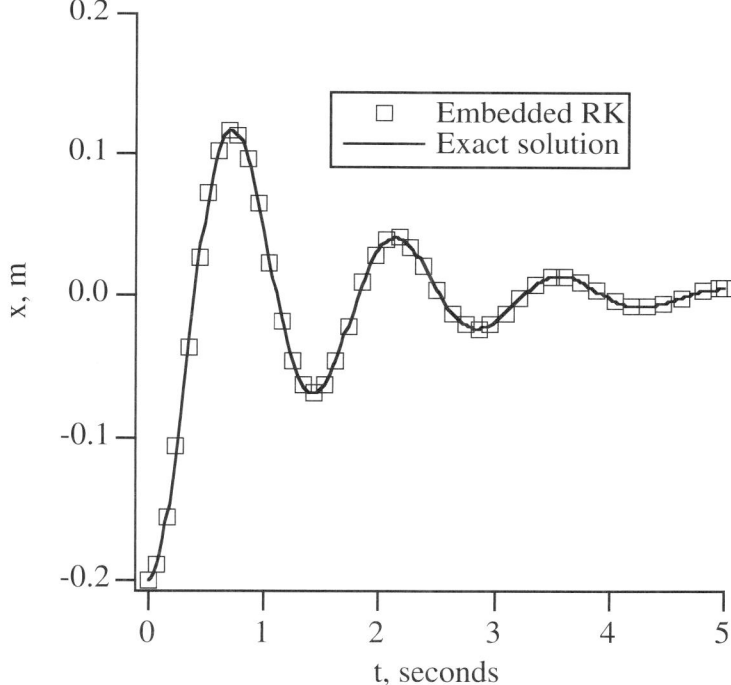

FIGURE 20.3 Spring position as a function of time

OTHER ODE SOLUTION TECHNIQUES

There are other techniques for solving initial value ODEs including Richardson extrapolation and predictor-corrector methods. We won't go into any more detail on these methods in this chapter, nor will we implement them. If you want to implement another ODE solver, the process will be the same as was used in this chapter. You would define your solver as a `public, static` method. The method would take as input arguments an ODE object and whatever additional input arguments were required. You would then write the body of the method to perform whatever solution technique you were implementing.

Two-Point Boundary Problems

Initial value problems are relatively simple to solve. All of the dependent variables are assigned values at the start of the range of integration. The solution then marches out from the starting point to whatever independent variable value is desired. The only decision is which integration algorithm to use.

With two-point boundary problems, boundary conditions are specified at both ends of the integration range. Some of the variables at each end of the integration range will be unspecified by boundary conditions. These are called *free variables*. Not only do you have to integrate the ODEs, but you also must assign values to the free variables at the beginning of the integration range such that the boundary conditions at the end of the range of integration are satisfied. Unless you make a very good initial guess, it is likely that the solution will have to be iterated. In addition to selecting an integration algorithm you must also develop an iteration scheme that will efficiently converge to the proper solution.

As you probably guessed, there are several techniques to solve two-point boundary problems. The method that we will implement in this chapter is called *shooting*.

Shooting Methods

Consider a two-point boundary problem that is to be solved from an initial independent variable value $x = x_0$ to a far-field location $x = x_e$. Not all of the dependent variables will be known at $x = x_0$ and some boundary conditions will need to be maintained at $x = x_e$. One way to solve this type of problem is by using a technique known as shooting. An initial guess is made for the free variables at $x = x_0$. The ODE is then integrated out to $x = x_e$. If the far-field boundary conditions are not met, the $x = x_0$ free variables are updated. The iteration continues until the $x = x_e$ boundary conditions are met to within a specified tolerance.

The trick with shooting methods is to develop a rapidly converging algorithm to obtain updates to the $x = x_0$ free variables. The method we will use is called multi-dimensional, globally convergent Newton-Raphson. Consider two arrays, V[] that contains the values of the free variables at the $x = x_0$ boundary and E[] that contains the difference between the computed value of the boundary condition variables at the $x = x_e$ boundary and their true boundary condition values. The size of the V[] and E[] arrays must be the same. To find an array δV[] that will zero the elements of the E[] array requires the solution of the system of equations shown in Eq. (20.21).

$$\frac{dE}{dV} \delta V = -E \qquad (20.21)$$

The updated values of the free variables at the $x = x_0$ boundary can then be obtained, Eq. (20.22).

$$V^{n+1} = V^n + \delta V \qquad (20.22)$$

Unfortunately, there is no general analytic expression for the dE/dV matrix. The matrix elements can be estimated in a finite-difference manner, as in Eq. (20.23).

$$\frac{dE}{dV} = \frac{\Delta E}{\Delta V} \qquad (20.23)$$

The process to calculate the $\Delta E/\Delta V$ matrix takes a number of steps. With an initial guess for the free variables at the $x = x_0$ boundary, integrate the ODE to get an initial value for the error vector at $x = x_e$. You then increment the first free variable at $x = x_0$ by a small amount and reintegrate the ODE to see how the E[] array values change. Subtracting the updated E[] array from the original gives you the first column of the $\Delta E/\Delta V$ matrix. You then continue the process by incrementing the other free variables at $x = x_0$ and reintegrating the ODE until the entire $\Delta E/\Delta V$ matrix is filled. You then invert the matrix and obtain the updates to the V[] array.

It may take more than one update to the V[] array until the far-field boundary conditions are satisfied. This sounds like a lot of work and it is when compared to the solution process for initial value problems. However, with a reasonably good initial guess for the free variables at $x = x_0$, the solution should converge within three to four iterations.

One final conceptual note about shooting is that sometimes if the initial guess for V[] is not very good the computed updates δV may overshoot physically allowable values. Depending on the ODE, you might get things like a square root of a negative number when you evaluate the ODE right-hand side. One way to enhance the stability of the solution process is to scale the δV updates by a number between 0 and 1. This procedure is called *under-relaxation*.

We will write an `ODEshooter()` method that will implement the ODE shooting technique we have just described. This method, like the others that preceded it in this chapter, will be placed inside the `ODESolver` class and will be a `public`, `static` method. The `ODEshooter()` method makes use of the matrix inversion method `EqnSolver.invertMatrix()` from Chapter 19 so an appropriate `import` declaration is placed at the top of the `ODESolver` class code listing.

After initializing the dependent variables at $x = x_0$, the `ODEshooter()` method solves the ODE by calling the `embeddedRK5()` method. A first calculation of the error at the $x = x_e$ boundary is performed by having the ODE object call its `getError()` method. Any ODE subclass that represents a two-point boundary problem will override the `getError()` method from the ODE class to compute error in the proper manner for that ODE.

The `ODEshooter()` method then enters a `while()` loop that updates the free variables at $x = x_0$ until the error in the far-field boundary conditions is below a specified tolerance. The `V[]` array updates are under-relaxed by a factor of 0.5. When convergence is achieved, the method exits and returns the number of dependent variable steps used to integrate the ODE. The `ODEshooter()` method source code is shown next.

```
public static int ODEshooter(ODE ode, double V[],
        double range, double dx, double tolerance) {

  //  Define some convenience variables to make
  //  the code more readable.

  int numEqns = ode.getNumEqns();
  int numVar = ode.getNumFreeVariables();
  double x[] = ode.getX();
  double y[][] = ode.getY();

  // define some local variables. The E[] array
  // holds the error at the end of the range of
  // integration.

  double E[] = new double[numVar];

  double dxInit = dx;
  double maxE, dVtotal;
  double deltaV = 0.0001;
  double underRelax = 0.5;

  int i, j, numSteps;

  double dV[][] = new double[numVar][numVar];
  double dEdV[][] = new double[numVar][numVar];
  double Etmp[] = new double[numVar];
```

```
// load initial conditions

ode.setInitialConditions(V);

// Solve the ODE over the desired range and compute
// the initial error at the end of the range

numSteps =
    ODESolver.embeddedRK5(ode, range, dx, tolerance);
ode.getError(E, y[numSteps-1]);

// If the E[]  array doesn't meet the desired
// tolerance try again with new initial conditions.

maxE = 0.0;
for(i=0; i<numVar; ++i) {
  maxE = Math.max(maxE,Math.abs(E[i]));
}

while (maxE > tolerance) {

  // Fill the dV array.  Each row of the array
  // is the original V  array with one of its
  // elements perturbed.

  for(i=0; i<numVar; ++i) {
    for(j=0; j<numVar; ++j) {
      dV[i][j] = V[j];
    }
    dV[i][i] += deltaV;
  }

  // Fill the dEdV matrix by determining how the E[]
  // elements change when one of the V[] elements is
  // incremented.

  for(j=0; j<numVar; ++j) {

    // Set initial conditions for a given row

    ode.setInitialConditions(dV[j]);
    dx = dxInit;

    // Solve ODE again with V+dVj

    numSteps =
     ODESolver.embeddedRK5(ode, range, dx, tolerance);

    // Recompute error for V+dVj.

    ode.getError(Etmp, y[numSteps-1]);

    // Compute dEdV
```

```
        for(i=0; i<numVar; ++i ) {
          dEdV[i][j] = ( Etmp[i] - E[i] )/deltaV;
        }
      }

      //   Invert dEdV matrix

      EqnSolver.invertMatrix(dEdV);

      //   Update V[] matrix. The updates to V[] are
      //   under-relaxed to enhance stability

      for(i=0; i<numVar; ++i) {
        dVtotal = 0.0;
        for(j=0; j<numVar; ++j) {
          dVtotal += -dEdV[i][j]*E[j];
        }
        V[i] += underRelax*dVtotal;
      }

      //  update initial conditions of y[][] using V[]

      ode.setInitialConditions(V);

      //   Integrate ODE with new initial conditions

      numSteps =
          ODESolver.embeddedRK5(ode, range, dx, tolerance);

      //   Compute new E[]  array and determine maximum
      //   error

      ode.getError(E, y[numSteps-1]);

      maxE = 0.0;
      for(i=0; i<numVar; ++i) {
        maxE = Math.max(maxE,Math.abs(E[i]));
      }

    } //   end of while loop

    return numSteps;
  }
```

Example Problem: Compressible Boundary Layer

For an example of a two-point boundary problem we will look at the equations that characterize a steady gas flow over a flat plate. Every gas is subject to viscous effects, the ability of one molecule of the gas to transfer momentum or energy to another molecule. The magnitude of the momentum or energy transfer is a function of the gradients of velocity or temperature in the flow. There is also a mass transfer mechanism called diffusion, but we won't concern ourselves with that here.

Consider a uniform flow of air over a flat plate. The flow velocity can have a component normal to the plate that we will call v and a component parallel to the plate that we will call u. The freestream conditions, the conditions far away from the plate, are that the flow has a constant u velocity and no v velocity. At the surface of the plate, except under very low-density conditions, both velocity components will be zero.

This sets up a velocity gradient and viscous effects come into play. The plate surface slows down the air molecules close to it. Molecules traveling at the freestream velocity try to speed up any slower molecules they encounter. The result is a velocity profile called the momentum boundary layer shown in Figure 20.4. Boundary layers have a finite thickness. At some distance above the flat plate the velocity will return to freestream conditions. The transition

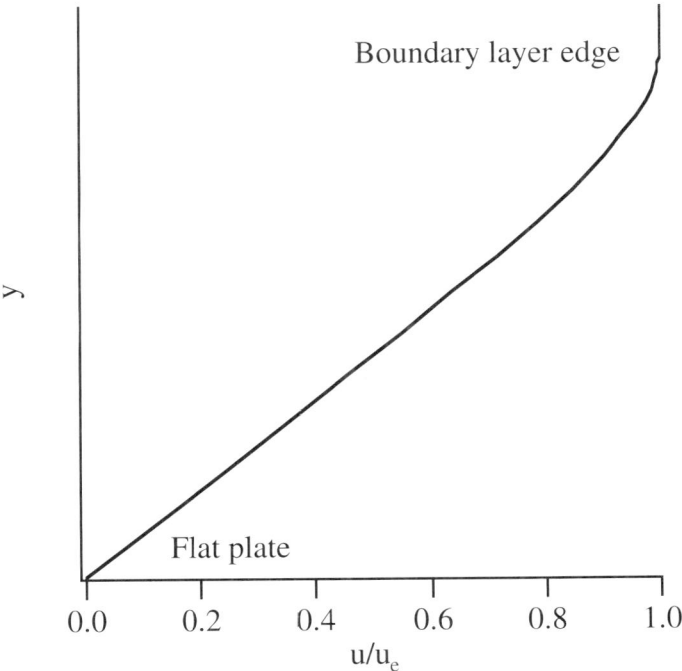

FIGURE 20.4 Boundary layer velocity profile

line between freestream and boundary layer conditions is known as the boundary layer edge.

There can be a thermal boundary layer as well. When the molecules slow down close to the flat plate, they lose kinetic energy. If the flat plate is insulated, adiabatic conditions exist and the lost kinetic energy is recovered in the form of increased temperature at the wall. If the flat plate is conducting, the kinetic energy will be transferred into the flat plate material. In either case, a temperature profile known as a thermal boundary layer is created.

The equations used to describe boundary layer flow start with the Navier-Stokes equations that represent the conservation of mass, momentum, and energy within a gas mixture. If the flow is steady and laminar, and if the boundary layer thickness is assumed to be small compared with the length scale of the flat plate, the original Navier-Stokes equations can be simplified into the following partial differential equations—

$$\frac{\partial \rho u}{\partial x} + \frac{\partial \rho v}{\partial y} = 0$$

$$\rho u \frac{\partial u}{\partial x} + \rho v \frac{\partial u}{\partial y} + \frac{\partial p}{\partial x} = \frac{\partial}{\partial y}\left(\mu \frac{\partial u}{\partial y}\right)$$

$$\frac{\partial p}{\partial y} = 0$$

$$\rho u \frac{\partial h}{\partial x} + \rho v \frac{\partial h}{\partial y} = u\frac{\partial p}{\partial x} + \frac{\partial}{\partial y}\left(\kappa \frac{\partial T}{\partial y}\right) + \mu\left(\frac{\partial u}{\partial y}\right)^2$$

(20.24)

The ρ term in Eq. (20.24) is the density of the gas and p is the pressure. The μ and κ terms are the coefficient of viscosity and thermal conductivity. The h term is the enthalpy and T is the temperature.

You could solve the system of equations given by Eq. (20.24) if you like, but you would most likely need to use a finite-difference or finite-element technique. This can be a difficult and computationally intensive process. Fortunately, the compressible boundary layer equations can be converted to a system of two ODEs with a single independent variable. For a flat plate, the independent variable is defined by Eq. (20.25).

$$\eta = \sqrt{\frac{u_e}{2\rho_e \mu_e x}} \int_{y1}^{y2} \rho dy$$

(20.25)

The e subscript in Eq. (20.25) denotes conditions at the boundary layer edge, equal to the freestream conditions for a flat plate. Two other variables,

Eq. (20.26) and Eq. (20.28) are introduced. The first is a nondimensional stream function.

$$f = \frac{\Psi}{\sqrt{2\rho_e u_e \mu_e x}} \tag{20.26}$$

It turns out that the derivative of f with respect to η is equal to the ratio of the local streamwise velocity to the boundary layer edge velocity.

$$\frac{df}{d\eta} = \frac{u}{u_e} \tag{20.27}$$

The second variable used in the transformation is the enthalpy ratio.

$$g = \frac{h}{h_e} \tag{20.28}$$

Without going through all the details of the derivation, using Eq. (20.25), (20.26), and (20.28), the conservation of mass, momentum, and energy expressions shown in Eq. (20.24) can be transformed into two ordinary differential equations.

$$\frac{d}{d\eta}\left(C\frac{d^2f}{d\eta^2}\right) + f\frac{d^2f}{d\eta^2} = 0$$
$$\frac{d}{d\eta}\left(\frac{C}{\Pr}\frac{dg}{d\eta}\right) + f\frac{dg}{d\eta} + C\frac{u_e^2}{h_e}\left(\frac{d^2f}{d\eta^2}\right)^2 = 0 \tag{20.29}$$

The Pr parameter in Eq. (20.29) is the Prandtl number, and C is given by the expression in Eq. (20.30).

$$C = \frac{\rho\mu}{\rho_e \mu_e} \tag{20.30}$$

The boundary conditions for flat plate boundary layer flow with an adiabatic surface are listed in Eq. (20.31). The physical condition corresponding to each boundary condition is shown in parentheses.

At $\eta = 0$ (flat plate surface)

$$f = 0 \quad (v = 0)$$
$$\frac{df}{d\eta} = 0 \quad (u = 0) \tag{20.31}$$
$$\frac{dg}{d\eta} = 0 \quad (\text{adiabatic wall})$$

At $\eta = \eta_e$ (boundary layer edge)

$$\frac{df}{d\eta} = 1 \quad (u = u_e)$$

$$\frac{d^2 f}{d\eta^2} = 0 \quad (\frac{du}{dy} = 0)$$

$$g = 1 \quad (h = h_e) \tag{20.32}$$

$$\frac{dg}{d\eta} = 0 \quad (\frac{dh}{dy} = 0)$$

To solve the compressible flat-plate boundary layer equations, the two ODEs shown in Eq. (20.29) are expressed as a system of five first-order differential equations.

$$\frac{d}{d\eta}\left(C \frac{d^2 f}{d\eta^2}\right) = -f \frac{d^2 f}{d\eta^2}$$

$$\frac{d}{d\eta}\left(\frac{df}{d\eta}\right) = \frac{d^2 f}{d\eta^2}$$

$$\frac{d}{d\eta}(f) = \frac{df}{d\eta} \tag{20.33}$$

$$\frac{d}{d\eta}\left(\frac{C}{\Pr} \frac{dg}{d\eta}\right) = -f \frac{dg}{d\eta} - C \frac{u_e^2}{h_e}\left(\frac{d^2 f}{d\eta^2}\right)^2$$

$$\frac{d}{d\eta}(g) = \frac{dg}{d\eta}$$

You can see from Eq. (20.33) that the first-order form of the compressible boundary layer equations has five dependent variables. From Eq. (20.31), the $\eta = 0$ boundary specifies three boundary conditions. This problem is therefore a two-point boundary problem with two free variables, one that we will solve using the shooting technique. Once we have computed the profiles of $df/d\eta$ and g, we can determine the velocity and enthalpy profiles from Eq. (20.27) and Eq. (20.28).

The CompressODE Class

The first step in the solution process is to write a class that represents the compressible boundary layer ODEs. We will name the class CompressODE. In addition to the members it inherits from the ODE class, the CompressODE class declares a number of other fields specific to the compressible boundary layer equations. These include the boundary layer edge enthalpy, velocity, and temperature, the Mach number of the freestream flow, the Prandtl number, and the *C* ratio defined in Eq. (20.30).

The `CompressODE` class defines one constructor. The constructor first calls the `ODE` class constructor passing it the numbers 5 (number of first-order ODEs) and 2 (number of free variables). The constructor then initializes the fields declared in the `CompressODE` class. Strictly speaking, the Prandtl number is a function of temperature. At low to moderate temperatures it is more or less a constant value. We use the constant value 0.75 in the `CompressODE` constructor. This was the same value used by Van Driest,[2] whose results we will compare against.

The `CompressODE` class then overrides the three sub methods declared in the `ODE` class. The `getFunction()` method is overridden to return the right-hand sides of Eq. (20.33). The `setInitialConditions()` method enforces the boundary conditions shown in Eq. (20.31). Before we override the `getError()` method we must decide how we will implement it. There are two free variables at the $\eta = 0$ boundary. There are four specified boundary conditions at the far-field boundary. Since the `V[]` and `E[]` arrays must be the same size, we must choose two of the far-field boundary conditions with which to compute the errors. The `getError()` method is written to compute the error vector based on the $df/d\eta = 1$ and $g = 1$ boundary conditions.

The `CompressODE` class source code is shown here.

```java
package TechJava.MathLib;

import TechJava.Gas.*;

public class CompressODE extends ODE
{
  double he, ue, Te, mach, Pr, C;
  double ratio1, ratio2;

  //  The CompressODE constructor calls the ODE
  //  constructor passing it some compressible
  //  boundary layer specific values. There are five
  //  first order ODEs and two free variables.

  public CompressODE(double Te, double mach) {
    super(5,2);
    this.Te = Te;
    this.mach = mach;

    he = 3.5*AbstractGas.R*Te/0.02885;
    ue = mach*Math.sqrt(1.4*AbstractGas.R*Te/0.02885);
```

```
    ratio1 = ue*ue/he;
    ratio2 = 110.4/Te;
    Pr = 0.75;
  }

  //  The getFunction() method returns the right-hand
  //  sides of the five first-order compressible
  //  boundary layer ODEs
  //    y[0] = delta(C*f'') = delta(n)*(-f*f'')
  //    y[1] = delta(f')  = delta(n)*(f'')
  //    y[2] = delta(f)   = delta(n)*(f')
  //    y[3] = delta(Cg') = delta(n)*(-Pr*f*g' -
  //                        Pr*C*(ue*ue/he)*f''*f'')
  //    y[4] = delta(g)   = delta(n)*(g')

  public void getFunction(double x, double dy[],
                          double ytmp[]) {
    C = Math.sqrt(ytmp[4])*(1.0+ratio2)/
        (ytmp[4]+ratio2);
    dy[0] = -ytmp[2]*ytmp[0]/C;
    dy[1] = ytmp[0]/C;
    dy[2] = ytmp[1];
    dy[3] = -Pr*(ytmp[2]*ytmp[3]/C +
            ratio1*ytmp[0]*ytmp[0]/C);
    dy[4] = ytmp[3]/C;
  }

  //  The getE() method returns the error, E[], in
  //  the free variables at the end of the range
  //  that was integrated.

  public void getError(double E[], double endY[]) {
    E[0] = endY[1] - 1.0;
    E[1] = endY[4] - 1.0;
  }

  // This method initializes the dependent variables
  // at the start of the integration range. The V[]
  // contains the current guess of the free variable
  // values

  public void setInitialConditions(double V[]) {
    setOneY(0, 0, V[0]);
    setOneY(0, 1, 0.0);
    setOneY(0, 2, 0.0);
    setOneY(0, 3, 0.0);
    setOneY(0, 4, V[1]);
    setOneX(0, 0.0);
  }
}
```

Solving the Compressible Boundary Layer Equations

Solving the compressible boundary layer equations for a given set of conditions is quite simple now. All we need to do is to create a `CompressODE` object and send the object to the `ODEshooter()` method. In this sample problem we are going to compute a Mach 8 boundary layer with a boundary layer edge temperature of 218.6 K. The `dx` parameter holds the initial increment value for the dependent variable (η in this case). The `V[]` array contains the initial guesses for $C\partial^2 f/\partial \eta^2$ and g at $\eta = 0$.

The class that does all this is named `ShootingCompress`. Its source code is—

```
import TechJava.MathLib.*;

public class ShootingCompress
{
  public static void main(String args[]) {

    //  Create a CompressODE object

    CompressODE ode = new CompressODE(218.6, 8.0);

    //  Solve the ODE over the desired range with the
    //  specified tolerance and initial step size.
    //  The V[] array holds the initial conditions of
    //  the free variables.

    double dx = 0.1;
    double range = 5.0;
    double tolerance = 1.0e-6;
    double V[] = {0.0826, 25.8};

    //  Solve the ODE over the desired range

    int numSteps =
      ODESolver.ODEshooter(ode, V, range, dx, tolerance);

    //  Print out the results

    System.out.println("i    eta    Cf''   f'    f");
    for(int i=0; i<numSteps; ++i) {
      System.out.println(
        ""+i+"   "+ode.getOneX(i)+"   "+ode.getOneY(i,0)+
        "   "+ode.getOneY(i,1)+"   "+ode.getOneY(i,2));
    }
    System.out.println();
    System.out.println("i    eta    Cg'    g");
    for(int i=0; i<numSteps; ++i) {
      System.out.println(
```

```
                    ""+i+"   "+ode.getOneX(i)+
            "   "+ode.getOneY(i,3)+"   "+ode.getOneY(i,4));
        }
    }
}
```

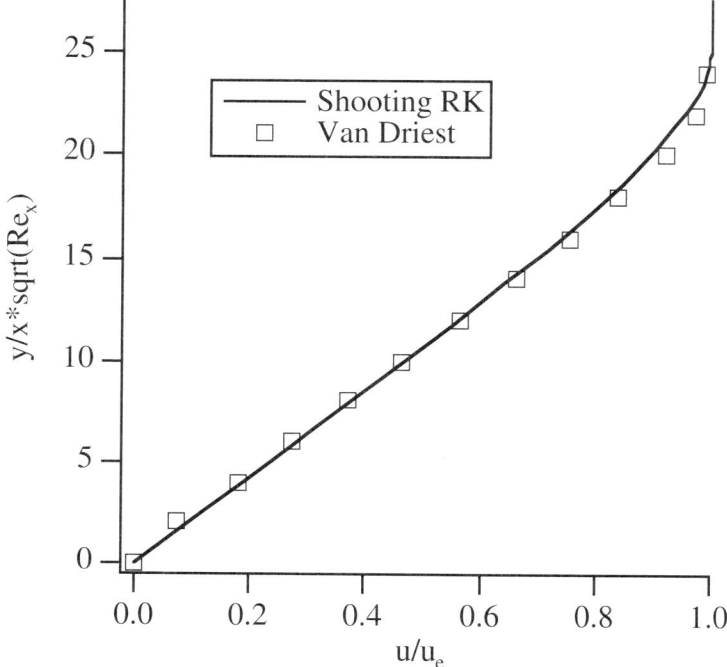

FIGURE 20.5 Velocity profile, Mach 8 boundary layer

As with the damped spring problem, it is more meaningful to show the compressible boundary layer results in plot form rather than as columns of data. Figure 20.5 shows the velocity profile computed by the shooting method as well as data from Van Driest[2] obtained by an analytical method known as Crocco's method. The two methods produce very similar velocity profile results. The independent variable, η, in Figure 20.5 has been converted into the nondimensional length $y/x \sqrt{Re_x}$, where Re_x is the Reynolds number per unit length.

The nondimensional temperature profile results are shown in Figure 20.6. There are slight discrepancies between the shooting and Van Driest data but overall the two methods produce very similar results. You can see by Figure 20.6 the effects of using an adiabatic wall boundary condition. Since energy cannot be conducted into the flat plate surface, the loss of kinetic energy near

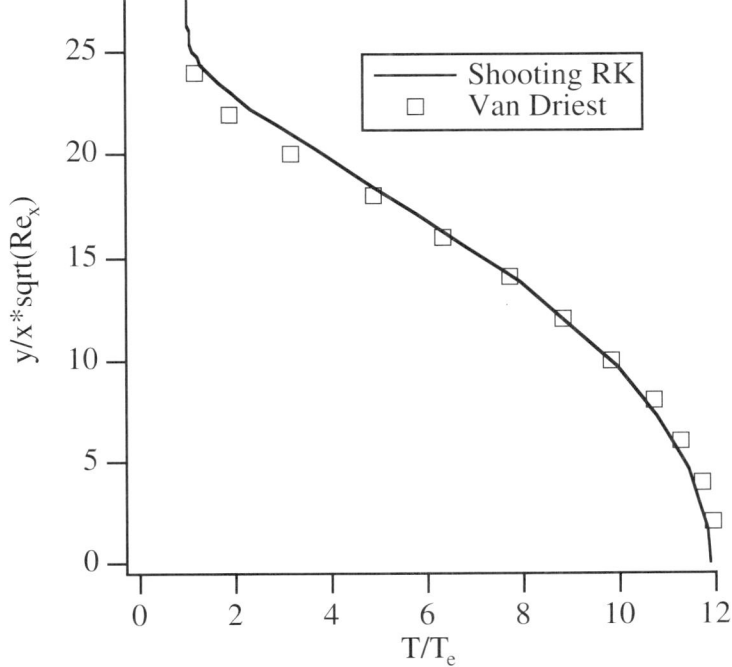

FIGURE 20.6 Temperature profile, Mach 8 boundary layer

the flat plate surface shows up as increased thermal energy. The temperature of the gas at the surface is 12 times that at the boundary layer edge.

OTHER TWO-POINT BOUNDARY SOLUTION TECHNIQUES

As with initial value problems, there are techniques other than shooting for solving two-point boundary problems. The most commonly used alternative technique is called *relaxation*. Relaxation methods divide the integration range into a 1-D grid of points. The ODE is represented by finite-difference equations that are solved at each point over the integration domain. The solution is iterated on until the required boundary conditions are met.

We won't implement a relaxation method in this chapter, but if you wanted to you probably know how to do it by now. You would define a `public`, `static` method that would take an `ODE` object as one of its input arguments. The body of the method would then implement whatever relaxation technique was desired.

PARTIAL DIFFERENTIAL EQUATIONS

So far in this chapter we have been exploring ways to solve ordinary differential equations. These are equations with one independent variable. A PDE is one that has more than one independent variable. An example of a PDE is the conservation of mass equation used in fluid dynamics. shown in Eq. (20.34).

$$\frac{\partial \rho}{\partial t} + \frac{\partial \rho u}{\partial x} + \frac{\partial \rho v}{\partial y} = 0 \qquad (20.34)$$

As you probably guessed, solving the typical PDE is more complicated and more treacherous than solving an ODE. Another complicating factor is that many physical models involve coupled sets of PDEs. The most commonly used ways to solve PDEs are by using finite-difference or finite-element techniques. The computational domain is subdivided into smaller domains called *cells*. The cells will characterize a 1-, 2-, or 3-D space. The collection of cells that model the computational domain is called a *grid*. The PDEs are then discretized and solved at each cell. A cumulative record of the solution error is computed. The solution is iterated on until the error falls below a certain convergence criteria.

A detailed discussion of methods to solve partial differential equations is beyond the scope and intent of this book. There are entire books devoted to the subject of solving PDEs. The Java language is well suited to developing methods to solve PDEs. Classes would be defined to represent the PDEs, the computational grid, and each cell within the computational grid. The PDE solvers themselves could be written as `public static` methods and stored in a package that could be readily accessed by other programs.

REFERENCES

1. Shampine, L. F., and M. K., Gordon, *Computer Solution of Ordinary Differential Equations: The Initial Value Problem,* W.H. Freeman Press, San Francisco, 1975.

2. Van Driest, E. R., "Investigation of Laminar Boundary Layer in Compressible Fluids Using the Crocco Method," NACA TN-2597, Jan. 1952.

21

INTEGRATION OF FUNCTIONS

The task of finding the area enclosed by a given curve is an old problem. The ancient Egyptians, for example, tried to find the area of a circular field by relating it to the area of a square field. The search for a solution to the area problem gave rise to the field of integral calculus, where the integral of a function between two limits is equal to the area under that function. In modern science and engineering, integral equations are widely used to model physical phenomena including things such as aerodynamic analysis and radiation computations.

Integral equations can be divided into two types—proper and improper. A proper integral is one with finite integration limits and whose function can be evaluated at every point along the range of integration. An improper integral is one that has a singularity at some point in the range of integration and/or has one or both integration limits equal to positive or negative infinity. In some cases you can recast an improper integral into a proper one by using a change of variables.

In this chapter we will discuss numerical techniques to solve both proper and improper integrals. In either case the algorithms involve deriving a polynomial expression that, when evaluated, approximates the integral value. The solution process involves dividing the integration range into subelements. Generally speaking, the more subelements used the greater the precision of the final result. Many of the numerical techniques are iterative, beginning with an initial division of the integration range and then refining the solution by increasing the number of subelements until the change in the solution is less than a specified error tolerance.

At the end of the chapter we will briefly discuss the more general families of integrals known as Fredholm and Volterra integrals. We will then use one of the solution methods developed earlier in the chapter to determine the lift and moment coefficient of a NACA 2412 airfoil according to thin airfoil theory. The specific topics we will discuss in this chapter are—

- Trapezoidal algorithms
- Simpson's rule
- Solving improper integrals
- Gaussian quadrature formulas
- General integral types
- Example: thin airfoil theory

GENERAL COMMENTS

The general form of a simple integral equation is shown in Eq. (21.1).

$$y = \int_a^b f(x)dx \tag{21.1}$$

Eq. (21.1) is an example of a larger class of integrals known as Fredholm integrals of the first kind. Fredholm integrals are discussed in more detail at the end of this chapter, but for the time being let's consider the simple integral shown in Eq. (21.1). The evaluation of the integral equation computes the area under the curve $f(x)$ from $x = a$ to $x = b$.

If the integration limits a and b are finite numbers and the function $f(x)$ is nonsingular over the integration range, the integral is termed a proper integral. Proper integrals are usually solved using *closed* techniques, those that evaluate the function at the endpoints, $f(a)$ and $f(b)$. If either integration limit is ∞ or $-\infty$, or if there is a singularity in the function $f(x)$ anywhere in the integration range, the integral is improper. An improper integral that evaluates to a finite value is convergent. Convergent improper integrals can be solved using what are known as *open* techniques that only evaluate $f(x)$ between $x = a$ and $x = b$. An improper integral that is infinite is a divergent integral. Obviously, divergent integrals cannot be solved because their values diverge.

Some integrals have precise, closed-form solutions. For those that do not, numerical methods have been developed to approximate the integral value. The numerical methods we will discuss in this chapter approximate the integral value by developing a polynomial expression based on values of the function being integrated at discrete locations along the range of integration. We will start by examining trapezoidal algorithms.

TRAPEZOIDAL ALGORITHMS

Trapezoidal algorithms are a general class of solution methods used to estimate the area under the curve $f(x)$ from $x = a$ to $x = b$. The algorithms we will discuss in this section will be for proper integrals whose function $f(x)$ can be evaluated at all points between a and b. A typical curve is shown in Figure 21.1.

The simplest way to approximate the area under $f(x)$ is to draw a line between $f(a)$ and $f(b)$ and compute the area under the resulting trapezoidal figure.

$$y = \int_a^b f(x)dx = \Delta x \left[\frac{1}{2} f(a) + \frac{1}{2} f(b) \right] \qquad (21.2)$$

The Δx term in Eq. (21.2) is the width of the trapezoid and for the two-point trapezoid method is given by the expression $\Delta x = b - a$. Of course for most curves, Eq. (21.2) is not a very good approximation. Looking at the curves in Figure 21.1, we are missing the area between the actual curve and the

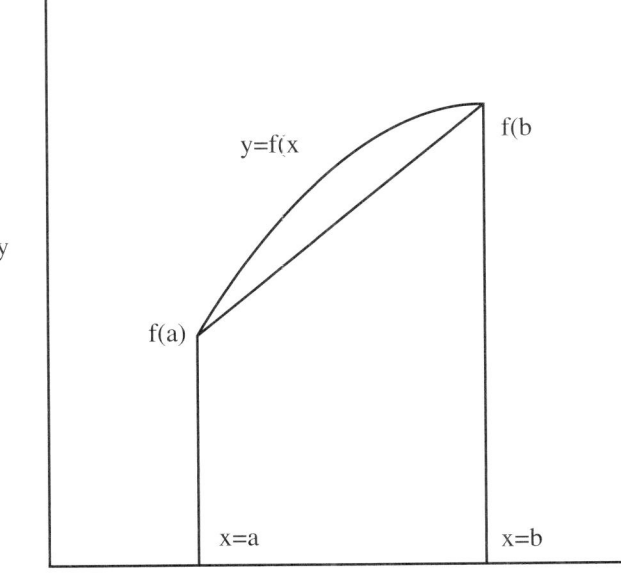

FIGURE 21.1 Two-point trapezoidal method

straight line. To improve the accuracy of the solution, we can divide the range of integration into two sections at the midpoint x location between $x = b$ and $x = a$. In this case, we have to compute the area of two trapezoids, and the approximate value of the integral becomes the following.

$$y = \int_a^b f(x)dx = \Delta x \left[\frac{1}{2} f(a) + f\left(\frac{a+b}{2}\right) + \frac{1}{2} f(b) \right] \quad (21.3)$$

In Eq. (21.3), the width of each of the two trapezoids is half as large as when only one trapezoid was considered so $\Delta x = (b - a)/2$. You can easily see that Eq. (21.3) can be extended to a general form with an arbitrary number of divisions of Δx.

$$y = \int_a^b f(x)dx = \Delta x \left[\frac{1}{2} f_1 + f_2 + f_3 + \ldots + f_{N-1} + \frac{1}{2} f_N \right] \quad (21.4)$$

In Eq. (21.4) $\Delta x = (b - a)/(N - 1)$ where N is the number of trapezoids considered between $x = a$ and $x = b$. Eq. (21.4) is called the *trapezoidal method*. It is a second-order method because its error is proportional to $1/N^2$. One thing to note about the trapezoidal method is that the Δx increments are uniform over the entire integration range.

But how do you know how many times to divide up the integration range for a given integral equation? You keep adding points until the computed integral value changes less than a specified convergence tolerance. If you are clever about how you add points, you can reuse the values from the previous approximation. For example, consider an integration range between $x = 0$ and $x = 1$. If three points are used the expression to evaluate is the following.

$$y_1 = \frac{1}{2} \left[\frac{1}{2} f(0) + f\left(\frac{1}{2}\right) + \frac{1}{2} f(1) \right] \quad (21.5)$$

Keep in mind when looking at Eq. (21.5) that $\Delta x = (b - a)/2 = (1 - 0)/2 = 1/2$. If you add two additional points for the next approximation, the expression becomes Eq. (21.6).

$$y_2 = \frac{1}{4} \left[\frac{1}{2} f(0) + f\left(\frac{1}{4}\right) + f\left(\frac{1}{2}\right) + f\left(\frac{3}{4}\right) + \frac{1}{2} f(1) \right] = \frac{1}{2} y_1 + \frac{1}{4} \left[f\left(\frac{1}{4}\right) + f\left(\frac{3}{4}\right) \right] \quad (21.6)$$

Adding four additional points for the next approximation yields Eq. (21.7).

$$y_3 = \frac{1}{8} \left[\frac{1}{2} f(0) + f\left(\frac{1}{8}\right) + f\left(\frac{1}{4}\right) + f\left(\frac{3}{8}\right) + f\left(\frac{1}{2}\right) + f\left(\frac{5}{8}\right) + f\left(\frac{3}{4}\right) + f\left(\frac{7}{8}\right) + \frac{1}{2} f(1) \right]$$

$$= \frac{1}{2} y_2 + \frac{1}{8} \left[f\left(\frac{1}{8}\right) + f\left(\frac{3}{8}\right) + f\left(\frac{5}{8}\right) + f\left(\frac{7}{8}\right) \right] \quad (21.7)$$

You can see that a pattern is developing. If you start by adding one point to the two-point trapezoidal approximation and then double the number of additional points with each iteration, the next approximation to the integral is one half the previous approximation plus the factors due to the additional points. An equation for a general update to an integral approximation is shown in Eq. (21.8).

$$y_n = \frac{1}{2} y_{n-1} + \Delta x \sum_{j=1}^{2^{n-1}} f\left(\frac{2j-1}{2^n}\right) \qquad (21.8)$$

where

$$\Delta x = \frac{b-a}{2^n} \qquad (21.9)$$

Now let's write a method to implement the trapezoidal method. As we did with our system of equation and differential equation solvers, the trapezoidal method will be defined as a `public`, `static` method and its name will be `trapezoidal()`. The method will be defined in a class named `Integrator`. This is a mathematical routine so the `Integrator` class will be placed in the `TechJava.MathLib` package.

The `trapezoidal()` method takes four arguments. The first is a `Function` object that represents the mathematical function being integrated. We'll discuss the `Function` class in more detail later in this section. The second and third arguments define the range of integration. The fourth argument defines the convergence criteria for the iteration that will be performed.

After defining some variables, the `trapezoidal()` method computes an approximation to the integral using the two-point trapezoidal algorithm shown in Eq. (21.2). Subsequent (and better) approximations are produced by successively adding points to the integration range according to Eq. (21.8). When the change in the computed value of the integral is less than the specified convergence tolerance, the method returns. If the iteration does not converge, the value `12345.6` is returned.

The `trapezoidal()` method source code is—

```
package TechJava.MathLib;

public class Integrator
{
    public static double trapezoidal(Function function,
            double start, double end, double tolerance) {
        double dx = end - start;
        double value, oldValue, sum, scale;
        int maxIter = 20;
```

```
    //  Compute an initial value for the integral using
    //   the two-point trapezoidal rule.

    value = 0.5*dx*( function.getValue(start) +
                     function.getValue(end) );

    // Subdivide the integration range by adding more
    // points, first 1 point, then two more, then four
    // more and so on. Recompute the integral value
    // each time. If the solution converges, return the
    // value.

    for(int i=0; i<maxIter; ++i) {
      sum = 0.0;
      scale = Math.pow(0.5,i+1);
      for(int j=0; j<Math.pow(2,i); ++j) {
        sum += function.getValue(
                    start + scale*(2*j + 1.0)*dx);
      }

      oldValue = value;
      value = 0.5*value + scale*dx*sum;

      if ( Math.abs(value-oldValue) <=
           tolerance*Math.abs(oldValue) ) {
        return value;
      }
    }

    //  Solution did not converge

    return 12345.6;
  }
}
```

The `trapezoidal()` method makes use of a reference to a `Function` object. The `Function` class is defined to be the abstract parent class of classes that represent mathematical functions. The class declares one method named `getValue()` that simply returns the value of the function evaluated at a given independent variable value. The `Function` class listing is—

```
package TechJava.MathLib;

public abstract class Function
{
   abstract double getValue(double u);
}
```

Let's test the `trapezoidal()` method by having it integrate two mathematical functions. Both functions have an exact, closed-form solution, so an exact value of the integral can be computed. The two functions, their integral solutions, and the numerical values of their solutions are shown in Eq. (21.10) and Eq. (2.11). In Eq. (21.11), if $a = 2$, $y = 7.797853348$.

$$y = \int_{x=2}^{4} x\ln(x)dx = \frac{x^2}{2}\left(\ln(x) - \frac{1}{2}\right)\bigg|_{2}^{4} = 6.704060528 \quad (21.10)$$

$$y = \int_{x=0}^{3} \sqrt{x^2 + a^2}\, dx = x\frac{\sqrt{x^2 + a^2}}{2} + \frac{a^2}{2}\ln(x + \sqrt{x^2 + a^2})\bigg|_{0}^{3} \quad (21.11)$$

To use the `trapezoidal()` method on these functions, we will have to create two `Function` subclasses to represent the functions. The `LogFunction` class encapsulates Eq. (21.10). Its code listing is shown here.

```
package TechJava.MathLib;

// This class represents the function
//   y = u*ln(u)

public class LogFunction extends Function
{
   public double getValue(double u) {
      return u*Math.log(u);
   }
}
```

The `SqrtFunction` class represents the expression shown in Eq. (21.11) and here is its source code.

```
package TechJava.MathLib;

// This class represents the function
//   y = sqrt(u^2 + a^2)

public class SqrtFunction extends Function
{
   private double a;

   public SqrtFunction(double a) {
      this.a = a;
   }

   public double getValue(double u) {
      return Math.sqrt(u*u + a*a);
   }
}
```

All that remains is to write a driver program that will send the appropriate input to the `trapezoidal()` method and display the results. The `TestTrap` class performs this function. It simply creates a `Function` subclass object and sends a reference to the object to the `trapezoidal()` method. The computed integral value is then printed to standard output. The `TestTrap` class source code is shown next.

```
import TechJava.MathLib.*;

public class TestTrap
{
  public static void main(String args[]) {

    double value;

    //  Integrate the function y = x*ln(x) from
    //  x=2 to x=4 with an error tolerance of 1.0e-4

    LogFunction function = new LogFunction();
    value = Integrator.trapezoidal(
                    function,2.0,4.0,1.0e-4);
    System.out.println("value = "+value);

    //  Integrate the function y = sqrt(x^2 + 2^2) from
    //  x=0 to x=3 with an error tolerance of 1.0e-4

    SqrtFunction function2 = new SqrtFunction(2.0);
    value = Integrator.trapezoidal(
                    function2,0.0,3.0,1.0e-4);
    System.out.println("value = "+value);
  }
}
```

Output—

```
value = 6.704116936052852
value = 7.798005701125523
```

The results from the `trapezoidal()` method are the same as the exact results to within four decimal places, which is the value to which the convergence tolerance was set.

SIMPSON'S RULE

The trapezoidal algorithm is a second-order function integration technique. There are many other integration schemes with the same general form as Eq. (21.4). A commonly used example is the fourth-order technique known as Simpson's rule.

$$y = \int_a^b f(x)dx = \Delta x \left[\frac{1}{3}f_1 + \frac{4}{3}f_2 + \frac{2}{3}f_3 + \ldots + \frac{4}{3}f_{N-1} + \frac{1}{3}f_N \right] \quad (21.12)$$

In Eq. (21.12), the 4/3 and 2/3 factors alternate for the interior points and $\Delta x = (b - a)/(N - 1)$. The number of divisions, N, must be odd since Simpson's rule uses parabolas rather than lines to approximate the intervals.

Simpson's rule shares a common characteristic with the trapezoidal algorithm in that one approximation can be used as a building block toward a more accurate approximation. In the case of Simpson's rule, this feature is accomplished by adding three times the points that were added in the previous approximation. Another interesting feature of Simpson's rule is that the expression for any given level of approximation is related to the corresponding trapezoidal rule expressions. For example, consider an integration range between $x = 0$ and $x = 1$. If you multiply 4/3 times Eq. (21.6) and subtract 1/3 times Eq. (21.5) you obtain the following expression.

$$\frac{4}{3} y_2 - \frac{1}{3} y_1 = \frac{1}{4}\left[\frac{1}{3}f(0) + \frac{4}{3}f\left(\frac{1}{4}\right) + \frac{2}{3}f\left(\frac{1}{2}\right) + \frac{4}{3}f\left(\frac{3}{4}\right) + \frac{1}{3}f(1)\right] \quad (21.13)$$

Eq. (21.13) is the five-point version of Simpson's rule. Indeed, the Simpson's rule value at any given level of refinement can always be expressed in terms of the corresponding trapezoidal expressions.

$$S_n = \frac{4}{3} y_n - \frac{1}{3} y_{n-1} \quad (21.14)$$

The S term in Eq. (21.14) is Simpson's rule's evaluation of the integral and the y terms are the trapezoidal approximations.

Using Eq. (21.14) it is very easy to implement Simpson's rule with only slight modifications to the `trapezoidal()` method. We will call our Simpson's rule method `simpsonsRule()` and place it inside the `Integrator` class. The method computes successive approximations to the integral function with the trapezoidal rule and uses the trapezoidal results to compute Simpson's rule approximations according to Eq. (21.14).

The method takes the same input arguments as the `trapezoidal()` method. After declaring some variables, the method computes initial values of the trapezoidal and Simpson's rule approximations. The `simpsonsRule()` method then goes through the same iteration sequence as the `trapezoidal()` method. Points are added to the integration domain, each iteration adding twice as many points as the one before it. The Simpson's rule approximation is computed from the current and previous trapezoidal values. When the Simpson's rule values converge to within a certain tolerance, the method returns.

The `simpsonsRule()` method source code is—

```
public static double simpsonsRule(Function function,
        double start, double end, double tolerance) {
  double dx = end - start;
  double value, oldValue, sum, scale;
  double valueSimpson, oldValueSimpson;
  int maxIter = 20;

  //  Set initial values for the trapezoidal
  //  method (value) and Simpson's rule (valueSimpson)

  value = 0.5*dx*( function.getValue(start) +
                   function.getValue(end) );
  valueSimpson = 1.0e+6;

  //  Subdivide the integration range by adding more
  //  points, first one point, then two more, then
  //  four more, and so on. Recompute the extended
  //  trapezoidal value and the Simpson's rule value.
  //  If the Simpson's rule value converges, return
  //  the value.

  for(int i=0; i<maxIter; ++i) {
    sum = 0.0;
    scale = Math.pow(0.5,i+1);
    for(int j=0; j<Math.pow(2,i); ++j) {
      sum += function.getValue(
               start + scale*(2*j + 1.0)*dx);
    }

    oldValue = value;
    value = 0.5*value + scale*dx*sum;
    oldValueSimpson = valueSimpson;
    valueSimpson = (4.0*value - oldValue)/3.0;

    if ( Math.abs(valueSimpson-oldValueSimpson) <=
         tolerance*Math.abs(oldValueSimpson) ) {
      return valueSimpson;
    }
  }

  //  Solution did not converge

  return 12345.6;
}
```

Let's apply the `simpsonRule()` method to the same two problems as were solved by the `trapezoidal()` method. The driver to do this computation is called `TestSimpson.java` and its source code is shown here.

```java
import TechJava.MathLib.*;

public class TestSimpson
{
  public static void main(String args[]) {

    double value;

    //  Integrate the function y = x*ln(x) from
    //   x=2 to x=4 with an error tolerance of 1.0e-4

    LogFunction function = new LogFunction();
    value = Integrator.simpsonsRule(
                      function,2.0,4.0,1.0e-4);
    System.out.println("value = " + value);

    //  Integrate the function y = sqrt(x^2 + 2^2) from
    //   x=0 to x=3 with an error tolerance of 1.0e-4

    SqrtFunction function2 = new SqrtFunction(2.0);
    value = Integrator.simpsonsRule(
                      function2,0.0,3.0,1.0e-4);
    System.out.println("value = " + value);

  }
}
```

Output—

```
value = 6.704064541919408
value = 7.7978469366358025
```

The `simpsonsRule()` method provides better accuracy than the `trapezoidal()` method with fewer iterations and function evaluations required to achieve a converged solution. The `simpsonsRule()` method results match the exact results to eight and five decimal places respectively. The `simpsonsRule()` method converged in three iterations requiring nine function evaluations. The `trapezoidal()` method, on the other hand, required five iterations and 65 function evaluations to achieve convergence.

SOLVING IMPROPER INTEGRALS

So far in this chapter, we have been exploring methods to solve proper integrals, expressions where the function can be evaluated across the entire integration range and where the limits of integration are finite numbers. Now we turn to the issue of solving improper integrals. If you recall, an improper integral is one that either has an infinite integration limit or one or more singularities in the range of integration.

In some cases, you can turn an improper integral into a proper one and then apply the trapezoidal or Simpson's rule methods. If one or both of the integration limits is positive or negative infinity you can sometimes perform a change of variables to eliminate the infinite limit. For example, the transformation in Eq. (21.15) could be performed on an integral with an upper integration limit of ∞ to convert the integral from improper to proper.

$$y = \int_a^\infty f(x)dx = \int_0^{\frac{1}{a}} \frac{1}{t^2} f\left(\frac{1}{t}\right) dt \qquad (21.15)$$

Eq. (21.15) would require that the function $f(x)$ decrease faster than $1/x^2$ as $x \to \infty$. A similar transformation could be achieved for an integration limit of $-\infty$. If both limits are infinity or if one is infinity and the other 0, the best thing to do is to split the integration into pieces and apply the change of variables to one or both.

Now let's look at the case where the integration limits are finite but there is a singularity at one of the limits. We can't use the trapezoidal or Simpson's rule methods because they evaluate the function at the integration limits. Fortunately, there is a family of what are called *open* formulas that approximate an integral using only points interior to the integration limits. The algorithm we will implement in this chapter is called the *midpoint rule* and is given by the expression in Eq. (21.16).

$$y = \int_a^b f(x)dx = \Delta x \left[f_{\frac{3}{2}} + f_{\frac{5}{2}} + f_{\frac{7}{2}} + \ldots + f_{N-\frac{1}{2}} \right] \qquad (21.16)$$

The midpoint method is second-order accurate similar to the trapezoidal algorithm. It is called a midpoint method because the function evaluations are performed midway between the Δx intervals. For example, consider an integration domain between $x = 0$ and $x = 1$. A three-point trapezoidal algorithm would evaluate the function at $x = 0$, $x = 1/2$, and $x = 1$. To model that same situation with the midpoint rule, you would evaluate the equation at $x = 1/4$ and $x = 3/4$.

$$y_1 = \int_a^b f(x)dx = \frac{1}{2}\left[f\left(\frac{1}{4}\right) + f\left(\frac{3}{4}\right)\right] \qquad (21.17)$$

As with the trapezoid and Simpson's rule methods, a more accurate midpoint solution can be obtained by adding more evaluation points. Once again, if you increase the number of points wisely you can reuse previous evaluations of $f(x)$. For example, let's say you start with the two-point midpoint formula shown in Eq. (21.17). If you want to reuse the two function evaluations, the next level in the approximation uses six points (adds four to the two existing points). The six-point midpoint method is defined by the expression in Eq. (21.18).

$$y_2 = \frac{1}{6}\left[f\left(\frac{1}{12}\right) + f\left(\frac{1}{4}\right) + f\left(\frac{5}{12}\right) + f\left(\frac{7}{12}\right) + f\left(\frac{3}{4}\right) + f\left(\frac{11}{12}\right)\right]$$
$$= \frac{1}{3}y_1 + \frac{1}{6}\left[f\left(\frac{1}{12}\right) + f\left(\frac{5}{12}\right) + f\left(\frac{7}{12}\right) + f\left(\frac{11}{12}\right)\right]$$
(21.18)

To reuse the function evaluations from the six-point level, the next level in the approximation would add 12 points to the existing six for an 18-point midpoint algorithm.

$$y_3 = \frac{1}{18}\left[f\left(\frac{1}{36}\right) + f\left(\frac{3}{36}\right) + f\left(\frac{5}{36}\right) + \ldots + f\left(\frac{33}{36}\right) + f\left(\frac{35}{36}\right)\right]$$
$$y_3 = \frac{1}{3}y_2 + \frac{1}{18}\left[f\left(\frac{1}{36}\right) + f\left(\frac{5}{36}\right) + f\left(\frac{7}{36}\right) + f\left(\frac{11}{36}\right) + f\left(\frac{13}{36}\right)\right.$$
$$\left. + \ldots + f\left(\frac{29}{36}\right) + f\left(\frac{31}{36}\right) + f\left(\frac{35}{36}\right)\right]$$
(21.19)

Once again, we can see a pattern developing. Each level in the midpoint approximation adds three times the number of points that were added at the previous level. The value at each new level of approximation is equal to one-third the value at the previous approximation added to the contributions of the additional points added at the current level.

The midpoint method can evaluate an integral with a singularity at one or both of the integration limits, but what happens if a singularity occurs in the middle of the range of integration. The answer is to split the range of integration into two pieces at the singular point. The singularity now occurs at one of the integration limits and the midpoint methodology can be applied.

We will implement the midpoint technique in a method named `midpoint()` that will be defined in the `Integrator` class. The method will take the same four input arguments as the `trapezoidal()` and `simpsonsRule()` methods. The first argument is a reference to a `Function` object that is used to evaluate the function being integrated. The second and third arguments are the integration limits. The fourth argument is the convergence tolerance.

After declaring some variables, the method computes a two-point midpoint approximation to the integral equation. It then refines the integral value with successive approximations adding points to the integration domain with each approximation. The first iteration adds four points, the second adds 12 points, the third adds 36 points, and so on. If the integration value converges, the method returns the value.

Here is the `midpoint()` method source code.

```
public static double midpoint(Function function,
        double start, double end, double tolerance) {
  double dx = end - start;
  double value, oldValue, sum, temp;
  double scale = 1.0/3.0;
  int numPoints, numPairs;
  int maxIter = 20;

  //  Start with a two-point midpoint
  //  evaluation.

  value = 0.5*dx*(
            function.getValue(start + 0.25*dx) +
            function.getValue(end - 0.25*dx) );

  //  Refine the solution by adding points to the
  //  integration domain. Each iteration adds three
  //  times as many points as the previous iteration.
  //  When the solution converges, return the result.

  for(int i=0; i<maxIter; ++i) {

    numPoints = 4*(int)Math.pow(3,i);
    numPairs = (numPoints - 2)/2;
    temp = 1.0/(3.0*numPoints);

    //  Add the two endpoint values to the sum

    sum = function.getValue(start + temp*dx) +
            function.getValue(end - temp*dx);

    //  Add in each pair to the sum

    for(int j=0; j<numPairs; ++j) {
      sum = sum +
         function.getValue(start + (6*j + 5)*temp*dx) +
         function.getValue(start + (6*j + 7)*temp*dx);
    }

    oldValue = value;
    value = value/3.0 +
          0.5*Math.pow(scale,i+1)*dx*sum;

    if ( Math.abs(value-oldValue) <=
         tolerance*Math.abs(oldValue) ) {
      return value;
    }
  }
```

```
    //  Solution did not converge

    return 12345.6;
}
```

Let's test the `midpoint()` method by applying it to solve two integral equations. Midpoint methods can also be applied to proper integrals, so the first equation to be solved will be the logarithmic integral in Eq. (21.10). The `midpoint()` method will then be applied to the following improper integral.

$$y = \int_{2}^{3} \frac{dx}{\sqrt{x-2}} \qquad (21.20)$$

The integral shown in Eq. (21.20) has a singularity at $x = 2$, but is convergent and has a value of $y = 2$. To represent this function, we will define another `Function` subclass called the `SqrtFunction2` class. Its code listing is—

```
package TechJava.MathLib;

//  This class represents the function
//   y = 1/sqrt(x-2)

public class SqrtFunction2 extends Function
{
   public double getValue(double u) {
       return 1.0/Math.sqrt(u-2.0);
   }
}
```

Next we'll create a driver program similar to the ones developed in the previous sections. The code will simply create the proper `Function` subclass object, call the `midpoint()` method, and display the result. The class is called `TestMidpoint` and its source code is—

```
import TechJava.MathLib.*;

public class TestMidpoint
{
  public static void main(String args[]) {

    double value;

    //  Integrate the function y = x*ln(x) from
    //   x=2 to x=4 with an error tolerance of 1.0e-4

    LogFunction function = new LogFunction();
    value = Integrator.midpoint(
                       function,2.0,4.0,1.0e-4);
    System.out.println("value = " + value);
```

```
            //  Integrate the function y = 1/sqrt(x-2) from
            //   x=2 to x=3 with an error tolerance of 1.0e-4

            SqrtFunction2 function2 = new SqrtFunction2();
            value = Integrator.midpoint(
                            function2,2.0,3.0,1.0e-4);
            System.out.println("value = " + value);
        }
    }
```

Output—

```
value = 6.7040209108022335
value = 1.9998044225262488
```

The `midpoint()` method successfully evaluated the integrals to four-decimal place precision. Improper integrals are tougher to compute and generally take significantly more iterations to achieve convergence. In this example, three iterations were required for the proper logarithmic integral but 14 were necessary to converge the improper integral computation.

GAUSSIAN QUADRATURE METHODS

The three techniques to solve integral equations that we have implemented so far in this chapter divide the integration domain into constant-sized increments of Δx. This is acceptable for smoothly varying functions but may be inefficient or even inaccurate for functions with widely varying slopes. In this case, you would want to use a variable step size with small Δx increments in regions of high gradients and larger Δx increments in smoothly varying regions.

The trapezoidal, Simpson's rule, and midpoint methods are really specialized cases of a more general class of integration techniques called *Gaussian quadrature formulas*. Gaussian quadrature formulas assume that an integral equation can be approximated by a summation of weights multiplied by function evaluations at various x locations along the integration domain, as shown in Eq. (21.21).

$$y = \int_a^b W(x)f(x)dx = \sum_{j=1}^{N} w_j f(x_j) \qquad (21.21)$$

The x locations at which the function is evaluated are called the *abscissas*. The coefficients in front of the function evaluations are called the *weights*. The determination of the weights depends on the choice for the $W(x)$ function. There are a number of classical forms for $W(x)$, each designed to be used for a certain type of integral equation. In this section, we will work with a commonly used form called the *Gauss-Legendre formula,* which assumes that $W(x) = 1$.

The implementation of the Gauss-Legendre formula requires two methods, one to compute the weights and abscissas and a second to integrate a specified function. You could alternately use a hard-coded array of weight and abscissa data, but evaluating this data directly gives you more flexibility in choosing the number of points to be considered in the integration domain.

Without going into all of the details, the `computeGaussWeights()` method uses Newton's method to determine the roots of the orthogonal polynomial equation associated with the Gauss-Legendre formula. The weights and abscissas are computed from the polynomial roots and are normalized for an integration ranging from $x = 0$ to $x = 1$. The weights and abscissas can be applied to any integration domain by multiplying the resulting integral value by $b - a$, where a and b are the limits of integration.

The `computeGaussWeights()` method source code follows.

```
public static void computeGaussWeights(
          double x[], double w[], int numPoints) {
  int i,j,m;
  double z, zOld, root, p3, p2, p1;
  double EPS = 1.0e-10;

  //  The weights and abscissa values are normalized
  //  for an integration range between 0 and 1. The
  //  values are symmetric about x=0.5 so you only
  //  have to compute half of them.

  m = (numPoints + 1)/2;

  //  Compute the Legendre polynomial, p1, at point
  //  z using Newton's method.

  for(i=0; i<m; ++i) {
    z = Math.cos(Math.PI*(i+0.75)/(numPoints+0.5));
    do {
      p1 = 1.0;
      p2 = 0.0;
      for(j=0; j<numPoints; ++j) {
        p3 = p2;
        p2 = p1;
        p1 = ((2.0*(j+1) - 1.0)*z*p2 - j*p3)/
             (j+1.0);
      }
      root = numPoints*(z*p1 - p2)/(z*z - 1.0);
      zOld = z;
      z = zOld - p1/root;
    } while ( Math.abs(z-zOld) > EPS);
```

```
        // Compute the weights and abscissas. The values
        //   are symmetric about the point z=0.5

        x[i] = 0.5*(1.0 - z);
        x[numPoints-1-i] = 0.5*(1.0 + z);
        w[i] = 1.0/((1.0- z*z)*root*root);
        w[numPoints-1-i] = w[i];
    }
}
```

Once we have the weight and abscissa data, the rest of the implementation is simple. The `gaussLegendre()` method integrates a function using the Gauss-Legendre weighting coefficients and abscissa data. The method takes the same four input arguments as the `trapezoidal()`, `simpsonsRule()`, and `midpoint()` methods.

After declaring some variables, the method enters an iteration loop. Starting with 10 points in the integration domain, the `computeGaussWeights()` method is called to obtain the 10-point Gauss-Legendre weights and abscissas. The integral value is then obtained by summing up the weights and function evaluations at the abscissas. The number of abscissa points is then doubled, the process is repeated, and the current solution is compared against the previous solution. If the two results are within the convergence tolerance, the value is returned. Otherwise, the number of points is again doubled and the process repeats itself.

The `gaussLegendre()` method source code is—

```
public static double gaussLegendre(Function function,
    double start, double end, double tolerance) {
  double dx = end - start;
  double value = 1.0e+10;
  double oldValue;
  int numPoints = 10;
  int maxPoints = 100000;
  double x[] = new double[maxPoints];
  double w[] = new double[maxPoints];

  // Compute the integral value adding points
  //   until the solution converges or maxPoints
  //   is reached.

  while(true) {

    // Calculate the Gauss-Legendre weights and
    //   abscissas

    computeGaussWeights(x, w, numPoints);

    // Compute the integral value by summing up the
    //   weights times the function value at each
    //   abscissa
```

```
      oldValue = value;

      value = 0.0;
      for(int i=0; i<numPoints; ++i) {
       value += w[i]*function.getValue(start + x[i]*dx);
      }
      value *= dx;

      //  If the solution is converged, return the
      //  value. Otherwise, double the points in the
      //  integration domain and try again.

      if ( Math.abs(value-oldValue) <=
           tolerance*Math.abs(oldValue) ) {
        return value;
      }

      numPoints *= 2;
      if (numPoints >= maxPoints) break;
    }

    //  Solution did not converge

    return 12345.6;
  }
```

The Gaussian quadrature technique can be applied to both proper and improper integrals so we use the `gaussLegendre()` method to solve Eq. (21.10) and Eq. (21.20). The driver class is called `TestGauss` and its source code is:

```
import TechJava.MathLib.*;

public class TestGauss
{
  public static void main(String args[]) {

    double value;

    //  Integrate the function y = x*ln(x) from
    //  x=2 to x=4 using 10 points in the integration

    LogFunction function = new LogFunction();
    value =
        Integrator.gaussLegendre(function,2.0,4.0,1.0e-4);
    System.out.println("value = " + value);

    //  Integrate the function y = 1/sqrt(x-2) from
    //  x=2 to x=3 using 10 points in the integration

    SqrtFunction2 function2 = new SqrtFunction2();
    value =
        Integrator.gaussLegendre(function2,2.0,3.0,1.0e-4);
```

```
        System.out.println("value = " + value);
    }
}
```

Output—

```
value = 6.70406052759485
value = 1.9998289705958587
```

The `gaussLegendre()` method successfully reproduced the exact solutions to within four decimal places for both the proper and improper integrals. The logarithmic integral converged on the first iteration. The improper integral took longer—10 iterations—but this was somewhat more efficient than the midpoint method that required 14 iterations to converge.

GENERAL INTEGRAL TYPES

The integral equations that we have been working with in this chapter are part of a larger class of equations known as Fredholm integrals. There are Fredholm integrals of the first and second kind that take the general form of Eq. (21.22) and Eq. (21.23).

$$g(t) = \int_a^b K(t,s)f(s)ds \tag{21.22}$$

$$f(t) = \lambda \int_a^b K(t,s)f(s)ds + g(t) \tag{21.23}$$

The quantity $K(t,s)$ is known as the kernel. The equations used in the examples in this chapter have been Fredholm integrals of the first kind with $K(t,s) = 1$. Another important type of integral is a Volterra integral that is similar to a Fredholm integral of the first kind except the upper integration limit is t. We won't implement methods to solve general Fredholm or Volterra integrals, but they are typically solved using Gaussian quadrature methods described in the previous section.

EXAMPLE: THIN AIRFOIL THEORY

As a practical application of the tools we developed in this chapter, let's use the `simpsonsRule()` method to solve for the lift and moment coefficients of an airfoil using thin airfoil theory. Once again, when reading through this

Example: Thin Airfoil Theory

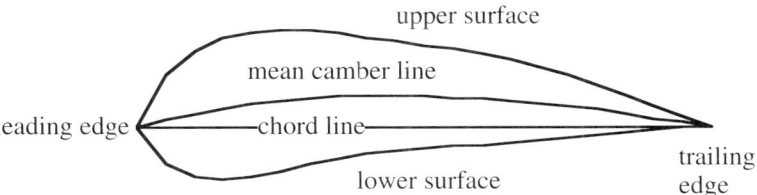

FIGURE 21.2 Generic airfoil configuration

section concentrate on the process. Even if you never need to compute the aerodynamic characteristics of a thin airfoil, you can apply the same solution process to your own integral problems.

Before we discuss what thin airfoil theory is, let's define some terminology about an airfoil. Consider the airfoil shown in Figure 21.2. A straight line drawn from the wing leading edge to trailing edge is called the *chord line*. The length of the chord line is the *chord* of the wing. The *mean camber line* is the line from the leading to trailing edge such that there is an equal airfoil thickness above and below the line. The difference between the mean camber and chord lines is the *camber* of the wing. A symmetrical airfoil would be one that has zero camber. The angle that an airfoil's chord line makes with the airfoil's direction of travel is called the *angle of attack*.

Now let's move on to thin airfoil theory. The German aerodynamicist Ludwig Prandtl developed this theory in the early 1900s. It starts by modeling an airfoil as a thin plate that follows the mean camber line. Because you can't have air flow through the solid surface of the airfoil, the normal velocity at the airfoil surface is balanced by the induced normal velocity of a sheet of vortices distributed along the airfoil. This assumption results in the following integral equation.

$$\frac{1}{2\pi U_\infty} \int_0^c \frac{\gamma(x')}{x - x'} dx' = \alpha - \frac{\partial z}{\partial x} \quad (21.24)$$

In Eq. (21.24), U_∞ is the freestream velocity, c is the chord length, α is the angle of attack, and $z = z(x)$ is the equation that describes the mean camber line. The quantity γ is the unknown vorticity distribution function that we need to compute. It turns out that the vorticity distribution can be approximated using a Fourier series.

$$\gamma(\theta) = 2U_\infty \left[A_0 \cot\left(\frac{\theta}{2}\right) + \sum_{n=1}^\infty A_n \sin(n\theta) \right] \quad (21.25)$$

Eq. (21.25) uses a change of variables from x to θ with the relation in Eq. (21.26).

$$x = \frac{c}{2}(1 - \cos(\theta)) \qquad (21.26)$$

The θ quantity varies from 0 to π. After performing some trigonometric manipulations, we arrive at the expressions in Eq. (21.27) for A_0 and A_n.

$$A_0 = \alpha - \frac{1}{\pi}\int_{\theta=0}^{\pi} \frac{\partial z}{\partial x} d\theta \qquad A_n = \frac{2}{\pi}\int_{\theta=0}^{\pi} \frac{\partial z}{\partial x} \cos(n\theta) d\theta \qquad (21.27)$$

Once the A coefficients are known, the lift and leading edge moment coefficients can be computed from the relations shown in Eq. (21.28) and Eq. (21.29). The terms ρ_∞ and U_∞ are the freestream density and velocity, L is the lifting force on the airfoil, and M is the moment about the leading edge.

$$C_l = \frac{L}{\frac{1}{2}\rho_\infty U_\infty^2} = \pi(2A_0 + A_1) \qquad (21.28)$$

$$C_{M_{LE}} = \frac{M}{\frac{1}{2}\rho_\infty U_\infty^2 l} = -\frac{\pi}{2}\left(A_0 + A_1 - \frac{A_2}{2}\right) \qquad (21.29)$$

We will now write a program to compute the A coefficients for an arbitrarily cambered wing using Simpson's rule integration method we developed earlier in this chapter. Once the A coefficients have been found, the program will calculate the lift and leading edge moment coefficients for the airfoil.

We will apply our program to compute the aerodynamic coefficients for a NACA 2412 airfoil traveling at an angle of attack of 5 degrees. The NACA 2412 is an airfoil with a maximum thickness of 0.12*chord and has a 2 percent maximum camber at 40 percent chord. The equation for its camber line is defined in two pieces.

$$\begin{aligned} z(x) &= 0.125(0.8x - x^2) & \frac{x}{c} &\leq 0.4 \\ z(x) &= 0.0555(0.2c + 0.8x - x^2) & \frac{x}{c} &> 0.4 \end{aligned} \qquad (21.30)$$

Taking the derivatives of Eq. (21.30) and converting x to θ, we obtain expressions (Eq. 21.31) for $\partial z/\partial x$ that we need to compute the A coefficients.

$$\frac{\partial z}{\partial x} = 0125\cos(\theta) - 0.025 \quad \frac{x}{c} \leq 0.4$$
$$\frac{\partial z}{\partial x} = 0.0555\cos(\theta) - 0.0111 \quad \frac{x}{c} > 0.4$$
(21.31)

The first code to write is a `Function` subclass that will return the function $\partial z/\partial x \cos(n\theta)$. This function is needed to evaluate the A integrals. The class is named `CamberFunction` and its source code is shown next. The power to be applied to the cosine term is passed to the `CamberFunction` constructor.

```
package TechJava.MathLib;

//  This class represents the camber
//  function for a NACA 2412 airfoil

public class CamberFunction extends Function
{
  private int n;

  public CamberFunction(int n) {
    this.n = n;
  }

  //  getValue() returns the height of the camber
  //  line for a given theta where
  //  cos(theta) = 1.0 - 2x/c

  public double getValue(double theta) {
    if (theta < 1.36944) {
      return (0.125*Math.cos(theta) - 0.025)*
              Math.cos (theta*n);
    } else {
      return (0.0555*Math.cos(theta) - 0.0111)*
              Math.cos (theta*n);
    }
  }
}
```

Now we can write our thin airfoil analysis code, which we will call `ThinAirfoil.java`. In this case, the program computes the aerodynamic coefficients for a 5 degree angle of attack. With a little extra effort, you could modify the code to take the angle of attack as an input argument. After declaring some variables, the code calculates the A_0, A_1, and A_2 coefficients. It does this by creating a `CamberFunction` object and then integrating the associated function using the `simpsonsRule()` method. Once the A coefficients are in hand, the lift and moment coefficients are computed and the results are printed to the console.

Here is the `ThinAirFoil` class source code—

```java
import TechJava.MathLib.*;

public class ThinAirfoil
{
  public static void main(String args[]) {

    double alpha, Cl, Cm;
    double A[] = new double[3];
    CamberFunction naca2412;

    //  Compute the conditions for a 5 degree
    //  angle of attack.

    alpha = 5.0*Math.PI/180.0;

    //  Calculate the A0, A1, and A2 coefficients

    double temp = 1.0/Math.PI;

    naca2412 = new CamberFunction(0);
    A[0] = alpha - temp*Integrator.simpsonsRule(
                naca2412,0.0,Math.PI,1.0e-4);

    for(int i=1; i<3; ++i) {
      naca2412 = new CamberFunction(i);
      A[i] = 2.0*temp*Integrator.simpsonsRule(
                naca2412,0.0,Math.PI,1.0e-4);
    }

    //  Compute Cl and Cm(leading edge)

    Cl = Math.PI*(2.0*A[0] + A[1]);
    Cm = -0.5*Math.PI*(A[0] + A[1] - 0.5*A[2]);

    //  Print out the results

    for(int i=0; i<3; ++i) {
      System.out.println("A["+i+"] = "+A[i]);
    }
    System.out.println("\nCl = "+Cl);
    System.out.println("Cm = "+Cm);
  }
}
```

Output—

```
A[0] = 0.08274980955387196
A[1] = 0.08146092605250739
A[2] = 0.01387204625538765

Cl = 0.7758494344019757
Cm = -0.02470465406592427
```

The compute lift coefficient value is within 3.5 percent of the experimentally obtained value[1] of 0.75.

REFERENCES

1. University of Tennessee Aerodynamic Database, *www.engr.ut.edu/~rbond/airfoil.html*.

22

FOURIER TRANSFORMS

An endeavor common to a wide variety of scientific and engineering disciplines is the need to analyze or process a signal from a data source. A signal can be characterized either in the time domain (amplitude versus time) or in the frequency domain (frequency magnitude versus frequency). Sometimes it may be more convenient to work in the time domain, sometimes in the frequency domain, and there are times when you will want to switch back and forth between the two domains.

A Fourier transform is a way of switching between time and frequency domains. It is based on the theory that a signal can be decomposed into an infinite series of sinusoidal functions. The sinusoidal functions can identify the frequencies and amplitudes associated with the signal. The forward Fourier transform is usually defined to convert from the time to frequency domains. The inverse Fourier transform converts a signal from the frequency domain to the time domain and can be used to reconstitute a signal from a frequency spectrum. Fourier transforms are widely used in science and engineering in such differing fields as acoustics, image processing, seismology, astronomy, optics, and digital filtering.

The integral form of the Fourier transform is applicable only if the signal can be expressed as a mathematical equation. If no such expression exists, a discrete Fourier transform (DFT) can be used. The DFT samples values of the input signal at locations along a specified range and applies a Fourier transform to the sampled data. The transformed results are also at discrete points along either the time or frequency domains.

DFTs work well, but are computationally expensive if a large number of data samples is used. The standard form of the DFT has an operation count proportional to the square of the number of samples. If you are taking a million or so data samples, this can be a real problem. To overcome this limitation, variations on the standard DFT have been developed that require a substantially reduced operation count. These methods are referred to as fast Fourier transforms (FFTs).

In this chapter we will go over the general theory of the Fourier transform and show how the DFT and FFT algorithms are derived. We will write methods that implement a DFT and FFT and apply the methods to several sample problems. This chapter will pass rather quickly through Fourier transform theory and is not meant to be a comprehensive treatment on the subject. For example, we won't cover such topics as convolution theorem, Parseval's theorem, or windowing. The purpose of this chapter is to show how general workhorse DFT and FFT methods can be written in Java with the tools and concepts we have learned in this book. For a more complete treatment of Fourier transforms consult *The Fast Fourier Transform and Its Applications* by E. Oran Brigham.

The topics we will cover in this chapter are

- The Fourier transform
- Discrete Fourier transform
- Analyzing composite signals
- Sampling theory
- Spectral leakage
- Fast Fourier transform

The Fourier Transform

As mentioned in the introduction to this chapter, there are two ways in which you can characterize a signal. The first way is in the time domain where the signal amplitude is expressed as a function of time, as in Eq. (22.1).

$$x = x(t) \tag{22.1}$$

The signal can also be characterized in the frequency domain by expressing the frequency amplitude as a function of frequency, as in Eq. (22.2).

$$X = X(f) \tag{22.2}$$

The frequency, f, in Eq. (22.2) is in units of 1/sec or Hz and is equal to $1/T$, where T is the period of the function. The frequency domain is sometimes characterized using, $\omega = 2\pi f$, the angular frequency in units of radians/sec.

The Fourier transform is used to switch back and forth between the time and frequency domains. It is based on the Fourier series that allows you to express any periodic function, $g(t)$, as an infinite series of sinusoidal functions.

$$f(t) = \frac{a_0}{2} + \sum_{n=1}^{\infty} a_n \cos(\omega_n t) + \sum_{n=1}^{\infty} b_n \sin(\omega_n t) \tag{22.3}$$

The ω_n term in Eq. (22.3) is given by the expression $\omega_n = 2\pi n f$. The signal energy at a given frequency, f_n, is equal to the sum of the square of the a and b coefficients, $E_n = (a_n^2 + b_n^2)$. Determining the energy spectrum of a signal is an important use of Fourier transforms.

The Fourier series can be also expressed in complex form.

$$g(t) = \sum_{-\infty}^{\infty} c_n e^{i\omega_n t} \tag{22.4}$$

The variables on the right-hand side of Eq. (22.4) are defined in Eq. (22.5).

$$\begin{aligned} i &= \sqrt{-1} \\ c_0 &= \frac{a_0}{2} \\ c_n &= \frac{1}{2}(a_n - ib_n) \quad n > 0 \\ c_n &= \frac{1}{2}(a_n + ib_n) \quad n < 0 \end{aligned} \tag{22.5}$$

The continuous or integral Fourier transform is based on Eq. (22.4). It relates the characterization of a signal in the frequency domain to its characterization in time domain.

$$X(f) = \int_{-\infty}^{\infty} x(t) e^{-i\omega t} dt \tag{22.6}$$

The inverse Fourier transform, going from frequency to time domains, is given by a similar expression.

$$x(t) = \int_{-\infty}^{\infty} X(f) e^{i\omega t} df \tag{22.7}$$

The reason to define both forward and inverse transforms is to provide the ability to switch back and forth between the time and frequency domains. The inverse transform of the forward transform of a function should return the original function. The only differences between Eq. (22.6) and Eq. (22.7) are

TABLE 22.1 Time and Frequency Function Relationships	
x(t)	X(f)
Real and even	Real and even
Real and odd	Imaginary and odd
Imaginary and even	Imaginary and even
Imaginary and odd	Real and odd

the change of sign in the exponential power term and the different function and variable of integration. The time-frequency domains are not the only ones to which Eq. (22.6) and Eq. (22.7) can be applied. They could be used, for instance, to switch between the position and inverse wavelength domains.

One reason to use the complex form of the Fourier series is that the time and frequency equations may be complex, containing both real and imaginary parts. Even if the original signal is completely real, the frequency response obtained from the Fourier transform may have both real and imaginary components. The characteristics of the frequency response depend on whether the function is real or imaginary and whether the function is even or odd. An odd function, such as the sine function, is one where $g(t) = -g(-t)$. An even function, such as the cosine function, is one where $g(t) = g(-t)$. Table 22.1 summarizes some of the relationships between the two domains.

One thing to notice about Table 22.1 is that when you transform a sine wave, which is a real, odd function, the resulting frequency response is in the imaginary plane.

What we have discussed in this section and will cover in the rest of this chapter is a 1-D Fourier transform that is used to travel between time and frequency domains. This type of transform is typically applied to electronic or acoustic signal analysis. There are also multidimensional Fourier transforms that are used for optical or image analysis applications. We won't discuss multidimensional Fourier transforms in this book. For more information on them, consult an appropriate Fourier transform reference.

Discrete Fourier Transform

The integral form of the Fourier transform equations is only useful if you have a mathematical function that characterizes the signal to be analyzed. A more common situation is to have a series of measurements of a given signal taken at a discrete time or frequency increments. The DFT is a way to apply a Fourier transform to a discrete set of data.

Let's say the amplitude of a signal is measured N times at equal time increments over a total sampling time of T. You would then have N measurements of $x(t)$, $[x_0, x_1, x_2, ..., x_{N-1}]$. Any one discrete x value would be given by the following equation.

$$x_n = x(t_n) = x(n\Delta t) = x\left(n\frac{T}{N}\right) \quad n = 0, 1, 2, ..., N-1 \quad (22.8)$$

Eq. (22.8) assumes that the sampling started at time $t = 0$. We can discretize the frequency domain in a similar manner. The overall sampling frequency is $F = N/T$. We will take N discrete values of the frequency amplitude, $[X_0, X_1, X_2, ..., X_{N-1}]$; where any individual frequency amplitude is given by the expression in Eq. (22.9).

$$X_k = X(f_k) = X(k\Delta f) = X\left(\frac{k}{N\Delta t}\right) \quad k = 0, 1, 2, ..., N-1 \quad (22.9)$$

Eqs. (22.6), (22.8), and (22.9) can be used to derive a forward transform for a discrete value of X_k along the sampling range, Eq. (22.10).

$$X(f_k) = \int_0^T x(t_n) e^{-i2\pi f_k t_n} dt = \Delta t \sum_{n=0}^{N-1} x(t_n) e^{-i\frac{2\pi kn}{N}} \quad k = 0, 1, 2, ..., N-1 \quad (22.10)$$

Using the same process, an equation can also be derived for the inverse transform.

$$x(t_n) = \int_0^F X(f_k) e^{i2\pi f_k t_n} df = \frac{1}{N\Delta t} \sum_{k=0}^{N-1} X(f_k) e^{i\frac{2\pi kn}{N}} \quad n = 0, 1, 2, ..., N-1 \quad (22.11)$$

The Δf term to the left of the summation in Eq. (22.11) has been replaced with $\Delta f = 1/(N\Delta T)$. The standard form of the DFT equations can be obtained by using the following relations.

$$X(f_k) = \Delta t X_k \quad \text{and} \quad x(t_n) = x_n \quad (22.12)$$

Using the variables from Eq. (22.12), the DFT equations take their commonly expressed form shown in Eq. (22.13) and Eq. (22.14).

$$X_k = \sum_{n=0}^{N-1} x_n e^{-i\frac{2\pi kn}{N}} \quad k = 0, 1, 2, ..., N-1 \quad (22.13)$$

$$x_n = \frac{1}{N} \sum_{k=0}^{N-1} X_k e^{i\frac{2\pi kn}{N}} \quad n = 0, 1, 2, ..., N-1 \quad (22.14)$$

Because Eq. (22.13) is a summation, the magnitude of the X_k terms will increase with increasing sample number. If you are taking millions of samples, this can make the frequency response output difficult to plot. To avoid this situation, the $1/N$ term is sometimes incorporated into the forward transform equation by using the expression $X(f_k) = N\Delta t X_k$.

As it turns out, the Java implementation of the DFT equations is quite simple. We will write a method named `discreteFT()` that will perform a forward or inverse DFT analysis on an array of data. The method will be `public` and `static` and will be declared in a class named `Fourier`. The `Fourier` class will be placed in the `TechJava.MathLib` package.

Before we can implement the `discreteFT()` method, we need to convert Eq. (22.13) and Eq. (22.14) back into trigonometric form. We will do this conversion using the following relations.

$$e^{i\theta} = \cos(\theta) + i\sin(\theta)$$
$$e^{-i\theta} = \cos(\theta) - i\sin(\theta) \quad (22.15)$$

The other important thing to consider is that both the initial and transformed data can have real and imaginary components.

$$x_n = x_{n,r} + ix_{n,i}$$
$$X_k = X_{k,r} + iX_{k,i} \quad (22.16)$$

When Eq. (22.15) and Eq. (22.16) are incorporated into Eq. (22.13) and Eq. (22.14), we come up with the following expressions for a forward and inverse DFT. We will use the $1/N$ term in the forward transform.

$$X_k = \frac{1}{N}\sum_{n=0}^{N-1}[x_{n,r}\cos(\omega_{kn}) + x_{n,i}\sin(\omega_{kn})] + i[-x_{n,r}\sin(\omega_{kn}) + x_{n,i}\cos(\omega_{kn})] \quad (22.17)$$

$$x_n = \sum_{k=0}^{N-1}[X_{n,r}\cos(\omega_{kn}) - X_{n,i}\sin(\omega_{kn})] + i[X_{n,r}\sin(\omega_{kn}) + X_{n,i}\cos(\omega_{kn})] \quad (22.18)$$

If you look at Eq. (22.17) and Eq. (22.18), you will see that the equations are very similar. The only differences are the $1/N$ term and the leading edge coefficient on the sin() terms. This similarity means that we can implement the forward and inverse Fourier transforms with a single method. You should also note that, generally speaking, the transformed values will have both real and imaginary components whether the initial data is real, imaginary, or both.

The `discreteFT()` method is really very simple. It takes three arguments. The first is the array of data to be transformed. This array will contain real-imaginary data pairs for each sample point. The second argument is the number of sample points. The final argument is a `boolean` that is true if this is a forward transform calculation (from time domain to frequency domain) or false if it is a reverse transform (from frequency to time).

The method initializes a temporary variable omega that represents $\omega = 2\pi/N$. If this calculation is for an inverse transform, a negative sign is placed in front of the variable. This will cause the `Math.sin()` method evaluations later on to flip their signs. The `discreteFT()` method then goes through the summations from Eq. (22.17) and Eq. (22.18). If this is a forward transform, the resulting X_k values are scaled by $1/N$.

The `discreteFT()` method source code is shown here.

```
package TechJava.MathLib;

public class Fourier
{

  //  Discrete Fourier transform

  public static double[] discreteFT(double[] data,
                        int N, boolean forward) {
    double X[] = new double[2*N];
    double omega;
    int k, ki, kr, n;

    //  If this is a inverse transform, reverse the
    //  sign of the angle so the sin() terms will
    //  change sign.

    if (forward) {
      omega = 2.0*Math.PI/N;
    } else {
      omega = -2.0*Math.PI/N;
    }

    //  Perform the discrete Fourier transform.
    //  The real and imaginary data are stored in the
    //  x[] and X[] vectors as pairs, one real and
    //  one imaginary value for each sample point.

    for(k=0; k<N; ++k) {
      kr = 2*k;
      ki = 2*k + 1;
      X[kr] = 0.0;
      X[ki] = 0.0;
      for(n=0; n<N; ++n) {
        X[kr] += data[2*n]*Math.cos(omega*n*k) +
                 data[2*n+1]*Math.sin(omega*n*k);
        X[ki] += -data[2*n]*Math.sin(omega*n*k) +
                 data[2*n+1]*Math.cos(omega*n*k);
      }
    }

    //  If this is a forward transform, multiply
    //  in the 1/N terms
```

```
      if ( forward ) {
        for(k=0; k<N; ++k) {
          X[2*k]   /= N;
          X[2*k + 1] /= N;
        }
      }

      //  Return the transformed data.

      return X;
   }
}
```

Let's apply the `discreteFT()` method to compute an FFT on a 2 Hz cosine wave. The amplitude as a function of time for this wave is given by the equation below.

$$x(t) = \cos(4\pi t) \tag{22.19}$$

We will take 64 data samples over a 2-second sample period. The `discreteFT()` method will first compute a FFT to obtain the frequency spectrum for a 2 Hz cosine wave. The `discreteFT()` method will then be used to perform an inverse transform that will reconstruct a 2 Hz cosine wave from its frequency spectrum. The program that will do all this is named `TestDFT.java`. Its code listing follows. When the transformed data is written to the console, the sample indexes are converted to units of time or frequency.

```
import TechJava.MathLib.*;

public class TestDFT
{
  public static void main(String args[]) {
    int N = 64;
    double T = 2.0;
    double tn, fk;
    double data[] = new double[2*N];

    //  A 2 Hz cosine function that is sampled
    //  for two seconds. First load the amplitude data

    for(int i=0; i<N; ++i) {
      data[2*i] = Math.cos(4.0*Math.PI*i*T/N);
      data[2*i+1] = 0.0;
    }

    //  Compute the DFT

    double X[] = Fourier.discreteFT(data, N, true);

    //  Print out the frequency spectrum
```

```
    for(int k=0; k<N; ++k) {
      fk = k/T;
      System.out.println("f["+k+"] = "+fk+"Xr["+k+
              "] = "+X[2*k]+ "  Xi["+k+"] = "+X[2*k + 1]);
    }

    //  Reconstruct a 2 Hz cosine wave from its
    //  frequency spectrum. First load the frequency
    //  data.

    for(int i=0; i<N; ++i) {
      data[2*i] = 0.0;
      data[2*i+1] = 0.0;
      if (i == 4 || i == N-4 ) {
        data[2*i] = 0.5;
      }
    }

    //  Compute the DFT

    double x[] = Fourier.discreteFT(data, N, false);

    //  Print out the amplitude vs time data.

    System.out.println();
    for(int n=0; n<N; ++n) {
      tn = n*T/N;
      System.out.println("t["+n+"] = "+tn+"xr["+n+
              "] = "+x[2*n]+"  xi["+n+"] ="+x[2*n + 1]);
    }
  }
}
```

The results of the FFT are shown in Figure 22.1. The frequency amplitude data was converted to decibels using the `Math2.log10()` method we developed in Chapter 17. There are two peaks in the data. The first is at 2 Hz, the frequency of the cosine signal. The second is at 30 Hz. This may seem a bit confusing but is the result of starting our summations at $n = 0$. We took samples at a rate of 32 samples a second for this analysis. The DFT actually computes the spectrum from −16 to 16 Hz, but we have shifted it over to start at 0 so the negative part of the spectrum has been mapped onto the frequency range 16 to 32 Hz. The peak at 30 Hz on the figure really corresponds to a peak at −2 Hz. Having peaks at ±2 Hz is the correct solution. The imaginary part of the frequency part of the spectrum as computed by the `discreteFT()` method was uniformly zero as it should be since a cosine wave is a real, even function.

The results of the inverse Fourier transform are shown in Figure 22.2. In this case we reconstructed a 2 Hz cosine wave from a frequency spectrum using the `discreteFT()` method. The DFT method did an excellent job of

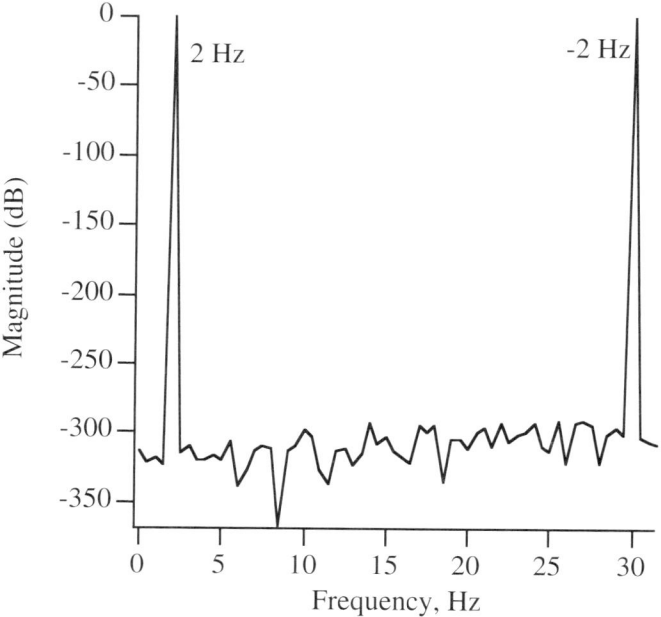

FIGURE 22.1 Frequency response of 2 Hz cosine wave

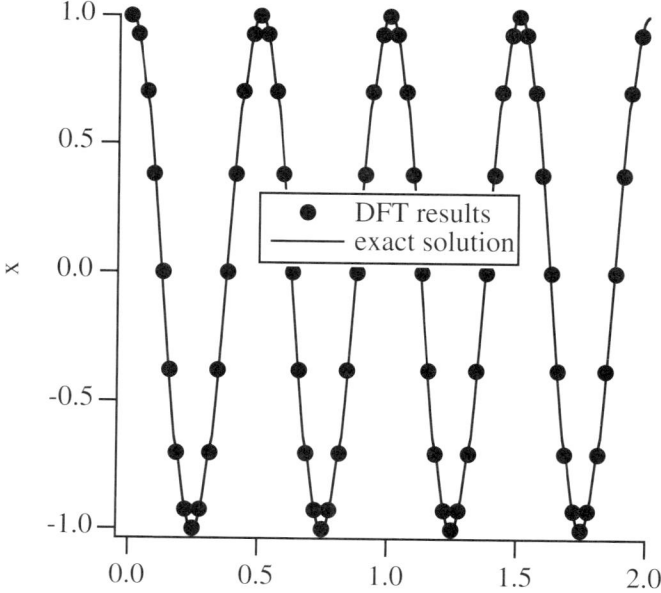

FIGURE 22.2 Cosine wave reconstruction

reconstructing the cosine wave. The computed points lie right on the exact solution curve.

ANALYZING COMPOSITE SIGNALS

One of the powerful uses of Fourier transforms is analyzing composite signals, those that are made up of multiple frequency components. You can transform a composite signal into the frequency domain and this will often provide insight into the nature of the signal. For example, consider the signal shown in Figure 22.3. It is difficult to say very much about the signal by looking at its amplitude-time curve.

But when the signal is transformed into the frequency domain using the `discreteFT()` method a much clearer picture arises. The signal was sampled 64 times in a total sample time of 1 second. The frequency spectrum for the range 0 to 32 Hz is shown in Figure 22.4. The negative part of the spectrum

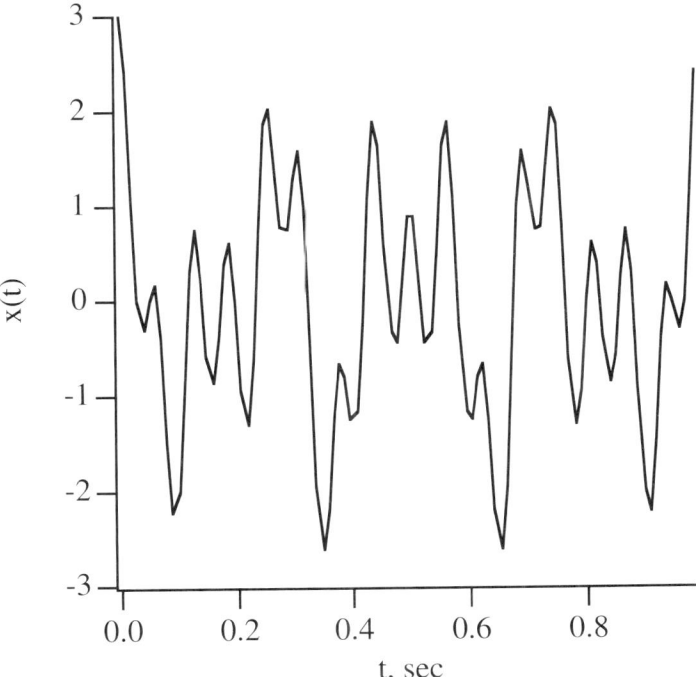

FIGURE 22.3 Composite signal

(the data from 32 to 64 Hz) was not plotted. We can see in Figure 22.4 that there are three components to the composite signal. There is a 4 Hz wave, a 7 Hz wave, and a 16 Hz wave. This result is completely correct, because the signal shown in Figure 22.3 was created using Eq. (22.20).

$$x(t) = \cos(8\pi t) + \cos(14\pi t) + \cos(32\pi t) \qquad (22.20)$$

The code to produce the data shown in Figures 22.3 and 22.4 is shown next. It is named TestComplex.java and is just a slight variation on the TestDFT.java program described earlier.

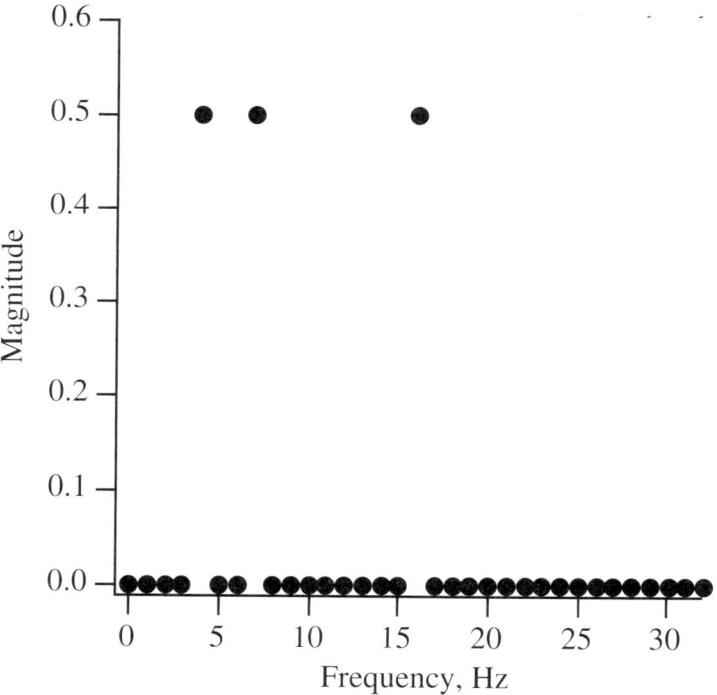

FIGURE 22.4 Composite signal frequency response

```
import TechJava.MathLib.*;

public class TestComplex
{
  public static void main(String args[]) {
    int N = 64;
    double T = 1.0;
    double tn, fk;
    double data[] = new double[2*N];
```

```
    //  A composite cosine function that is sampled
    //  for one second at 64 samples/sec

    for(int i=0; i<N; ++i) {
      data[2*i] = Math.cos(8.0*Math.PI*i*T/N) +
                  Math.cos(14.0*Math.PI*i*T/N) +
                  Math.cos(32.0*Math.PI*i*T/N);
      data[2*i+1] = 0.0;
    }

    //  Compute the Fourier transform

    double X[] = Fourier.discreteFT(data, N, true);

    //  Print out the frequency spectrum

    System.out.println();
    for(int k=0; k<N; ++k) {
      fk = k/T;
      System.out.println("f["+k+"] = "+fk+
                  "   Xr["+k+"] = "+X[2*k]+
                  "   Xi["+k+"] = "+X[2*k + 1]);
    }
  }
}
```

SAMPLING THEORY

DFTs are based on a finite number of samples taken of an input signal, but who is to say what the sampling rate should be? If you don't take enough samples, the signal won't be properly characterized. If you take more samples than you need, you will waste computer resources. Fortunately, there is something called *sampling theory* to help resolve this issue.

What sampling rate to use depends on whether or not a signal is bandwidth limited. A bandwidth-limited signal is one that has no spectral components beyond a certain frequency. An example of a bandwidth-limited signal would be one that was passed through an amplifier with a finite frequency response. According to the sampling theory, a bandwidth-limited signal with a maximum frequency of B can be reconstructed without error from samples taken at the Nyquist frequency, shown in Eq. (22.21).

$$f_c = 2B \quad \frac{samples}{sec} \qquad (22.21)$$

For a sine or cosine function, the Nyquist sampling frequency corresponds to taking a sample at each peak and trough of the function. One way to think of the Nyquist frequency is that it is the minimum sampling rate that should be used to properly sample a bandwidth-limited signal. A signal sampled at less than Nyquist sampling frequency is said to be undersampled. If the sampling rate is greater than the Nyquist frequency, the signal is oversampled.

Another way to look at the Nyquist sampling frequency is to reverse-engineer the problem. Let's say you are going to take N samples per second for a given signal. The maximum signal frequency that can be correctly modeled by the resulting Fourier transform is given by Eq. (22.22).

$$f_{max} = \frac{1}{2\frac{1}{N}} = \frac{N}{2} \quad Hz \tag{22.22}$$

For example, if you are taking 64 samples per second for a given signal, the maximum frequency component of the signal should be less than or equal to 32 Hz. The quantity f_{max} is also referred to as the Nyquist critical frequency.

A problem arises if there are any components to the input signal that are above the Nyquist critical frequency for the chosen sampling rate. When a Fourier transform is performed on such a signal, all of the power spectral density that lies outside of the sampling frequency is spuriously moved into the frequency range. This is a phenomenon known as *aliasing*, and can make properly interpreting a frequency spectrum a difficult task. One way to prevent aliasing is to pass the signal though an analog signal filter that will low-pass the signal below some upper cutoff frequency, f_h. Naturally, this upper cutoff frequency must be higher than any signal frequency of interest. You then set the sampling rate to be at least twice the upper cutoff frequency of the filter used, $f_N > 2f_h$. Sampling at a rate roughly five times the upper cutoff frequency of the low-pass filter is a good rule of thumb.

To see the effects of aliasing, let us revisit the composite cosine function we looked at in the previous section. The maximum frequency in the composite signal was 16 Hz. This corresponds to a Nyquist minimum sampling rate of 32 samples per second. When we analyzed the signal in the previous section, we used a sampling rate of 64 samples per second so everything was fine.

But what happens if we use a sampling rate of 18 samples per second instead? To do this, modify the `TestComplex.java` program by replacing the line `int N = 64;` with the line `int N = 18;`. The results of this change are shown in Figure 22.5. Instead of peaks at 4, 7, and 16 Hz, there are peaks at 2, 4, and 7 Hz. Because the 16 Hz component of the signal was beyond the Nyquist critical frequency for this case (9 Hz), its frequency amplitude peak has been aliased into the 2 Hz location.

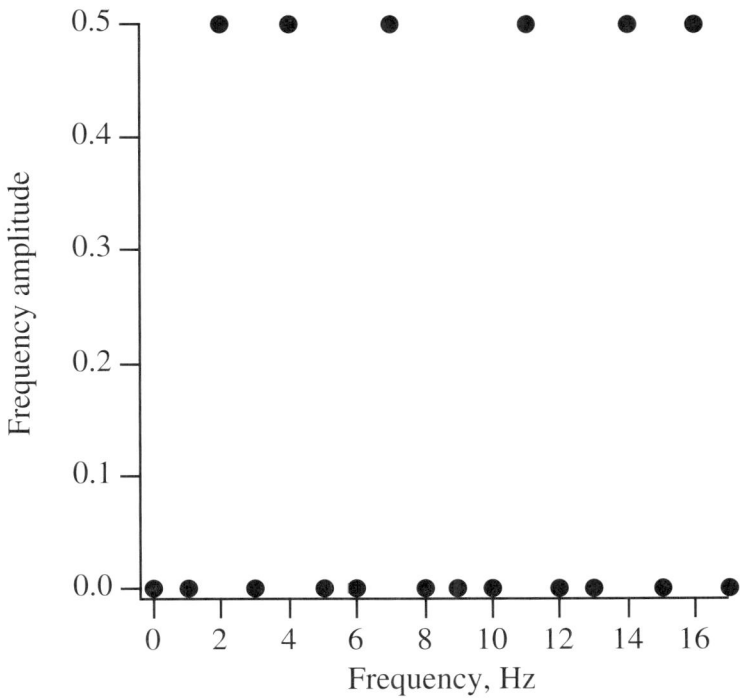

FIGURE 22.5 Effect of signal aliasing

SPECTRAL LEAKAGE

The DFT creates a frequency spectrum by mapping the signal amplitude at various discrete time samples into frequency amplitudes at various discrete frequencies. Each discrete frequency location (f_k) in the frequency response is called a *bin*. The frequency of a particular bin depends on its location in the frequency response (its k value), the sample rate, and the total sample time.

If there is a bin corresponding to the frequency of each component of the signal, the result is a nice, sharp computed frequency spectrum. But what happens if a signal frequency lies between two bins? For example, let's say a signal has a component at 8.33 Hz and the DFT uses frequency bins 1 Hz apart. Since there isn't a bin that exactly corresponds to the signal frequency, the DFT will distribute the frequency amplitude among the 8 and 9 Hz bins and surrounding bins. This effect is called *spectral leakage*. The frequency response no longer shows sharp peaks but the frequency amplitude is spread out along the spectrum.

To demonstrate what spectral leakage looks like, let's modify the previous composite cosine function to include a component at 4.4 Hz. The steps are shown in Eq. (22.23).

$$x(t) = \cos(8.8\pi t) + \cos(14\pi t) + \cos(32\pi t) \qquad (22.23)$$

When we sample the signal at the same 64 samples a second for 1 second and send the data to the `discreteFT()` method, Figure 22.6 shows the resulting frequency response. (The negative frequency spectrum has again been omitted.)

The 2 Hz frequency amplitude peak in Figure 22.6 is now lower and the amplitude of neighboring bins has increased both positively and negatively. The other interesting thing about this figure is that an imaginary component has been introduced to the frequency response. Because there were bins at 7 Hz and 16 Hz, the peaks at those frequencies are not subject to spectrum leakage and still show sharp peaks.

What is the answer to spectral leakage? One solution is to modify the sample number and/or sample time such that there is a bin at the frequency of

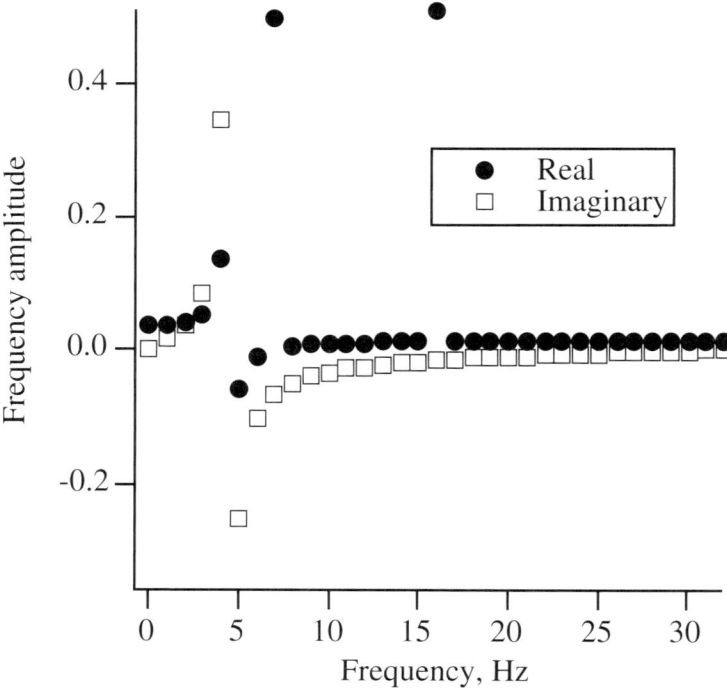

FIGURE 22.6 Effect of spectrum leakage

every component in the signal. In the previous example, if we had taken 32 samples per second over a 10 second sample time (320 total samples) there would have been a bin at 4.4 Hz and the frequency response would have come out cleanly.

Fast Fourier Transform

The DFT algorithm is simple to understand. It's easy to program. Everything is wonderful, right? Not exactly. The operation count of the DFT algorithm is proportional to the square of the number of sample points. When we are taking 32 or 64 samples this is not a big deal. However, there are applications of the Fourier transform, such as in the field of seismology, that require millions of data sample points. In this case the efficiency of the DFT algorithm is a big concern.

A number of algorithms have been developed over the years to perform a DFT in a more efficient manner. These algorithms are known as FFT methods. When an FFT performs a transform it requires an operation count proportional to $N\log_2 N$ rather than N^2. For a one million sample analysis the FFT reduces the required operations by a factor of 50,000. There are many variations of FFT algorithms out there today. In this section, we will examine the "standard" radix 2 Decimation in Time (DIT) technique based on the method of Danielson and Lanczos.

FFT methods start with the fact that a DFT can be subdivided into half-size transforms containing the even and odd elements of the original transform.

$$X_k = \sum_{n=0}^{N-1} x_n e^{-i\omega_N kn} = \sum_{m=0}^{\frac{N}{2}-1} x_{2m} e^{-i\omega_N k 2m} + \sum_{m=0}^{\frac{N}{2}-1} x_{2m+1} e^{-i\omega_N k(2m+1)} \quad (22.24)$$

The ω_N term in Eq. (22.24) is equal to $2\pi/N$. If you start with the forward Fourier transform as was done in Eq. (22.24) and split the time domain sequence, it is called DIT. If we had started with the inverse Fourier transform and divided the frequency domain, it would be *Decimation in Frequency (DIF)*. The odd-term summation can be cleaned up a little bit using the following relation.

$$e^{-i\omega_N k(2m+1)} = e^{-i\omega_N k} e^{-i\omega_N k 2m} = W_N^k e^{-i\omega_N k 2m} \quad (22.25)$$

Inserting Eq. (22.25) into Eq. (22.24), we get a form of Eq. (22.24) where the exponential term is the same in both summations.

$$X_k = \sum_{n=0}^{N-1} x_n e^{-i\omega_N kn} = \sum_{m=0}^{\frac{N}{2}-1} x_{2m} e^{-i\omega_N k2m} + W_N^k \sum_{m=0}^{\frac{N}{2}-1} x_{2m+1} e^{-i\omega_N k2m} \quad (22.26)$$

So far, you may be wondering what all the fuss is about. The reason that Eq. (22.26) is significant is that it is only the beginning of the possible transform subdivisions. The two summations on the right-hand side of Eq. (22.26) are themselves DFTs each with half as many points as the original. Indeed, we could rewrite Eq. (22.26) as Eq. (22.27).

$$X_k = X_k^{even} + W_N^k X_k^{odd} \quad (22.27)$$

The DFTs X_k^{even} and X_k^{odd} can themselves be divided into even and odd pieces just as was done by Eq. (22.26). You can continue the decimation process until you are left with a collection of two-point transforms.

This process can probably be best illustrated by the simple example of an eight-point forward Fourier transform. The DFT version of this transform is shown in Eq. (22.28).

$$X_k = [x_0 W_N^0 + x_2 W_N^{2k} + x_4 W_N^{4k} + x_6 W_N^{6k}] + W_N^{1k}[x_1 W_N^0 + x_3 W_N^{2k} + x_5 W_N^{4k} + x_7 W_N^{6k}]$$
$$X_k = X_k^e + W_N^{1k} X_k^o \quad (22.28)$$

As before, $W_N^{kn} = e^{-i 2\pi mk/N}$. The transforms X_k^e and X_k^o are themselves divided into even and odd subtransforms.

$$X_k^e = [x_0 W_N^0 + x_4 W_N^{4k}] + W_N^{2k}[x_2 W_N^0 + x_6 W_N^{4k}] = X_k^{ee} + W_N^{2k} X_k^{eo}$$
$$X_k^o = [x_1 W_N^0 + x_5 W_N^{4k}] + W_N^{2k}[x_3 W_N^0 + x_7 W_N^{4k}] = X_k^{oe} + W_N^{2k} X_k^{oo} \quad (22.29)$$

The X_k^{ee} level terms are defined by the two-point transforms in the brackets of Eq. (22.29). The two-point transforms are relatively easy to compute requiring only a single complex multiplication and a single complex addition.

The process we have just described is actually the reverse of the FFT solution process. The FFT starts at the lowest subdivided transform level, the two-point transforms, and works its way back up, recombining the divided transforms until the full, N-point transform has been recreated. The transform reconstruction algorithm can be done recursively so no additional memory allocation is required for the transformed data. The transform process overwrites the array of input data with the transformed output data. Several other tricks are used to further increase efficiency. The algorithm restricts sine and cosine calls to outer iteration loop and also makes use of the periodic nature of DFTs to evaluate only half of the divided subtransforms by using Eq. (22.30).

$$X_k = X_k^e + W_N^{nk} X_k^o \quad k = 0, 1, \ldots, \frac{N}{2} - 1 \quad (22.30)$$

$$X_{k+\frac{N}{2}} = X_k^e - W_N^{nk} X_k^o$$

One caveat about the FFT algorithm that we have described so far is that it depends on dividing a Fourier transform in two. This fact implies that the length of the input data array should also be a multiple of two. If the data set you are using does not have a length equal to a multiple of two, you can simply add zeros to the end of it until its length is the next power of two.

Now it is time to implement an FFT as a Java method. The method is called fastFT() and is declared to be public and static. It is defined in the Fourier class that also defines the discreteFT() method. The first thing the fastFT() method does after declaring and initializing some variables is to rearrange the order of the input data. If you look at Eq. (22.29), you will see that the input data is used in the order $[x_0, x_4, x_2, x_6, x_1, x_5, x_3, x_7]$. It is convenient for the FFT algorithm to place the input data in this type of order before starting the solution process. It turns out the input data can be placed in the proper sequence by reversing the bits of the input data indices. For example, for a system with eight data points, the index number 1 has a binary representation of 001. If you reverse the order of the bits you create the binary number 100, which is equal to the decimal number 4. This tells you to exchange x[1] and x[4] elements in the input data array.

After the bit reversal, the method computes the Fourier transform by recursively building up subtransforms starting with the two-point transforms. The initial data vector is overwritten with the transformed values. If this is a forward transform, the output data is scaled by $1/N$. The fastFT() method source code is shown here.

```
public static void fastFT(double[] data, int N,
                boolean forward) {
  double omega, tempr, tempi, scale;
  double xtemp, cos, sin, xr, xi;
  int i, j, k, n, m, M;

  //  bit-shift the input data. Remember that N
  //  is the number of samples. There is a real and
  //  a complex component to each data point.

  j=0;
  for(i=0; i<N-1; i++) {
    if (i<j) {
      tempr = data[2*i];
      tempi = data[2*i + 1];
```

```
      data[2*i] = data[2*j];
      data[2*i + 1] = data[2*j + 1];
      data[2*j] = tempr;
      data[2*j + 1] = tempi;
    }
    k = N/2;
    while (k <= j)  {
      j -= k;
      k >>= 1;
    }
    j += k;
  }

  //  Perform the FFT. Recursively build up the
  //  full transform from the sub-transforms

  if (forward) {
    scale = 1.0;
  } else {
    scale = -1.0;
  }

  M = 2;
  while( M < 2*N ) {
    omega = scale*2.0*Math.PI/M;
    sin = Math.sin(omega);
    cos = Math.cos(omega) - 1.0;
    xr = 1.0;
    xi = 0.0;
    for (m=0; m<M-1; m+=2) {
      for (i=m; i<2*N; i+=M*2) {
        j = i + M;
        tempr = xr*data[j] - xi*data[j+1];
        tempi = xr*data[j+1] + xi*data[j];
        data[j] = data[i] - tempr;
        data[j+1] = data[i+1] - tempi;
        data[i] += tempr;
        data[i+1] += tempi;
      }
      xtemp = xr;
      xr = xr + xr*cos - xi*sin;
      xi = xi + xtemp*sin + xi*cos;
    }
    M *= 2;
  }

  //  If this is a forward transform, multiply
  //  in the 1/N terms

  if ( forward ) {
    for(k=0; k<N; ++k) {
      data[2*k] /= N;
```

```
        data[2*k + 1] /= N;
      }
    }

    return;
  }
```

Let's test the `fastFT()` method by applying it to the composite cosine signal we processed in the "Analyzing Composite Signals" section. The `TestFFT.java` program sets up and runs this case. The program is very similar to the `TestComplex.java` program we looked at earlier. The amplitude-time history for a signal containing 4, 7, and 16 Hz components is generated and sent to the `fastFT()` method. The resulting frequency spectrum is written to the console. The `TestFFT` class source code follows.

```
import TechJava.MathLib.*;

public class TestFFT
{
  public static void main(String args[]) {
    int N = 64;
    double T = 1.0;
    double tn, fk;
    double data[] = new double[2*N];

    //  A composite cosine function that is sampled
    //  for one second at 64 samples/sec

    for(int i=0; i<N; ++i) {
      data[2*i] = Math.cos(8.0*Math.PI*i*T/N) +
                  Math.cos(14.0*Math.PI*i*T/N) +
                  Math.cos(32.0*Math.PI*i*T/N);
      data[2*i+1] = 0.0;
    }

    //  Compute the Fourier Transform

    Fourier.fastFT(data, N, true);

    //  Print out the frequency spectrum

    System.out.println();
    for(int k=0; k<N; ++k) {
      fk = k/T;
      System.out.println("f["+k+"] = " + fk +
                         "  Xr["+k+"] = " + data[2*k] +
                         "  Xi["+k+"] = " + data[2*k+1]);
    }
  }
}
```

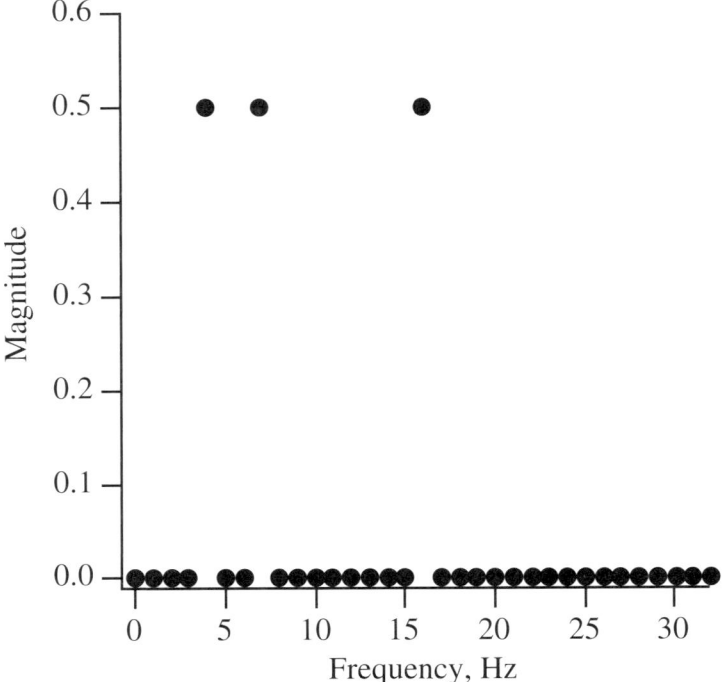

FIGURE 22.7 FFT results for composite cosine signa

The results for this test case are shown in Figure 22.7. The `fastFFT()` method correctly computed the frequency spectrum with peaks at the 4, 7, and 16 Hz frequencies. Just to get a feeling for the efficiency difference between DFT and FFT, this case was rerun through the `discreteFT()` and `fastFT()` methods using 131072 (2^{17}) samples. On a 1.6 GHz Pentium 4 PC, the `fastFT()` method took about one second to execute. The `discreteFT()` method, on the other hand, required over 2 hours to perform the same calculation.

23

GENERIC CLASS LIBRARIES

Consider the following common programming situation. You write an analysis method where part of the analysis is generic and part is specific to a given problem. As a good Java programmer, you don't want a different version of the method for every problem it might be used to solve. What you want is to write one generic version of the method that accepts the problem-specific information as an argument.

In C the answer would be to use a *function pointer*. As the name implies, it is a pointer to a generic function with a certain input parameter list. Java doesn't have function pointers, but you can do the same thing by using classes. A class can be defined to contain problem-specific information. An instance of the class is then passed to the generic analysis tool.

A collection of generic analysis tools is called a *generic class library*. You may not have realized it, but we created a generic class library in Chapters 20, 21, and 22. In Chapter 20, the ODE solver methods integrated a generic ordinary differential equation. Information about the specific ODE to be solved was encapsulated in an instance of the `ODE` class that was passed to the ODE solver method as an argument. Among other things, the `ODE` object defined a method named `getFunction()` that computed the right-hand side of the ordinary differential equations being solved.

In this chapter we will formalize the process for developing a generic class library using as an example the development of a method to compute a least squares curve fit to a collection of data. The specific topics we will discuss are—

- Analyzing the problem
- Example: least squares fit
- Implementing the generic part
- Implementing the problem-specific part
- Testing the generic class library

Analyzing the Problem

The first thing to decide when writing a generic class library is whether the analysis in question should be implemented as such. As the name implies, generic class libraries define methods that perform a generic analysis useful to a variety of applications. Any problem-specific components of the analysis are separated from the generic class library methods. Problem-specific information is generally passed to the generic method as an argument.

So when considering implementing a method as part of a generic class library, ask yourself if the method can be used by more than one application. If the answer is no, stop right there. If the answer is yes, decide if the analysis can be separated into generic and problem-specific parts. If it can, develop the generic part of the analysis as part of a generic class and incorporate the problem-specific part into a separate class.

An example of a generic class library is the `ODESolver` class we developed in Chapter 20. The `ODESolver` class defined a number of methods to solve ordinary differential equations using the Runge-Kutta integration technique. The Runge-Kutta solution process is generic. Since they can be applied to any ordinary differential equation, the Runge-Kutta methods were declared inside a generic class. The generic ODE solvers need to know what equation they are supposed to solve. This is problem-specific information. The `ODE` class was written to encapsulate an ordinary differential equation. An instance of the `ODE` class or one of its subclasses is passed to the Runge-Kutta method as an argument.

Example: Least Squares Fit

To demonstrate the process of developing a generic class library, let's use the example of implementing a least squares curve fit to a collection of data. We'll go over the details of the least squares fit methodology in the next chapter, but the general objective is to come up with a polynomial expression that models a collection of data such that the sum of the square of the errors at each data point is minimized. The procedure comes down to solving the matrix equation shown in Eq. (23.1).

$$A^T A x = A^T b \qquad (23.1)$$

The x vector contains the coefficients of the curve fit polynomial equation. The b vector contains the data being fitted. The process of solving a system of equations is, of course, generic, but the contents and size of the A, b, and x arrays are problem-specific. Since the analysis can be broken up into generic and problem-specific components, the least squares fit functionality can be built into a generic class library.

There are three generic parts to the least squares fit analysis—the arrays must be loaded with the appropriate data, the system of equations shown in Eq. (23.1) is solved, and the polynomial coefficients are returned. The generic elements of the analysis will be placed in a method named `leastSquaresFit()` that is defined in the `DataModeling` class.

The problem-specific elements of the least squares fit process are the form of the curve fit polynomial equation, the data that will be modeled, and the size and contents of the arrays. This information, and the methods used to access it, is stored in a class named `Polynomial`. The `Polynomial` class will also take care of filling the arrays $A^T A$ and $A^T b$. An instance of the `Polynomial` class, or one of its subclasses, is passed to the `leastSquaresFit()` method as an argument.

IMPLEMENTING THE GENERIC PART

We will define the generic part of the least squares fit analysis in a class called `DataModeling`. The `leastSquaresFit()` method declared in the `DataModeling` class will be written to implement the generic part of the least squares fit process, which is essentially defining and solving a system of equations. Before you can solve the system of equations, the arrays must be loaded with the appropriate data. Before you fill the arrays you need two things—the data that will be fit and the equation to which the data will be fit.

The `leastSquaresFit()` method takes three arguments. The data to be modeled is passed to the method in two arrays, `x[]` and `y[]`. Information about the curve fit polynomial equation is encapsulated in an instance of the

Polynomial class or by an instance of a Polynomial subclass. We'll discuss and define the Polynomial class in the next section.

The arrays $A^T A$ and $A^T b$ are filled by having the Polynomial object call its loadArrays() method. Once the arrays are loaded with data, the gaussian() method from the EqnSolver class solves the system of equations. When the solution process is finished, the $A^T b$ vector is overwritten to contain the coefficients for the curve fit equation. The coefficients are copied into the Polynomial object's coeffs[] data member using the setCoefficients() method.

The DataModeling class source code is shown here.

```
package TechJava.MathLib;

public class DataModeling
{
  public static void leastSquaresFit(
      Polynomial equation, double x[], double y[]) {

    // Load the AT*A and AT*b arrays using the data in
    // x[] and y[].

    equation.loadArrays(x,y);

    // Solve the system of equations AT*A*x = AT*b
    // The b[] array is overwritten to contain the
    // curve fit coefficients.

    EqnSolver.gaussian(equation.getA(),
                      equation.getB());

    // Copy the curve fit coefficient values into
    // the Polynomial object's coeffs[] array.

    equation.setCoefficients(equation.getB());
  }
}
```

IMPLEMENTING THE PROBLEM-SPECIFIC PART

Now it's time to implement the problem-specific part of the least squares fit analysis. The problem-specific elements of the analysis are the type of polynomial equation to be used and the data that will be modeled. The data to be modeled can be stored in 1-D arrays. Information about the curve fit polynomial equation will be stored in an instance of the Polynomial class, which encapsulates a general polynomial equation.

Implementing the problem-specific part

$$y = c_N x^N + c_{N-1} x^{N-1} + \ldots + c_1 x + c_0 \qquad (23.2)$$

The order of the polynomial equation in Eq. (23.2) is equal to the largest exponent in the equation. For example, the quadratic equation, $y = c_2 x^2 + c_1 x + c_0$, would be a second-order polynomial expression.

The `Polynomial` class defines four data members. The first is an integer variable that stores the order of the equation. The `A[][]` array stores the values of $A^T A$. The `b[]` array stores the values of $A^T b$. The `coeffs[]` array stores the coefficients of the polynomial curve fit equation.

The `Polynomial` class then defines a series of methods to get or set the values of its data members. The `getA()` and `getB()` methods return a reference to the `A[][]` and `b[]` arrays. In the `leastSquaresFit()` method, the `getA()` and `getB()` methods are used to send the `A[][]` and `b[]` arrays to the `gaussian()` method. The `setA()` and `setB()` methods are used by `Polynomial` subclasses.

The `loadArrays()` method loads the values for $A^T A$ and $A^T b$ into the `A[][]` and `b[]` arrays. The implementation is to load the arrays for a general polynomial equation. The mathematical formulation of the $A^T A$ and $A^T b$ arrays for a general polynomial is provided in Chapter 24. Finally, the `getValue()` method returns a value along the curve fit equation. This method would be called after the least squares fit had been performed.

The `Polynomial` class source code is shown here.

```
package TechJava.MathLib;

public class Polynomial
{
  private int order;
  private double A[][];
  private double b[];
  private double coeff[];

  public Polynomial(int order){
    this.order = order;
    A = new double[order+1][order+1];
    b = new double[order+1];
    coeff = new double[order+1];
  }

  // These methods return the current value
  // of the data members.

  public int getOrder() {
    return order;
  }
```

```
    public double[][] getA(){
      return A;
    }

    public double[] getB() {
      return b;
    }

    public double getCoefficient(int index) {
      return coeff[index];
    }

    public double[] getCoefficients() {
      return coeff;
    }

    //  These methods are to change one or more elements
    //  of the A[][], b[], or coeff[] arrays

    public void setA(int i, int j, double value){
      A[i][j] = value;
    }

    public void setB(int j, double value) {
      b[j] = value;
    }

    public void setCoefficients(double coeff[]) {
      this.coeff = coeff;
    }

    //  Load the A[][] and b[] arrays. The A[][] array
    //  stores the values of AT*A. The b[] array stores
    //  the values of AT*b. This implementation
    //  is for a general polynomial expression

    public void loadArrays(double x[], double y[]) {
      int numPoints = x.length;

      for(int j=0; j<order+1; ++j) {
        b[j] = 0.0;
        for(int k=0; k<numPoints; ++k) {
          b[j] += Math.pow(x[k],order - j)*y[k];
        }
      }

      for(int i=0; i<order+1; ++i) {
        for(int j=0; j<order+1; ++j) {
          A[i][j] = 0.0;
          for(int k=0; k<numPoints; ++k) {
            A[i][j] += Math.pow(x[k],2.0*order - i - j);
          }
```

```
        }
      }
    }

    //  Return a value along the least squares fit line.
    //  This implementation is for a general polynomial
    //  expression.

    public double getValue(double x) {
      double y = 0.0;

      for(int i=0; i<getOrder()+1; ++i) {
        y += coeff[i]*Math.pow(x,order - i);
      }
      return y;
    }
}
```

TESTING THE GENERIC CLASS LIBRARY

Let's see how the generic and problem-specific parts work together by writing a simple test program. The `LineDemo` class loads data to be curve fit into arrays `x[]` and `y[]`. The data is to be fit to a straight line, so a `Polynomial` object representing a first-order polynomial is created by sending the value 1 to the `Polynomial` class constructor. The `leastSquaresFit()` method is then called with the `Polynomial` object and the `x[]` and `y[]` arrays as arguments.

The `leastSquaresFit()` method performs a least squares fit analysis on the data and computes the straight-line coefficients. The coefficients are listed as well as the value of the curve fit line when $x = 0$. The following is the `LineDemo` source code.

```
import TechJava.MathLib.*;

public class LineDemo
{
  public static void main(String args[]) {
    double x[] = { 5.0, 10.0, 15.0, 20.0 };
    double y[] = { 2281.9, 3205.3, 4302.5, 5445.0 };

    //  Create a Polynomial object that represents a
    //  straight line, y = Cx + D.

    Polynomial straightLine = new Polynomial(1);

    //  Curve fit the data to a straight line.
```

```
        DataModeling.leastSquaresFit(straightLine, x, y);

        //  Show the resulting curve-fit equation

        double coeff[] = straightLine.getCoefficients();
        System.out.println("y = " + coeff[0] + "x + " +
                        coeff[1]);

        //  Get the curve fit value at x=0.0

        System.out.println();
        System.out.println("x = 0.0 y = " +
                        straightLine.getValue(0.0));
    }
}
```

Output—

```
y = 211.729999999x + 1162.05
x = 0.0    y = 1162.05
```

Figure 23.1 shows a plot of the original data and the computed curve fit. You can see that some data points are below the line and some are above, but

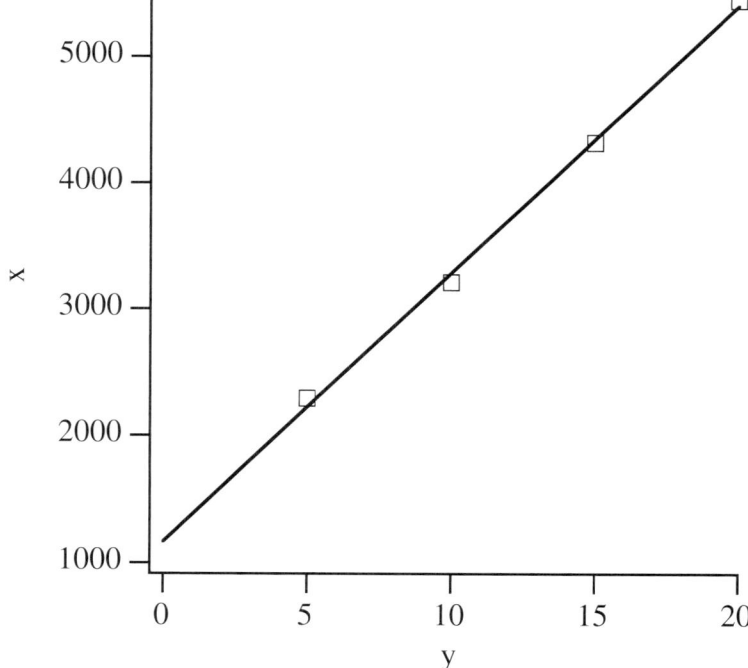

FIGURE 23.1 Least squares curve fit

the computed curve fit line does a good job representing the data. Another benefit of the curve fit line is it lets you estimate the intercept of the data, the value of y when $x = 0$.

Since the `Polynomial` class can be used to represent any polynomial equation (and therefore is generic) you might wonder why we didn't incorporate the `Polynomial` class functionality into the `leastSquaresFit()` method. The answer is that the least squares fit process can be applied to types of equations other than polynomials, and other equation types will fill the arrays $A^T A$ and $A^T b$ in different ways. To maintain the integrity of the generic class library, it is necessary to represent the curve fit equation in a separate class. We will discuss how to model nonpolynomial equations in the next chapter.

24

DATA MODELING AND CURVE FITS

Two main branches of science are experimental and theoretical. While the two parties don't always see eye-to-eye, there is a symbiotic relationship between them. The experimentalist is chiefly concerned with observation and measurement of physical phenomenon. The theoretician incorporates the experimental data into mathematical models to analyze situations for which no experimental data exists.

Experimental data, particularly when different measurement techniques and facilities are used, generally has some scatter to it. Even if scatter is minimal, the data may very well follow a nonlinear curve with respect to its independent variable. An engineer or scientific analyst usually requires an analytical expression for a collection of data, one or more mathematical expressions that provide a good representation of the data collection.

In this chapter we will look at ways to model a collection of data and to develop curve fit relations to that data. A common method used to curve fit data is by using a least squares approximation. The coefficients of a mathematical expression are determined that minimize the sum of the square of the errors between the curve fit equation and the original data points.

The least squares fit process is generic and can be applied to any number of problems. Because it is generic, we will define it as part of a generic class library. Much of the code development work for the least squares fit source code was performed in Chapter 23. The generic part of the least squares fit solution process was implemented in a method defined in the `DataModeling` class. Problem-specific information is encapsulated in the `Polynomial` class, an instance of which is sent to the `leastSquaresFit()` method as an input argument.

In Chapter 23 we developed many of the classes and methods needed to implement a least squares fit to a collection of data. In this chapter we will outline the mathematical derivation of the least squares method showing the governing equations for both polynomial and nonpolynomial curve fit equations. We will also briefly discuss other techniques used to model a collection of data. The topics we will discuss in this chapter are—

- Least squares fit to a polynomial equation
- The `DataModeling` class
- The `Polynomial` class
- Example problem: curve fitting specific heat data
- Fitting to nonpolynomial equations
- The `Power` class
- Other data modeling techniques

LEAST SQUARES FIT TO A POLYNOMIAL EQUATION

Consider a set of data $[y_1, y_2, ..., y_N]$ taken at discrete points $[x_1, x_2, ..., x_N]$. The data might be beam displacement as a function of load factor, specific heat as a function of temperature, or any other data you might wish to consider. Now let us assume that we want to define a straight line, a first-order polynomial expression, through the data.

$$y = c_1 x + c_0 \tag{24.1}$$

If we apply Eq. (24.1) to each data point in our collection of data, we obtain the following matrix equation.

$$\begin{pmatrix} x_1 & 1 \\ x_2 & 1 \\ \vdots & \vdots \\ x_N & 1 \end{pmatrix} \begin{bmatrix} c_1 \\ c_0 \end{bmatrix} = \begin{bmatrix} y_1 \\ y_2 \\ \vdots \\ y_N \end{bmatrix} \tag{24.2}$$

We will also refer to Eq. (24.2) by the shorthand notation, $Ac = y$. If there is any scatter to the data, the left-hand side of Eq. (24.2) will not equal the right hand side. There will be a difference, or error, between the computed value of y_i and the actual data point value. At any point the error is equal to Eq. (24.3).

Least Squares Fit to a Polynomial Equation

$$E_i = y_i - (c_1 x_i + c_0) \tag{24.3}$$

The total error of the system can be estimated by summing the square of the error at each individual point, as in Eq. (24.4).

$$E_{total} = \frac{1}{N} \sum_{i=1}^{N} (y_i - c_1 x - c_0)^2 \tag{24.4}$$

One way to find a best fit to the data is to compute the coefficients c_0 and c_1 such that the total error of the system is minimized. This is known as a least squares fit to a collection of data. It turns out that the least square coefficients can be determined by multiplying the transpose of the A matrix to the left and right hand sides of Eq. (24.2). The result is Eq. (24.5).

$$A^T A c = A^T y \tag{24.5}$$

If the left- and right-hand sides of Eq. (24.2) are multiplied by A^T you obtain the following matrix equation.

$$\begin{bmatrix} \sum_{i=1}^{N} x_i^2 & \sum_{i=1}^{N} x_i \\ \sum_{i=1}^{N} x_i & N \end{bmatrix} \begin{bmatrix} c_1 \\ c_0 \end{bmatrix} = \begin{bmatrix} \sum_{i=1}^{N} x_i y_i \\ \sum_{i=1}^{N} y_i \end{bmatrix} \tag{24.6}$$

When the system of equations shown in Eq. (24.6) is solved, the coefficients vector, $[c_1, c_o]$, will contain the least squares fit coefficients.

The least squares fit procedure can be applied to any polynomial expression. The contents and size of the arrays $A^T A$ and $A^T y$ will depend on the type of equation used. The number of columns and/or rows of the arrays $A^T A$ and $A^T y$ will be equal to the order of the polynomial equation used for the data fit plus one. Consider the case of the general polynomial expression shown in Eq. (24.7).

$$y_i = \sum_{j=0}^{M} c_j x_i^j \quad i = 1, 2, \ldots, N \tag{24.7}$$

In Eq. (24.7) the order of the equation is M. The array $A^T A$ will be an $(M+1) \times (M+1)$ array shown in Eq. (24.8).

$$A^T A = \begin{bmatrix} \sum_{i=1}^{N} x_i^{2M} & \sum_{i=1}^{N} x_i^{2M-1} & \cdots & \sum_{i=1}^{N} x_i^{M} \\ \sum_{i=1}^{N} x_i^{2M-1} & \sum_{i=1}^{N} x_i^{2M-2} & \cdots & \sum_{i=1}^{N} x_i^{M-1} \\ \vdots & \vdots & \ddots & \vdots \\ \sum_{i=1}^{N} x_i^{M} & \sum_{i=1}^{N} x_i^{M-1} & \cdots & N \end{bmatrix} \tag{24.8}$$

The $A^T y$ vector for the general polynomial shown in Eq. (24.7) is shown in Eq. (24.9).

$$A^T y = \begin{bmatrix} \sum_{i=1}^{N} y_i x_i^M \\ \sum_{i=1}^{N} y_i x_i^{M-1} \\ \vdots \\ \sum_{i=1}^{N} y_i \end{bmatrix} \quad (24.9)$$

The DataModeling Class

Let us develop (or revisit) the capability to compute a least squares fit to a collection of data according to Eq. (24.8) and Eq. (24.9). The least squares fit analysis process has three parts—you decide which polynomial equation to use for the curve fit expression, you load the arrays $A^T A$ and $A^T y$, and you solve the system of equations and return the polynomial coefficients.

The third part of the process is generic and can be implemented by a generic class. In Chapter 23 we defined the DataModeling class that contains the leastSquaresFit() method. The method takes three input arguments. A Polynomial equation is used to store information about the polynomial equation used for the data fit. The other two arguments are arrays used to store the data that will be fit.

The leastSquaresFit() method is simple. It only does three things. It first fills the $A^T A$ and $A^T y$ arrays calling the loadArrays() method on the Polynomial object. The least squares system of equations is then solved using the gaussian() method from the EqnSolver class. Finally, the polynomial coefficients are copied into a storage array using the setCoefficients() method.

The leastSquaresFit() method source code is shown next.

```
public static void leastSquaresFit(Polynomial equation,
                                   double x[], double y[]) {

    //  Load the AT*A and AT*b arrays using the data in
    //  x[] and y[].

    equation.loadArrays(x,y);
```

```
        //  Solve the system of equations AT*A*c = AT*y
        //  The b[] array is overwritten to contain the
        //  curve fit coefficients.

        EqnSolver.gaussian(equation.getA(),
                           equation.getB());

        //  Copy the curve fit coefficient values into
        //  the Polynomial object's coeffs[] array.

        equation.setCoefficients(equation.getB());
    }
```

The Polynomial Class

The `leastSquaresFit()` method is generic and can be applied to any type of polynomial expression for any collection of data. Its main purpose is to solve the least squares system of equations. The problem-specific components of the analysis are passed to the method as input arguments. One of the input arguments is an instance of the `Polynomial` class. The `Polynomial` class code listing is shown in Chapter 23. It is somewhat long and won't be repeated in its entirety here, but we will review some of its more important elements.

The `Polynomial` class represents a general polynomial. An integer argument passed to the `Polynomial` class constructor specifies the order of the polynomial expression. If the number 1 is passed as an argument to the constructor the `Polynomial` represents a straight line. If the number 2 is passed, the `Polynomial` represents a quadratic equation, and so on.

In addition to storing the order of the polynomial it represents, the `Polynomial` class defines three other data members. The `A[][]` array stores the values of the $A^T A$ matrix. The `b[]` array stores the values of the $A^T y$ matrix. The `coeffs[]` array is used to store the coefficients of the polynomial equation once they are computed.

The `loadArrays()` method is used to fill the `A[][]` and `b[]` array elements following the expressions shown in Eq. (24.8) and Eq. (24.9). The `getValue()` method is used to return a value of the polynomial equation. The `loadArrays()` and `getValue()` method code listings are shown here.

```
    //  Load the A[][] and b[] arrays. This implementation
    //  is for a general polynomial expression

    public void loadArrays(double x[], double y[]) {
      int numPoints = x.length;
```

```
    for(int j=0; j<order+1; ++j) {
      b[j] = 0.0;
      for(int k=0; k<numPoints; ++k) {
        b[j] += Math.pow(x[k],order-j)*y[k];
      }
    }

    for(int i=0; i<order+1; ++i) {
      for(int j=0; j<order+1; ++j) {
        A[i][j] = 0.0;
        for(int k=0; k<numPoints; ++k) {
          A[i][j] += Math.pow(x[k],2.0*order-i-j);
        }
      }
    }
  }

  // Return a value along the least squares fit line.
  // This implementation is for a general polynomial
  // expression.

  public double getValue(double x) {
    double y = 0.0;

    for(int i=0; i<getOrder()+1; ++i) {
      y += coeff[i]*Math.pow(x,order-i);
    }
    return y;
  }
```

Example Problem: Curve Fitting Specific Heat Data

Let's apply the `DataModeling` and `Polynomial` classes to a practical problem—developing a curve fit expression for the specific heat data of diatomic oxygen. The specific heat data is from the JANAF Thermochemical Tables.[1] As the name would suggest, this reference provides tables of specific heat, enthalpy, and entropy values as a function of temperature for a wide variety of chemical species. When developing chemical or thermodynamic analysis tools it is often useful to have a mathematical expression for specific heat as a function of temperature. We will obtain such an equation by applying a least squares analysis to the JANAF data. The data we will curve fit is shown in Table 24.1.

If you went through the examples from Chapter 23, you should have already placed the DataModeling.java and Polynomial.java source files in the

Example Problem: Curve Fitting Specific Heat Data

TABLE 24.1 Diatomic Oxygen-Specific Heat Data

Temperature, K	Specific Heat, $\dfrac{J}{mole - K}$
200	29.106
500	31.091
1000	34.870
2000	37.741
3000	39.864
4000	41.421
5000	42.675
6000	44.387

TechJava\MathLib directory and compiled the files from the package root directory. If you haven't already done that, do it now.

The `FifthOrderDemo` class is written to curve fit the specific heat data. The code listing is shown next. The first thing the class does is to define `x[]` and `y[]` arrays to store the data from Table 24.1. We'll use a fifth-order polynomial expression for the curve fit, so a `Polynomial` object is created passing the number 5 to the constructor. The `leastSquaresFit()` method is then called to compute the polynomial coefficients. The resulting polynomial equation is printed to standard output as well as a column of specific heat results.

```
import TechJava.MathLib.*;

public class FifthOrderDemo
{
  public static void main(String args[]) {
    double x[] = { 200.0, 500.0, 1000.0, 2000.0,
                   3000.0, 4000.0, 5000.0, 6000.0 };

    //  diatomic oxygen specific heat data
    double y[] = { 29.126, 31.091, 34.870, 37.741,
                   39.864, 41.421, 42.675, 44.387 };

    //  Create a Polynomial object that represents a
    //  fifth-order polynomial equation of the form
    //  y = A5*x^5 + A4*x^4 + A3*x^3 + A2*x^2 + A1*x + A0

    Polynomial fifthOrder = new Polynomial(5);

    //  Perform a least squares fit on the data.

    DataModeling.leastSquaresFit(fifthOrder, x, y);
```

```
      //  Print out the polynomial equation and some
      //  results over a range of temperatures.

      double coeff[] = fifthOrder.getCoefficients();
      System.out.println("cp = " + coeff[0] + "x^5 + " +
           coeff[1] + "x^4 + " + coeff[2] + "x^3 + " +
           coeff[3] + "x^2 + " + coeff[4] + "x + " +
           coeff[5]);

      System.out.println();
      double T;
      for (int i=0; i<60; ++i) {
        T = 100*(i+1);
        System.out.println("T = "+T+" cp = "+
                             fifthOrder.getValue(T));
      }
    }
  }
}
```

Output (removing some decimal places for clarity)—

```
cp = 9.82625E-18x^5 + -1.80028E-13x^4 + 1.32458E-9x^3 + -5.03019E-
6x^2 + 0.01157x + 26.82537
```

The column of data printed by the `FifthOrderDemo` class is plotted in Figure 24.1. Also shown on the plot are the original data points. The curve fit

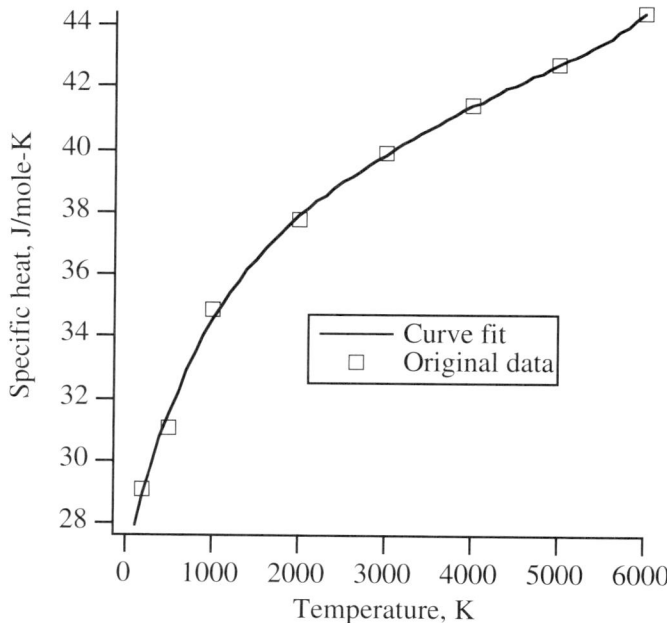

FIGURE 24.1 Least squares curve fit to specific heat data

equation does an excellent job of reproducing the original data over the entire temperature range. One thing to note, however, is that the curve fit equation would only be reliable for the temperature range over which it was constructed, 200 K to 6000 K. At temperatures below 200 K or above 6000 K, the curve fit equation might give erroneous specific heat values.

Fitting to Nonpolynomial Equations

The least squares methodology we've discussed so far is applicable to polynomial equations. But what happens when you want to use another type of equation, such as an exponential, logarithmic, or power function? You can still use the least squares analysis process if you can recast the function you want to use into polynomial form.

The best way to explain this is by example. In Chapter 19 we developed a method to compute the viscosity of a real gas mixture. To perform this computation you need to calculate the collision integrals of every species pair in the gas mixture. A collision integral can be thought of as an orientationally and thermally averaged collision probability between two molecules. Collision integral data can be measured experimentally at low temperatures but more often is computed in tabular form by analytical techniques. To use this collision integral data in an analysis program, it is usually convenient to create a curve fit to the tabular data. One commonly used curve fit expression is shown in Eq. (24.10).

$$\Omega^{(l,s)*} = DT^{[A(\ln T)^2 + B\ln T + C]} \qquad (24.10)$$

Clearly, Eq. (24.10) is not a polynomial equation but it can be converted into a polynomial form by taking the natural logarithm of the left- and right-hand sides. When this operation is performed, Eq. (24.10) becomes the following third-order equation.

$$\ln(\Omega^{(l,s)*}) = A(\ln T)^3 + B(\ln T)^2 + C(\ln T) + \ln(D) \qquad (24.11)$$

We can see from Eq. (24.11) that the original equation has been transformed into polynomial form. The independent variable is $\ln T$ and we are now trying to match values of $\ln(\Omega^{(l,s)*})$ instead of $\Omega^{(l,s)*}$, but the bottom line is that the least squares analysis can be applied to Eq. (24.11). As you might expect, the arrays $A^T A$ and $A^T y$ are somewhat different when using Eq. (24.11) than they are for a standard polynomial equation. The $A^T A$ array elements for Eq. (24.11) are shown in Eq. (24.12).

$$A^T A = \begin{bmatrix} \sum_{i=1}^{N}(\ln T_i)^6 & \sum_{i=1}^{N}(\ln T_i)^5 & \sum_{i=1}^{N}(\ln T_i)^4 & \sum_{i=1}^{N}(\ln T_i)^3 \\ \sum_{i=1}^{N}(\ln T_i)^5 & \sum_{i=1}^{N}(\ln T_i)^4 & \sum_{i=1}^{N}(\ln T_i)^3 & \sum_{i=1}^{N}(\ln T_i)^2 \\ \sum_{i=1}^{N}(\ln T_i)^4 & \sum_{i=1}^{N}(\ln T_i)^3 & \sum_{i=1}^{N}(\ln T_i)^2 & \sum_{i=1}^{N}\ln T_i \\ \sum_{i=1}^{N}(\ln T_i)^3 & \sum_{i=1}^{N}(\ln T_i)^2 & \sum_{i=1}^{N}\ln T_i & N \end{bmatrix} \quad (24.12)$$

The $A^T y$ vector for Eq. (24.11) is shown in Eq. (24.13).

$$A^T y = \begin{bmatrix} \sum_{i=1}^{N}(\ln T_i)^3 \ln(\Omega_i^{(l,s)*}) \\ \sum_{i=1}^{N}(\ln T_i)^2 \ln(\Omega_i^{(l,s)*}) \\ \sum_{i=1}^{N}\ln T_i \ln(\Omega_i^{(l,s)*}) \\ \sum_{i=1}^{N}\ln(\Omega_i^{(l,s)*}) \end{bmatrix} \quad (24.13)$$

THE Power CLASS

Extending our least squares capability to include an equation of the form shown in Eq. (24.11) is quite simple. We have already done most of the work. The generic part of the analysis, the `leastSquaresFit()` method from the `DataModeling` class, doesn't need to be changed at all. All we have to do is to write a `Polynomial` subclass that will model Eq. (24.11).

We will call this class the `Power` class. Its code listing is shown next. Eq. (24.11) is a third-order polynomial equation so the `Power` constructor simply calls the `Polynomial` constructor passing it the value 3. The only other thing the `Power` class must do is to override the `loadArrays()` and `getValue()` methods. The `loadArrays()` method is overridden according to Eq. (24.12) and Eq. (24.13). The `getValue()` method is overridden to return a value according to Eq. (24.10).

```
package TechJava.MathLib;

public class Power extends Polynomial
{
```

```java
// This models the third-order equation
// lnY = A*(lnT)^3 + B*(lnT)^2 + C*lnT + E

public Power(){
  super(3);
}

// Override the loadArray() method for a power
//   function.

public void loadArrays(double x[], double y[]) {
  int numPoints = x.length;
  double order = getOrder();
  double A, b;

  for(int j=0; j<order+1; ++j) {
    b = 0.0;
    for(int k=0; k<numPoints; ++k) {
      b += Math.pow(Math.log(x[k]),order - j)*y[k];
    }
    setB(j,b);
  }

  for(int i=0; i<order+1; ++i) {
    for(int j=0; j<order+1; ++j) {
      A = 0.0;
      for(int k=0; k<numPoints; ++k) {
        A += Math.pow(Math.log(x[k]),order - i)*
             Math.pow(Math.log(x[k]),order - j);
      }
      setA(i,j,A);
    }
  }
}

// Return a value along the least squares fit line.
// This implementation is for a power function

public double getValue(double T) {
  double tmp;
  double A, B, C, D;
  double lnT = Math.log(T);

  A = getCoefficient(0);
  B = getCoefficient(1);
  C = getCoefficient(2);
  D = Math.exp(getCoefficient(3));

  tmp = A*lnT*lnT + B*lnT + C;
  return D*Math.pow(T,tmp);
}
}
```

TABLE 24.2 Collision Integral Data

TEMPERATURE, K	$\Omega^{(2,2)*}$, SOURCE 1	$\Omega^{(2,2)*}$, SOURCE 2
200	10.892	14.914
500	9.648	11.435
1000	9.723	9.877
2000	9.351	8.701
3000	8.945	8.076
4000	8.585	7.635
5000	8.269	7.289
6000	7.991	7.003

To test if the Power class is working properly, let's try to curve fit the collision integral data shown in Table 24.2. In this case the data is for the $\Omega^{(2,2)*}$ collision integral for the $O_2 - O_2$ collision pair. Data will be used from two sources,[2,3] so there will be two data points at each of the temperature values.

The PowerDemo class fits the data shown in Table 24.2 to an expression of the type shown in Eq. (24.10). The process is very similar to the specific heat curve fit example earlier in this chapter. Arrays named x[] and y[] are defined to store the data from Table 24.2. Since the modified curve fit expression shown in Eq. (24.11) uses the natural logarithm of the collision integral data, the elements of the y[] array are replaced with their natural logarithms.

A Power object is created and sent along with the arrays x[] and y[] to the leastSquaresFit() method. The resulting coefficients are printed as well as a column of collision integral data calculated using the curve fit equation.

```
import TechJava.MathLib.*;

public class PowerDemo
{
  public static void main(String args[]) {
    double x[] = { 200.0, 500.0, 1000.0, 2000.0,
                   3000.0, 4000.0, 5000.0, 6000.0,
                   200.0, 500.0, 1000.0, 2000.0,
                   3000.0, 4000.0, 5000.0, 6000.0 };

    double y[] = { 10.892, 9.648, 9.723, 9.351,
                   8.945, 8.585, 8.269, 7.991,
                   14.914, 11.435, 9.877, 8.701,
                   8.076, 7.635, 7.289, 7.003 };
```

```
    // replace the y[] array elements with their
    // natural logarithm

    for(int i=0; i<y.length; ++i) {
      y[i] = Math.log(y[i]);
    }

    // Create a Power object that represents the eqn
    // y = D*Math.pow(T, A*lnT*lnT + B*lnT + C)

    Power power = new Power();

    // Perform the least squares fit

    DataModeling.leastSquaresFit(power, x, y);

    // Write out the power function coefficients
    // and some data values. Remember that the
    // D coefficient is computed as ln(D)

    System.out.println("A = " +
                      power.getCoefficient(0));
    System.out.println("B = " +
                      power.getCoefficient(1));
    System.out.println("C = " +
                      power.getCoefficient(2));
    System.out.println("D = " +
              Math.exp(power.getCoefficient(3)));

    System.out.println();
    double T;
    for (int i=2; i<61; ++i) {
      T = 100*i;
      System.out.println("T = " + T + " Omega = " +
                        power.getValue(T));
    }
  }
}
```

Output—

```
A = -0.017596459962575077
B = 0.37349043457915776
C = -2.748620708686359
D = 10292.688325352558
```

Figure 24.2 shows a plot of the computed curve fit equation along with the initial data. You can see that there is a considerable amount of scatter between the two data sources. The least squares curve fit equation lies pretty much halfway between the two sets of original data.

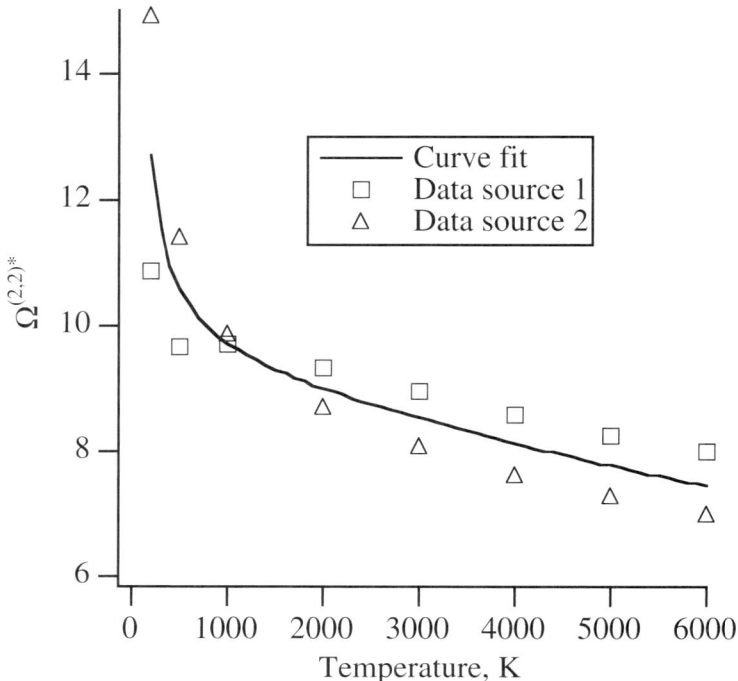

FIGURE 24.2 Curve fit to collision integral data

OTHER DATA MODELING TECHNIQUES

There are other techniques besides least squares fitting to model data and develop curve fit relations. Other data modeling techniques include inverse-Hessian, steepest descent, and Levenberg-Marquadt methods that are used to map data to general nonlinear functions. Monte Carlo algorithms use statistical techniques to model data according to a probability distribution.

We won't implement any of these data modeling techniques in this chapter, but if you were to do so you would follow a similar procedure as was used to implement the least squares curve fit method. First, you would determine if the algorithm could be implemented as a generic class library and, if so, divide the analysis into generic and problem-specific parts. You would then most likely implement the data modeling technique as a `public static` method accepting any problem-specific data as arguments to the method.

References

1. Chase, M., "NIST-JANAF Thermochemical Tables," *Journal of Physical and Chemical Reference Data,* Monograph No. 9, 1998, p. 1745.

2. Gupta, R. N., J. M. Yos, and R. A. Thompson, "A Review of Reaction Rates and Thermodynamic and Transport Properties for the 11 Species Air Model for Chemical and Thermal Nonequilibrium Calculations to 30000 K," NASA RP-1232, Aug. 1990.

3. Capitelli, M., et al, "Transport Properties of High Temperature Air Species," AIAA Paper 98-2936, June 1998.

25

JAVA I/O

So far in this book, we have demonstrated most of the classes we developed using simple driver programs that hard-coded the input arguments required by the class. This approach is okay for demonstration programs but not for real-life scientific and engineering applications. Ideally, you want to compile your analysis classes and driver programs once and have them be flexible enough to accept different input arguments every time the program is executed. What's more, you may wish to do different things with the output from your applications. Sometimes, printing the output to the screen may be sufficient. Other times you may want to write the output to a file. You may even wish to permanently save the data structure associated with an object.

Java provides a rich library of I/O classes, interfaces, and methods to meet a wide variety of data input and output needs. Java uses stream-based I/O. A stream can be thought of as a flow of data from a source to a destination. The data source might be a Java program, an input file, or the keyboard. The destination might be the console, an output file, or a Java program. In either case, the basic process is the same. A stream is opened between a source and destination and data is read from or written to the stream. Most of the traditional I/O classes can be found in the java.io package. The release of Java version 1.4 saw the introduction of the java.nio package and its subpackages that define additional I/O functionality. The contents of java.nio and its subpackages will be discussed briefly at the end of this chapter.

There are two general types of Java I/O streams—byte and character. Byte streams are used to read or write 8-bit byte data, either a single byte or the contents of a byte array. Byte streams are useful for reading image or sound files or any other binary data set. Since reading and writing to text files is such a common programming activity, Java also provides a family of character I/O classes that read and write 16-bit character data. While byte streams can be used to read character data, you should generally use character streams for this purpose. Character streams can read any Unicode character, whereas byte streams can only read ISO-Latin-1 8-bit bytes.

There are five basic ways for a scientific or engineering program to read and write data—through command line arguments, by using the standard I/O streams, by reading from or writing to a file, by putting a GUI front-end on the application, or by turning the application into a web-based program. In this chapter we will discuss the first three methods. An introduction to Java GUI development is provided in Chapter 26. A discussion of how to create Web-based applications using Java servlets is part of Chapter 27.

This chapter will be presented in a task-oriented manner. The Java I/O libraries are extensive and there isn't room to provide comprehensive coverage of all of them in this book. This chapter will provide a big-picture look at the I/O classes and methods you will most likely use in your scientific and engineering programming. It will also demonstrate three commonly used ways to read and write data. The topics covered in this chapter are—

- General concepts
- Byte input streams
- Byte output streams
- Character input streams
- Character output streams
- Test case: an atmosphere modeling tool
- Getting input from command line arguments
- Using the standard I/O streams
- Reading and writing to a file
- Saving and restoring objects
- The `java.nio` packages

GENERAL CONCEPTS

Java uses stream-based I/O. A data stream is simply a flow of data from a data source to a destination. An input stream connects a data destination to a source. Data is read from the stream. An output stream connects a data source to a destination. Data is written to the stream. The data source might be an array of data, a `String`, the contents of a file, or input received from the keyboard. Possible destinations include the console, a file, a Java program, or even another data stream.

As you might expect, I/O streams are encapsulated in classes, largely found in the `java.io` package. To open a stream, you create an instance of the appropriate I/O class. The stream object will invoke methods to read or write data to its stream. There are two general types of Java I/O streams—byte and character. Byte streams are used to read and write byte data, either 1 byte at a time or an array of bytes. Byte streams are useful for I/O operations on things like images or sound files. Byte streams can also be used to save and restore objects.

One of the most common I/O tasks is to either read data from a file or write data to a file. Using a byte stream to read or write character data is a bit inconvenient. The data has to be first read as byte data, then converted into character data. In addition, byte streams can only read 8-bit bytes, meaning they cannot read all Unicode characters. To make things easier for you and to provide I/O capability for all Unicode characters, Java provides a family of character I/O streams that read or write 16-bit character data. These classes allow you to read and write character data directly as characters or `Strings`.

The Java I/O libraries provide classes that allow buffered I/O for improved performance. Rather than reading or writing each byte or character individually, the data is first stored in an internal buffer. When the buffer reaches its capacity, its contents are read in or written out. Buffering improves efficiency by reducing the number of low-level system calls required for the read or write. This efficiency gain is particularly important when reading or writing to a file. There are also classes that define streams that are wrapped around other streams to add additional functionality to the underlying stream. For example, an `InputStreamReader` can be wrapped around the standard input stream, allowing you to read keyboard input as character data.

The next few sections are meant to provide a brief overview of the I/O classes and methods that you will most likely use in your scientific and engineering programming work. It is not meant to be comprehensive and won't discuss every class and method in detail. The Java I/O libraries are so large that it is easy to get bogged down in detail and lose sight of the important concepts. We'll try to focus on the key byte and character stream classes and on the key methods of each class.

Byte Input Streams

The byte input stream class hierarchy is shown in Figure 25.1. The `InputStream` class is the abstract superclass of all byte input stream classes. It defines methods to read one or more bytes of data, to flush the contents of an input buffer, to close an input stream, and to determine how much data is available from an input stream. These methods are often overridden by `InputStream` subclasses.

The `InputStream` class has a number of subclasses that provide additional functionality or are used for specialized purposes. The `FileInputStream` class allows you to read data from a file. The `ObjectInputStream` class lets you restore an object that was previously saved using an `ObjectOutputStream`. The `ByteArrayInputStream` class reads data from a byte array.

The `FilterInputStream` class is the direct superclass of two classes that wrap other `InputStream` objects to provide additional functionality. The `BufferedInputStream` class provides a memory buffer that results in more efficient reading of data. The `DataInputStream` class defines meth-

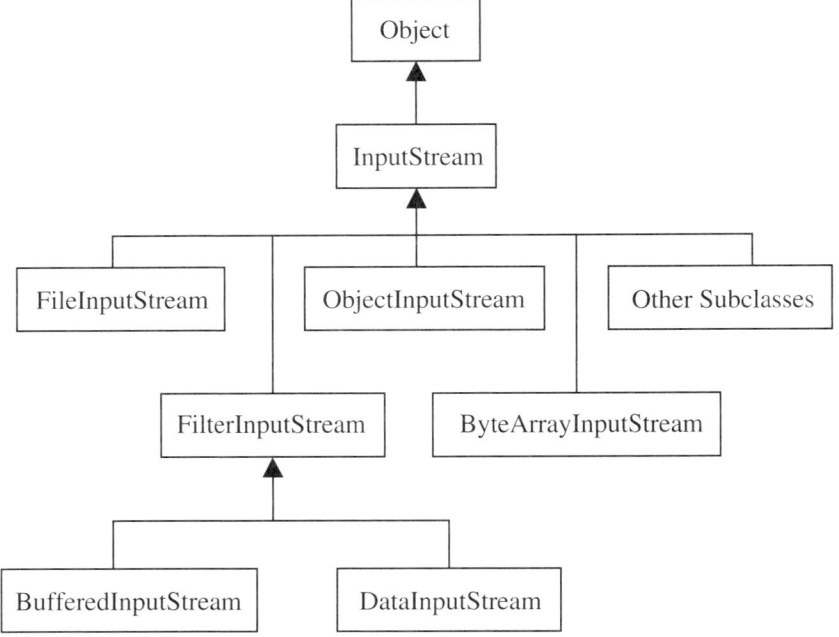

FIGURE 25.1 Byte input class hierarchy

ods that can read a primitive value directly from the stream or to fill a byte array with data from the stream.

The byte input stream classes should be primarily used for data that would normally be stored as bytes such as image, audio, or binary data files. For reading text files, or other character data, you are probably better off using a character input stream.

InputStream Class

The InputStream class is an abstract class that is the superclass of all byte input stream classes and defines methods common to all byte input streams. Among the important methods defined in the InputStream class are the available(), close(), and read() methods.

```
public int available() throws IOException
public void close() throws IOException
public abstract int read() throws IOException
public int read(byte[] buf) throws IOException
public int read(byte[] buf, int offset, int length) throws IOException
```

The available() method returns the number of bytes that can be read from the input stream. This method can be useful for sizing a byte array that will store input data. The close() method closes the input stream and releases any resources associated with it. It's always a good idea to close your I/O streams when you are finished with them.

The read() method reads one or more bytes from the input stream. The no-argument version reads a single byte from the stream and returns the byte as an integer value between 0 and 255. The return value is –1 when the end of the stream is reached. The second and third versions fill a byte array with data from the stream. The return value is the number of bytes actually read. An exception is thrown if the byte array argument is null.

BufferedInputStream Class

A BufferedInputStream is used to provide an underlying byte input stream with a memory buffer for more efficient data reading. Instead of reading data byte-by-byte, a large number of bytes are read into an internal buffer. Higher level system functions can read data from the memory buffer. Using a memory buffer improves performance by reducing the number of times the disk must be accessed. A `BufferedInputStream` object is always wrapped around an underlying `InputStream`.

The `BufferedInputStream` class defines two public constructors.

```
public BufferedInputStream(InputStream stream)
public BufferedInputStream(InputStream stream, int bufferSize)
```

You can specify the buffer size in the constructor if you wish. In addition to the constructors, the `BufferedInputStream` class overrides some of the `InputStream` methods, including the `read()` methods, but does not define any new methods for reading byte data.

`ByteArrayInputStream` Class

The `ByteArrayInputStream` class is a subclass of the `InputStream` class that is used to read one or more bytes from a byte array passed to the `ByteArrayInputStream` constructor. The class defines two constructors.

```
public ByteArrayInputStream(byte[] buf)
public ByteArrayInputStream(byte[] buf, int offset, int length)
```

With the first constructor the entire byte array is available for reading. The second constructor specifies that a maximum of `length` bytes will be read from the byte array starting at position `offset`. The `ByteArrayInputStream` class overrides many of the methods from the `InputStream` class including the `read()` methods.

`DataInputStream` Class

A `DataInputStream` object allows primitive type values to be read directly from an underlying byte input stream. This can be convenient, for instance, when reading data from a file. The `DataInputStream` class defines one constructor.

```
public DataInputStream(InputStream stream)
```

A `DataInputStream` object is always wrapped around an underlying `InputStream`. In addition to the `read()` methods it inherits from the `InputStream` class, the `DataInputStream` class defines the following methods to read data.

```
public final boolean readBoolean() throws IOException
public final byte readByte() throws IOException
public final char readChar() throws IOException
public final double readDouble() throws IOException
public final float readFloat() throws IOException
public final int readInt() throws IOException
public final long readLong() throws IOException
public final short readShort() throws IOException
public final int readUnsignedByte() throws IOException
public final int readUnsignedShort() throws IOException
```

The `DataInputStream` class methods are all used to read one or more bytes from the underlying stream and return the data read as a primitive type value. The `DataInputStream` also defines a method that can be used to fill a byte array with data from the stream.

```
public final void readFully(byte[] buf) throws IOException
public final void readFully(byte[] buf, int offset, int length)
  throws IOException
```

The `readFully()` method will fill the specified byte array with data from the input stream. Either the entire byte array will be filled or a specified number of bytes, starting at the specified offset. If you want to read all of the available bytes in the stream, the `available()` method can be used to size the byte array before calling this method.

FileInputStream Class

A `FileInputStream` object associates an input stream with an input file, allowing you to read data from the file. The `FileInputStream` class defines three constructors.

```
public FileInputStream(FileDescriptor fd)
public FileInputStream(File file) throws FileNotFoundException
public FileInputStream(String path) throws FileNotFound-
  Exception
```

There are three ways to specify the file. The most direct way is to specify the path to the file. The `FileInputStream` class provides overridden versions of the three `read()` methods from the `InputStream` class. If you want to read primitive data from the file, you can wrap a `DataInputStream` around the `FileInputStream`. If you want to read an object that was stored to disk, you can wrap an `ObjectInputStream` around a `FileInputStream`.

For an example of using the `FileInputStream` class, look at the "Saving and Restoring Objects" section later in this chapter.

`FilterInputStream` Class

`FilterInputStream` is the superclass for byte input streams that are wrapped around other streams to provide additional functionality to the underlying stream. Subclasses of `FilterInputStream` include the `DataInputStream` and `BufferedInputStream` classes. The `FilterInputStream` class overrides the `InputStream` methods to pass all requests to the underlying stream, but does not define any new methods.

`ObjectInputStream` Class

The `ObjectInputStream` class is used to restore primitive data and objects that have been serialized using an `ObjectOutputStream`. When used in conjunction with a `FileInputStream`, an `ObjectInputStream` object can be used to read objects that have been saved to disk. Although the `ObjectInputStream` class is wrapped around another input stream, it is not a subclass of `FilterInputStream`. The `ObjectInputStream` class defines one public constructor.

```
public ObjectInputStream(InputStream stream)
```

In addition to overriding the methods defined in the `InputStream` class, the `ObjectInputStream` class defines the following methods to read a primitive value that was previously saved using an `ObjectOutputStream`.

```
public boolean readBoolean() throws IOException
public byte readByte() throws IOException
public char readChar() throws IOException
public double readDouble() throws IOException
public float readFloat() throws IOException
public int readInt() throws IOException
public long readLong() throws IOException
public short readShort() throws IOException
public int readUnsignedByte() throws IOException
public int readUnsignedShort() throws IOException
```

The ObjectInputStream class defines two versions of the read-Fully() method that fill a byte array with data read from the input stream.

```
public void readFully(byte[] buf) throws IOException
public void readFully(byte[] buf, int offset, int length)
throws IOException
```

The readFully() method will fill the specified byte array with data from the input stream. Either the entire byte array will be filled or a specified number of bytes, starting at the specified offset. If you want to read all of the available bytes in the stream, the available() method can be used to size the byte array before calling this method.

One of the more useful features of the ObjectInputStream class is that it defines a method that can restore a previously serialized object.

```
public final Object readObject() throws IOException, ClassNotFoundException
```

The readObject() method is used to restore an instance of a class that was previously stored using an ObjectOutputStream. Typically, the object will have been written to a file. The default implementation restores the value of all nonstatic and nontransient data members to the return Object. The return value of the method can be cast into another data type if desired. An ObjectInputStream can only restore instances of classes that implement the Serializable interface. The Serializable interface is defined in the java.io package. It declares no methods or constants but is used as a marker to indicate a class that can be serialized (persistently stored).

The "Saving and Restoring Objects" section later in this chapter contains an example of saving and restoring an object to disk.

Other InputStream Subclasses

There are other subclasses of InputStream that you probably won't use much in your technical programming, including the StringBufferInputStream, AudioInputStream, PipedInputStream, and SequenceInputStream classes. We won't discuss details of these classes in this book. If you want more information on any of them, consult the Sun Java doc pages.

Byte Output Streams

The byte output stream class hierarchy is shown in Figure 25.2. The `OutputStream` class is the abstract superclass of all byte output stream classes. It defines methods to close an output stream, to write the contents on a buffer to the stream, and to write 1 byte or an array of bytes to the stream. The `OutputStream` class has a number of subclasses that override the `OutputStream` methods and/or provide additional functionality.

The `FileOutputStream` class connects an output stream to a file allowing you to write data to that file. The `ObjectOutputStream` class lets you write the data from an object to an output stream. If the `ObjectOutputStream` is wrapped around a `FileOutputStream`, you can write the data for an object to a file. A saved object can be restored using an `ObjectInputStream`. The `ByteArrayOutputStream` class writes data to a byte array.

The `FilterOutputStream` class is the superclass of three classes that are wrapped around other `OutputStream` objects to provide additional functionality. The `BufferedOutputStream` class provides an intermediate buffer that improves I/O performance. The `DataOutputStream` class defines methods that can write a primitive value directly to the stream without

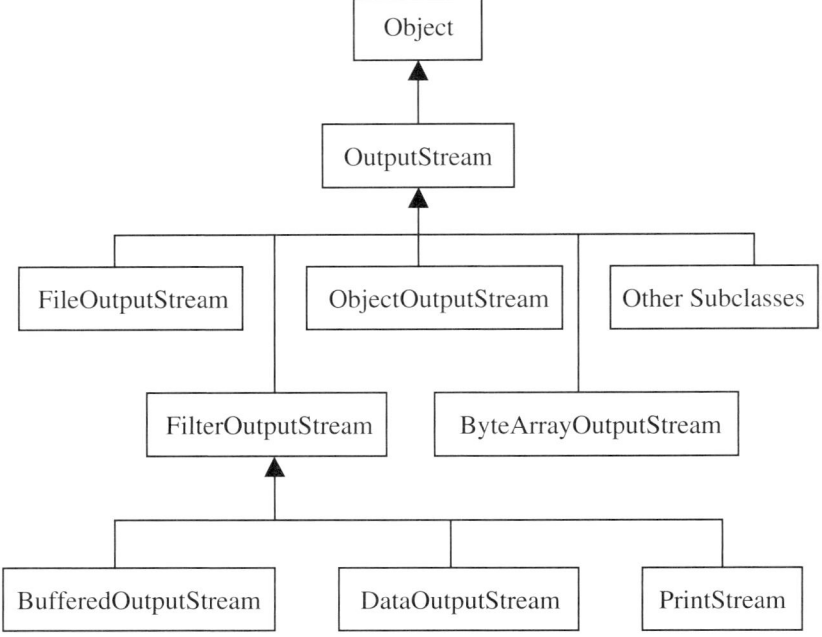

Figure 25.2 Byte output stream class hierarchy

first having to convert it to bytes. The `PrintStream` class provides the `print()` and `println()` methods that print a `String` or a `String` representation of a primitive type value or `Object` to the output stream.

`OutputStream` Class

The `OutputStream` class is the abstract superclass of all byte output stream classes and defines methods available to all byte output streams. `OutputStream` subclasses will often override these methods to suit their own needs.

```
public void close() throws IOException
public void flush() throws IOException
public abstract void write(int b) throws IOException
public void write(byte[] b) throws IOException
public void write(byte[] b, int offset, int length) throws IOException
```

The `close()` method is overridden by `OutputStream` subclasses to close the output stream and release any resources allocated to it. The `flush()` method is overridden by `OutputStream` subclasses to force any bytes stored in an output buffer to be written to the stream. The `write()` method is used to write one or more bytes to the output stream. The first version, when overridden by an `OutputStream` subclass, writes a single byte (the input argument is really an `int`) to the output stream. The second version writes the contents of an array of bytes to the stream. The third version writes `length` bytes to the stream from the specified byte array starting at position `offset`.

`BufferedOutputStream` Class

A `BufferedOutputStream` is wrapped around another `OutputStream` to provide buffered output. Rather than writing bytes to the output stream one at a time, the bytes are first written to an internal buffer. When the buffer reaches its capacity the contents are written to the output stream. This operation improves performance by reducing the number of low-level system calls required. The `BufferedOutputStream` class defines two public constructors.

```
public BufferedOutputStream(OutputStream stream)
public BufferedOutputStream(OutputStream stream, int bufferSize)
```

The second constructor allows you to specify the size of the internal buffer. The `BufferedOutputStream` class overrides some of the methods from the `OutputStream` class but does not define any new methods.

ByteArrayOutputStream Class

A `ByteArrayOutputStream` object is an output stream that writes data into a byte array. The class defines two public constructors.

```
public ByteArrayOutputStream()
public ByteArrayOutputStream(int bufferSize)
```

The second constructor allows you to specify the size of the output stream byte array. In addition to overriding some of the methods from the `OutputStream` class, the `ByteArrayOutputStream` defines the following methods.

```
public int size()
public byte[] toByteArray()
public String toString()
public void writeTo(OutputStream stream) throws IOException
```

The `size()` method returns the current size of the byte array. The `toByteArray()` method returns the contents of the output stream byte array. The `toString()` method returns the contents of the output stream byte array as a `String` by converting the bytes to character data. The `writeTo()` method writes the contents of the output stream byte array to another output stream. This method could be used, for instance, to write the contents of the byte array to a file.

DataOutputStream Class

The `DataOutputStream` class allows you to write primitive type values to a byte output stream. A `DataOutputStream` object is always wrapped around another `OutputStream` object. If you want to write primitive types to a file, you could wrap a `DataOutputStream` around a `FileOutputStream`. The `DataOutputStream` class defines one public constructor.

```
public DataOutputStream(OutputStream stream)
```

In addition to overriding some of the `OutputStream` class methods, the `DataOutputStream` class defines the following methods to write primitive values or `String` objects to the output stream.

```
public final void writeBoolean(boolean b) throws IOException
public final void writeByte(int b) throws IOException
public final void writeBytes(String str) throws IOException
public final void writeChar(int c) throws IOException
public final void writeChars(String str) throws IOException
public final void writeDouble(double d) throws IOException
public final void writeFloat(float f) throws IOException
public final void writeInt(int i) throws IOException
public final void writeLong(long l) throws IOException
public final void writeShort(short s) throws IOException
public final void writeUTF(String str) throws IOException
```

These methods are used to write a primitive value or `String` to the output stream. The `writeBytes()` method writes a `String` as a sequence of bytes. The `writeChars()` method writes a `String` as a sequence of characters. The `writeUTF()` method writes a `String` as a sequence of bytes using the UTF-8 character encoding scheme.

`FileOutputStream` Class

The `FileOutputStream` class is used to connect an output stream with a file on disk. Whatever is written to the output stream will be written to the file. The `FileOutputStream` class defines five public constructors.

```
public FileOutputStream(File file) throws FileNotFoundException
public FileOutputStream(File file, boolean append) throws FileNotFoundException
public FileOutputStream(FileDescriptor desc)
public FileOutputStream(String name) throws FileNotFoundException
public FileOutputStream(String name, boolean append) throws FileNotFoundException
```

The file can be specified by a `File` object, a `FileDescriptor` object, or by providing the name and, if necessary, path of the file. If the file does not exist, it will be created. If you specify a path, the directory structure must already exist. If `append` is true, data is written starting at the end of the file. The default is false, meaning that data is written from the beginning of the file.

The `FileOutputStream` class overrides the three `write()` methods from the `OutputStream` class but does not provide any new methods to write data to the output stream.

`FilterOutputStream` Class

The `FilterOutputStream` is the superclass for byte output streams that are wrapped around other output streams to provide additional functionality to the underlying stream. Child classes of the `FilterOutputStream` class include the `BufferedOutputStream`, `DataOutputStream`, and `PrintStream` classes. The `FilterOutputStream` class overrides the `OutputStream` methods to pass all requests to the underlying stream, but does not define any new methods.

`ObjectOutputStream` Class

An `ObjectOutputStream` object can be used to write primitive types and objects to an output stream. An `ObjectOutputStream` is always wrapped around another output stream. If the `ObjectOutputStream` is wrapped around a `FileOutputStream`, you can save an object or primitive type value to a file. A saved object or value can be restored using an `ObjectInputStream`. The class defines one public constructor.

```
public ObjectOutputStream(OutputStream stream) throws IOException
```

In addition to overriding some of the `OutputStream` class methods, the `ObjectOutputStream` class provides the following methods for writing a primitive value to an output stream. The description of these methods is the same as previously given in the "DataOutputStream Class" section.

```
public void writeBoolean(boolean b) throws IOException
public void writeByte(int b) throws IOException
public void writeBytes(String str) throws IOException
public void writeChar(int c) throws IOException
public void writeChars(String str) throws IOException
public void writeDouble(double d) throws IOException
public void writeFloat(float f) throws IOException
public void writeInt(int i) throws IOException
public void writeLong(long l) throws IOException
public void writeShort(short s) throws IOException
public void writeUTF(String str) throws IOException
```

The `ObjectOutputStream` class also defines a method for writing an object to an output stream.

```
public final void writeObject(Object obj) throws IOException
```

The `writeObject()` method writes the class of the object, the class signature, and the values of the nonstatic and nontransient data members to the underlying output stream. If the underlying stream is a `FileOutputStream`, the object will be saved as a file. Only objects that are instances of classes that implement the `Serializable` interface can be passed to this method. An attempt to write an object that does not implement `Serializable` will cause an exception to be thrown. An object written by this method can be restored using an `ObjectInputStream`.

For an example of how an `ObjectOutputStream` can store an object to disk, see the "Saving and Restoring Objects" section later in this chapter.

`PrintStream` Class

A `PrintStream` object can be wrapped around another output stream allowing the underlying stream access to the `print()` and `println()` methods. The standard output stream is implemented as an instance of the `PrintStream` class. One useful feature of the `PrintStream` class is that its methods never throw an `IOException` and don't have to be enclosed in a `try` block.

The `PrintStream` class defines three public constructors.

```
public PrintStream(OutputStream stream)
public PrintStream(OutputStream stream, boolean autoFlush)
public PrintStream(OutputStream stream, boolean autoFlush,
 String encoding)
```

If the argument `autoFlush` is true, the output buffer is flushed whenever a byte array is written. You can also specify a character encoding scheme if you wish. Examples of character encoding schemes include Unicode and UTF8. In addition to overriding some of the `OutputStream` class methods, the `PrintStream` class defines the following methods.

```
public void print(boolean b)
public void print(char c)
public void print(char[] chars)
public void print(double d)
public void print(float f)
public void print(int i)
public void print(long l)
public void print(Object obj)
public void print(String str)
```

The `print()` method prints a `String` or a `String` representation of a primitive type value or `Object` to the output stream without appending a newline character to the end of the `String`.

```
public void println()
public void println(boolean b)
public void println(char c)
public void println(char[] chars)
public void println(double d)
public void println(float f)
public void println(int i)
public void println(long l)
public void println(Object obj)
public void println(String str)
```

The `println()` method prints a `String` or a `String` representation of a primitive type value or `Object` to the output stream. A newline character is appended to the end of the `String`. The no-argument version simply writes a newline to the output stream. The `println()` method that has been used dozens of times in the examples of this book is usually called by the standard output stream.

Character Input Streams

The character input stream class hierarchy is shown in Figure 25.3. The `Reader` class is the abstract superclass of all character input stream classes. Among other things, it defines methods to read one or more characters from the input stream.

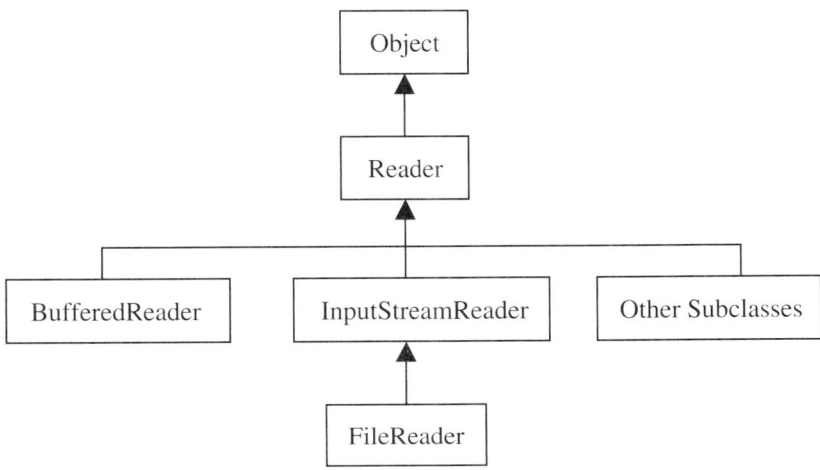

FIGURE 25.3 Character input stream classes

The `BufferedReader` class provides an internal buffer to improve I/O performance. It also defines the `readLine()` method that can read an entire line of data at a time. The `InputStreamReader` class is a bridging class between character and byte input streams. It can be wrapped around a byte stream allowing data from the byte stream to be read as characters. The `FileReader` class connects an input stream to a file so character data can be read from the file.

Reader Class

The `Reader` class is the abstract superclass of all character input stream classes. It provides methods that are available to all character input streams. The most important of these methods are the `close()` and `read()` methods.

```
public abstract void close() throws IOException
public int read() throws IOException
public int read(char[] chars) throws IOException
public int read(char[] chars, int offset, int length) throws
IOException
```

The `close()` method, when overridden by a `Reader` subclass, closes the input stream and releases any resources associated with it. The `read()` method is used to read one or more characters from the input stream. The first version reads one character and returns the character as an integer value between 0 and 65535. The second version reads characters into the specified character array. The return value is the number of characters read or –1 if the end of the stream has been reached. The third version does the same thing as the second version except `length` characters are read into the array starting at array index `offset`.

`BufferedReader` Class

A `BufferedReader` provides a memory buffer for more efficient reading of character data. The class also defines the `readLine()` method that can read an entire line of text from an input file and return the line as a `String`. A `BufferedReader` is wrapped around another character input stream. The class defines two public constructors.

```
public BufferedReader(Reader stream)
public BufferedReader(Reader stream, int bufferSize)
```

The second version of the constructor allows you to specify the buffer size. In addition to overriding some of the methods from the `Reader` class, the `BufferedReader` class defines the following method.

```
public String readLine() throws IOException.
```

The `readLine()` method reads a line of text from the input stream and returns the line as a `String`. The read operation will continue until a linefeed, carriage return, or carriage return immediately followed by a linefeed is encountered.

To see how a `BufferedReader` is used to read input data from a file, see the "Reading and Writing to a File" section later in this chapter.

`FileReader` Class

The `FileReader` class represents a character input stream that is connected to a file, allowing you to read data from the file. The class does not define any new methods or override any of the methods inherited from the `InputStreamReader` or `Reader` classes, but it does define three public constructors.

```
public FileReader(File file) throws FileNotFoundException
public FileReader(FileDescriptor desc)
public FileReader(String name) throws FileNotFoundException
```

You can specify the file using a `File` object, a `FileDescriptor` object, or by providing a `String` containing the name and/or path of the file. An example of using the `FileReader` class is provided in the "Reading and Writing to a File" section later in this chapter.

`InputStreamReader` Class

The `InputStreamReader` class provides a bridge between the byte and character input stream worlds. An `InputStreamReader` object (a character stream) is wrapped around an `InputStream` object (a byte stream). The `InputStreamReader` reads the input data as bytes and then converts the bytes to character data using a character set mapping.

The `InputStreamReader` class allows you to do some interesting things. For example, if you wrap an `InputStreamReader` around the standard input stream, you can read keyboard input as character data. If you wanted to read a line of keyboard input at a time, you could wrap a `BufferedReader` around the `InputStreamReader`.

The `InputStreamReader` class does not define any new methods to read data but does define four public constructors.

```
public InputStreamReader(InputStream stream)
public InputStreamReader(InputStream stream, Charset cs)
public InputStreamReader(InputStream stream, CharsetDecoder dec)
public InputStreamReader(InputStream stream, String charsetName) throws UnsupportedEncodingException
```

The first constructor version uses the default character set mapping scheme. The other three versions allow you to specify a character mapping to be used. For an example of using an `InputStreamReader` to read keyboard input, see the "Using the Standard I/O Streams" section later in this chapter.

Other `Reader` Subclasses

There are other `Reader` subclasses in the `java.io` package that you probably won't use much in your scientific and engineering programming work. These include `CharArrayReader`, `FilterReader`, `PipedReader`,

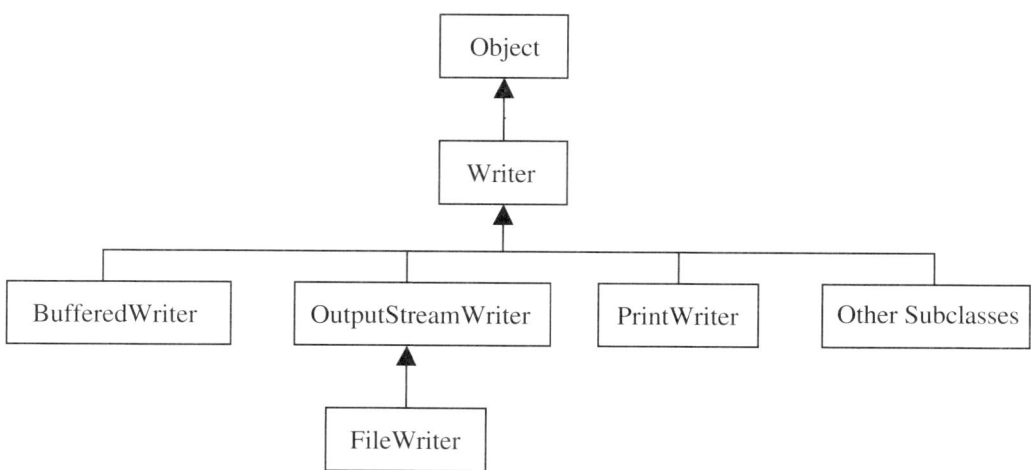

FIGURE 25.4 Character Output Streams

`PushbackReader`, and `StringReader`. We won't discuss these classes in this chapter. If you want more details on them, consult the Sun Java doc pages.

CHARACTER OUTPUT STREAMS

The character output stream class hierarchy is shown in Figure 25.4. At the top of the hierarchy is the `Writer` class that defines methods to write one or more characters to the output stream. The `BufferedWriter` class provides a buffer for improved I/O performance. The `PrintWriter` class can be wrapped around either a character or byte output stream and gives the underlying stream access to the `print()` and `println()` methods. The `OutputStreamWriter` class allows you to wrap a character output stream around a byte output stream. The `FileWriter` class connects an output stream to a file allowing you to write data to the file.

`Writer` Class

The `Writer` class is the abstract superclass for all character output stream classes. It defines methods that are available to all character output streams, including methods to close an output stream, write the contents of a buffer to the stream, or write character or `String` data to the stream.

```
public abstract void close() throws IOException
public abstract void flush() throws IOException
public void write(int c) throws IOException
public void write(char[] cbuf) throws IOException
public void write(char[] cbuf, int offset, int length)
throws IOException
public void write(String str) throws IOException
public void write(String str, int offset, int length) throws
IOException
```

The `close()` method closes the output stream and releases any resources allocated to it. The `flush()` method causes any data stored in a memory buffer to be written to the stream. The `write()` method is used to write a single character, the contents of a character array, or a `String` to the output stream. You can also write a subset of a character array or `String` to the output stream.

BufferedWriter Class

The `BufferedWriter` class provides an intermediary buffer for writing data resulting in more efficient I/O performance. Instead of writing characters or `Strings` immediately to a file, for instance, the character data is first written to the buffer. When the buffer reaches its capacity, its contents are written to the file. The `BufferedWriter` class defines two public constructors.

```
public BufferedWriter(Writer stream)
public BufferedWriter(Writer stream, int bufferSize)
```

A `BufferedWriter` object is always wrapped around another character output stream. The second constructor version allows you to specify the size of the buffer. The `BufferedWriter` class overrides some of the `Writer` class methods but defines no new methods to write character data. To see an example of using a `BufferedWriter`, see the "Reading and Writing to a File" section later in this chapter.

FileWriter Class

The `FileWriter` class allows you to connect a character output stream to a file. `FileWriter` objects can be used on their own, but they are often used in conjunction with a `BufferedWriter` or `PrintWriter` object to take advantage of the extra functionality provided by those classes. The `File-`

Writer class does not define any new methods, nor does it override any methods inherited from the OutputStreamWriter or Writer classes. The FileWriter class does define five constructors.

```
public FileWriter(File file) throws IOException
public FileWriter(File file, boolean append) throws IOException
public FileWriter(FileDescriptor desc)
public FileWriter(String name) throws IOException
public FileWriter(String name,boolean append) throws IOException
```

The file can be specified either by a File object, a FileDescriptor object, or by providing the name and, if necessary, path of the file. If append is true, data is written starting at the end of the file. The default is false meaning that data is written from the beginning of the file.

OutputStreamWriter Class

The OutputStreamWriter class provides a way to wrap a character output stream around a byte output stream. Character data is converted to bytes and stored in an intermediate buffer before being written to the underlying stream. The OutputStreamWriter class overrides some of the Writer class methods but defines no new methods to write data. The class defines four public constructors.

```
public OutputStreamWriter(OutputStream stream)
public OutputStreamWriter(OutputStream stream, Charset cs)
public OutputStreamWriter(OutputStream stream, CharsetDecoder dec)
public OutputStreamWriter(OutputStream stream,
  String charsetName) throws UnsupportedEncodingException
```

The first constructor version uses the default character set mapping scheme. The other three versions allow you to specify a character mapping to be used.

PrintWriter Class

The PrintWriter class provides an underlying output stream access to the print() and println() methods. These methods never throw an IOException and do not need to be enclosed in a try block. The Print-

Writer class is unique in that it can be wrapped around either a character or byte output stream. The four PrintWriter class constructors are as follows.

```
public PrintWriter(OutputStream stream)
public PrintWriter(OutputStream stream, boolean autoFlush)
public PrintWriter(Writer stream)
public PrintWriter(Writer stream, boolean autoFlush)
```

If autoFlush is true, any call to the println() method will flush the output buffer. In addition to overriding some of the Writer class methods, the PrintWriter class defines the following methods.

```
public void print(boolean b)
public void print(char c)
public void print(char[] chars)
public void print(double d)
public void print(float f)
public void print(int i)
public void print(long l)
public void print(Object obj)
public void print(String str)
```

The print() method prints a String or a String representation of a primitive type value or Object to the output stream without appending a newline character to the end of the String.

```
public void println()
public void println(boolean b)
public void println(char c)
public void println(char[] chars)
public void println(double d)
public void println(float f)
public void println(int i)
public void println(long l)
public void println(Object obj)
public void println(String str)
```

The println() method prints a String or a String representation of a primitive type value or Object to the output stream. A newline character is appended to the end of the String. The no-argument version simply writes a newline to the output stream.

Other Writer Subclasses

The Writer class has some other subclasses that you probably won't use much in your scientific and engineering programming work. These include the CharArrayWriter, FilterWriter, PipedWriter, and StringWriter classes. We won't discuss these classes in this chapter. If you want more details, consult the Sun Java doc pages.

TEST CASE: AN ATMOSPHERE MODELING TOOL

The preceding sections have provided an overview of some of the more significant classes and methods provided by the Java I/O libraries. Now, let's apply some of those classes and other built-in I/O capabilities to a real-life situation—providing the I/O functionality for an atmosphere modeling tool. As with previous chapters, the important thing here is to focus on the process. Don't worry about whether you would ever use an atmosphere modeling tool.

The modeling tool computes the conditions in the Earth's atmosphere at a given altitude by interpolating the pressure and temperature between known data points. The data is from the U.S. 1976 Standard Atmosphere model.[1] The temperature interpolation is performed using a linear expression. The pressure is interpolated using either an exponential or power function. The density is calculated based on the pressure and temperature. The molar mass is assumed to be constant.

The USatm76 class source code is shown next. The USatm76 class implements the Serializable interface to indicate that a USatm76 object can be saved and restored. At the top of the code, instance variables and some constants are declared. The arrays h[], T[], and p[] contain the known altitude, temperature, and pressure data. The lambda coefficients are used in the interpolation process. The methods computeTemperature() and computePressure() interpolate the temperature and pressure values. The rest of the methods are used to the return the values of pressure, temperature, density, molar mass, altitude, geo-potential altitude, and labels that define the units for each quantity.

The USatm76 constructor takes two input arguments—a String that defines whether the SI or English system of units will be used and the altitude at which the conditions will be computed. In the next few sections we will examine three ways to read the input data into the program and two ways to write out the results.

```java
  import java.io.Serializable;

public class USatm76 implements Serializable
{
  String units;
  private double altitude, geoAltitude, tmpAltitude;
  private double temperature, pressure, molarMass;
  private double G = 9.80665;
  private double radiusEarth = 6356766.0;
  private double Rgas = 8.31432;

  //  These are the known conditions at 8 different
  //  altitudes. lambda[] determines how the data
  //  is interpolated between points.

  private double h[] = {0.0, 11000.0, 20000.0, 32000.0,
               47000.0, 51000.0, 71000.0, 84000.8520};
  private double T[] = {288.15, 216.65, 216.65, 228.65,
                  270.65, 270.65, 214.65, 186.946};
  private double p[] = {101325.0,22631.9468,5474.8335,
         868.0044, 110.9036, 66.9371, 3.95628, 0.373367};
  private double lambda[] = {-0.0065, 0.0, 0.001,
                   0.0028, 0.0, -0.0028, -0.002};

  //  These arrays are used in the printData() method.

  private String labelSI[] = {" m"," m", " K",
                " N/m^2", " kg/mole", " kg/m^3"};
  private String labelEnglish[] = {" ft"," ft", " R",
              " psi", " lbm/lbmole", " lbm/ft^3"};

  //  If the units are "English" the input altitude
  //  is converted from feet to meters.

  public USatm76(String units, double alt) {
    this.units = units;
    if ( units.equals("English") ) {
      altitude = 0.3048*alt;
      tmpAltitude = alt;
    } else {
      altitude = alt;
    }
    geoAltitude = radiusEarth*altitude/
             (radiusEarth + altitude);
    molarMass = 0.0289645;
    computeTemperature();
    computePressure();
  }
```

```java
//   These methods compute temperature and pressure
//   by interpolating between the known data points.

private void computeTemperature() {
  int i = 0;
  if (geoAltitude > h[1]) i = 1;
  if (geoAltitude > h[2]) i = 2;
  if (geoAltitude > h[3]) i = 3;
  if (geoAltitude > h[4]) i = 4;
  if (geoAltitude > h[5]) i = 5;
  if (geoAltitude > h[6]) i = 6;
  if (geoAltitude > h[7]) i = 7;

  temperature = T[i] + lambda[i]*
                (geoAltitude - h[i]);
}

private void computePressure() {
  double AA, BB;

  int i = 0;
  if (geoAltitude > h[1]) i = 1;
  if (geoAltitude > h[2]) i = 2;
  if (geoAltitude > h[3]) i = 3;
  if (geoAltitude > h[4]) i = 4;
  if (geoAltitude > h[5]) i = 5;
  if (geoAltitude > h[6]) i = 6;
  if (geoAltitude > h[7]) i = 7;

  if (lambda[i] != 0.0) {
    AA = T[i]/
        (T[i] + lambda[i]*(geoAltitude - h[i]));
    BB = G*molarMass/(Rgas*lambda[i]);
    pressure = p[i]*Math.pow(AA,BB);
  } else {
    AA = G*molarMass*
        (geoAltitude - h[i])/(Rgas*T[i]);
    pressure = p[i]*Math.exp(-AA);
  }
}

//   These methods return the values of the altitude,
//   temperature, pressure, density, molar mass,
//   and number density.

public double getAltitude() {
  if ( units.equals("English") ) {
    return tmpAltitude;
  } else {
    return altitude;
  }
}
```

```java
//  SI units = m
//  English units = ft

public double getGeoPotentialAltitude() {
  if ( units.equals("English") ) {
    return 3.28084*geoAltitude;
  } else {
    return geoAltitude;
  }
}

//  SI units = K
//  English units = R

public double getTemperature() {
  if ( units.equals("English") ) {
    return 1.8*temperature;
  } else {
    return temperature;
  }
}

//  SI units = N/m^2
//  English units = lb/in^2

public double getPressure() {
  if ( units.equals("English") ) {
    return 1.45037e-4*pressure;
  } else {
    return pressure;
  }
}

//  SI units = kg/m^3
//  English units = lbm/ft^3

public double getDensity() {
  if ( units.equals("English") ) {
    return 6.24279e-2*pressure*molarMass/
              (Rgas*temperature);
  } else {
    return pressure*molarMass/(Rgas*temperature);
  }
}

//  SI units = kg/mole
//  English units = lbm/lbmole

public double getMolarMass() {
  if ( units.equals("English") ) {
    return 1000.0*molarMass;
  } else {
```

```
      return molarMass;
    }
  }

  public String[] getLabels() {
    if ( units.equals("English") ) {
      return labelEnglish;
    } else {
      return labelSI;
    }
  }
}
```

GETTING INPUT FROM COMMAND LINE ARGUMENTS

One way to provide input to the atmosphere modeling code is through command line arguments. If you recall, command line arguments are strings typed after the "java <classfile>" command to run a Java program. White space is the standard delimiter for command line arguments. Compound words can be treated as a single command line argument by enclosing them in double quotes.

Command line arguments are passed to the `main()` method as a `String` array, conventionally named `args[]`. The elements of the `String` array can be parsed as required and the arguments can then be used as needed. The advantage of command line arguments is the I/O code is easy to program. There are no menus to code or input files to read and parse. The I/O code is contained within the driver code. No additional files are required.

Using command line arguments is impractical if you have a large number of input arguments. The user also has to know the number, type, and order of the input arguments, although you can build in code to help the user if she makes a mistake. This method of I/O is also unforgiving of typographical errors. You have to type in all the arguments every time the code is run, and if you make one mistake you must repeat that process.

The `CmdLineDemo` class demonstrates how to acquire input data from command line arguments. The `main()` method of the `CmdLineDemo` class creates a `USatm76` object using command line arguments to provide the necessary inputs to the `USatm76` constructor. The first part of the `main()` method makes sure that the user provides two command line arguments. The first argument to the `USatm76` constructor is a `String` indicating the system of units that will be used. The second argument to the constructor is a `double` value containing the altitude. Command line arguments are always read in as `Strings`. The second command line argument is converted from type

`String` to type `double`. The `USatm76` object is then created and the atmospheric conditions are written to standard output.

The `CmdLineDemo` class source code is shown here.

```java
public class CmdLineDemo
{
  public static void main(String args[]) {

    //  Make sure the user provides two
    //  command line arguments

    if (args.length != 2) {
      System.out.println(
          "usage: java CmdLineDemo <units> <altitude>");
      System.exit(1);
    }

    //  Convert the second command line argument
    //  into a double

    double altitude = Double.parseDouble(args[1]);

    //  Create a USatm76 object with the recently
    //  acquired input values.

    USatm76 atm = new USatm76(args[0], altitude);

    //  Print out the results to standard output

    String label[] = atm.getLabels();

    System.out.println("\ngeometric altitude   = " +
                  atm.getAltitude() + label[0]);
    System.out.println("geopotential altitude = " +
              atm.getGeoPotentialAltitude() + label[1]);
    System.out.println("temperature          = " +
                  atm.getTemperature() + label[2]);
    System.out.println("pressure             = " +
                  atm.getPressure() + label[3]);
    System.out.println("molar mass           = " +
                  atm.getMolarMass() + label[4]);
    System.out.println("density              = " +
                  atm.getDensity() + label[5]);
  }
}
```

Output—

If the code is run using the syntax

```
java CmdLineDemo SI 20000.0
```

The resulting output will be—

```
geometric altitude     = 20000.0 m
geopotential altitude  = 19937.27227876952 m
temperature            = 216.65 K
pressure               = 5529.256361823237 N/m^2
molar mass             = 0.0289645 kg/mole
density                = 0.08890932913275061 kg/m^3
```

Using the Standard I/O Streams

A second way to read and write program data is to use the standard I/O streams. If you remember from Chapter 6, the standard input and output streams are `static` variables defined in the `System` class. The standard input stream is `System.in`. The standard output stream is `System.out`. Since the standard I/O streams are `public static` variables from the `java.lang` package, you can access them anywhere in any program.

The standard input stream is an instance of the `InputStream` class, which is a byte stream. The default is for the standard input to come from the keyboard. The standard input stream has access to the `read()` method that is used to read a byte or an array of bytes. It is often convenient to wrap a character stream such as an `InputStreamReader` around the standard input stream allowing you to read character or `String` data directly.

The standard output stream is an instance of the `PrintStream` class, which is a byte output stream. The default for the standard output is to write to the console. The standard output stream has access to the `print()` and `println()` methods, which write a `String` or a `String` representation of a primitive value or object to the output stream. The standard output stream and the `print()` and `println()` methods have been used hundreds of times in the examples in this book.

The main advantage of using the standard I/O streams is that a lot of the work has been done for you. You don't need to create an I/O stream object. There are no input files to parse or create. One disadvantage is that there is no permanent record of what you have done. Unless you write a script of some sort, you must type in all of the input every time you run the program and the output will similarly not be saved.

To demonstrate the use of standard I/O we will write a class named `StdIODemo`. The `main()` method of this class creates a `USatm76` object using the standard input stream to acquire the necessary inputs from the keyboard. In order to read the inputs as character data, an `InputStreamReader` is wrapped around the standard input stream. A `BufferedReader` is wrapped around the `InputStreamReader` to give access to the `readLine()` method that can read a line of input at a time.

The user is prompted for the units and altitude inputs. When the input is typed in and the Enter or Return key is pressed, the `readLine()` method returns the line of input as a `String`. The `String` corresponding to the altitude is converted to type `double` before it is passed to the `USatm76` constructor. After the `USatm76` object is created, the corresponding atmospheric conditions are printed to the console using the standard output stream and the `println()` method.

The `StdIODemo` class source code is shown next.

```java
import java.io.*;

public class StdIODemo
{
  public static void main(String args[]) {
    BufferedReader reader;
    String units, altitude;

    //  Wrap a BufferedReader and InputStreamReader
    //  around the standard input stream.

    try {
      reader = new BufferedReader(
                new InputStreamReader(System.in));

    //  The user is prompted for the system of units
    //  and the altitude.

    System.out.print("Select units (SI or English):  ");
      units = reader.readLine();

      System.out.print("Select altitude (m or ft):  ");
      altitude = reader.readLine();
      reader.close();

      //  Create a USatm76 object with the recently
      //  acquired input values.

      USatm76 atm =
       new USatm76(units, Double.parseDouble(altitude));

      //  Print out the results using the standard
      //  output stream

      String label[] = atm.getLabels();

      System.out.println("\ngeometric altitude    = " +
                    atm.getAltitude() + label[0]);
      System.out.println("geopotential altitude = " +
```

```
                    atm.getGeoPotentialAltitude() + label[1]);
      System.out.println("temperature             = " +
                    atm.getTemperature() + label[2]);
      System.out.println("pressure                = " +
                        atm.getPressure() + label[3]);
      System.out.println("molar mass              = " +
                     atm.getMolarMass() + label[4]);
      System.out.println("density                 = " +
                        atm.getDensity() + label[5]);

    } catch (IOException ioe) {
      System.out.println("IO Exception occurred");
      System.exit(1);
    }
  }
}
```

Output (will vary depending on the input provided)—

```
Select units (SI or English): SI
Select altitude (m or ft) : 20000.0

geometric altitude    = 20000.0 m
geopotential altitude = 19937.27227876952 m
temperature           = 216.65 K
pressure              = 5529.256361823237 N/m^2
molar mass            = 0.0289645 kg/mole
density               = 0.08890932913275061 kg/m^3
```

READING AND WRITING TO A FILE

A third way to implement I/O functionality is to read data from or write data to a file. File I/O is achieved by connecting an I/O stream to a file. File I/O can be done with either byte or character streams. To read or write byte data, you can use the `FileInputStream` or `FileOutputStream` classes. To read or write character data, you can use the `FileReader` or `FileWriter` classes. Another I/O stream is usually wrapped around the file I/O stream to make it easier to read and write data from the file.

One advantage of using file I/O is it can handle a large number of input parameters. There is no maximum length to an input file. You can also place descriptive comments inside the input file. Another advantage is that you have a permanent record of the input and output. You can reuse an input file or modify a large input file by making only a few changes.

Disadvantages include having to write code to parse the input file. The structure of the input file has to match what the parsing algorithm expects.

There are more things that can go wrong with file I/O than the other methods; an input file may not be found, for example.

The `FileDemo` class demonstrates how input data can be read from a file and output data can be written to a file. It is especially true about file I/O that there are many ways to accomplish the reading and writing of data. The `FileDemo` class uses character streams but you could (although it wouldn't be advisable) rewrite the program using byte streams instead.

A `FileReader` object is created that connects to an input file named "USatm76.inp." A `BufferedReader` is wrapped around the `FileReader` to allow the `readLine()` method to read a line of data at a time. The contents of the "USatm76.inp" file used in this example consist of the following two lines.

```
units (SI or English) = SI
altitude (m or ft)    = 20000.0
```

The first line of the input file contains the system of units to be used. The `BufferedReader` reads this line as a `String`, which is then split into substrings using the `split()` method with the = character as the delimiter. The last substring is the one we want, so we assign it to a `String` variable named `units`. The `BufferedReader` then reads the second line of the input file. Once again the resulting `String` is split into substrings. The last substring, containing the altitude value we want, is converted into a value of type `double` and assigned to a variable named `altitude`. The two inputs are then sent to the `USatm76` constructor.

The resulting atmospheric conditions are written to a file using `FileWriter` and `BufferedWriter` objects. The `FileWriter` is connected to a file named "USatm76.out." The `BufferedWriter` is wrapped around the `FileWriter` to improve I/O performance. The `BufferedWriter` object uses its `write()` method to write a sequence of `String` objects to the file. The `FileDemo` class source code is shown here.

```java
import java.io.*;

public class FileDemo
{
  public static void main(String args[]) {
    BufferedReader reader;
    BufferedWriter writer;
    String line, units;
    String strings[];
    double altitude;

    //  BufferedReader and FileReader objects are
    //  used to read input data from a file.
```

```java
try {
  reader = new BufferedReader(
              new FileReader("USatm76.inp"));

  //  Read the first line of the input file and
  //  split it into substrings.  The last substring
  //  is the one we want to keep after any leading
  //  and trailing white space is trimmed.

  line = reader.readLine();
  strings = line.split("=");
  units = strings[strings.length-1].trim();

  //  Read the second line of the input file.
  //  Convert the last substring of the line into a
  //  double value containing the altitude.

  line = reader.readLine();
  strings = line.split("=");
  altitude =
      Double.parseDouble(strings[strings.length-1]);

  //  Create a USatm76 object with the recently
  //  acquired input values. Print out the
  //  atmospheric data.

  USatm76 atm = new USatm76(units, altitude);

  //  Use a BufferedWriter and FileWriter object to
  //  write the output to a file.

  writer = new BufferedWriter(
              new FileWriter("USatm76.out"));

  String label[] = atm.getLabels();

  //  The write() method will not automatically
  //  add a newline character.

  writer.write("\ngeometric altitude    = " +
               atm.getAltitude() + label[0]);
  writer.write("\ngeopotential altitude = " +
       atm.getGeoPotentialAltitude() + label[1]);
  writer.write("\ntemperature           = " +
               atm.getTemperature() + label[2]);
  writer.write("\npressure              = " +
               atm.getPressure() + label[3]);
  writer.write("\nmolar mass            = " +
               atm.getMolarMass() + label[4]);
  writer.write("\ndensity               = " +
               atm.getDensity() + label[5]);

  //  Close the streams
```

Saving and Restoring Objects

```
      reader.close();
      writer.flush();
      writer.close();

   } catch (IOException ioe) {
     System.out.println("IO Exception occurred");
     System.exit(1);
   }
  }
}
```

Output (contents of "USatm76.out" file)—

```
geometric altitude    = 20000.0 m
geopotential altitude = 19937.27227876952 m
temperature           = 216.65 K
pressure              = 5529.256361823237 N/m^2
molar mass            = 0.0289645 kg/mole
density               = 0.08890932913275061 kg/m^3
```

Saving and Restoring Objects

A Java class can define a complicated data structure. An object can manipulate its data members using methods defined in its class such that the current values of its fields might be very different than when the object was first created. One nice feature about the Java I/O capability is that it defines a class that allows you to write the data associated with an object to an output stream. You can later restore the object by reading its data from an input stream. This capability can save you a lot of work. You no longer have to create the object's data structure from scratch.

As an example, in Chapter 23 a class named `Polynomial` was developed that stores as one of its data members the coefficients of an equation that models an ordinary differential equation. Rather than solving the ODE each time it was needed, it would be nice to solve it once and maintain the data in a `Polynomial` object that was stored on disk or onto a CD.

In this section, we will write a class named `SaveObject` that will save the data structure of a `USatm76` object. The first thing the `main()` method of this class does is create a `USatm76` object corresponding to the conditions using English units at an altitude of 40,000 feet. The method then creates an instance of the `ObjectOutputStream` class. We will save the object to a file, so we will wrap the `ObjectOutputStream` around a `FileOutputStream` connected to a file named "atm40kft.dat."

The data structure of the `USatm76` object is saved by having the `ObjectOutputStream` call its `writeObject()`, passing the method a reference to the `USatm76` object. The source code for the `SaveObject` class is shown here.

```java
import java.io.*;

public class SaveObject
{
  public static void main(String args[]) {

    USatm76 atm = new USatm76("English", 40000.0);

    //  An ObjectOutputStream object is used
    //  to write a USatm76 object to a file

    try {
      ObjectOutputStream writer =
          new ObjectOutputStream(
            new FileOutputStream("atm40kft.dat"));

      writer.writeObject(atm);

      writer.close();

    } catch (IOException ioe) {
      System.out.println("IO Exception occurred: " +
                         ioe);
      System.exit(1);
    }
  }
}
```

When you run this program, you will notice that a file named "atm40kft.dat" has been created on your system. Remember that only instances of classes that implement the `Serializable` interface can be saved in this manner.

The data structure of an object that has been saved using an `ObjectOutputStream` can be restored using an `ObjectInputStream` object. The `RestoreObject` class will restore the previously saved `USatm76` object. An `ObjectInputStream` object is wrapped around a `FileInputStream` object that is associated with the file "atm40kft.dat." The `ObjectInputStream` object calls its `readObject()` method and the return value is cast into a `USatm76` object. The data associated with the object is printed to standard output.

The source code of the `RestoreObject` class is shown next.

```java
import java.io.*;
```

```
public class RestoreObject
{
  public static void main(String args[]) {

    //  An ObjectInputStream object is used
    //  to read a USatm76 object from a file

    try {
      ObjectInputStream reader =
          new ObjectInputStream(
              new FileInputStream("atm40kft.dat"));

      USatm76 atm = (USatm76)reader.readObject();

      //  Print out the data from the object.

      String label[] = atm.getLabels();

      System.out.println("\ngeometric altitude   = " +
                        atm.getAltitude() + label[0]);
      System.out.println("geopotential altitude = " +
              atm.getGeoPotentialAltitude() + label[1]);
      System.out.println("temperature          = " +
                        atm.getTemperature() + label[2]);
      System.out.println("pressure             = " +
                        atm.getPressure() + label[3]);
      System.out.println("molar mass           = " +
                        atm.getMolarMass() + label[4]);
      System.out.println("density              = " +
                         atm.getDensity() + label[5]);

      reader.close();

    } catch (ClassNotFoundException cnfe) {
      System.out.println("Class not found: " + cnfe);
      System.exit(1);
    } catch (IOException ioe) {
      System.out.println("IO Exception occurred: " +
                           ioe);
         System.exit(1);
    }
  }
}
```

Output—

```
geometric altitude    = 40000.0 ft
geopotential altitude = 39923.42988235446 ft
temperature           = 389.97 R
pressure              = 2.7300260343469853 psi
molar mass            = 28.9645 lbm/lbmole
density               = 0.018895018156005174 lbm/ft^3
```

The java.nio Packages

All of the classes we have discussed so far are found in the java.io package. Up until Java 1.3, the java.io package is where most I/O functionality could be found. One of the additions to Java 1.4 was the java.nio family of packages. Notable features of the java.nio packages include buffer classes for primitive data types to improve I/O performance, classes that define character set encoders and decoders to convert bytes to Unicode characters and vice versa, and a regular expression pattern matching capability.

With respect to scientific and engineering programming applications, the features provided by the java.nio packages are refinements that are beyond the scope of this book, which is to explore the core elements of applying Java to technical programming. For more information on java.nio, consult the Sun Java doc pages.

References

1. U.S. Standard Atmosphere, 1976, U.S. Government Printing Office, Washington, D.C., 1976. Or *http://nssdc.gsfc.nasa.gov/space/model/atmos/us_standard.html*

26

AN INTRODUCTION TO JAVA GUIs

In Chapter 25, we discussed three ways to read input data into an application and two ways to write the output out. Using command line arguments, the standard I/O streams, or file I/O are good choices for many applications. There is another way for an application to read and write data—by creating a GUI front end to the application. The GUI provides a visual display of both the inputs and outputs from an application.

There are many benefits to using GUIs with your analysis tools. The application becomes more visual. The user can see the inputs and outputs on her console. A GUI can clearly present the acceptable input choices to the user. For example, if a particular input argument has only three acceptable values you can place these values in a list component that displays only those values. The user will have to select one of the three choices from the list, eliminating the possibility of mistyping or not knowing the proper input argument choices. A GUI provides self-contained I/O. There are no input files to create or edit.

It would take an entire book to cover all the details and possibilities of the Java GUI libraries. The purpose of this chapter is to outline the process of developing a Java GUI. It will highlight the various steps in building a GUI and talk about the basic elements common to all GUIs. We will also go over some of the design decisions that you will have to make when you create a GUI. We will introduce some of the GUI classes and methods, but for a comprehensive look at the Java GUI libraries, consult *Graphic Java 2, Volume 2: Swing (3rd ed.)* by David Geary.

The topics we will discuss in this chapter are—

- The Java GUI libraries
- The `AtmGUI` class
- Choosing a container
- Selecting the GUI components
- Adding the components to the container
- Event handlers
- Other GUI elements
- The final form of the `AtmGUI` class

The Java GUI Libraries

Before we demonstrate the process of creating a GUI, let's talk about the Java GUI libraries, what is in them, their history, and some of the design philosophy behind Java GUI development. The older Java GUI components, used during the Java 1.0 and 1.1 releases, can be found in the `java.awt` package. The `java.awt` GUI components are limited in functionality and flexibility. A lot of the style and features of the AWT components are hard-coded and can't be changed. For example, the size of a `Button` object and its border style is determined by the system and can't easily be altered. The AWT containers were similarly limited in what you could do with them. They consisted of only one layer and components are added directly to the container.

As Java became more sophisticated so did its GUI capability. The Swing packages were introduced with Java 1.2. These contain an entirely new class of GUI components. While the AWT components rely on a component peer, written in a non-Java language such as C, to display the component on the screen, Swing components are pure Java. One great advantage of the Swing components is that much of the control over what a component looks like or does has been turned over to the programmer. You can change a component's border, its size, even how it looks when it is rendered on the screen. You can create custom components by modifying the data model of an existing component.

Swing containers were redesigned as well. Instead of having only one layer on which to add components, Swing containers have multiple layers called panes with which to work. There are three types of panes—content, layered, and glass. You no longer add components directly to the container, instead you place them on one of the panes associated with the container. Using the different layers of a Swing container you can make components appear to be stacked, or temporarily disable the GUI display.

The Swing GUI components have not totally forgotten their AWT roots. The Swing components borrowed what functionality they could from their AWT predecessors. The superclass of the Swing components, JComponent, is itself a subclass of the AWT component superclass, Component. The high-level Swing container classes JFrame, JWindow, and JDialog are direct subclasses of AWT Frame, Window, and Dialog, respectively.

One aspect about Java GUIs that is different from the GUI capability of other languages is that Java retains a fair amount of control over how the GUI will look and behave. For example, you do not position components at a fixed location on the screen. An entity called a layout manager determines the component positions according to its own internal rules. If you change the size of the GUI window, for instance, the layout manager will likely change the location of the components as well. Java also has internal rules about style. You can make suggestions as to things like component size or margins, but the system reserves the right to ignore you if what you want to do violates its internal guidelines.

For the GUI that we will develop in this chapter, we will use Swing GUI components, but we will need to use some event handling and support classes from the java.awt package. Keep in mind that this is a relatively simple GUI example. The Java GUI capability is quite extensive. We won't discuss things like data models and will only briefly touch on subjects such as event handling. That all being said, let's create a GUI.

The AtmGUI Class

To demonstrate the process of developing a GUI front-end to a scientific or engineering application, we will create a GUI to handle the I/O requirements of the atmospheric modeling program we developed in Chapter 25. A USatm76 object requires two input arguments, the system of units to be used and the altitude at which to compute the atmospheric conditions. Once a USatm76 object is created, the object can access methods defined in the USatm76 class to return the atmospheric conditions the object represents. The name of our GUI class will be AtmGUI.java.

The first step in the GUI design process is to select a container to hold the other GUI components. Following that, we must decide which GUI components we will use to receive the input parameters and display the output from the atmosphere modeling tool. There are two input arguments to the `USatm76` constructor, so we will need two GUI components to accept the input data. The atmospheric conditions will be printed out as a series of `Strings`, so we need another GUI component that can display these `Strings`.

The `AtmGUI` class will also have to define a mechanism for determining when a `USatm76` object should be created and its atmospheric conditions displayed on the GUI. Under the Java GUI framework this mechanism is called an event handler. There are different ways to implement event handlers. For the example in this chapter, the `AtmGUI` class will serve as its own event handler.

Choosing a Container

The first step in developing a GUI is to decide which underlying container will be used to store the other GUI components. A container is a GUI component on which you can place other components. There are a variety of container classes defined in the `java.awt` and `javax.swing` packages. Most GUI applications will use a high-level container as their base container. High-level containers are those that have the different layers, or panes, we discussed earlier. The most commonly used high-level container is a `JFrame` that comes with a title, border, and other platform-specific features such as minimize/maximize, iconify, and close buttons. The atmosphere modeling GUI will use a `JFrame` as its container.

To create the GUI front-end for the `USatm76` program, we will define a class named `AtmGUI` that is a subclass of `JFrame`. We will need to import the `JFrame` class into the program, but just to simplify things later on we will import the entire `javax.swing` package. We will define an `AtmGUI` constructor that at this point will simply set the title and size of the frame and make the frame visible. The `setDefaultCloseOperation()` method ensures that the application will terminate if the window is closed.

We will also build the `main()` method into the `AtmGUI` class. When the `AtmGUI` class is compiled and run, the GUI is launched and appears on your screen. Here is the initial `AtmGUI` class source code.

```
import javax.swing.*;

public class AtmGUI extends JFrame
{
  public AtmGUI() {

    // Add a title to the JFrame, size it, and make it
    // visible.
```

```
    setTitle("Atmosphere Modeling Tool");
    setDefaultCloseOperation(JFrame.EXIT_ON_CLOSE);
    setBounds(100,100,500,300);
    setVisible(true);
  }

  public static void main(String args[]) {
    AtmGUI gui = new AtmGUI();
  }
}
```

When you compile and run this program, an empty frame will appear on your screen.

SELECTING THE GUI COMPONENTS

Now that we have our container it is time to define the GUI components that will be placed in it. The GUI components will be used to receive the input data, create a `USatm76` object, and display the resulting atmospheric conditions inside the GUI. Keep in mind that Java GUI development is another one of those areas where there is more than one way to do things. There is nothing magical about the selection of GUI components used in this example. The key is to evaluate what you want to do, and then decide which components will best allow you to do it.

There are two input arguments to the `USatm76` constructor, so we need to identify two GUI components to accept the input data. The first component will accept the system of units under which the results will be displayed. There are only two choices for the system of units, `"SI"` and `"English"`. To make it easy on the user and to prevent bad input for this parameter, we will build the two choices into a list-type GUI component called a `JComboBox`. A `JComboBox` presents the user with one or more choices. The currently selected item is displayed on the screen. If you click on the `JComboBox`, the other available choices become visible. We will add two items to the `JComboBox`. One is the `String` `"SI"` and the other the `String` `"English"`.

The second input parameter is the altitude at which the atmospheric conditions will be computed. The altitude can theoretically be any nonzero floating point number. To accept the altitude input we will use a `JTextField` component. This component provides a box containing a single line of text into which the user can type input. The `JTextField` will be given an initial value of `"20000.0"` and will have 10 columns with which to input data. The altitude model that we implemented in the `USatm76` class is valid for any altitude greater than 0 and less than 86,400 meters. To be rigorous about the process, we could include code that would reject negative altitudes or those above 86,400 meters, but for purposes of code listing simplicity and clarity we will omit that step.

There also has to a component that tells the GUI that the atmospheric conditions should be computed using the currently selected system of units and altitude. The logical choice here is a button component. We will use a `JButton` that represents a simple, rectangular button. We will give the `JButton` the label "Compute" and will make some changes to the default style. For one thing, we will give the `JButton` a bevel border that makes the button appear raised from the screen.

The final GUI component we need is one that will display the atmospheric conditions at the specified altitude using the specified system of units. We will use a `JTextArea` component that represents a rectangular, multiline text box. The `JTextArea` is given an initial size of 10 rows and 55 columns. The display font of the `JTextArea` is changed to Courier so the output will line up nicely.

It's usually a good idea to label your GUI components so the user knows what input is required. Three `JLabel`s are created, one each for the `JComboBox`, `JTextField`, and `JTextArea`. The updated `AtmGUI` class code listing is shown here. We've added code to create each of the GUI components discussed in the preceding paragraphs.

```
import javax.swing.*;
import java.awt.*;
import javax.swing.border.BevelBorder;

public class AtmGUI extends JFrame
{
  private JComboBox comboBox;
  private JTextField textField;
  private JButton runButton;
  private JTextArea textArea;
  private JLabel comboLabel, textFieldLabel;
  private JLabel textAreaLabel;

  public AtmGUI() {

    //  Create a JComboBox to choose between
    //  English and SI units.

    comboLabel = new JLabel("Units");
    comboBox = new JComboBox();
    comboBox.addItem("SI");
    comboBox.addItem("English");
```

```java
      // Create a JTextField for the input altitude.

      textFieldLabel = new JLabel("Altitude");
      textField = new JTextField("20000.0",10);

      // Create a JButton that will compute the
      // atmospheric conditions when pressed. Register an
      // ActionListener for the JButton

      runButton = new JButton("Compute");
      runButton.setBorder(
                 new BevelBorder(BevelBorder.RAISED));
      runButton.setPreferredSize(new Dimension(60,35));

      // Create a JTextArea that will display the results

      textAreaLabel = new JLabel("Results");
      textArea = new JTextArea(10,55);
      textArea.setFont(new Font("Courier",Font.PLAIN,12));

        // Add a title to the JFrame, size it, and make it
        // visible.

        setTitle("Atmosphere Modeling Tool");
        setDefaultCloseOperation(JFrame.EXIT_ON_CLOSE);
        setBounds(100,100,500,300);
        setVisible(true);
    }
    public static void main(String args[]) {
      AtmGUI gui = new AtmGUI();
    }
}
```

When you compile and run this code, you still get the same blank frame on your screen. That is because although we have defined our GUI components, we haven't added the GUI components to one of the panes of the JFrame.

ADDING THE COMPONENTS TO THE CONTAINER

Once we have selected the GUI components we will use, we can then add the components to the container. Java maintains a certain amount of control over how components are positioned inside a container. You don't position the GUI components yourself; you define something called a layout manager that arranges the components for you. If the GUI window is resized or changed in some other manner, the layout manager will reposition the GUI components.

Even with layout managers, you still have a lot of control over the look of your GUI display. You can specify a component's preferred size, its orientation, and the margins between it and neighboring components, to name a few.

Most of the Java layout manager classes can be found in the `java.awt` package. The `CardLayout` class is a layout manager that stacks components like a deck of cards. The `FlowLayout` class places the components in a line from left to right. When the right edge of the container is reached, the layout continues on the left-hand side below the previous row. The `GridLayout` class is a layout manager that places the components in a two-dimensional grid. Each cell in the grid has the same size. The `GridBagLayout` class is the most sophisticated layout manager in the `java.awt` package and gives you the most control over the size and position of your components.

The layout manager we will use for the `AtmGUI` class is an instance of the `BorderLayout` class. This type of layout manager was chosen to keep things simple and because we have a relatively small number of components to place. A `BorderLayout` object places components in five sections of the container—north, south, east, west, and center.

A container can change its current layout manager by invoking the `setLayout()` method, passing it a reference to an instance of the desired layout class. Components are added to the container using the `add()` method. When a `BorderLayout` layout manager is used, the `add()` method takes two arguments—the component to be placed and the quadrant of the container in which to place it. We will place the `JComboBox`, `JTextField`, and `JButton` in the north section and the `JTextArea` in the center section.

If you remember, with higher level Swing containers you don't add GUI components directly to the container. If you try to do this, you will generate an error. Components are added to one of the panes associated with the container, usually the content pane. A higher level container can get a reference to its content pane using the `getContentPane()` method. The `setLayout()` and `add()` methods are called on the content pane object.

There is one more issue to consider before we conclude this section. The `BorderLayout` layout manager has a quirk— it will resize components to fill the available space in a given section (north, center, etc.). This can result in really large, strange looking components. The `FlowLayout` layout manager does not do this resizing; instead it maintains the component's preferred size. To prevent the `BorderLayout` manager from resizing our components, we can first place the components on a `JPanel` (the default layout manager of `JPanel` objects is `FlowLayout`) and then place the `JPanel` on the content pane of our `JFrame`. Because a `JPanel` is a low-level container, it does not have the various subpanes. You can add components directly to a `JPanel`.

To lay out our GUI components according to the previous discussion, we will add the following lines of code to the `AtmGUI` class immediately after the GUI component definition statements. The blank `JLabel` components are used for spacing.

```
//  The components are placed on a JPanel before
//  being added to the content pane to maintain
//  their preferred sizes.

JPanel northPanel = new JPanel();
northPanel.add(comboLabel);
northPanel.add(comboBox);
northPanel.add(new JLabel("     "));
northPanel.add(textFieldLabel);
northPanel.add(textField);
northPanel.add(new JLabel("     "));
northPanel.add(runButton);

JPanel centerPanel = new JPanel();
centerPanel.add(textAreaLabel);
centerPanel.add(textArea);

//  Add the JPanel objects to the content pane

getContentPane().setLayout(new BorderLayout());
getContentPane().add(northPanel, BorderLayout.NORTH);
getContentPane().add(centerPanel, BorderLayout.CENTER);
```

When you add this code to the `AtmGUI` class and compile and run the code, a frame with all of the GUI components appears on your screen. Figure 26.1 at the end of this chapter is a typical screen shot.

EVENT HANDLERS

If you were to run the code developed in the previous section and press the Compute button, nothing would happen because we have not built in the code that will detect and respond to when the button is pressed. Before we do that, we need to back up and discuss the concept of events.

When you interact with a GUI you expect that something will happen. For example, when you press the Compute button, you expect the application to run. For this to happen, there has to be a mechanism that (a) detects when the button has been pressed and (b) calls the appropriate method or block of code to respond to that action.

The way Java implements this functionality is by using what are known as events. An event is an instance of an event class. Though not limited to GUI applications, events are typically used to encapsulate some sort of GUI interaction. Almost everything you do around a GUI window will generate events. If you move the mouse across the window you will generate `MouseEvents`. If you press a `JButton` you will generate an `ActionEvent`. If you change the selected value of a `JList` you will generate a `ListSelectionEvent`. The system takes care of all of the event generation for you.

Now that we are generating events, we need to be able to respond to them. Java does this using what is known as a delegation model. All this means is that the event handling is disconnected from the event source. When an event is generated, the system checks to see if there are any event handlers of the appropriate type registered to the event source. If there are, the system sends the event object to one of the methods defined by the event handler. To define event handlers, Java uses a type of interface known as an event listener interface. These interfaces declare methods that respond to a given type of event. An instance of a class that implements one of these interfaces is an event listener.

A GUI component registers an event listener by adding the event listener to a list maintained by the component. A component can register any number of event listeners. A `JButton` might register both an `ActionListener` and a `MouseListener`, for example. One great feature of the delegation model is that you can pick and choose which events you will respond to. For example, the `JComboBox` object of the `AtmGUI` class will generate an `ItemEvent` when the selected item changes. We don't need to do anything with this event, so we simply ignore it.

This has been a brief overview of the Java event model. We haven't discussed all of the possible event classes and event listener interfaces, nor have we covered things like user-defined event classes or how to manipulate the event dispatching thread. For more information on events and event handling, see *Java Event Handling* by Grant Palmer.

Now that we know a little bit about events, let's add event handling capability to the `AtmGUI` class. The component we want to do this for is the Compute button. When this button is pressed, we want a `USatm76` object to be created and the corresponding atmospheric conditions to be written into the `JTextArea`. Whenever a `JButton` is pressed, an `ActionEvent` is generated. We need to create an `ActionListener` class, register the `ActionListener` with the `JButton`, and implement the `actionPerformed()` method of the `ActionListener` to respond to the event.

The first thing to do is to create an `ActionListener` class. This is done simply by defining a class that implements the `ActionListener` interface and the `actionPerformed()` method defined in that interface. Under the delegation model, any class can serve as an `ActionListener`. We could define the `ActionListener` to be a separate class from `AtmGUI` or an inner class of `AtmGUI`. To keep things simple, we will define the `AtmGUI` class itself to be the `ActionListener`.

```
public class AtmGUI extends JFrame
                         implements ActionListener
```

The `ActionListener` interface declares one method named `actionPerformed()`. Because the `AtmGUI` class now implements the `ActionListener` interface, it must also implement the `actionPerformed()` method. The first thing `actionPerformed()` does is create a `USatm76` object using the current values of the `JComboBox` and `JTextField` components. The value of the `JTextField` component is converted to a value of type `double`. The previous contents of the `JTextArea` are cleared using the `setText()` method. The current atmospheric results are then written into the `JTextArea` using the `append()` method. The `actionPerformed()` method source code follows.

```
public void actionPerformed(ActionEvent event) {
  String units = (String)comboBox.getSelectedItem();
  double altitude =
          Double.parseDouble(textField.getText());
  atm = new USatm76(units, altitude);

  String label[] = atm.getLabels();

  textArea.setText("");
  textArea.append("geometric altitude    = " +
              atm.getAltitude()+label[0]);
  textArea.append("\ngeopotential altitude = " +
          atm.getGeoPotentialAltitude()+label[1]);
  textArea.append("\ntemperature           = " +
              atm.getTemperature()+label[2]);
  textArea.append("\npressure              = " +
              atm.getPressure()+label[3]);
  textArea.append("\nmolar mass            = " +
              atm.getMolarMass()+label[4]);
  textArea.append("\ndensity               = " +
              atm.getDensity()+label[5]);
}
```

The final thing to do is to have the Compute button register the `ActionListener` by calling the `addActionListener()` method on it. Because the `AtmGUI` class itself is serving as the `ActionListener`, the method is passed the `this` reference.

```
runButton.addActionListener(this);
```

This code is placed in the `AtmGUI` code listing after the Compute button is created.

Other GUI elements

Let's talk briefly about some other GUI elements that are commonly used but weren't applied to the `AtmGUI` class. For example, Java defines a number of menu and menu item classes. A menu bar can be defined that contains menus. The menus can contain menu items or other menus. There are varieties of menu items including check boxes and radio buttons. There are also pop-up menus that appear next to other GUI components when certain combinations of mouse buttons are pressed. Java also defines a variety of dialog windows that can be used for everything from selecting a file to confirming a certain action.

The Final Form of the AtmGUI class

Here is the final form of `AtmGUI` class that we developed in this chapter. You can see that the code really isn't that long, nor is it all that complicated.

```java
import javax.swing.*;
import java.awt.*;
import javax.swing.border.BevelBorder;
import java.awt.event.*;

public class AtmGUI extends JFrame
                implements ActionListener
{
  private JComboBox comboBox;
  private JTextField textField;
  private JButton runButton;
  private JTextArea textArea;
  private JLabel comboLabel, textFieldLabel;
  private JLabel textAreaLabel;
  private USatm76 atm;

  public AtmGUI() {

    //  Create a JComboBox to choose between
    //  English and SI units.

    comboLabel = new JLabel("Units");
    comboBox = new JComboBox();
```

The Final Form of the AtmGui Class 431

```java
comboBox.addItem("SI");
comboBox.addItem("English");

//  Create a JTextField for the input altitude.

textFieldLabel = new JLabel("Altitude");
textField = new JTextField("20000.0",10);

//  Create a JButton that will compute the
//  atmospheric conditions when pressed. Register an
//  ActionListener for the JButton

runButton = new JButton("Compute");
runButton.setBorder(
            new BevelBorder(BevelBorder.RAISED));
runButton.setPreferredSize(new Dimension(60,35));
runButton.addActionListener(this);

//  Create a JTextArea that will display the results

textAreaLabel = new JLabel("Results");
textArea = new JTextArea(10,55);
textArea.setFont(new Font("Courier",Font.PLAIN,12));

//  The components are added to a JPanel before
//  being added to the content pane to maintain
//  their preferred sizes.

JPanel northPanel = new JPanel();
northPanel.add(comboLabel);
northPanel.add(comboBox);
northPanel.add(new JLabel("     "));
northPanel.add(textFieldLabel);
northPanel.add(textField);
northPanel.add(new JLabel("     "));
northPanel.add(runButton);

JPanel centerPanel = new JPanel();
centerPanel.add(textAreaLabel);
centerPanel.add(textArea);

//  Add the JPanel objects to the content pane

getContentPane().setLayout(new BorderLayout());
getContentPane().add(
                northPanel, BorderLayout.NORTH);
getContentPane().add(
                centerPanel, BorderLayout.CENTER);

//  Add a title to the JFrame, size it, and make it
//  visible.
```

```
    setTitle("Atmosphere Modeling Tool");
    setDefaultCloseOperation(JFrame.EXIT_ON_CLOSE);
    setBounds(100,100,500,300);
    setVisible(true);
  }

  //  The actionPerformed() method is called when
  //  the "Compute" button is pressed. A USatm76
  //  object is created and the atmospheric conditions
  //  written to the JTextArea.

  public void actionPerformed(ActionEvent event) {
    String units = (String)comboBox.getSelectedItem();
    double altitude =
            Double.parseDouble(textField.getText());
    atm = new USatm76(units, altitude);

    String label[] = atm.getLabels();

    textArea.setText("");
    textArea.append("geometric altitude    = "+
                atm.getAltitude()+label[0]);
    textArea.append("\ngeopotential altitude = "+
          atm.getGeoPotentialAltitude()+label[1]);
    textArea.append("\ntemperature           = "+
                atm.getTemperature()+label[2]);
    textArea.append("\npressure              = "+
                atm.getPressure()+label[3]);
    textArea.append("\nmolar mass            = "+
                atm.getMolarMass()+label[4]);
```

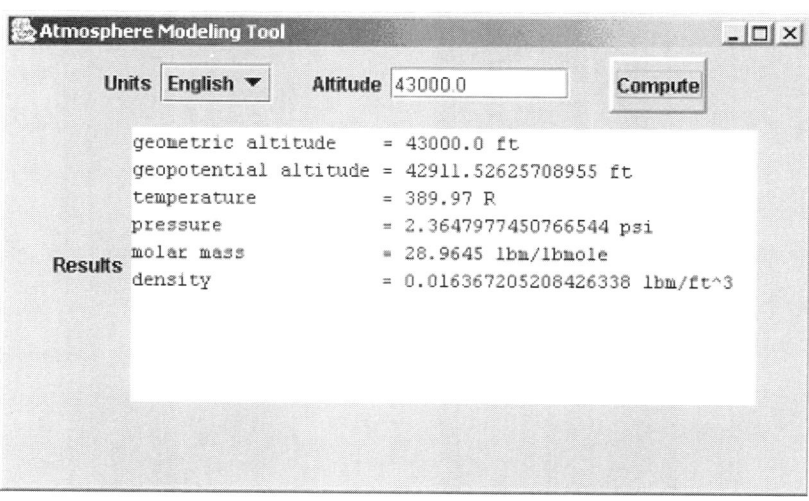

FIGURE 26.1 Atmosphere modeling tool GUI

```
    textArea.append("\ndensity              = "+
                    atm.getDensity()+label[5]);
  }

  public static void main(String args[]) {
    AtmGUI gui = new AtmGUI();
  }
}
```

When you compile and run the AtmGUI program, Figure 26.1 is a typical screen shot of what you will see.

27

CREATING WEB-BASED APPLICATIONS USING JAVA SERVLETS

So far, all of the examples we have developed have been stand-alone applications, meaning the application is run on the same machine on which it resides. This is fine for personal use-type programs or applications that are shared among a local group of colleagues, but what happens if you develop an application that will be widely disseminated and/or used on different, remote computer platforms. All of sudden you are faced with accessibility, maintainability, and version control issues.

Anyone who wants to use the application will either have to install it on his or her own computer or have direct access to a computer on which the application is installed. This raises a security concern in that it might be undesirable to give users direct access to the server on which the application resides. When the tool is updated, an updated version will have to be sent to everyone having an interest in using it. Further, there is no way of knowing if everyone is using the same version of the tool. Software maintenance and version control become a problem.

The advent of the Internet has provided a way around all these problems. You can deploy a scientific or engineering analysis program as a web-based application. A single version of the application exists on a central server. Any number of client machines can access the tool by connecting to the server via a web browser. The application is easier to update and maintain. When a new version of the tool is developed, it only has to be updated on the server. Every client machine is, therefore, assured of using the latest version. Security is enhanced in that users are not given direct access to the server. The front-end to the tool is implemented as a GUI on the client web browser providing all of the benefits that a GUI provides.

In this chapter we will look at how you can turn a Java program into a web-based application using Java servlets. We will discuss what a servlet is and go over step-by-step how to write one. This chapter will be similar to Chapter 26 in that it will give a broad overview of the process of developing Java servlets without providing comprehensive coverage of the subject. There simply isn't room in this book to explore all the possibilities of servlets and web-based Java programs. For a detailed look at all the ins and outs of Java servlets, consult *Inside Servlets: Server-Side Programming for the Java™ Platform* by Dustin Callaway.

The specific topics we will discuss in this chapter are—

- Web-based application basics
- Java servlets
- Required libraries and tools
- Example: a web-based atmosphere modeling tool
- `HttpServlet` class
- General form of an `HttpServlet` subclass
- Extracting input parameters
- Running server-based applications
- Sending output back to the client machine
- The `AtmServlet` class
- Deploying the web-based application

WEB-BASED APPLICATION BASICS

The basic schematic diagram of the client-server interaction for a web-based application is shown in Figure 27.1. The application resides on the server machine. Client machines send requests to access the application to the server through a web browser running on the client machine. The request will include any input parameters needed to run the application. The application is then executed on the server and the results sent back to the client. The web browser on the client machine displays the output received from the server.

The server-side application waits passively for client requests. When the server receives a client request, it extracts the input parameters and runs the ap-

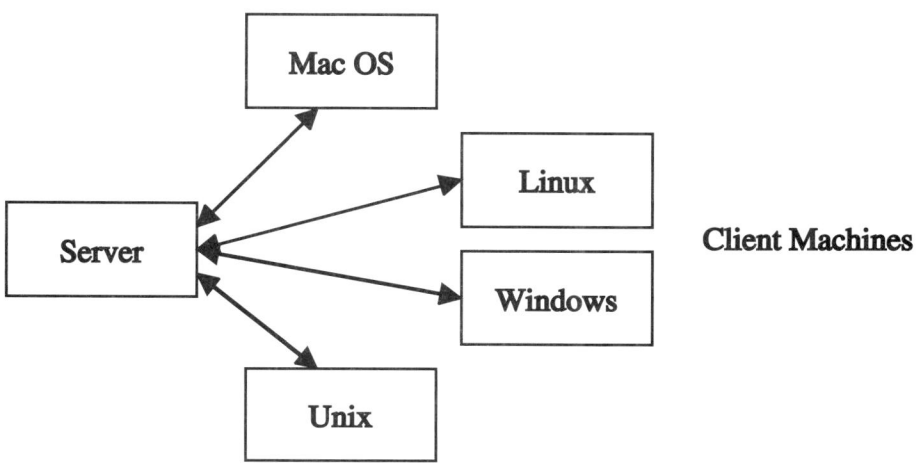

FIGURE 27.1 Client-server relationship diagram

plication. The server then sends the output back to the client machine. It is up to the server to define a mechanism that will interface with the client machine and receive and respond to client requests.

JAVA SERVLETS

One way to create the interface between the server and client machines is by using Java servlets. A Java servlet is simply a specialized type of Java program that does all of the work of implementing the web-based application. The servlet extracts the input arguments from the client request, runs the application, and sends the output back to the client. Java servlets can take advantage of the built-in security features of the Java language and give the developer access to the enormous code libraries in the Java API.

Servlets work in conjunction with a Java web server that is running on the server machine. When a Java web server detects a request from a client machine, it invokes the servlet. In this chapter we will discuss servlets that respond to the seven HTTP commands—DELETE, GET, HEAD, OPTIONS, POST, PUT, and TRACE.

In addition to supporting the concept of a servlet, Java is a particularly well-suited language for developing web-based applications. Java can handle all of the data transfer between client and server and can be used for all of the other server-side code as well. Being able to do everything with a single programming language is a great advantage when developing web-based applications.

Required Libraries and Tools

In order to write and execute Java servlets, several software packages must be installed onto the machine that will be used to develop and compile the servlets. You will need to download and install the J2EE SDK from the Sun Java website. The servlet libraries will be included in the SDK. Because Java is platform-independent, the servlets don't have to be compiled on the server. It is possible to install the SDK and servlet libraries on another machine and perform the servlet development work there. The server will have to have a JVM installed on it so it can run the servlet.

The final bit of infrastructure to install is a Java web server. A web server is an application that runs in the background on a server and can send things such as HTML pages back to client browsers. A Java web server is one that can also execute Java servlets. There are many commercial Java web servers on the market today. There are also Java web servers that can be acquired without charge. The Tomcat and Apache servers, for instance, can be found at *http://jakarta.apache.org*.

For the servlet example in this chapter, the Apache web server with the JServ module was installed on an SGI workstation that was used as the server.

Example: A Web-Based Atmosphere Modeling Tool

In Chapter 25, we developed a class named `USatm76` that represents the conditions in the Earth's atmosphere at a given altitude. In this chapter we will use that class and a Java servlet to create a web-based atmosphere modeling tool. The client machine will send an `HTTP` request along with the altitude and system-of-units inputs to the server, which will then invoke the servlet. The servlet will create a `USatm76` object using the client-specified parameters and send the resulting atmospheric conditions back to the client machine. To see the `USatm76` class code listing and sample outputs of when the atmosphere modeling tool is run, refer to Chapter 25.

HttpServlet Class

The next several sections of this chapter describe the technical details of writing a Java servlet. Like any other Java program, the code to implement a Java servlet is contained in a class. This chapter will focus on servlets that respond to HTTP commands. The HttpServlet class defined in the javax.servlet.http package can be used to create an HTTP servlet. The header for the HttpServlet class is:

```
public abstract class HttpServlet extends GenericServlet
                              implements Serializable
```

You will notice that HttpServlet is an abstract class, so you won't use the HttpServlet class directly, but instead write a subclass of it. The HttpServlet class defines a number of methods for responding to an HTTP request. The headers of these methods are

```
protected void doDelete(HttpServletRequest req,
                   HttpServletResponse res)
protected void doGet(HttpServletRequest req,
                   HttpServletResponse res)
protected void doHead(HttpServletRequest req,
                   HttpServletResponse res)
protected void doOptions(HttpServletRequest req,
                   HttpServletResponse res)
protected void doPost(HttpServletRequest req,
                   HttpServletResponse res)
protected void doPut(HttpServletRequest req,
                   HttpServletResponse res)
protected void doTrace(HttpServletRequest req,
                   HttpServletResponse res)
```

There is one method for each of the seven HTTP commands. For instance, the doGet() method corresponds to the HTTP GET command. When the Java web server receives a client request, the Java runtime will call one of these methods according to the type of HTTP command. If an HTTP GET command is received, the doGet() method is called, and so on. These methods as defined in the `HttpServlet` class are *stubs* (methods with no body). It is up to subclasses of `HttpServlet` to provide implementation of one or more of these methods.

Each method takes two input arguments. The `HttpServletRequest` object is used to extract the input parameters that accompanied the HTTP command. The `HttpServletResponse` object is used to send the output data back to the client. These input arguments are generated automatically by the system by the container that creates and controls servlets for the web server. You never need to worry about creating an `HttpServletRequest` or `HttpServletResponse` object.

GENERAL FORM OF AN `HttpServlet` SUBCLASS

To create an HTTP servlet, you must first create a subclass of `HttpServlet`. This process is a fairly simple matter because of inheritance. An `HttpServlet` subclass will inherit all of the methods declared in the `HttpServlet` class. The subclass only needs to override the methods the subclass will use. For example, the following is the general form for an `HttpServlet` subclass that will respond to HTTP GET commands.

```
import javax.servlet.*;
import javax.servlet.http.*;

public class MyServlet
       extends HttpServlet
{

  public void doGet(
       HttpServletRequest request,
       HttpServletResponse response)
         throws ServletException,
                IOException
  {
    //  code to extract and parse inputs

    //  code to run application

    //  code to return output to client
  }
}
```

This servlet class only concerns itself with GET commands, so it only overrides the `doGet()` method. If any other HTTP commands are received from the client, the `HttpServlet` class stub methods are called and nothing happens. There is no reason that a servlet class couldn't override more than one of the `HttpServlet` class methods. The `import` declarations at the top of the program give the `MyServlet` class access to the classes and interfaces contained in the `javax.servlet` and `javax.servlet.http` packages.

The code inside the `doGet()` method will perform three functions. It will extract and parse the input parameters that came with the client request, it will run the desired application, and it will send the output from the application back to the client machine. Now for the details.

EXTRACTING INPUT PARAMETERS

When a client machine sends an `HTTP` command to the server, it also provides the input arguments required to run the application. The most common `HTTP` commands used with web-based applications are `GET` and `POST`. With the `GET` command, the input arguments are concatenated into a single string called the *query string* that is passed to the server. This method is appropriate for applications that don't require a large number of input arguments. When the `POST` command is used, the arguments are included in an HTML form that accompanies the `POST` command.

In either case, the input parameter data will consist of a series of name-value pairs. The "name" is the name of the input parameter as it is defined in the HTML form on the client web browser. The "value" is the value of the input parameter expressed as a string. The `getParameter()` method from the `ServletRequest` interface can be used to return the value associated with a given parameter name. Here is the syntax of this method.

```
public String getParameter(String name)
```

For example, if the HTML form on the client machine defined input parameters named `"units"` and `"altitude"` the servlet could extract the values associated with the input parameters using the following syntax—

```
String units = request.getParameter("units");
String altitude = request.getParameter("altitude");
```

The `request` variable is a reference to the `HttpServletRequest` object passed to the `doGet()` or `doPost()` method. The value associated with the `"altitude"` parameter is returned as a `String`. It would then be converted into a floating point value before it was used as an input value for the application.

Running Server-Based Applications

Once the input values are extracted and converted into their appropriate forms, the servlet is ready to run the requested application. A servlet will run two basic types of applications—those written in Java and those written in some other language. The simplest case is when the servlet runs a Java application. The application invocation is simply incorporated into the servlet code listing. In the case of the atmosphere modeling tool, the servlet creates a `USatm76` object with the appropriate input parameters.

The situation becomes somewhat more complicated if the application is legacy code written in a language such as Fortran, C, or C++. The application needs to be one that can be run from the command line because Java has the ability to execute command line instructions. Executing an application from the command line is accomplished by using instances of the `Runtime` and the `Process` classes. `Runtime` defines the `exec()` method that executes a command line instruction. The `exec()` method returns a `Process` object that is used to suspend further activity until the command being executed by the `exec()` method is finished. For example, to run an application named `MyApplication`, you could use this syntax.

```
Runtime r = Runtime.getRuntime();
Process p = null;

String str = "MyApplication";

try
{
  p = r.exec(str);
  p.waitFor();
}
catch (Exception e)
{
  System.out.println("error "+e);
}
```

The `Runtime` object is acquired by calling the static `getRuntime()` method. The argument to the `exec()` method is a `String` containing the command line instruction to be executed. The `waitFor()` method blocks further activity until the instruction finishes its execution. The `exec()` and `waitFor()` methods are placed in a `try` block because either of them can cause an `IOException` if something unexpected happens during their execution.

Sending Output Back to the Client Machine

Once the server-side application has been run, the only remaining task for the servlet is to send the output data back to the client machine. The `HttpServletResponse` object that was initially passed to the `doGet()` or `doPost()` method sends output data to the client in a most interesting way. It first opens an I/O data stream between the server and client. If the `HttpServletResponse` instance were named `response`, the syntax would be—

```
response.setContentType("text/html");
PrintWriter writer = response.getWriter();
```

The `getWriter()` method returns a `PrintWriter` instance that is used to write character data to an output stream. The `PrintWriter` object writes the output to the client web browser in the form of an HTML file. The client web browser reads the HTML form as if it were loading a standard HTML file and displays it on the screen.

```
writer.println("<HTML><HEAD><TITLE>"+
        "Atmospheric Model Application</TITLE>");
writer.println("</HEAD><BODY>");

// more println() statements follow
```

In the example code fragment, the `PrintWriter` object calls the `println()` method to print HTML header and title information to the client web browser. Each line of the HTML file is written by the `println()` method as a `String`.

The AtmServlet Class

We will declare a class named `AtmServlet` that will serve as the servlet for our web-based atmosphere modeling application. The class will extend the `HttpServlet` class. Since the `USatm76` object only requires two input parameters, we will use an HTTP GET command for the client request. In order to respond to GET commands, the `AtmServlet` class will override the `doGet()` method.

The first thing the `doGet()` method does is to extract the input parameters from the query string. If this is the first time the servlet is accessed, there won't be a query string. In this case, the inputs are given default values. If there is a query string, the values are extracted from it using the `HttpServletRequest` object and the `getParameter()` method.

Next the `doGet()` method writes the GUI front end for the atmosphere modeling application back to the client machine. The `HttpServletResponse` object acquires a `PrintStream` that is connected to the client machine. The `PrintStream` uses the `println()` method to send an HTML page with GUI components back to the client machine. In this case, the GUI components consist of a list component that define the system of units to be used, a text field into which the desired altitude is typed, and a button that when pressed sends the `HTTP` request to the server. If you try this example, you will have to change *www.JackZack.com* to whatever the name of your server is.

If this is not the first time the servlet is run, the `doGet()` method then creates a `USatm76` object. The atmospheric conditions represented by the `USatm76` object are written back to the client machine. One interesting thing to note about the `AtmServlet.java` code is that when the Compute button is pressed, the servlet creates a `USatm76` object and then calls itself to update the display on the client machine. When the servlet is initially invoked, the `HTTP GET` command won't include a query string. In this case, the application is not run and the servlet simply displays the GUI front-end with default input values.

The `AtmServlet` class source code is shown here.

```
import javax.servlet.*;
import javax.servlet.http.*;
import java.io.*;

public class AtmServlet extends HttpServlet
{
  // The doGet() method is called when the servlet
  // is invoked

  public void doGet(HttpServletRequest request,
                    HttpServletResponse response)
              throws ServletException, IOException {
    String line, units, altitude;
    boolean firstTime = false;
    USatm76 atm;

    // The first time this servlet is accessed, the
    // query string might be null. If this is the case,
    // provide defaults for the inputs. Otherwise,
    // extract the inputs from the query string using
    // the HttpServletRequest object.

    if ( request.getQueryString() == null ) {
      units = "SI";
      altitude = "20000.0";
      firstTime = true;
```

The AtmServlet Class

```
      } else {
        units = request.getParameter("units");
        altitude = request.getParameter("altitude");
      }

      // Use the HttpServletResponse object to specify
      // the response type and to open an output stream.

      response.setContentType("text/html");
      PrintWriter pw = response.getWriter();

      // Start creating the output HTML file that will
      // be displayed by the browser.

      char dq = '\"';

      pw.println("<HTML><HEAD><TITLE>"+
                 "Atmospheric Model Application</TITLE>");
      pw.println("</HEAD><BODY>");

      // Create the Client GUI.  This contains the input
      // parameter components and the "run" button.  When
      // the "Compute" button is selected, the HTTP
      // request is sent to the server.

      pw.println("<FORM  METHOD=GET ACTION=" + dq +
        http://www.JackZack.com:8080/servlets/AtmServlet +
                 dq+">");

      // Create the units list component.  The if
      // statement insures that whatever species is
      // selected will still be selected when the screen
      // is refreshed.

      pw.println("Units");
      pw.println("<SELECT NAME=units SIZE=1 >");
      if ( units.equals("English") ) {
        pw.println("<OPTION VALUE=SI>SI</OPTION>");
        pw.println("<OPTION SELECTED
                    VALUE=English>English"+
                   "</OPTION SELECTED>");
      } else {
        pw.println("<OPTION VALUE=SI>SI</OPTION>");
        pw.println("<OPTION
                    VALUE=English>English</OPTION>");
      }
      pw.println("</SELECT><BR><BR><BR>");

      // Create the altitude text field component

      pw.println("altitude (ft or m) ");
      pw.println("<INPUT TYPE=TEXT NAME=altitude
                  VALUE="+altitude+"><BR><BR>");
```

```java
      //  Create the run button component

      pw.println("Compute atmospheric conditions");

      pw.println("<INPUT TYPE=submit NAME=compute
                  VALUE="+dq+"Compute"+dq+">");
      pw.println("</FORM>");

      //  If this is not the first time the servlet is
      //  accessed (i.e., if nondefault input parameters
      //  exist), create a USatm76 object

      if ( !firstTime )
      {
        atm = new USatm76(units,
                          Double.parseDouble(altitude));

      //  Display the results in a nice, column-aligned
      //  table

        pw.println("<HR WIDTH=100% ALIGN=LEFT>");
        pw.println("<BR>");
        pw.println("Results");
        pw.println("<BR><BR>");

        String label[] = atm.getLabels();

        pw.println("<TABLE BORDER=0 CELLSPACING=0
                    CELLPADDING=0>");
        pw.println("<TR>");
          pw.println("<TD ><TT> geometric altitude
                      </TT></TD>");
          pw.println("<TD WIDTH=20> = </TD>");
          pw.println("<TD ALIGN=RIGHT><TT>"+
                      atm.getAltitude()+"</TT></TD>");
          pw.println("<TD WIDTH=10> </TD>");
          pw.println("<TD><TT>"+label[0]+"</TT></TD>");
        pw.println("</TR>");
        pw.println("<TR>");
          pw.println("<TD ><TT> geopotential altitude
                      </TT></TD>");
          pw.println("<TD WIDTH=20> = </TD>");
          pw.println("<TD ALIGN=RIGHT><TT>"+
              atm.getGeoPotentialAltitude()+"</TT></TD>");
          pw.println("<TD WIDTH=10> </TD>");
          pw.println("<TD><TT>"+label[1]+"</TT></TD>");
        pw.println("</TR>");
        pw.println("<TR>");
          pw.println("<TD ><TT> temperature
                      </TT></TD>");
          pw.println("<TD WIDTH=20> = </TD>");
          pw.println("<TD ALIGN=RIGHT><TT>"+
                      atm.getTemperature()+"</TT></TD>");
          pw.println("<TD WIDTH=10> </TD>");
```

```
          pw.println("<TD><TT>"+label[2]+"</TT></TD>");
      pw.println("</TR>");
      pw.println("<TR>");
          pw.println("<TD ><TT> pressure </TT></TD>");
          pw.println("<TD WIDTH=20> = </TD>");
          pw.println("<TD ALIGN=RIGHT><TT>"+
                     atm.getPressure()+"</TT></TD>");
          pw.println("<TD WIDTH=10> </TD>");
          pw.println("<TD><TT>"+label[3]+"</TT></TD>");
      pw.println("</TR>");
      pw.println("<TR>");
          pw.println("<TD ><TT> molar mass
                   </TT></TD>");
          pw.println("<TD WIDTH=20> = </TD>");
          pw.println("<TD ALIGN=RIGHT><TT>"+
                     atm.getMolarMass()+"</TT></TD>");
          pw.println("<TD WIDTH=10> </TD>");
          pw.println("<TD><TT>"+label[4]+"</TT></TD>");
      pw.println("</TR>");
      pw.println("<TR>");
          pw.println("<TD ><TT> density </TT></TD>");
          pw.println("<TD WIDTH=20> = </TD>");
          pw.println("<TD ALIGN=RIGHT><TT>"+
                     atm.getDensity()+"</TT></TD>");
          pw.println("<TD WIDTH=10> </TD>");
          pw.println("<TD><TT>"+label[5]+"</TT></TD>");
      pw.println("</TR>");
      pw.println("</TABLE>");

  }  /*  End of "if ( !firstTime )" block   */

  //  The HTML form is complete

  pw.println("</BODY></HTML>");
  pw.close();
 }
}
```

DEPLOYING THE WEB-BASED APPLICATION

The servlet has been written, the USatm76.java program is ready, and it's time to deploy our web-based application. The first step is to start the Java web server. Once this is done, you must compile the USatm76 and AtmServlet source code and place the resulting .class file in the proper directory on the server. Where you place the .class file is server-dependent but will generally be in a subdirectory to the server root directory. For the example in this chapter, the server root directory was /usr/jserv. The .class files were placed in the /usr/jserv/servlets directory.

At this point, we can access the server-based application from a client machine by typing the appropriate address into the location window of the browser. For example, let's say the server is a machine named *www.Jack-Zack.com* and is listening on port number 8080. If the server root directory were /usr/jserv and if we placed the application byte code into the directory /usr/jserv/servlets, a client machine could invoke the servlet by typing the following into the location window of the browser—

```
http://www.JackZack.com:8080/servlets/AtmServlet
```

Figure 27.2 shows a typical result when the web-based atmosphere modeling application is run.

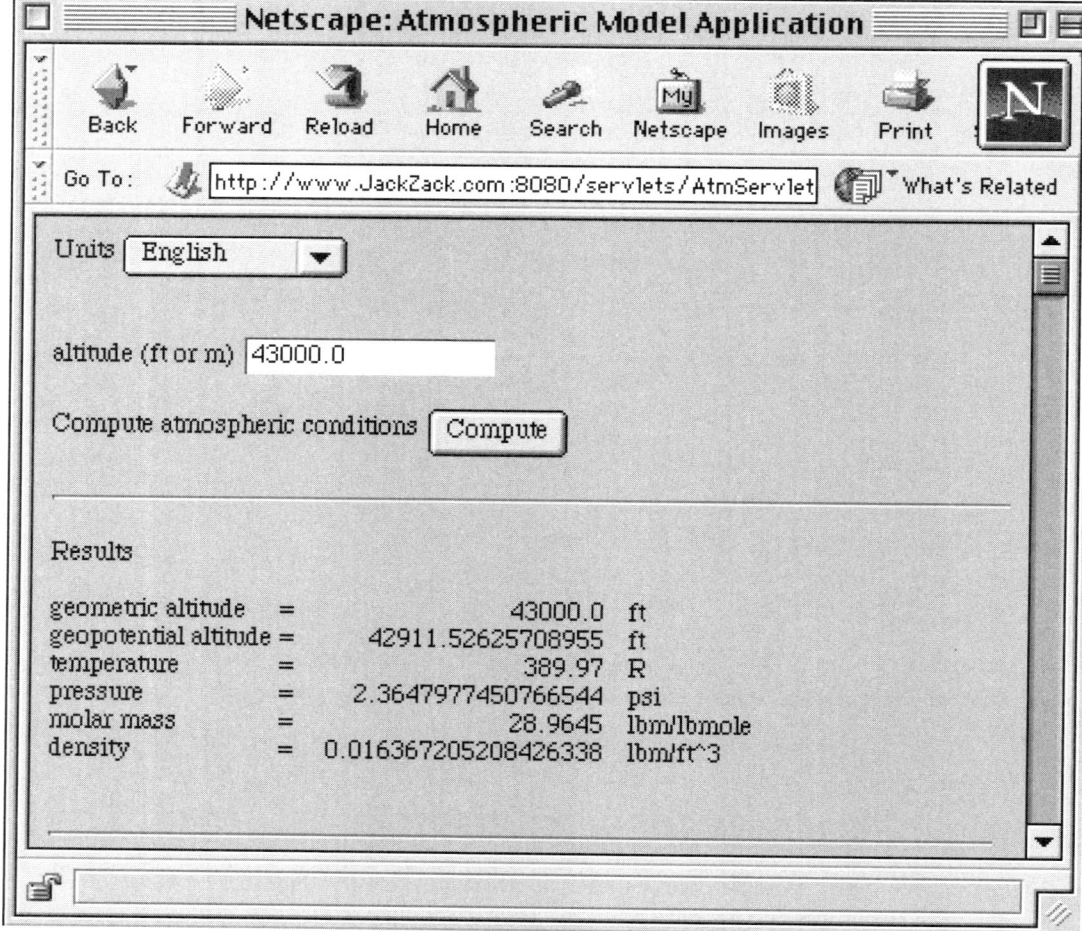

FIGURE 27.2 Web-based atmosphere modeling tool

APPENDIX

JAVA KEYWORDS

Throughout this book we have discussed words that have special meaning in the Java language. These words are referred to as Java *keywords*. The keywords are used to declare, modify, and define things, and some of them are operators. Because they have special meaning, keywords cannot be used as identifiers. You can't declare a variable named "final," for instance.

Here is a list of the Java keywords and a brief description of how they are used in the Java language. A more complete description of the keywords and examples of how to use them can be found throughout this book.

`abstract`—A modifier applied to a class or method. An `abstract` class is one that cannot be instantiated. An `abstract` method is one that must be overridden by a nonabstract subclass.

`assert`—Part of an assertion statement declaration.

`boolean`—A type that contains a logical true or false value.

`break`—A statement used to exit from a `switch`, `while`, `do`, or `for` statement or from a labeled block of code.

`byte`—A type representing a single byte of data.

`case`—A label that defines a value that is compared against the expression following a `switch` statement.

`catch`—A clause used to catch and process an exception of a specified type.

`char`—A type representing a 16-bit Unicode character.

`class`—Used to declare a class.

`const`—A reserved keyword that is not currently used by Java.

`continue`—A statement that causes program execution to return to the top of the current loop.

`default`—The code following the `default` label is run if none of the `case` label values match the expression of a `switch` statement.

`do`—A `do-while` loop will execute a block of code until a condition is met. The condition is tested after the block of code executes.

`double`—A type representing a 64-bit double precision floating-point value.

`else`—Part of an `if-else` statement. Defines a block of code that is executed if the condition after the `if` statement is not met.

`extends`—Indicates inheritance.

`final`—A modifier applied to classes, methods, and variables. A `final` class cannot be subclassed. A `final` method cannot be overridden. A `final` variable cannot change its value once it is set.

`finally`—A clause that can be optionally placed at the end of a `try` statement. The block of code after a `finally` clause will be executed whether or not an exception is thrown and whether or not a thrown exception is caught.

`float`—A type representing a 32-bit single precision floating-point value.

`for`—A flow of control structure that can be used to execute a block of code a number of times.

`goto`—Not used in the Java language. Making `goto` a keyword means you can't use it in your programs even if you wanted to.

`if`—A conditional branch statement.

`implements`—Used to indicate that a class will implement one or more interfaces.

`import`—A statement that allows you to refer to classes and interfaces by their simple names.

`instanceof`—Type comparison operator.

`int`—A type representing a 32-bit integer value.

`interface`—Used to declare an interface.

`long`—A type representing a 64-bit integer value.

`native`—Indicates that a method is implemented in a language other than Java.

new—Object creation operator.

package—A declaration indicating that the contents of a source file will be placed inside a package.

private—An access modifier. A member with private access is only accessible inside the class in which it is defined.

protected—An access modifier. A member with protected access is accessible inside the class in which it is defined and by subclasses.

public—An access modifier. A member with public access is accessible anywhere.

return—Used to return from the current method.

short—A type representing a 16-bit integer value.

static—A member associated with a class rather than with an instance of a class.

strictfp—A modifier that forces float or double expressions in a class, interface, or method declaration to be explicitly FP-strict.

super—Refers to a superclass member.

switch—A flow of control structure that compares an expression against one or more values.

synchronized—A synchronized method is one that ensures thread-safe data access.

this—A reference to the current object.

throw—A statement used to explicitly throw an exception.

throws—A clause used to declare the exception types that a method can throw.

transient—Indicates that a member variable should not be serialized.

try—An exception handling statement. Code that can generate an exception is placed inside a block of code after the try statement.

void—Indicates that a method does not return a value.

volatile—If a variable is declared to be volatile, the compiler will not perform certain synchronization optimizations on it.

while—A construct that executes a block of code as long as a condition is met.

INDEX

A

abs() method, 199–201
Abscissas, 322
AbsDemo class, 200–201
Absolute value methods, 199–201
Abstract classes, 87–89
   compared to interfaces, 132
   using, 88–89
Abstract methods, 123–24
Abstract Window Toolkit (AWT), 4, 176
AbstractGas class, 227–28, 229
Access control, and packages, 144
Access modifiers:
   and inheritance, 84–85
   methods, 114–16
   variables, 102–3
Access privileges, 67–68
   types of access, 67
AccessDemo class, 115–16
AccessDriver class, 116
Accessibility API, 4
acos() method, 204
ActionListener class, 78
ActionListener interface, 428–29
Air class, 160–61, 233–34
Air2 class, 165
Air3 class, 166–67
AirDriver class, 233–34
Aliasing, 346–47
Angle of attack, 327
Angles, converting, 207
AnonDemo class, 80–81
Anonymous inner classes, 77, 80–81
Apache server, 438
ArgDemo class, 137–38, 168–69
Arguments, passing by value, 16
Arithmetic operators, 44–45
ArithOpDemo class, 45

Array elements:
   accessing, 166–67
   initializing, 164–67
ArrayList class, 170
Arrays, 159–72
   accessing an element in, 17
   array elements:
      accessing, 166–67
      initializing, 164–67
   collection classes in the Java API, 170–71
   defined, 159
   indices, 16–17
   length, 169–70
   as method arguments and return types, 167–69
   of more than two dimensions, 164
   moving from C to Java, 26–27
   moving from Fortran to Java, 16–17
   one-dimensional, 160–61
   passing as a method argument, 168–69
   size of, 16
   two-dimensional, 161–64
asin() method, 204
Assignment operators, 45–46
AssignOpDemo class, 46
atan() method, 204
AtmGUI class, 421–23
   final form of, 430–33
AtmServlet class, 443–47
   source code, 444–47
AudioInputStream class, 389
available() method, InputStream class, 385

B

Basic syntax, *See* Syntax:
BigDecimal class, 197
BigInteger class, 197
Binary operators, 44

453

Bins, 347–49
Bitwise operators, 50–51
`BitWiseDemo` class, 51
`BlackBody` class, 96–97, 119
`BlackBody2` class, 104
`BlackBody2Driver` class, 104–5
`BlackBody3` class, 105–6
`BlackBody4` class, 128–29
Blottner curve fit expression, 203
`Boolean` class, 185
boolean data type, 14–15, 24, 93
Boolean operators, 48–50
`BooleanOpDemo` class, 50
`BorderLayout` class, 426
Braces, 13
break statements, 60–61
`BreakDemo` class, 61
Brigham, E. Oran, 334
`BufferedInputStream` class, 384, 385–86
`BufferedOutputStream` class, 390, 391
`BufferedReader` class, 175, 397–98
`BufferedWriter` class, 175, 400–401
Built-in math functions, 19, 197–214, *See also* User-defined math functions
  absolute value methods, 199–201
  angles, converting, 207
  comparing built-in math capability of C/C++/Fortran/Java, 212–14
  conversion methods, 206–7
  `java.math` package, 212
  `Math` class, 198
  mathematical constants, 199
  maximum methods, 208–9
  minimum methods, 208–9
  moving from C to Java, 29
  moving from C++ to Java, built-in math functions, 34–35
  `pow()` method, 201–2
  random number generator methods, 211–12
  remainder methods, 209–11
  rounding methods, 209–11
  `sqrt()` method, 201–2
  `StrictMath` class, 198
  transcendental math functions, 203–4
  trigonometric methods, 204–6
`Byte` class, 184–86
byte data type, 14–15, 24, 93
Byte input streams:
  `AudioInputStream` class, 389
  `BufferedInputStream` class, 384, 385–86
  `ByteArrayInputStream` class, 384, 386
  `DataInputStream` class, 384, 386–87
  `FileInputStream` class, 384, 387–88
  `FilterInputStream` class, 384, 388

  `InputStream` class, 385
  `ObjectInputStream` class, 384, 388–89
  `PipedInputStream` class, 389
  `SequenceInputStream` class, 389
  `StringBufferInputStream` class, 389
Byte output streams, 389–96
  `BufferedOutputStream` class, 391
  `ByteArrayOutputStream` class, 391–92
  `DataOutputStream` class, 392–93
  `FileOutputStream` class, 393
  `FilterOutputStream` class, 393
  `ObjectOutputStream` class, 393–95
  `OutputStream` class, 390–91
  `PrintOutputStream` class, 395–96
Byte streams, 20, 382
`ByteArrayInputStream` class, 384, 386
`ByteArrayOutputStream` class, 391–92
Bytecode, 6

C

C/C++, 442
Camber, 327
`CamberFunction` class, 329
  constructor, 329
`CardLayout` class, 426
`CastDemo` class, 107–8
Casting, 106–8
catch clause, 152–53
Catenary, 222–23
`ceil()` method, 209
`ChainDemo` class, 125
char data type, 14–15, 24, 93
  double data type, 24
`Character` class, 185
Character input streams, 396–99
  `BufferedReader` class, 397–98
  `CharArrayReader` class, 399
  `FileReader` class, 398
  `FilterReader` class, 399
  `InputStreamReader` class, 383, 398–99
  `PipedReader` class, 399
  `PushbackReader` class, 399
  `Reader` class, 396–97
  `StringReader` class, 399
Character output streams, 399–403
  `BufferedWriter` class, 400–401
  `CharArrayWriter` class, 403
  `FileWriter` class, 401
  `FilterWriter` class, 403
  `OutputStreamWriter` class, 401–2
  `PipedWriter` class, 403
  `PrinterWriter` class, 402–3
  `StringWriter` class, 403
  `Writer` class, 399–400

Character streams, 20, 382
`CharArrayReader` class, 399
`CharArrayWriter` class, 403
Chord, 327
Chord line, 327
`CircCylGrid` class, 162–63
.class files, using the CLASSPATH to locate, 143–44
Class hierarchies, 225–46
   `AbstractGas` class, 227–28, 229
   `Air` class, 233–34
   gas mixture, defining state/behavior of, 226–27
   general class hierarchy structure, 227–29
   `N` class, 241–42
   `N2` class, 240–41
   `NitrogenGas` class, 242–45
   `PerfectGas` class, 227–28, 230–33
   `RealGas` class, 227–28, 234–38
   `Species` class, 238–40
     class hierarchy, 228
Class loader, 7
Class method, 70
Class variables, 24, 69–70, 91, 95–98
Classes, 12–13, 22, 23, 37, 65–90, *See also* Abstract classes; Anonymous inner classes; Final classes; Instance (inner) nested classes; Nested classes; Static nested classes
   abstract, 87–89
     using, 88–89
   access privileges, 67–68
   constructors, 65, 72–74
   declaration syntax, 66–67
   defined, 65
   encapsulation, 81–82
   fields, declaring, 69–70
   final, 89
   garbage collector, 89–90
   inheritance, 82–84
   initializers, 65
   members, 65
   methods, declaring, 70–71
   nested, 77–81
   and object structure, 13
   objects, 68–69
     copying, 75–77
   static initialization blocks, 74
   `super` keyword, 86
   `this` keyword, 86–87
CLASSPATH environment variable, 143–44
Client machine, 436
   sending output back to, 443
Client-server relationship, 437
`close()` method:
   `InputStream` class, 385
   `OutputStream` class, 391

   `Reader` class, 396–97
   `Writer` class, 400
`CmdLineDemo` class, 408–9
Code blocks, 13
Code libraries, moving from Fortran to Java, 18–19
Collection classes, 170–71
`Collection` interface, 137
Collision integrals, 373
`Color` class, 176
Command line arguments, getting input, 407–9
`CommandLine` class, 120
Comment statements, 13
`CommentDemo` class, 43
Common Gateway Interface (CGI), 7
Comparator, 191
Comparator, defined, 191
`compareTo()` method, 190
`CompareToIgnoreCase()` method, 190
Compiler, 6, 8–9
   and exception handling, 18
   obtaining, 7
   options, 8
   output of, 9
Compressible boundary layer (example problem), 296–305
   `CompressODE` class, 300–302
   `ShootingCompress` class, 303–5
`CompressODE` class, 300–302
`computeGaussWeights()` method, 323–24
`computeMolarMass()` method, 235
`computepressure()` method, 404
`computeTemperature()` method, 404
`ConcatDemo` class, 189–90
Constants, 133
Constructors, 72–74
   classes, 65
Content panes, 420–21
`continue` statements, 61–62
Control statements, 54–60
   transfer of, 60–62
     `break` statements, 60–61
     `continue` statements, 61–62
     `return` statements, 62
`ConvertDemo` class, 207
CORBA Object Request Broker (ORB), 4
Core J2SE libraries, 174–76, *See also* Java 2 Platform Standard Edition (J2SE)
   `java.io` package, 174–75
   `java.lang` package, 174–75
   `java.math` package, 174–75
   `java.util` package, 175–76
Core JDBC API, 174
`cos()` method, 204
`CreateDemo` class, 69

`CreateString` class, 188–89
`CreateWrapper` class, 183–84
Crocco's method, 304
Curve fitting specified heat data (example problem), 370–73

D

Damped spring motion (example problem), 280–85
 solution, 283–85
 `SpringODE` class, 282–83
Damping forces, 281
Data modeling, 365–79
 curve fitting specified heat data (example problem), 370–73
 `DataModeling` class, 368–69
 least squares fit to a polynomial equation, 366–68
 nonpolynomial equations, fitting to, 373–74
 `Polynomial` class, 369–70
 `Power` class, 374–78
Data streams, 382–83
Data types, moving from C++ to, 33
`DataInputStream` class, 384, 386–87
`DataModeling` class, 354, 358, 368–69, 374
`DataOutputStream` class, 392–93
Decimation in Frequency (DIF) technique, 349
Decimation in Time (DIT) technique, 349
`DeclareDemo` class, 99–100, 113–14
Default access, 67–68
 variables, 102
Deitel, Harvey M., 124
Deitel, Paul J., 124
Differential equations, 271–307
 compressible boundary layer (example problem), 296–305
 damped spring motion (example problem), 280–85
 solution, 283–85
 `SpringODE` class, 282–83
 defined, 271
 embedded Runge-Kutta algorithms, 285–91
 initial value problems, 275–76
 `ODE` class, 273–75
 `ODESolver` class, 279–80
 ordinary, 272–73
 first-order ODE, 272–73
 second-order ODE, 272
 partial, 306
 Runge-Kutta schemes, 276–80
 `rungeKutta4()` method, 279–83
 shooting methods, 292–96
 two-point boundary problems, 292, 305–6
`Dimension` class, 176
Discrete Fourier transform (DFT), 333–34, 336–43
 defined, 336

`discreteFT()` method, 338–41
 `TestDF` class, 340–41
`discreteFT()` method, 338–41, 343, 354
`do-while` loops, 56–57
`do-while` statement, 14
Documentation comments, 13
`Double` class, 184–86
`double` data type, 14–15, 16, 24, 93, 208
`doubleValue()` method, 183–84, 185
`DoWhileDemo` class, 57
Dynamic memory allocation, 17
 moving from C to Java, 27–28

E

Eckel, Bruce, 225
`Electrostatic` interface, 133
Embedded Runge-Kutta algorithms, 285–91
`embeddedRK5()` method, 287–91
`EmbedSpring` class, 290–91
Empty statement, 112
Encapsulation, 37–38, 81–82, 111
Enterprise JavaBeans, 30
Enthalpy ratio, 299
Enumerations, moving from C++ to Java, 34
`EqnSolver` class, 249
 methods, testing, 263–65
`equals()` method, 191
Essential JNI: Java Native Interface (Gordon), 124
Euler's number, 199
Event handlers, 427–30
`EventDemo` class, 79–80
Exception handling, 149–57
 `Exception` class hierarchy, 150–51
 moving from C to Java, 28
 moving from Fortran to Java, 18
 passing exceptions to another method, 156–57
 `throw` and `throws` keywords, 155–57
 `try` statements, 151–55
 `catch` clause, 152–53
 `finally` clause, 153
 `try` keyword, 152
 using, 154–55
`exp()` method, 203–4
Extensible Markup Language (XML), 173–78
 Java API for, 4

F

Fast Fourier Transform and Its Applications (Brigham), 334
Fast Fourier transforms (FFTs), 334, 349–54
 Decimation in Frequency (DIF) technique, 349
 Decimation in Time (DIT) technique, 349

defined, 349–50
   `fastFT()` method, 351–53
   implementing as a Java method, 351
   `TestFFT` class, 353–54
`fastFT()` method, 351–53
`fastFt()` method, 351–54
`fastFT()` method, 354
Fields, 12–13
   declaring, 69–70
`FileDemo` class, 412–14
`FileInputStream` class, 384, 387–88
`FileOutputStream` class, 393
`FileReader` class, 398
`FileWriter` class, 399, 401
`FilterInputStream` class, 384, 388
`FilterOutputStream` class, 390, 393
`FilterReader` class, 399
`FilterWriter` class, 403
Final classes, 89
`final` keyword, 89
Final methods, 124
Final, methods, 124
Final variables, 105–6
`finally` clause, 153
First-order ODE, 272–73
`FithOrderDemo` class, 371–73
`Float` class, 184–86
`float` data type, 14–15, 24, 93, 208
`floor()` method, 209
FlowLayout layout manager, 426
`Fluids.Gas` package, 141–42
`flush()` method:
  `OutputStream` class, 391
  `Writer` class, 400
`Font` class, 176
`for` loops, 57–58
`ForDemo` class, 58
Fortran, 442
Forward transforms, 335–36
`Fourier` class, 339–40
Fourier transforms, 333–54
   composite signals, analyzing, 343–45
   defined, 333
   discrete Fourier transform (DFT), 333–34, 336–43
     defined, 336
     `discreteFT()` method, 338–41, 354
     `TestDF` class, 340–41
   fast Fourier transforms (FFTs), 334, 349–54
     Decimation in Frequency (DIF) technique, 349
     Decimation in Time (DIT) technique, 349
     defined, 349–50
     `fastFT()` method, 351–53, 354
     implementing as a Java method, 351
     `TestFFT` class, 353–54
   forward, 335–36
   generic part implementation, 354
     `leastSquaresFit()` method, 354, 361, 363
   inverse, 333, 335–36
   sampling theory, 345–47
     aliasing, 346–47
   signal characterization, 334–35
   spectral leakage, 347–49
   time and frequency function relationships, 336
Fredholm integrals, 308, 326
Free-form coding, 13
Free variables, 273
Freely Distributable Math Library (`fdlibm`), 19
Full pivoting, 250–51
Function pointer, 355
Functions:
   integration of, 307–31
   moving from C to Java, 25–26
   moving from Fortran to Java, 15–16

G

Gamma function, 219–20
Garbage collector, 17, 89–90
`GasDriver` class, 71
`GasDriver3` class, 73–74
`GasDriver4` class, 76–77
`GasDriver5` class, 95
Gauss-Jordan elimination, 253–55, 261
Gauss-Legendre formula, 323
Gaussian elimination, 255–57
`gaussian()` method, 256–57, 261, 267
Gaussian quadrature methods, 322–26
`gaussJordan()` method, 254–56
`gaussLegendre()` method, 324–25
Geary, David, 420
Generic class libraries, 355–63
   defined, 355
   least squares fit (example), 356–58
   `LineDemo` Class, 361–63
   problem analysis, 356
   problem-specific part, implementing, 358–61
   testing, 361–63
`getContentPane()` method, 426
`getDensity()` method:
  `PerfectGas` class, 230
  `RealGas` class, 235
`getEnthalpy()` method, 136
  `PerfectGas` class, 230
`getEntropy()` method, 136
  `PerfectGas` class, 230
`getField()` method, 136

getFunction() method, 355
    ODE class, 282, 301
getParameter() method, 443
getParameter() method, ServletRequest interface, 441
getPressure() method, RealGas class, 235
getTemperature() method, RealGas class, 235
getViscosity() method:
    PerfectGas class, 230
    RealGas class, 236, 267–68
getWriter() method, 443
Glass panes, 420–21
Gordon, Rob, 124
Graphic Java, Volume 2: Swing (3rd ed.) (Geary), 420
Graphical User Interface (GUI), 3, *See also* GUI libraries
Green Project, 2
Grid, 306
GridBagLayout class, 426
GUI libraries, 176–78, 420–21
    java.awt package, 176
    java.awt.event package, 176
    javax.swing package, 177
    javax.swing.border package, 177
    javax.swing.event package, 177
    javax.swing.table package, 177
    javax.swing.text package, 177
    javax.swing.tree package, 177
GUIs, 419–33
    AtmGUI class, 421–23
        final form of, 430–33
    container:
        adding components to, 425–27
        choosing, 422–23
    event handlers, 427–30
    GUI components, selecting, 423–25
    moving from C to Java, 30
    moving from Fortran to Java, 20

H

HashMap class, 170, 183
HashSet class, 170
Hashtable, 170
Header, 112
Hooke's law, 280–81
HttpServlet class, 439–40
    subclass, general form of, 440–41

I

I/O capability, 381–417
    atmosphere modeling tool (test case), 403–7
    byte input streams, 384–89
    byte output streams, 389–96
    character input streams, 396–99
    character output streams, 399–403
    command line arguments, getting input from, 407–9
    general concepts, 382–83
    java.nio package, 417
    moving from C++ to Java, built-in math functions, 35
    reading to a file, 412–14
    restoring objects, 414–16
    saving objects, 414–16
    streams, using, 409–11
    writing to a file, 412–14
IEEEremainder() method, 209
if-else statements, 54–55
IfDemo class, 55
ImplementDemo class, 135–36
import declarations, 142–43
Improper integrals, 308
    solving, 317–22
IncopDemo class, 47
Increment/decrement operators, 46–47
Indices, arrays, 16–17
InfiniteChargedPlate class, 134–35
Inheritance, 39, 67, 82–84, 111
    and access modifiers, 84–85
    and interfaces, 136
    member hiding/member overriding, 86
    and method arguments, 85
    moving from C++ to Java, 34
Initializers, classes, 65
Input streams, 382–83
InputDemo class, 122–23
InputStream class, 385
    close() method, 385
InputStreamReader class, 383, 398–99
Inside Servlets: Server-Side Programming for the Java Platform (Callaway), 436
Instance (inner) nested classes, 77, 78–80
Instance methods, 16, 70, 116–18
Instance variables, 70, 91, 95–98
InstanceDemo class, 117–18
int data type, 14–15, 24, 93, 208–9
Integer class, 184–86
Integral equations, 307–31
    closed-form solutions, 308–9
    Fredholm integrals, 308, 326
    Gaussian quadrature methods, 322–26
    general form of, 308
    general integral types, 326
    improper integrals, 308
        solving, 317–22
    open-form solutions, 308
    proper integrals, 308
    Simpson's rule, 314–17
    thin airfoil theory (example), 326–31

trapezoidal algorithms, 309–14
`Integrator` class, 311–12, 319
Interfaces, 67, 131–38
    compared to abstract classes, 132
    declaring, 132–33
    defined, 131
    as an example of polymorphism, 40
    implementing, 134–36
    and inheritance, 136
    instances as input parameters and return types, 136–38
    members, 133
    moving from C++ to Java, 34
Internet, 2
Inverse transforms, 335–36
`InvertDemo` class, 264–65
`invertMatrix()` method, 261–63
`Ionized` interface, 136
`IonizedSpecies` class, 84, 141

J

JANAF Thermochemical Tables, 370
`jar`, 4
`jar` utility, 145–49
    options, 145
`jarsigner`, 4
Java:
    access privileges, 67–68
    assignment operators, 14
    basic syntax, 41–64
        comments, 43
        general syntax, 41–43
        keyboard I/O, 62–64
        loops/control structures, 54–60
        operators, 44–54
        printing, 62–64
        simple Java program, 42–43
    braces, 13
    bytecode, 6
    class loader, 7
    classes, 12–13, 65–90
        declaration syntax, 66–67
    code blocks, 13
    comment statements, 13
    compiler, 6
    compiler options, 8
    expandability of, 7
    free-form coding, 13
    future of, 4
    history of, 2–4
    I/O capability, 381–417
    installing, 7–8
    as an interpreted language, 6
    Java APIs, 28–29
    keywords, 15
    loop and flow control structures, 14
    mathematical operators, 14
    memory model, 6
    moving from C to, 21–30
        arrays, 26–27
        basic printing, 30
        basic syntax, 23
        built-in math functions, 29
        C structs, 23
        classes, 22, 23
        dynamic memory allocation, 27–28
        exception handling, 28
        functions, 25–26
        GUIs, 30
        I/O capability, 30
        libraries, 28–29
        `main()` method, 22
        methods, 25–26
        pointers, 25
        program structure, 22
        strings, 29
        variables, 24–25
        Web-base applications, 30
    moving from C++ to, 31–36
        basic syntax, 32
        built-in math functions, 34–35
        data types, 33
        enumerations, 34
        I/O capability, 35
        inheritance, 34
        interfaces, 34
        memory management, 35–36
        pointers, 33–34
        preprocessor directives, 32–33
        strings, 35
        structures, 34
        unions, 34
    moving from Fortran to, 11–20
        arrays, 16–17
        basic syntax, 13–14
        built-in math functions, 19
        code libraries, 18–19
        dynamic memory allocation, 17
        exception handling, 18
        functions, 15–16
        GUIs, 20
        I/O capability, 19–20
        methods, 15–16
        pointers, 17–18
        program structure, 12–13
        subroutines, 15–16
        variables, 12, 14–15
        Web-base applications, 20

Java (*cont.*)
  as multithreaded language, 7
  object-oriented nature of, 5, 11
  packages, 19, 28–29, 67
  platform neutrality of, 5–6
  primitive types, 15, 16
  reference types, 15, 16
  robustness of, 6
  security of, 6–7
  simplicity/familiarity of, 5
  source code, initial release of, 3
  as a standard, 1
  as strongly typed language, 15
  types, 14–15, 24–25
  versatility of, 7
Java 1.0, 2–3
Java 1.1, 3
Java 1.2, 3–4
Java 1.3, 4
Java 1.4, 4
Java 2 Platform Enterprise Edition (J2EE), 3, 173
  downloading, 7
  SDK, 438
Java 2 Platform Micro Edition (J2ME), 3, 173
  downloading, 7
Java 2 Platform Standard Edition (J2SE), 3
  core J2SE libraries, 174–76
    java.io package, 174–75
    java.lang package, 174–75
    java.math package, 174–75
    java.util package, 175–76
  GUI libraries, 176–78
    java.awt package, 176
    java.awt.event package, 176
    javax.swing package, 177
    javax.swing.border package, 177
    javax.swing.event package, 177
    javax.swing.table package, 177
    javax.swing.text package, 177
    javax.swing.tree package, 177
  obtaining, 7
Java 2 Software Development Kit (SDK), 4
Java APIs, 28–29, 69
  collection classes in, 170–71
Java Archive (JAR) files, 139, 145–49
  creating, 146–47
  extracting files from, 147–48
  jar utility, 145–49
  running an application from, 148
  viewing the contents of, 147
Java Authentication and Authorization Service (JAAS), 4
Java class libraries, 173–78

Java Cryptography Extension (JCE), 4
Java Database Connectivity (JDBC), 3, 174
Java Event Handling (Palmer), 428
Java How-to Program (Deitel/Deitel), 124
Java Naming and Directory Interface (JNDI), 4
Java Native Interface (JNI), 3, 19
Java Print Service API, 4
Java programs, compiling/running, 8–9
Java Secure Socket Extension (JSSE), 4
Java servlets, *See* Servlets:
Java Virtual Machine (JVM), 6
  obtaining, 7
  options, 9
Java Vlrtuai Machine (JVM), 438
Java web server, 437–38
Java Web Start, 4
java.awt package, 176, 420, 426
java.awt.event package, 140, 176
JavaBeans, 3–4
javac, 4, 8
javadoc, 43
java.io package, 174–75, 381–83, 417
java.io.package, 19
java.lang package, 174–75, 197–98
java.math package, 174–75, 197, 212
java.nio package, 417
JavaServer Pages (JSPs), 30
java.swing.table package, 140
java.util package, 137, 159, 175–76
javaw, 4
javax.swing package, 177
javax.swing.border package, 177
javax.swing.event package, 177
javax.swing.table package, 177
javax.swing.text package, 177
javax.swing.tree package, 177
JButton, 426, 428
JButton class, 177
JComboBox, 423–24, 428–29
JFrame, 427
JPanel, 426–27
JRadioButton class, 177
JSplitPane class, 177
JTabbedPane class, 177
JTable class, 177–78
JTextArea, 424, 426, 429
JTextField, 423–24, 429
JToggleButton class, 177
JTree class, 177–78

K

Keyboard I/O, 62–64
Keywords, 15

INDEX

L
Layered panes, 420–21
Least squares fit to a polynomial equation, 366–68
`leastSquaresFit()` method, 354, 361, 363, 366, 368–69, 371, 374
Length, arrays, 169–70
`length()` method, 191
Levenberg-Marquadt methods, 378
`LexComparator` class, 191–92
Libraries:
    core J2SE libraries, 174–76
    generic class libraries, 355–63
    GUI libraries, 176–78
    Java class libraries, 173–78
    Java I/O libraries, 383
    moving from C to Java, 28–29
    moving from Fortran to Java, 18–19
`LineDemo` Class, 361–63
`LinkedHashmap` class, 170
`LinkedHashset` class, 171
`LinkedList` class, 171
`loadArrays()` method, 368–70, 374
    `Polynomial` class, 359–60
`log()` method, 203–4, 217
`log10()` method, 216–18
`LogDemo` class, 203–4
`logX()` method, 216–18
Long class, 184–86
`long` data type, 14–15, 93, 208
Loops, 54–60
Lower-upper decomposition (LU), 250, 257–61
`luDecomp()` method, 259–61

M
Maclaurin series, 216
`main ()` method, 13, 42, 407–9
    general syntax, 119
    using command-line arguments in, 120
Math class, 197, 198–204
Math functions, *See* Built-in math functions:
Math2 class, 126–27
    compiling, 222
    final version of, 220–22
    methods, 222–23
Mathematical constants, 199
Matrix inversion, 261–63
`max()` method, 208–9
`MaxDemo` class, 208–9
Maximum methods, 208–9
Mean camber line, 327
Member hiding/member overriding, and inheritance, 86

Members:
    classes, 65
    interfaces, 133
Memory management, moving from C++ to Java, 35–36
META-INF directory, 146
Method arguments:
    arrays as, 167–69
    and inheritance, 85
Method chaining, 124–25
Method overloading, 126–27
Method overriding, 127–29
`MethodArgDemo` class, 85
Methods, 12–13, 111–30
    abstract, 123–24
    access modifiers, 114–16
    chaining, 124–25
    declaring, 70–71, 112–14
    final, 124
    input parameters, 121–23
    instance, 116–18
    `main ()` method, 119–20
    moving from C to Java, 25–26
    moving from Fortran to Java, 15–16
    naming conventions/restrictions, 114
    `native` keyword, 124
    overloading, 126–27
    overriding, 127–29
    passing arguments to, 121–23
    `return` statement, 129–30
    signature, 40
    static, 118–19
    `synchronized` keyword, 124
    types of, 16
`MethodsDemo` class, 192
`midpoint()` method, 319–22
    source code, 320–21
    `TestMidpoint` class, 321–22
Midpoint rule, 318
`min()` method, 208–9
Minimum methods, 208–9
Miscellaneous operators, 51–53
`MiscOpDemo` class, 52–53
Monte Carlo algorithms, 378
Multiline comment, 13

N
N class, 241–42
N2 class, 240–41
Naming conventions:
    methods, 114
    variables, 101
`native` keyword, 124
Navier-Stokes equations, 271, 298

Nested classes, 77–81
    anonymous inner classes, 77, 80–81
    defined, 77–78
    instance (inner) nested classes, 77, 78–80
    static nested classes, 77, 78
Newton's second law, 281
`NitrogenGas` class, 242–45
Nonpolynomial equations, fitting to, 373–74
Nonstatic fields, 69–70
Nyquist sampling frequency, 345–46

O

Oak, 2
Object-oriented programming, 37–40
    classes, 37
    encapsulation, 37–38
    inheritance, 39, 67
    interfaces, 67
    objects, 37–38
    polymorphism, 40
`ObjectInputStream` class, 384, 388–89
`ObjectOutputStream` class, 393–95
Objects, 13, 37–38, 68–69
    copying, 75–77
ODE class, 273–75
`ODEshooter()` method, 294–96, 303–4
`ODESolver` class, 279–80, 356
One-dimensional arrays, 160–61
Open formulas, 318
Operators, 44–54
    arithmetic operators, 44–45
    assignment operators, 45–46
    bitwise operators, 50–51
    boolean operators, 48–50
    increment/decrement operators, 46–47
    miscellaneous operators, 51–53
    precedence, 53–54
    relational operators, 47–48
`OpPrecedence` class, 53
Ordinary differential equations (ODEs), 271, 272–73
    first-order ODE, 272–73
    second-order ODE, 272
Output streams, 382–83
`OutputStream` class, 390–91
    `close()` method, 391
`OutputStreamWriter` class, 401–2
`OverrideDemo` class, 129

P

Packages, 19, 28–29, 67, 139–48
    and access control, 144
    bytecode files of, 140

CLASSPATH environment variable, 143–44
    defining, 140–42
    definition of, 139
    `import` declarations, 142–43
    including classes in, 141–42
    user-defined package, importing, 142–43
Palmer, Grant, 428
Panes, 420–21
`ParallelPlate` class, 135
`parse()` methods, 185–86
`ParseDemo` class, 195–96
`parseDouble()` method, `Double` class, 195
Partial differential equations (PDEs), 271, 306
Partial pivoting, 250–51
`partialPivot()` method, 251–54
Passing arguments to methods, 121–23
Passing arrays as method arguments, 168–69
Passing exceptions to methods, 156–57
`PerfectGas` class, 227–28, 230–33
    `getDensity()` method, 230
    `getEnthalpy()` method, 230
    `getEntropy()` method, 230
    `getViscosity()` method, 230
`PipedInputStream` class, 389
`PipedReader` class, 399
`PipedWriter` class, 403
Pivoting, 250–53
    full, 250–51
    partial, 250–51
    `partialPivot()` method, 251–54
Pointers:
    moving from C to Java, 25
    moving from C++ to, Java, 3
Polymorphism, 40, 111–12
`Polynomial` class, 358–61, 369–70
`pow()` method, 201–2
`PowDemo` class, 202
Power class, 374–78
`PowerDemo` class, 376–77
Prandtl number, 299
Precedence, 53–54
    operators, 53–54
Preprocessor directives, moving from C++ to, 32–33
Primitive types, 15, 16
    converting to strings, 193
    input arguments, 122–23
Primitive variable wrapper classes, 179–81
    constructors, 182
    objects:
        converting to a primitive value, 184–85
        creating, 181–84
    `parse()` methods, 185–86

Index

print() method:
  PrintStream class, 393
  PrintWriter class, 402–3
printArray() method, 168
PrinterWriter class, 402–3
Printing, 62–64
println () method, 42
println() method:
  PrintStream class, 394
  PrintWriter class, 402–3
PrintOutputStream class, 395–96
PrintStream class, 390
PrintWriter class, 399
private access, 67–68
  variables, 102
Program structure:
  moving from C to Java, 22
  moving from Fortran to, 12–13
Proper integrals, 308
protected access, 67–68, 144
  variables, 102
public access, 67–68
  variables, 102
Public interface, 133
PushbackReader class, 399

Q
Query string, 441

R
Random number generator methods, 211–12
RandomDemo class, 211–12
read() method:
  InputStream class, 385
  Reader class, 396–97
Reader class, 396–97
  close() method, 396–97
readFully() method:
  DataInputStream class, 387
  ObjectInputStream class, 388–89
readLine() method, 396
  BufferedReader class, 398–99, 412
readObject() method, ObjectInputStream class, 389, 416
Real gas viscosity method, 265–69
RealGas class, 227–28, 234–38
  getDensity() method, 235
  getPressure() method, 235
  getTemperature() method, 235
  getViscosity() method, 236
RealGasDriver class, 244–45
Rectangle class, 176

Reference types, 15, 16
  converting to strings, 193
  input arguments, 122–23
Relational operators, 47–48
RelationalOpDemo class, 48
Remainder methods, 209–11
Remote Method Invocation (RMI), 3
RestoreObject class, 416–17
return statements, 62, 129–30, 218
Return types, arrays as, 167–69
ReturnDemo class, 130
rint() method, 209
rmic, 4
round() method, 209
RoundDemo class, 210–11
Rounding methods, 209–11
Runge-Kutta schemes, 276–80, 356
  orders of accuracy, 277–78
rungeKutta4() method, 279–84, 290

S
Sampling theory, 345–47
  aliasing, 346–47
SaveObject class, 415–16
Scope, variables, 108–10
ScopeDemo class, 109
Second-order ODE, 272
SequenceInputStream class, 389
Servlets:
  creating Web-based applications using, 435–48
  defined, 437
  and Java web server, 437
  required libraries/tools, 438
setContentPane() method, 426
setInitialConditions() class, ODE class, 282, 301
setLayout() method, 426
Shadowed variables, 108, 121
Shape class, 88
Shooting, 292
ShootingCompress class, 303–5
Short class, 184–86
short data type, 14–15, 24, 93
Signature, methods, 40
Simple Java program, 42–43
SimpleGas class, 70
SimpleGas2 class, 71
SimpleGas3 class, 73
SimpleGas4 class, 75–76
SimpleGas5 class, 94–95
SimpleGas6 class, 100–101
SimpleProgram class, 42

Simpson's rule:
  shared characteristic with trapezoidal algorithm, 315
  `TestSimpson` class, 316–17
`simpsonsRule()` method, 315–19, 326, 329
  source code, 316
`sin()` method, 205
Single-line comments, 13
`size()` method, `ByteArrayOutputStream` class, 391–92
Software Development Kit (SDK), 4, 7, 173
  obtaining, 8
`SolverDemo` class, 263–65
Sonine polynomial expansion, 266
`Species` class, 83–84, 238–40
  class hierarchy, 228
`Species2` class, 87
`SpeciesDriver` class, 142–43
Spectral leakage, 347–49
`split()` method, 191
`sqrt()` method, 201–2
`SqrtFunction2` class, 321
`Stack` class, 171
Static fields, 69–70
Static initialization blocks, 74
Static methods, 16, 70, 118–19
Static nested classes, 77, 78
`StaticDemo` class, 118–19
`StaticInitDemo` class, 74
`StdIODemo` class, 410–11
Stream-based I/O system, 20
Streams, 381
`StrictMath` class, 197, 198–204
`String` class, 14–15, 20, 186–87
  concatenating strings, 189–90
  constructors, 187
  converting primitive and reference types to strings, 193
  creating strings, 188–89
  methods, 190–92
  string objects, obtaining, 187–89
`StringBufferInputStream` class, 389
`StringReader` class, 399
Strings:
  concatenating, 189–90
  converting primitive and reference types to, 189–90
  converting to primitive values, 193–96
  creating, 188–89
  moving from C to Java, 29
  moving from C++ to Java, 35
`StringWriter` class, 403
`struct` type, 24

Structures, moving from C++ to Java, 4
Subroutines, moving from Fortran to Java, 15–16
`substring()` method, 191
`super` keyword, 86
Swing containers, 420–21
Swing GUI components, 421
Swing GUI libraries, 4
Swing packages, 4
`switch` statement, 14
`switch` statements, 59–60
`SwitchDemo` class, 60
`synchronized` keyword, 124
`synchronized` keyword, 133
Syntax, 41–64
  general syntax, 41–43
  keyboard I/O, 62–64
  loops/control statements, 54–62
    `do-while` loops, 56–57
    `if-else` statements, 54–55
    `for` loops, 57–58
    `switch` statements, 59–60
    `while` loops, 55–56
  moving from C to Java, 23
  moving from C++ to Java, 32
  moving from Fortran to, 13–14
  operators, 44–54
    arithmetic operators, 44–45
    assignment operators, 45–46
    bitwise operators, 50–51
    boolean operators, 48–50
    increment/decrement operators, 46–47
    miscellaneous operators, 51–53
    precedence, 53–54
    relational operators, 47–48
  printing, 62–64
  simple Java program, 42–43
Systems of equations:
  `EqnSolver` class, 249
    methods, testing, 263–65
  Gauss-Jordan elimination, 253–55
  Gaussian elimination, 255–57
  general considerations, 248
  lower-upper decomposition, 257–61
  matrix inversion, 261–63
  pivoting, 250–53
  real gas viscosity method, 265–69
  solving, 247–70
  test case, 249–50

T

`tan()` method, 205
`TechJava.Gas` package, 229, 231–33

INDEX

`TechJava.MathLib` package, 249, 273, 311, 313, 321
Ternary operators, 44
`TestComplex` class, 344–45
`TestDFT` class, 340–41
`TestFFT` class, 353–54
`TestGauss` class, 325–26
`TestMidpoint` class, 321–22
`TestPoint` class, 321–22
`TestSimpson` class, 316–17
`TestTrap` class, 314
Thermal boundary layer, 298
Thin airfoil theory (example), 326–31
`ThinAirFoil` class, 330
Thinking in Java (Eckel), 225
`this` keyword, 86–87
`throw` and `throws` keywords, 155–57
`ThrowDemo` class, 157
Tomcat server, 438
`toString()` method, 193
Transcendental math functions, 203–4
`transient` keyword, 133
Transient variables, 106
Trapezoidal algorithms, 309–14
Trapezoidal method, 310
`trapezoidal()` method, 311–14, 317, 319
    source code, 311–12
`TreeMap` class, 171
`TreeSet` class, 171
`TrigDemo` class, 205
Trigonometric methods, 204–6
`trim()` method, 191
`try` keyword, 152
`try` statements, 151–55
    `catch` clause, 152–53
    `finally` clause, 153
    `try` keyword, 152
    using, 154–55
`TryDemo` class, 154–55
Two-dimensional arrays, 161–64
Two-point boundary problems, 292, 305–6
`TwoDimDemo` class, 163–64
Types, 14–15

U

Unary operators, 44
Under-relaxation procedure, 293–94
`union` type, 24
Unions, moving from C++ to Java, 34
Universal Gas Constant, 226–27
`USatm76` class, 404–7, 438
User-defined math functions, 215–24
    basic plan of attack, 216
    comparing Java/C/Fortran values, 223–24
    gamma function, 219–20
    hyperbolic trigonometric methods, 218–19
    logarithm methods, 217–18
    `Math2` class, 216–17
        compiling, 222
        final version of, 220–22
        methods, 222–23
User-defined package, importing, 142–43
`UserMathDemo` class, 222–23
    source code, 223

V

`valueOf()` class, `Double` class, 185–86
Variables, 12, 24–25, 91–110
    access modifiers, 102–3
    casting, 106–8
    class, 69–70, 91, 95–98, 99
    creating, 98–101
    defined, 91
    final, 105–6
    free, 273
    initializing, example of, 100–101
    instance, 70, 91, 95–98
    moving from C to Java, 24–25
    moving from Fortran to Java, 14–15
    naming conventions/restrictions, 101
    primitive type, 92–95, 98
    reference type, 92–95, 98
    scope, 108–10
    shadowed, 108, 121
    transient, 106
    values, accessing, 103–5
    visible, 108
    volatile, 106
`Vector` class, 171
`ViscosityDemo` class, 268–69
`volatile` keyword, 133
Volatile variables, 106
Volterra integrals, 326

W

Web-base applications:
    moving from C to Java, 30
    moving from Fortran to Java, 20
Web-based applications:
    `AtmServlet` class, 443–47
    basics of, 436–37
    client machine, sending output back to, 443
    creating using servlets, 435–48
    deploying, 447–48

Web-based applications (*cont.*)
  `HttpServlet` class, 439–40
    subclass, general form of, 440–41
  input parameters, extracting, 441
  server-based applications, running, 442
  web-based atmosphere modeling tool, 438
Weights, 322
`while` loops, 55–56
`while` statement, 14
`write()` method:
  `OutputStream` class, 391
  `Writer` class, 400

`writeBytes()` method, `DataOutputStream` class, 393
`writeChars()` method, `DataOutputStream` class, 393
`writeObject()` method, `ObjectOutputStream` class, 393, 415
`Writer` class, 399–400
  `close()` method, 400
`writeUTF()` method, `DataOutputStream` class, 393

Wouldn't it be great

if the world's leading technical publishers joined forces to deliver their best tech books in a common digital reference platform?

They have. Introducing
InformIT Online Books
powered by Safari.

- **Specific answers to specific questions.**
InformIT Online Books' powerful search engine gives you relevance-ranked results in a matter of seconds.

- **Immediate results.**
With InformIt Online Books, you can select the book you want and view the chapter or section you need immediately.

- **Cut, paste and annotate.**
Paste code to save time and eliminate typographical errors. Make notes on the material you find useful and choose whether or not to share them with your work group.

- **Customized for your enterprise.**
Customize a library for you, your department or your entire organization. You only pay for what you need.

POWERED BY Safari

informit.com/onlinebooks

Get your first 14 days FREE!
InformIT Online Books is offering its members a 10 book subscription risk-free for 14 days. Visit **http://www.informit.com/onlinebooks** for details.

informIT

www.informit.com

YOUR GUIDE TO IT REFERENCE

Articles

Keep your edge with thousands of free articles, in-depth features, interviews, and IT reference recommendations – all written by experts you know and trust.

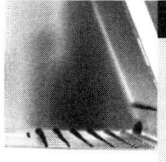

Online Books

Answers in an instant from **InformIT Online Book's** 600+ fully searchable on line books. Sign up now and get your first 14 days **free**.

POWERED BY

Catalog

Review online sample chapters, author biographies and customer rankings and choose exactly the right book from a selection of over 5,000 titles.

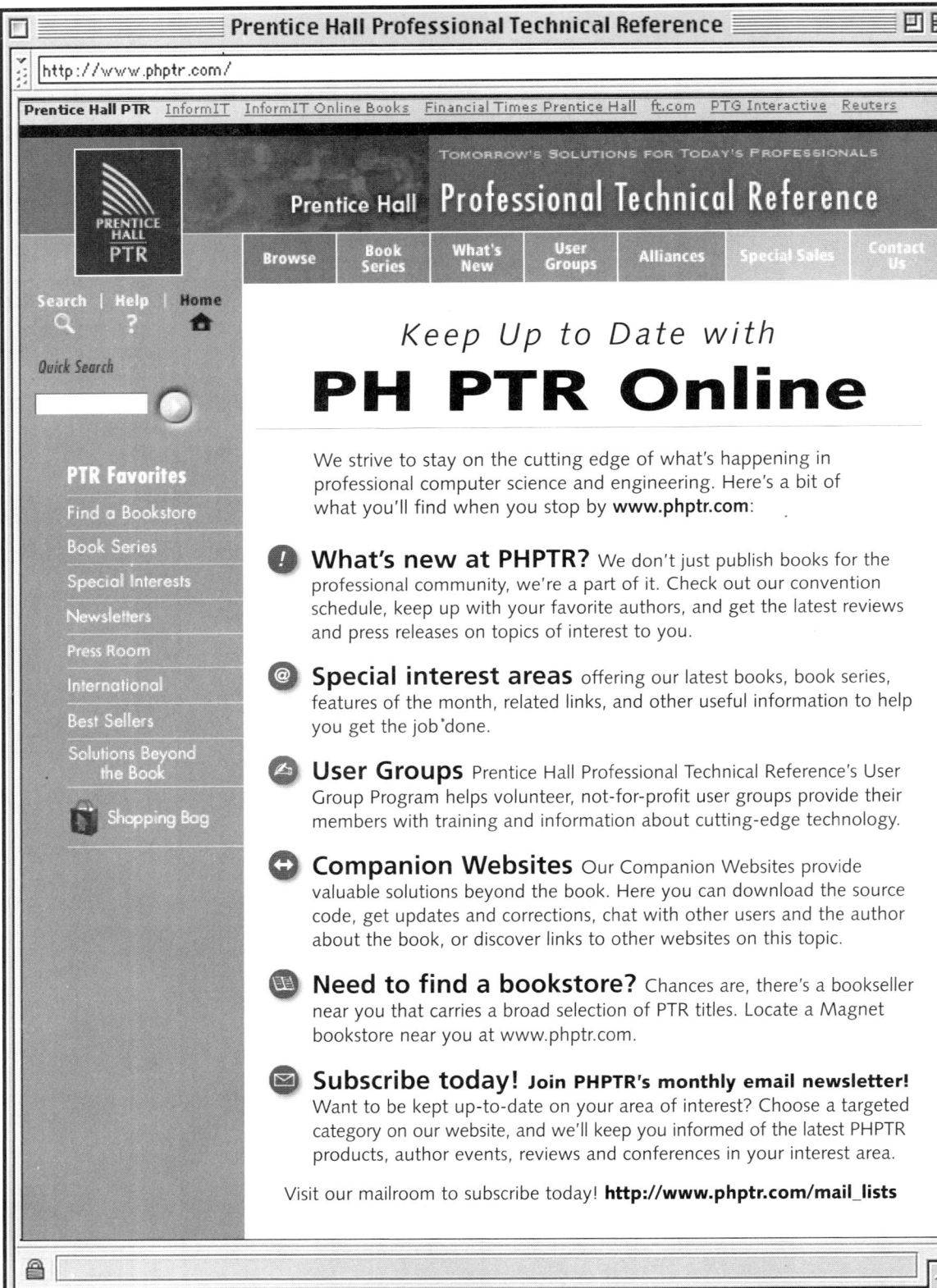